RE-INTRODUCING JESUS

You Know Him as God,
Know Him as Man

Charles A Thrall

Foreword by Kenneth Boa

Re-Introducing Jesus

You Know Him as God, Know Him as Man

Copyright © June 8th, 2024, by Charles A Thrall

ISBN: 9798332681769

Library of Congress Control Number: 2024914451

Independently Published

First Edition

Dedication

First of all, I want to most of all dedicate this book to my first love, God my Father and Messiah, Jesus His Son and Holy Spirit, the Triune God of all time and all universes. The only God and my "I still can't believe it" best friend.

Secondly, to my wife Shirley, who has put up with and hopefully enjoyed the outworking of God's love for me and mine for Him. I also want to say the same for my sons, daughters-in-law, daughter, grandchildren, and friends.

To the believer whom God used to first share the story of Jesus' redeeming love for me, Patrick Booth, who is now in the presence of the One he introduced me to.

To my Life Group at Lakepointe Church in Rockwall, I praise God for the wonderful privilege of teaching you Scriptures twice a week. It has been a pleasure in my mentoring of you and your mentoring of me.

To Kelly Freestone, my editor, who I owe a deep appreciation for helping me form this book.

To key men in my life whom God has used: Mr. Herbert Bray, a strong believer in the Messiah now in His presence, who took a risk on me never operating a big Caterpillar bulldozer and hired me as his 23-year-old operator. For Ken Boa, whom I met as a 17 yr. old hippy and he, a senior at Dallas Theological Seminary (DTS). God used Ken as a long-distance mentor, discipler and friend over most of my Christian life through his writings, audio, video, many e-mail exchanges and on-line live teaching. Ken was also an influencer in my pursuit of DTS. For Chuck Swindoll, in whom I heard his very first radio broadcast sitting on Mr. Bray's D7 Caterpillar bulldozer. Chuck was sponsored by The Lockman Foundation at that time, and the broadcast title was *New Standard for Living*. Mr. Bray's Scrap Metal guy,

Willie, was drawn to Jesus through me shutting down every day to listen to Chuck's message. God used the fire in Chuck's preaching also to influence me to pursue studies at DTS. For "Tad" Foran, now in the presence of Jesus, who was the leader in an Adult Bible Class I taught for several years. Please note that this Bible class had been together for over 50 years and Dr John Walvoord, former President at DTS, had taught this class. I always had a deep love and admiration for Tad and his wife, Peg. I remember Tad telling me whenever they were seeking a new Bible teacher for their class, "When your name first came up about teaching the class, I had my doubts. I said let's give him a chance. Looking back that was one of my better decisions. You have far exceeded all expectations and have been one of the best." That was Tad, truly a Barnabas, son of Encouragement. I also want to mention those elders who thought my emails were too long. You will surely think that I have lost my mind writing this book! (You must have a sense of humor, eh?)

Finally, to Napoleon Sergio, father of my daughter-in-law, Debie Thrall, and Pastor of Dagupan Baptist Church in the Ilocos Region, Philippines. He has recently stepped into eternity to be with the Lord and his Savior. Napoleon faithfully served with his life. I never had the honor to meet Napoleon, but I do know him through Jesus' character and heart. We will meet someday soon together with Jesus.

FOREWORD

I have given my life to discipling men and women in their walk with the risen Christ. My heart's desire has been to introduce them to the lifelong pursuit of the power of an eternal perspective in every component of life.

One such relationship started 53 years ago with the author of this book.

I met Charlie, a new believer in Jesus when I was at Dallas Theological Seminary. Over those years, as Charlie would put it, "The Spirit of God used you and your ministry as my spiritual ground of being many times over those years." Those are encouraging words for a discipler to hear.

This book explores the dramatic dilemma of human sin and divine grace from Genesis to Revelation. God is the Sacred Romancer who pursues, provides, and protects His beloved, and the Scriptures reveal the awful cost He paid for our redemption from the bondage of sin, the law, and death so that we could be set free to walk in His light, life, and love.

It illuminates three of Jesus' profound questions that I now stop and consider several times a day:

1. What do you seek? (John 1:38)
2. Who do you say that I am? (Matthew 16:15)
3. Do you love Me more than these? (John 21:15)

This book can assist you in clarifying your answers to these profound questions.

—Kenneth Boa
President, Reflections Ministries
Author, Speaker, Teacher
KenBoa.org

Table of Contents

Introduction

Do not skip this!
It's vital for understanding the rest of the book.

This book explores something little emphasized in the church. Namely the Man Jesus. Please know that the Scriptures present that Messiah Jesus is both *fully* God and *fully* Man. The Bible, as the sacred communication from God to mankind, holds both of these descriptions of Jesus totally equal and mutually exclusive. This is one of the Bible's mysteries. While most of the Word of God is clear in its meaning, there are descriptions and events that the Bible does not explain but renders them as truth all the same. It becomes more difficult for us since mutually exclusive events cannot occur at the same time in our world; this is why it is a Biblical mystery. Concerning Biblical mysteries, the Scriptures usually will give us the "what" side of the mystery but not a "why" or a "how."

I have come to know over the past fifty-plus years as a Christ follower that the Man Jesus is extremely important to understand and know as much as the Scriptures allow. I wrote "allow" because that is an important point. With any Biblical mystery such as the Trinity, the Word of God itself, the resurrection body, God's relation to time, etc., if we try to tip the scale in favor of one side or the other in order to make our intellectual sense out of it, we are on a slippery slope that can lead to a cult or worse. We must respect the intellectual boundaries God the Holy Spirit has erected within the Scriptures.

Isaiah 55:8-9 — *"For My thoughts are not your thoughts, Nor are your ways My ways," declares the LORD. 9 "For as the heavens are higher than the earth, So are My ways higher than your ways And My thoughts than your thoughts.*

Why is it important to know the Man Jesus? Simply put because I am a man. Because you, as a reader-participant, are a man or a woman. When I refer to man, I am referring to the Man-Adam that I am related to. But for a woman, she would relate as Man-Eve. Huh? Well, the Scripture teaches that God the Father made man in His image both male and female; He made them.

Genesis 1:26-27 — *Then God said,* **"Let Us make man in Our image, according to Our likeness***; and let them rule over the fish of the sea and over the birds of the sky and over the cattle and over all the earth, and over every creeping thing that creeps on the earth." 27 God created* **man** *in His own image,* **in the image of God He created him***; male and female He created them*.

To know Jesus as a Man is important for believers. My reasoning is because Jesus got it. He got God the Father like no other man before Him. Jesus got God more than Moses through Malachi, any of the Apostles, or anyone in the Church since then. I can hear you say, "Uh, hah!" Don't fall into the trap that you may think, "Of course, *sure* Jesus got God the Father, Jesus *was* God." But we are not discussing Jesus as God here but focusing on Him as a Man in particular.

We will discover on this journey that the Man Jesus had similar struggles as you and I. He laughed, He cried, He worried, He felt alone, He felt betrayed, He was disappointed, He was loyal, He was faithful, He was joyful, He was angry, He was tempted … He was like you and me in every way except for one great, glaring difference. He was sinless. But He was not Superman from our comic books. Untouchable.

Unreachable. Indestructible. He could have sinned, but He didn't. He chose to not break His fellowship with God the Father, not once.

> **Hebrews 4:14-16** — *Therefore, since we have a great high priest who has passed through the heavens, Jesus the Son of God, let us hold fast our confession. 15 For we do not have a high priest who cannot sympathize with our weaknesses, but One who has been tempted in all things as we are, yet without sin. 16 Therefore let us draw near with confidence to the throne of grace, so that we may receive mercy and find grace to help in time of need.*

I think these verses illustrate the interplay between Jesus as God and Jesus as Man. There is a doctrine among theologians called impeccability (the highest standards of propriety; faultless). It teaches that to suggest the capability or possibility of sinning would disqualify Christ as Savior. They reason that a peccable (capable of sinning) Christ would mean a peccable God. My question is how so? God the Father holds a lot of mystery relative to us. Just one example, we do not understand, nor does the Scriptures explain, how Satan can have access to God to accuse us. But God cannot be in the presence of sin. Is not Satan the embodiment of sin? Again a mystery. The Biblical fact that Jesus is both fully God and Man is also a mystery. Yet the Bible presents it to us as it is so. Hebrews 13:8 is cited: "Jesus Christ is the same yesterday and today and forever." My personal belief is that this doctrine of impeccability is in danger of "tipping the scale" as we discussed earlier.

The Scripture presents Jesus as God's Son, the second of the Trinity. The Scripture presents Jesus as the Man born of the virgin Mary and God's Spirit. We will discuss this more later, but Jesus the Man had the same starting point as Adam the man. Both were born, one by God the Father using dirt and His breath and the other from a woman's womb through the Holy Spirit but both created sinless perfection. Both were in a state of unconfirmed holiness. Adam confirmed his unholiness by his choice of disobedience to the Father.

Jesus the Man, the last Adam, confirmed His holiness by His obedience to the Father, sinlessness.

Adam, in his temptation, failed in disobedience. Jesus, the Man, in His temptation succeeded in His obedience. Jesus, the Man, confirmed His holiness and perfection. In their state of sinlessness, when tempted, they could have failed in disobedience. One did and One did not. That is why Jesus' righteousness is imputed (attributed) to us once we believe in His taking of our place on the cross.

Jesus truly showed us the way of salvation through His life, teaching, and preaching. Jesus lived not only to bring salvation to mankind but also, in spite of our disobedience to God the Father, to bring peace with the Father through His obedience. Jesus the Man lived to show us how to live daily through dependance in prayer and the Word so that we would grow to also choose not to break our fellowship with God the Father.

We need to start at the beginning of mankind's relationship with God in the Garden because they are foundational to us and our history. We will then broadbrush the love relationship between man and God throughout Biblical history and then to you and me in particular. That seems like a daunting task, but it will be very broad. I will not do a scholarly deep dive on any of these historical chunks, but I will give some resources at the end of the book and within the chapter notations.

I have always considered Christian authors acquaintances with whom I have engaged in a conversation. Through the pages of their books we will get to know one another and will go back and forth over the subject matter. We will agree. We will argue (in the healthy sense, which is foreign in today's world). You and I will, and I hope within these pages, should do the same. But do you know what I truly hope will happen? You will come, first of all, to discover how you love God in your relationship with Him. Secondly, you will learn to love God in a deeper new way or revive a way you allowed to be buried that enriches your living, dynamic daily relationship with each other, God and you. It is *not* about Christian religion in *any* form, Protestant or

Catholic; it is about relationship. And that will be worth the struggle. After all, relationship with God and others in your "community" are the currency of heaven not time, talent or treasures.

Jesus calls you and me to join Him daily on a walk with the Father in our Garden. Are you ready to join me on a journey to be re-introduced to Jesus the Man and find out the source of His joy with His and our Father?

1

Jesus God Before Jesus Man

I met Him as God first

I come from a typical Texas 1950s religious home. I say "religious" because I was never told of Jesus being my Savior. We believed in God, apple pie, and the American patriotic way of life. We were the typical middle-class, blue-collar family. My parents were children of the Great Depression. We went to church sometimes. My dad worked midnights and weekends most of my childhood. Since life had to be quiet inside the house in daylight hours, whatever I found to do outside the house was the call of the day. I was all boy, one could say, and so keeping quiet inside our house was an extreme challenge. My mom was the best. Always there for me. Through YMCA football and Boy Scouts all the way through to my Eagle Scout level, my mom was there. Dad, not so much. But I understood the need, his commitment to work and his schedule were out of his control. As a high school dropout himself during the Great Depression, I really understood, or at least I accepted it all. However, in our relationship, it was the extra time he chose to spend on himself that hurt.

My dad was into the CB Radio world (Citizen Band Radio). There were "CBer" events and dinners that the entire family was dragged to. He built a "radio shack" (a portable building) where he spent countless hours alone and away from his family. Then he progressed up the open community radio world into 2 meter and eventually became a fully licensed HAM (high frequency amateur) radio operator. But all alone. All of the time. He was an angry man and you did not want to get on his bad side.

It was obvious that my dad was selfish and angry. Not only that but he also had a very low self-esteem. I realized that whenever I would beg him to come to my Boy Scout meetings. He had days off during the weekdays so that he could come to those meetings. Other dads were there with their sons. It was not like I did not have a dad. I can remember the one and only night my dad came. While us boys would conduct our scout meeting, the dads would stand around, have a cup of coffee and talk. That was the night I witnessed my dad's low self-esteem. He stood off by himself. It was like he was in pain and could not wait for the meeting to be over. Both were very true. Dad never came back.

Besides that one scout meeting night, I have only two other memories of my dad and I having personal time together. One positive time, I remember that he threw a football to me in our front yard. The other time was a negative one; it was fishing. My dad loved to fish. He did not have any fishing buddies because he was a loner. He took me a couple of times, but I was a pain in his neck. I would ask questions but I was told that I scared the fish away with either my mouth or moving around. My dad made it *not* fun, and I was clearly unwanted. So I gave it to him; those experiences actually ruined fishing for me. I have gone fishing a few times in my lifetime, but it never became a thing for me because the pleasure was crushed out of it. That alternate choice became a life habit where the original emotional decision to have a relationship with my dad became buried.

I say all of this to give you a picture of my childhood years. My dad faithfully excelled at one thing. He was a good and faithful provider. Through my mom, I was not denied any reasonable request during my stages of growth. Those years came with an absent dad, and a lot of time with my mom giving the excuse of my dad's work schedule. She would go to bat for me behind the scenes if my dad tried to put a damper on things.

I was seventeen years old in November of 1970, and I was a shoulder-length-hair different kind of hippie than the 60's-70's era. There were clicks of "hippies" just as there are clicks of all manner in the high school culture. In my Texas hometown at that time, there were only a handful of us who had adopted the Woodstock type of "free love," using dope and rebellion against the perceived societal norms or authority of the day.

I was bored with school. I did not do homework, but I took tests, passed those tests, and sometimes aced them. However, I would fail the class because I did not do the homework, which frustrated my mom and teachers. I found out what I had to accomplish in order to pass and did that much.

It was during this time period I met a guy who walked to the pace of a different drummer. He was an artist with long hair and smoked dope. He introduced me to marijuana, aka Mary Jane, or Hooch. I would cut classes and go to his house to use.

From that point, my circle of "hippie" friends expanded. I did notice that as my old friends adopted the "long hair" look, most of their personalities remained the same. If they were rednecks and fighters with short hair, they were rednecks and fighters with long hair. It seemed that the purity of the movement became diluted the more personalities that got involved. I am sure that is true in most movements of any kind. I, too, was a different kind of "Texas long hair" or hippie.

Despite my long hair, dope smoking, free love, and against-the-rules attitude, I did love my country. I did not have the typical hippie view of politics. I supported the Vietnam War only because I hated Communism and its worldwide progression. However, I did not like the way that war was fought. To me, then and even now, the most merciful thing one can do in war is to win it as quickly and decisively as possible. There are fewer human casualties that way. I detested and thought the DMZs, or demilitarized zones, were a stupid idea. The enemy *never* played by those rules. So, as a long hair, during that time period, that was an odd perspective to maintain about the Vietnam War.

Bored with high school, I became enamored with hippie culture or art, fashion, posters, and all the hippie paraphernalia. I sold an expensive trumpet from my high school band days and decided to open a Head Shop in the mid-cities between Dallas and Ft. Worth. Most of the competition was in the bigger cities but not where I lived.

I found an owner of a strip mall who thought my wanting to be in business at the age of 17 was a novelty. She cut my rent in half. I found several resell product suppliers in Dallas and other cities. Very soon, "The AmeriKan Eye Misc." opened its doors. I built a stage in the back of the building. All of my merchandising islands were on wheels and I would push them aside on Saturday nights, throw big pillows on the floor, let a band play, and charged $1 at the door. People either liked me or they hated me. There was not a lot of middle ground. I was the only kid at my High School who was in the DECA (Distributive Education Clubs of America) program who signed and reviewed his own work report back to the school since I was the owner/manager. I thought that was pretty cool.

I recently had lunch with an old high school friend who was my only employee at The AmeriKan Eye Misc. That lunch was the first time we had seen each other in over 50 years. He disclosed something to me that I never knew and took me by utter surprise. He related to me that hiring him was a great encouragement to him at that time. He said that it made him feel good that someone would take a "chance on a tall, lanky kid like himself" by hiring him. He said that experience had inspired confidence to go on to other things later. He did become quite successful in the music world and hair salons. You just never know how decisions and actions involving others will affect them and their lives. Small things to you can be actually great to someone else.

During that time period, I had progressed from marijuana to dropping acid (LSD). I did that a lot. I had adopted some older friends.

We would drop acid and trip on Moody Blues, Pink Floyd, The Grateful Dead or other artists. They thought I was a novelty to do what I was doing, a head shop owner, at 17. They thought I had it more together than themselves in their mid-twenties.

Most of my close friends my age got busted and many were in a halfway house sponsored by the local Police Dept. A few of them approached me about a fundraising idea for their halfway house. Every fall our city hosted a community fair. The halfway house was called The Truth House. They wanted to sell non-drug paraphernalia products at their rented booth at the community fair. They asked me to be their supplier since I had wholesale product connections. Their product resale focus was blacklight posters, blacklights, strobe lights, leather goods, clothes, incense and the like.

I am sure you see the irony, right? A group of ex-dopers, residents in a halfway house sponsored by the local Police Department were supplied non-drug merchandise, and I was the legal dealer who also sold the pipes, papers, hookahs, etc. for illegal dope smoking.

I even went to that community fair and helped them man their booth! Ha-ha! I still shake my head at it all. No one can make this stuff up! However, it was in that scenario and that community fair that I met Messiah Jesus! Unbelievable. I am still amazed to this very day at God's sovereignty!

I was working a shift at the fair in the Truth House booth when a man approached me and asked me if I had ever heard of the Four Spiritual Laws. I replied that I had not. You need to know that my hippie culture at that time was open to doing a "sit down" and discussing almost anything you wanted to talk about. At least the purest heads had this attitude.

Dallas businessman Patrick Booth and I went into the blacklight booth, which was the only quiet place around. We sat down on the sawdust floor and we started through this little booklet called the *Four Spiritual Laws*. The Holy Spirit had me queued up and primed for that meeting. I had previously concluded that for any real peace, it had to come from outside of our world. I had come to the belief that real peace was not to be found on this earth.

The businessman went through the booklet. He gave me one and I followed along as he read out of his copy. Now that you know my background and where my head was at in this historical moment for me personally, I want to take you through that same experience. The businessman and I went through the booklet page by page. The booklet follows.

The Four Spiritual Laws

Just as there are physical laws
that govern the physical universe,
so are there spiritual laws that govern
your relationship with God.

—LAW 1—

God **loves** you and offers a
wonderful **plan** for your life.

(References contained in this booklet should be read in context from the Bible wherever possible.) Most Scriptures cited from the Amplified Bible (AMP).

GOD'S LOVE

John 3:16, AMP — *"For God so [greatly] loved and dearly prized the world, that He [even] gave His [One and] only begotten Son, so that whoever believes and trusts in Him [as Savior] shall not perish, but have eternal life."*

GOD'S PLAN

John 10:10b, AMP *[Christ speaking]* — *"I came that they may have and enjoy life, and have it in abundance"* *[to the full, till it overflows].*

Why is it that most people are not experiencing the abundant life?

Because...

—LAW 2—

Man is sinful (disobedient) and separated from God.
Therefore, he cannot know and experience
God's love and plan for his life.

MAN IS SINFUL

Romans 3:23, AMP — *"Since all have sinned {disobeyed} and continually fall short of the glory of God."*

Man was created to have fellowship with God; but, because of his own stubborn self-will, he chose to go his own independent way and fellowship with God was broken. This self-will, characterized by an attitude of active rebellion or passive indifference, is an evidence of what the Bible calls sin {disobedience}.

MAN IS SEPARATED

Romans 6:23a, AMP — *"The wages of sin {disobedience} is death"* *[spiritual separation from God].*

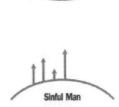

This diagram illustrates that God is holy and man is sinful. A great gulf separates the two. The arrows illustrate that man is continually trying to reach God and the abundant life through his own efforts, such as a good life, philosophy, or religion— but he inevitably fails.

The third law explains the only way to bridge this gulf...

—LAW 3—

Jesus Christ is God's **only** provision for man's sin {disobedience}. Through Him you can know and experience God's love and plan for your life.

HE DIED IN OUR PLACE

Romans 5:8, AMP — *"But God clearly shows and proves His own love for us, by the fact that while we were still sinners, Christ died for us."*

HE ROSE FROM THE DEAD

1 Corinthians 15:3–6, AMP — *"For I passed on to you as of first importance what I also received, that Christ died for our sins {disobedience} according to [that which] the Scriptures [foretold], 4 and that He was buried, and that He was [bodily] raised on the third day according to [that which] the Scriptures [foretold], 5 and that He appeared to Cephas (Peter), then to the Twelve. 6 After that He appeared to more than five hundred brothers and sisters at one time."*

HE IS THE ONLY WAY TO GOD

John 14:6, AMP — *"Jesus said to him, 'I am the [only] Way [to God] and the [real] Truth and the [real] Life; no one comes to the Father but through Me.'"*

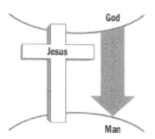

This diagram illustrates that God has bridged the gulf that separates us from Him by sending His Son, Jesus Christ, to die on the cross in our place to pay the penalty for our sins {disobedience}.

It is not enough just to know these three laws...

—LAW 4—

We must individually **receive** Jesus Christ
as Savior and Lord; then we can know and
experience God's love and plan for our lives.

WE MUST RECEIVE CHRIST

John 1:12, AMP — *"But to as many as did receive and welcome Him, He gave the right [the authority, the privilege] to become children of God, that is, to those who believe in (adhere to, trust in, and rely on) His name."*

WE RECEIVE CHRIST THROUGH FAITH

Ephesians 2:8-9, AMP — *For it is by grace [God's remarkable compassion and favor drawing you to Christ] that you have been saved [actually delivered from judgment and given eternal life] through faith. And this [salvation] is not of yourselves [not through your own effort], but it is the [undeserved, gracious] gift of God; 9 not as a result of [your] works [nor your attempts to keep the Law], so that no one will [be able to] boast or take credit in any way [for his salvation].*

WHEN WE RECEIVE CHRIST, WE EXPERIENCE A NEW BIRTH

(Read John 3:1–8.)

WE RECEIVE CHRIST THROUGH PERSONAL INVITATION

Revelations 3:20, NASB — *[Christ Speaking] "Behold, I stand at the door and knock; if anyone hears My voice and opens the door, I will come in to him and will dine with him, and he with Me."*

Receiving Christ involves turning to God from self (repentance) and trusting Christ to come into our lives to forgive our sins {disobedience} and to make us what He wants us to be. Just to agree **intellectually** that Jesus Christ is the Son of God and that He died on the cross for our sins is not enough. Nor is it enough to have an **emotional** experience. We receive Jesus Christ by **faith**, as an act of the **will** {intentional purposeful decision}. These two circles represent two kinds of lives:

Self-Directed Life
S – Self is on the throne
† – Christ is outside the life
● – Interests are directed by self, often resulting in discord and frustration

Christ-Directed Life
† – Christ is in the life and on the throne
S – Self is yielding to Christ
● – Interests are directed by Christ, resulting in harmony with God's plan

Which circle best represents your life?

Which circle would you like to have represent your life?

The following explains how you can receive Christ:

You Can Receive Christ Right Now by Faith Through Prayer

(Prayer is talking with God)

God knows your heart and is not so concerned with your words as He is with the attitude of your heart. The following is a suggested prayer:

Lord Jesus, I need You. Thank You for dying on the cross for my sins {disobedience}. I open the door of my life and receive You as my Savior and Lord. Thank You for forgiving my sins {disobedience} and giving me eternal life. Take control of the throne of my life. Make me the kind of person You want me to be.

Does this prayer express the desire of your heart? If it does, I invite you to pray this prayer right now, and Christ will come into your life, as He promised.

How to Know That Christ Is in Your Life

Did you receive Christ into your life? According to His promise in Revelation 3:20, where is Christ right now in relation to you? Christ said He would come into your life. Would He mislead you? On what authority do you know God has answered your prayer?

(The trustworthiness of God Himself and His Word.)

The Bible Promises Eternal Life to All Who Receive Christ

1 John 5:11–13, AMP — *"And the testimony is this: that God has given us eternal life [we already possess it], and this life is in His*

*Son[resulting in our spiritual completeness, and eternal companionship with Him]. 12 He who has the Son [by accepting Him as Lord and Savior] has the life [that is eternal]; he who does not have the Son of God [by personal faith] does not have the life. 13 These things I have written to you who believe in the name of the Son of God [which represents all that Jesus Christ is and does], so that you may **know** [with settled and absolute knowledge] that you have eternal life."*

Thank God often that Christ is in your life and that He will never leave you (Hebrews 13:5). You can know on the basis of His promise that Christ lives in you and that you have eternal life from the very moment you invite Him in. He will not deceive you.

An important reminder...

DO NOT DEPEND ON FEELINGS

The promise of God's Word, the Bible—not our feelings—is our authority. The Christian lives by faith (trust) in the trustworthiness of God Himself and His Word. This train diagram illustrates the relationship among **fact** (God and His Word), faith (our trust in God and His Word), and **feeling** (the result of our faith and obedience). (Read John 14:21.)

The train will run with or without the caboose. However, it would be useless to attempt to pull the train by the caboose. In the same way, as Christians we do not depend on feelings or emotions, but we place our faith (trust) in the trustworthiness of God and the promises of His Word.

NOW THAT YOU HAVE RECEIVED CHRIST

The moment you received Christ by faith, as an act of the will, many things happened, including the following:

- Christ came into your life (Revelation 3:20; Colossians 1:27).
- Your sins were forgiven (Colossians 1:14).
- You became a child of God (John 1:12).
- You received eternal life (John 5:24).
- You began the great adventure for which God created you (John 10:10; 2 Corinthians 5:17; 1 Thessalonians 5:18).

Can you think of anything more wonderful that could happen to you than receiving Christ? Would you like to thank God in prayer right now for what He has done for you? By thanking God, you demonstrate your faith.

To enjoy your new life to the fullest ...

SUGGESTIONS FOR CHRISTIAN GROWTH

Spiritual growth results from trusting Jesus Christ. "The righteous man shall live by faith" (Galatians 3:11). A life of faith will enable you to trust God increasingly with every detail of your life, and to practice the following:

G - Go to God in prayer daily (John 15:7).

R - Read God's Word daily (Acts 17:11); begin with the Gospel of John.

O - Obey God moment by moment (John 14:21).

W - Witness for Christ by your life and words (Matthew 4:19; John 15:8).

T - Trust God for every detail of your life (1 Peter 5:7).

H - Holy Spirit—allow Him to control and empower your daily life and witness (Galatians 5:16,17; Acts 1:8).

FELLOWSHIP IN A GOOD CHURCH

God's Word instructs us not to forsake "the assembling of ourselves together" (Hebrews 10:25). Several logs burn brightly together, but put one aside on the cold hearth and the fire goes out. So it is with your relationship with other Christians.

If you do not belong to a church, do not wait to be invited. Take the initiative; call the pastor of a nearby church where Christ is honored and His Word is preached. Start this week, and make plans to attend regularly.

SPECIAL MATERIALS ARE AVAILABLE FOR CHRISTIAN GROWTH

If you have come to know Christ personally through this presentation of the gospel or would like further help in getting to know Christ better, two sites are recommended:

www.startingwithGod.com or www.growinginChrist.com

If you still have questions, visit: www.whoisJesus-really.com or www.everystudent.com.[1]

---

[1] Bill Bright, *The Four Spiritual Laws* (Bright Media Foundation and Campus Crusade for Christ, 2007), All rights reserved. www.campuscrusade.org Alteration by this author: wherever the word "sin" was mentioned inserted {disobedience} for enhanced definition. The use of the Amplified Bible version (AMP) was used where appropriate. Inserted {intentional purposeful decision} to enhance the definition of the term "will." Used by permission.

Simple yet profoundly powerful don't you think? I placed the appropriate word "disobedience" in brackets next to the word "sin" because I think the word has lost its true meaning for most moderns or they have diluted it. For me, to replace the word "sin" with the word "disobedience" anchors its true meaning. That word levels the playing field. We moderns all know disobedience.

The Holy Spirit had me queued up for this experience through His Word. Regarding Law 2, I saw myself and all of the world I experienced personally or on TV. In Law 3, it hit home! That is it! Peace to this world and my world would come from outside of it. Mankind has never found it within himself. Look at our history then or now!

Whenever I saw Law 4, I was ready to jump in. Jesus would be my peace; Messiah Jesus would be my Savior! It was a gift from God.

My family knew and believed in God as Creator and Almighty. In my early years, my mom would take me and my sister to church. The more my dad worked midnights, the more we stopped going. But oddly enough, Jesus Christ was never introduced to me. He may have been or His name but it seems then that I did not have "ears to hear." I remember going to church when I visited my grandmother, MeeMaw, at the young age of 10 or so. At her church Sunday School, in a class for my age group, I did not know the answers to many of the Bible questions. I was made fun of by several kids in the class; that was the last time I ever went back.

However, fast forward seven or so years later, and it was Law 4 that introduced me to Jesus! But get this, even the faith it takes to believe in the Son of God is His gift of salvation. Look at the verse in Ephesians again:

Ephesians 2:8-9, AMP — *"For it is by grace [God's remarkable compassion and favor drawing you to Christ] that you have been saved [actually delivered from judgment and given eternal life] through faith. And this [salvation] is not of yourselves [not through your own effort], but it is the [undeserved, gracious] gift of*

God; 9 not as a result of [your] works [nor your attempts to keep the Law], so that no one will [be able to] boast or take credit in any way [for his salvation]."

Even over 50 years later, from that 17-year-old boy in that blacklight booth on a sawdust floor, I am still in awe and amazed at Messiah Jesus' saving grace and gift to me. Why me? His love is utterly amazing. While I was totally cut off from God because of my disobedience, it was His amazing grace that called out to my soul and gave me "ears to hear."

This is what God the Father said of His Son in His grace given to me and to you.

- God raised Jesus from the dead, freeing Him from the agony of death, because it was impossible for Him to be held by it. (Acts 2:24)
- Just as the Father raises the dead and gives them life, even so the Son gives life to whom He wishes. (John 5:21)
- God gives life to the dead and calls into being things that do not exist. (Romans 4:17)
- He who believes in the Son of God has everlasting life. (John 6:47)
- God raised both the Lord and who will also raise me up through His power. (1 Corinthians 6:14)[2]

The prayer I prayed on that sawdust floor started an adventure with the Living God through His Son, Jesus the Messiah, that will continue running past the date of my earthly death. There have been many ups and downs. Many three-steps-forward-and-ten-steps-back type experiences. But one thing is for sure, as my mom always prayed for me, "Please, Lord, never let go of my son's hand." That prayer has been answered over and over in my lifetime. And still is to this writing. Only our God is totally Sovereign over our lives.

---

[2] Kenneth Boa, *Handbook to Prayer* (Atlanta: 2021), 410-411.

My friend, a primary mentor and brother in Christ, Ken Boa, gave me a new view of God's sovereignty. When I shared with him about my absentee father as a child, he made this comment that gave me a deeper appreciation for God's Sovereignty especially when found on the negative or dark side of our life. Ken's response, "The description of your difficult relationship with your insecure and largely absent father clarified a dominant motif in your life and the power of the gospel to redeem what God has allowed." That statement, "God redeems what He allows" went directly to the spiritual bone marrow of my childhood hurt of a rejecting, absentee father. The Gospel of Christ truly has redeemed me and that broken childhood that God allowed. Thanks, Ken, and praise You, Jesus.

If you followed the *Four Spiritual Laws* booklet as I did and came to faith in Jesus for the first time, I pray you would drop me a note. There is an address at the end of this book so you can. I pray you do. I may even be able to point you to a good church.

My salvation did not happen in a void; neither did my growth as a believer. Just as Holy Spirit used people to make me aware of God's gift of redeeming grace, Holy Spirit also used people to nurture, disciple, and encourage growth. I began my salvation journey and hit some bumps in the road when left alone. Patrick hooked me up with another believer in my area. It was refreshing to be able to befriend another hipster who had found Jesus. I will call him TB. TB went to a small gathering of believers who met in a Dallas Dentist's home on Saturday nights. It was called Emmanuel's Fellowship. The Bible teaching there was handled by two Dallas Theological Seminary Seniors. TB was close to one of the two guys, Ken Boa. From that connection, Holy Spirit used Ken and his writing and teaching ministry to be whom I call "My Mentor from Afar" for the rest of my life to this writing. I had other influencers for sure; some I will mention within these pages and some I will not, but Ken has been the main Biblical influencer in my life. Later on I will discuss more of Emmanuel's Fellowship and Ken Boa.

For the rest of this book, I want to take you through a discussion of re-introducing Jesus. We know Him as God, and we get to know Him as Man also. I began this book with my own personal starting point when I first met Jesus as God. I personally think that is the starting point for all believers. To meet Jesus as God. It is through Jesus as God we come to the Father, He saves us from our disobedience, and restores our relationship. It is the miracle of the cross that Jesus, as God, secured our salvation. It is the miracle of the resurrection that Jesus, as God, imputed His righteousness to us as believers.

But it will be Jesus as Man, used by the Holy Spirit, that will be our model in the day-to-day warfare of life with the enemy of our souls. It will be Jesus the Man where we will see how to walk, how to pray, how to seek the Word of God, how to minister, how to challenge our world, how to share the Good News, how to be a disciple, how to walk in the Spirit, and how to disciple others in our Jerusalem, Judea and the uttermost parts of the world.

I pray you use this book as a discussion between you, me and God over a cup of coffee. I am not an expert. I am a fellow sojourner seeking how to interact with God's world, God's Word, and God's ways daily in my life. I am still on the journey, at times fumbling and bumbling, but always seeking to love the One Who loved me first!

> *"Nothing you can do can make Him love you more. Nothing you can do can make Him love you less. The One Who knows you best loves you most."* –Ken Boa[3]

---

[3] Ken Boa, Friday Morning Men's Bible Study, on 12/22/2023.

2

The First Relationships

Setting the Stage

In the first chapter of Genesis we find the creation account of all that is in existence. After God created the heavens, the earth and all living things, He created man. Throughout this book you may see me refer to Man as a collective of both male and female. At other times you will see me refer to Adam as Man: Adam and Eve as Man: Eve or just Adam and Eve. My point is to over emphasize that Adam and Eve are created equal. Both male and female make up the category of man. This equality of Adam and Eve is often lost in a host of Christian media over hundreds if not a couple thousand years.

> **Genesis 1:26-31** — *Then God said, "Let Us make man in Our image, according to Our likeness; and let them rule over the fish of the sea and over the birds of the sky and over the cattle and over all the earth, and over every creeping thing that creeps on the earth." 27 God created man in His own image, in the image of God He created him; male and female He created them. 28 God blessed them; and God said to them, "Be fruitful and multiply, and fill the earth, and subdue it; and rule over the fish of the sea and over the birds of the sky and over every living thing that moves on the earth." 29 Then*

God said, "Behold, I have given you every plant yielding seed that is on the surface of all the earth, and every tree which has fruit yielding seed; it shall be food for you; 30 and to every beast of the earth and to every bird of the sky and to every thing that moves on the earth which has life, I have given every green plant for food"; and it was so. 31 God saw all that He had made, and behold, it was very good. And there was evening and there was morning, the sixth day.

In the overview of all creation, God placed Adam and Eve as God's authority over all that God created.

Adam's Commitment to God

How was the stage set? It started with a commitment between God and Adam (and us by proxy) in Genesis 2.

Genesis 2:15 — *Then the LORD God took the man and put him into the garden of Eden to cultivate it and keep it. 16 The LORD God commanded the man, saying, "From any tree of the garden you may eat freely; 17 but from the tree of the knowledge of good and evil you shall not eat, for in the day that you eat from it you will surely die."*

God placed Adam (us) in the garden of Eden for the purpose of cultivating and keeping it. God then said, suggested, requested? No, He *commanded* Adam.

"Commanded," according to Webster's is "to direct authoritatively; order; commanded adherence to the rules."[4]

God used His authority to give Adam (us) a directive that contained both freedom and restriction. Freedom "from any tree of the garden you may eat freely" (Genesis 2:16). Restriction "from the tree of the knowledge of good and evil you shall not eat" (Genesis 2:17).

---

[4] "Commanded," Meriam-Webster, https://www.merriam-webster.com/dictionary/command. Accessed February 12, 2024.

God gave Adam (us) total freedom within the garden but with only one restriction. He was to not eat the fruit of the Tree of the Knowledge of Good and Evil.

While we focus on *the* "command," let's realize that *all the words* from God are authoritative. Therefore, when God states His purpose for man, "And let them rule over," it is made by God's own holy authority.

It is important to note "who" God gave this command to. It was Adam, the male side of man. Eve had not been created at this point in the Creation timeline. Note also what was the outcome of not obeying this command (His Word) of God, "For in the day that you eat from it you will surely die." We have to assume from the context that Adam (we) recognized God's authority and therefore knew his disobedience would have consequences. Adam had knowledge of the concepts that God was using in this command, else why would this have been recorded this way? Everything in Adam's world, God said it and it was so. Therefore, he has no reason not to take God at His Word here.

The recording of this exchange sets the stage for how God will choose to interact with the object of His love (us, all humanity). This is His pattern in dealing with us. God will give us a command and then state the consequences if we do not obey. The follow-up story, however, is equally loving if we choose to disobey, by God providing *redemption.* Even though God provides redemption, it is important to note that His commands are to be taken seriously. This is evident when you consider the consequence stated in the text, that if the command is not obeyed, "you will surely die."

Adam and Eve were eternal beings like angels. However, unlike angels, Adam and Eve were not immortal. They needed the fruit from the Tree of Life to sustain them. They had eternal life if we define eternal life as life in the physical presence of God. As long as they served and obeyed God, the fruit of the Tree of Life would sustain them forever. When they failed God's command to refrain from eating the fruit of the knowledge…it brought about eternal death. Death is the separation from the presence of God. But it also introduced physical death since they would be forever barred from the Garden and thus the Tree of Life.[5]

Right from the get-go, God states that obedience to His Word(s), His Command, is of the highest importance in His relationship between Adam (us) and Himself. We place the same importance on our words, don't we? Think about it. We have acted on all sorts of vows, oaths, and promises in our lives. We get this. We have done it and our government or authorities "commanded" it of others in our own lives.

Adam was created in the likeness of the Godhead as the first of humanity. He had a unique relationship with God among all creation and Adam was fully aware of that. After all, it was Adam who reviewed and named every other creature upon the earth. No other creature was made in the image of the Godhead. No other creature had the position given to them by God to name all the creatures of the earth. No other creature was given a charge by God and the freedom to accomplish it by the abilities given to them by their Creator. No other creature was given a command to obey or had the ability to choose not to obey.

Third Significant Creation

Genesis 2:18-24 — *Then the LORD God said, "It is not good for the man to be alone; I will make him a helper suitable for him." 19 Out of the ground the LORD God formed every beast of the field and every bird of the sky, and brought them to the man to see what he would call them; and whatever the man called a living creature, that was its name. 20 The man gave names to all the cattle, and to the birds of the sky, and to every beast of the field, but for Adam there was not found a helper suitable for him. 21 So the LORD God caused a deep sleep to fall upon the man, and he slept; then He took*

---

[5] For a great discussion about angels refer to an online article at Bible.org titled, "Angelology: The Doctrine of Angels"; https://bible.org/article/angelology-doctrine-angels

one of his ribs and closed up the flesh at that place. 22 The LORD God fashioned into a woman the rib which He had taken from the man, and brought her to the man. 23 The man said, "This is now bone of my bones, And flesh of my flesh; She shall be called Woman, Because she was taken out of Man." 24 For this reason a man shall leave his father and his mother, and be joined to his wife; and they shall become one flesh. 25 And the man and his wife were both naked and were not ashamed.

In the same chapter, we find the record of God's third most significant creation, Man: woman, Eve. First was the world creation and second is Man: Adam, and now third, Man: Eve.

It is significant to note the detail in which the Holy Spirit led Moses to write.

- First, we notice a relationship void in Adam's life that God sees: "It is not good for the man to be alone." In Adam's review of all the creatures, "There was not found a helper suitable for him."

- Second, God Himself says, "I will make him a helper suitable for him." No evolution here. The Scriptures record it as an act of creation as the will of the Sovereign God.

- Third, we have the contrast of "stuff" of creation: "Out of the ground the Lord God formed every beast of the field and every bird of the sky." When the Bible says, "Out of the ground," this is in contrast to when "the Lord God caused a deep sleep to fall upon the man, and he slept; then He took one of his ribs and closed up the flesh at that place. The Lord God fashioned into a woman from the rib which He had taken from the man"

The creation of Eve, Adam's wife and helpmate, is significant and unique. In her creation we see that she was Adam's equal in position but different in her function or role. Part of that role, we will discover, will not be that of the primary eternal command keeper. Recall I stated that it is important to note "who" God gave His command to not eat of the Tree of Knowledge. It was Adam, the male side of man. Eve had not been created at that point in the Creation timeline. Therefore, Eve was not the primary eternal command keeper; it was Adam.

Importance of Relationship

God (of course) saw that after Adam named all of the created living creatures, he did not have a suitable helpmate. I think it is important that God noted Adam's relationship void and declared it "not good for man to be alone." Why wasn't God enough? From the context, it apparently was by God's design that Adam was incomplete. In the text, all of God's creation had a pairing. In every created kind there were two compliments designed to procreate. But not so with Adam.

What can we derive from this? God puts a huge value on relationships. This matches the position God placed on His creation of man. All other creatures were not created in God's image. The creation of man was far more valuable than the other creatures. All creatures had value, but the creation of man was according to the likeness of the Triune God. In that likeness, it was to mirror the relationship that existed within the Trinity. "As a communion of three persons, God is a relational being. He is the originator of a personal relationship with us."[6] That relationship was now between God and man and also between Adam and Eve themselves. If you turn back to Genesis 1 where God shows an overview of His creation, you will read the highest value God places on the human relationship.

> **Genesis 1:26** — *Then God said, "Let Us make man in Our image, according to Our likeness; and let them rule over the fish of the sea and over the birds of the sky and over the cattle and over all*

---

[6] Kenneth Boa, *Conformed to His Image*, Revised Edition (Grand Rapids: Zondervan, 2020), 4

the earth, and over every creeping thing that creeps on the earth." 27 God created man in His own image, in the image of God He created him; male and female He created them.

God said, "Let us make man in Our image, according to Our likeness." "Let Us" shows the community relationship among the Godhead: Father, Son and Holy Spirit. Relationship is shown as important within the Godhead, and relationship will be shown as important to all of creation. No other living creature out of all creation held this intimate position with their Maker, nor did any other have God's image as their design guide. And the Scripture shows it was not just Adam-Man that held this position with God.

Genesis 1:27 — *God created man in His own image, in the image of God He created him;* **male and female He created them.**

In this overview of all creation we see additional detail. The term "man" was a class of humankind. Both Adam, male, and Eve, female, were considered "man." Both Man: Adam and Man: Eve God made in the likeness of "Us, Our" (Elohim, plural in form and singular in meaning) image. Both Adam and Eve held a special place in God's creation.

Both Adam and Eve possessed within their own being a special relationship and position with God the Creator. God was intimate with the creation of Adam, and God actually blew His own breath of life into Adam's nostrils, creating him in the form of His own image.

Genesis 2:7 — *Then the LORD God formed man of dust from the ground, and breathed into his nostrils the breath of life; and man became a living being.*

While God was intimately connected to the creation of Adam through His own breath, God was indirectly intimate in His creation of Eve. Life, through God's breath, was already in Adam and so God took from Adam his rib and formed his helpmate, Eve.

Relationships Were Set

The relationship stage was set. God had a more intimate relationship with Adam above all other created kinds, especially in the exchange of communication. In this intimate relationship, God created Adam first, then commanded Adam to obey His Word and not to eat of the tree of the knowledge of good and evil. God created a woman, Eve, out of man's rib to be Adam's helpmate. Both Adam and Eve were considered man made in God's image. Both Adam and Eve were commanded to "rule over the fish of the sea and over the birds of the sky and over the cattle and over all the earth, and over every creeping thing that creeps on the earth" (Genesis 1:26).

In this relationship set by God, there is an inherent created order. Man is at the pinnacle of God's creation in that only man was created after all living creatures and was the only creature that was created in the image of God. Man was given the Creator's command to rule over all of God's creatures and creation. But of the two types of man, Adam was given the specific garden command to obey. Eve was taken from Adam's flesh to be inherently connected to Adam, to be his helpmate to fulfill God's creation command to procreate and to obey the garden command.

The stage was set for the relationship with our Creator. Both Adam and Eve were created in the image of God's plural but singular self (Elohim). Both Adam and Eve were given the command to be God's stewards over all creation. But only Adam, the first man created, was given the specific instruction to not eat the fruit of only one tree. In Genesis, we are introduced to the first characters representing all of mankind. We met Adam. Now we meet Eve.

Let's look back at the intimate creation of Eve, the woman of man in Genesis 2:22-24.

Genesis 2:22-24 — *The LORD God fashioned into a woman the rib which He had taken from the man and brought her to the man. 23 The man said, "This is now bone of my bones, And flesh* *of my flesh; She shall be called Woman, Because she was taken out of Man." 24 For this reason a man shall leave his father and his mother and be joined to his wife; and they shall become one flesh. 25 And the man and his wife were both naked and were not ashamed.*

The Lord God fashioned from Adam's rib woman. God brought Eve to Adam. Chuck Swindoll, in his book. *Marriage: From Surviving to Thriving*, viewed this interaction this way:

"So God created the woman from Adam's rib (Genesis 2:21–23). Once Adam 'recovered from surgery' he opened his eyes and saw the woman. The Hebrew is emphatic so that his first words should be translated, 'Now, finally, at last!' She perfectly complemented his every strength and weakness the way no other creature could. Adam's declaration, 'This is now bone of my bones, and flesh of my flesh,' is the basis for a Hebrew expression describing closeness, oneness, or intimacy. It communicates that she is the fulfillment of everything he desired. And having seen every other creature God had made, he was in a good position to know. This is a magnificent scene played out in an idyllic setting, and it's the beginning of a wonderful love story."[7]

All men can relate to Adam's first meeting with Eve. For the men reading this, did you not have that "WOW" factor when you met the love of your life? I know I did!

Adam and Eve were created in the image of the Godhead. In that created image, they shared equality with each other before God, but their designed functional roles were significantly different. As with all pairings by the Creator in His creation, Adam and Eve complimented each other perfectly as the Designer intended.

---

[7] Charles R. Swindoll, *Marriage: From Surviving to Thriving* (Nashville: Thomas Nelson, 2008). 29-35

Final Significant Character

The final significant character in our Garden of Eden Play is Satan, the devil. A little backstory on Satan is appropriate. Who is Satan? For a very short description, I will give you GotQuestions.org answer.

> *People's beliefs concerning Satan range from the silly to the abstract— from a little red guy with horns who sits on your shoulder urging you to sin, to an expression used to describe the personification of evil. The Bible, however, gives us a clear portrait of who Satan is and how he affects our lives. Put simply, the Bible defines Satan as an angelic being who fell from his position in heaven due to sin and is now completely opposed to God, doing all in his power to thwart God's purposes.*
>
> *Satan was created as a holy angel. Isaiah 14:12 possibly gives Satan's pre-fall name as Lucifer. Ezekiel 28:12-14 describes Satan as having been created a cherub, apparently the highest created angel. He became arrogant in his beauty and status and decided he wanted to sit on a throne above that of God (Isaiah 14:13-14; Ezekiel 28:15; 1 Timothy 3:6). Satan's pride led to his fall. Notice the many "I will" statements in Isaiah 14:12-15. Because of his sin, God permanently removed Satan from his exalted position and role.[8]*

Satan is an angelic creature who is a spirit. As a spirit, he obviously, from the context, can inhabit flesh-and-blood creatures. This is no different, for instance, from the demon-possessed men of the country of the Gadarenes pleading with Jesus to cast them into the herd of pigs found in Matthew 8. While there are several examples of demon or spirit possession, another one in this example in Matthew 9 is that of a man whom the demon had made mute. Jesus cast out the demon and the man could speak plainly with everyone around.

---

[8] "Who/What is Satan?" Got Questions Ministries,
https://www.gotquestions.org/who-Satan.html. Accessed February 20, 2024.

The first verse of the third chapter of Genesis gives us insight into the character of Satan.

Genesis 3:1 — *Now the serpent was more crafty than any beast of the field which the Lord God had made.*[9]

Satan is obviously aware of the creation of man. Satan is also aware of God's relationship with man and of God's command to Adam, specifically the purpose of Eve's creation, their role, purpose, and the command of God to them both. Satan knows the Scriptures. Psalm 91:11–12 was quoted by Satan when he tempted Messiah Jesus in the desert (Matthew 4:6). Satan is well aware of the Word of God, but we need to remember even though Satan has great power, he is still a creature himself. He is a creation of God. like man. And just like man, as God is man's God, so God is Satan's God. I know that is odd sounding, but it is true. For God's sovereign reason, Satan is allowed a role in God's world. But I put it to you that Satan's role was intensified or solidified by man's disobedience.

1 Peter 1:12 — *"It was revealed to them [the prophets] that they were not serving themselves, but you, in these things which now have been announced to you through those who preached the gospel to you by the Holy Spirit sent from heaven—things into which angels long to look."*

Satan also has limited understanding because he is a creature. The Apostle Peter (1 Peter 1:12) said this of angels whenever he was discussing how God's plan of salvation was first revealed through His prophets to Israel but they did not fully grasp it. It was not until the Apostles' preaching of the Gospel of Messiah (Christ) that their prophecy was fulfilled and revealed to the Apostles by the Holy Spirit. These two themes were desired by angels to understand. But they were

---

[9] A note: I am not going to go into the two views held by evangelicals whether Satan was a literal snake or whether it was Satan controlling a snake. Our focus is the relationships and dynamic between the characters. There are good commentaries that can deal with these issues.

limited. Dr. Arnold G. Fruchtenbaum had this comment on the verse in 1 Peter 1:12:

> *"Now, the announcement of the fulfillment has come by means of the apostles who preached. Preaching was also accomplished through the power of the Holy Spirit Who indwelled the prophets. In the past, the Holy Spirit inspired the prophets, and now He uses the apostles as His agents to spread the Gospel. The Holy Spirit sent forth from Heaven, emphasizes His work of inspiration. Peter concludes that even angels desire to investigate and understand the two themes. The Greek word for look into means "to stoop down in order to get a better look" or "to stoop down in order to look at or to peer into." The point being made here is that the angels are characterized by an intense interest in what God is bringing about for the salvation of man. The present tense used here demonstrates a continuous inner yearning to understand. Peter is teaching that angels look at church truth "from the side" as the Greek implies. Angels are outside the work of redemption and, therefore, no redemption is provided for fallen angels. Because angels are outside the work of redemption, they cannot understand it in terms of their own experience. Angels are not participants; they are spectators. In Luke 15:7 and 10, angels rejoice when someone is saved. In I Corinthians 4:9, angels are spectators of believers' sufferings. Here, they are spectators of believers' salvation."[10]*

To round out our brief sketch of the Garden of Eden character named Satan, I submit this short summary of the person of Satan, as a fallen angel, by a Biblical resource I used previously called Got Questions.

> *Why did Satan fall from heaven? Satan fell because of pride. He desired to be God, not to be a servant of God. Notice the many "I*

---

[10] Dr. Arnold G. Fruchtenbaum, The Messianic Jewish Epistles : Hebrews, James, First Peter, Second Peter, Jude (San Antonio: Ariel Ministries, 2005), 225

will..." statements in Isaiah 14:12-15. Ezekiel 28:12-15 describes Satan as an exceedingly beautiful angel. Satan was likely the highest of all angels, the anointed cherub, the most beautiful of all of God's creations, but he was not content in his position. Instead, Satan desired to be God, to essentially "kick God off His throne" and take over the rule of the universe. Satan wanted to be God, and interestingly enough, that is essentially what Satan tempted Adam and Eve within the Garden of Eden (Genesis 3:1-5). How did Satan fall from heaven? Actually, a fall is not an accurate description. It would be far more accurate to say God cast Satan out of heaven (Isaiah 14:15; Ezekiel 28:16-17). Satan did not fall from heaven; rather, Satan was pushed.[11]

This final character in the Garden of Eden stage is Satan, an angelic being of significant position with God the Creator. But as with other angels being a creature, Satan does have limited understanding as does God's highest creation, man. The Garden stage is now set for the relationships to live out between God the Creator and His creatures Man: Adam, Man: Eve, and Satan.

Satan's Set Up

The setup for the crack in man's relationship with God starts out between the characters of Satan and Man: Eve.

> **Genesis 3:1-5** — *Now the serpent was more crafty than any beast of the field which the LORD God had made. And he said to the woman, "Indeed, has God said, 'You shall not eat from any tree of the garden'?" 2 The woman said to the serpent, "From the fruit of the trees of the garden we may eat; 3 but from the fruit of the tree which is in the middle of the garden, God has said, 'You shall not eat from it or touch it, or you will die.'" 4 The serpent said to the*

---

[11] "How, Why, and When Did Satan Fall from Heaven?" Got Questions Ministries, https://www.gotquestions.org/Satan-fall.html. Accessed February 20, 2024.

woman, "You surely will not die! 5 For God knows that in the day you eat from it your eyes will be opened, and you will be like God, knowing good and evil."

Hermeneutics, the best method for determining texts, demands that we do not assume anything about the text, and that context is the rule for the lens of content, grammar, language, culture and history. That entire process is observation of the text through all of these lenses. This process is really no different from reading any other book. The difference is that the author usually provides most of that for the reader. In the Bible, most of that is assumed by the author's audience. Therefore, we, as the modern reader, need to do some digging to provide all of these lenses. Observation is the first part of a process in accurate Bible study methods that sets up correct interpretation that leads to meaningful application of the truths of the text to our life. So, what can we observe?

In this initial interaction between Satan and Eve, let's observe from the text. First off, this is the first recorded conversation of Eve with Satan and of them together. What does that tell you from the content of their conversation? They seem familiar with each other and even comfortable. There is no surprise given by Eve that she is talking with an animal, a serpent. Their demeanor is comfortable enough to have some level of trust in each other, at least for the conversation. Why? Because the content of the conversation holds no conversational hedging or any strong objections, questioning, positioning, or argument. The conversation is just a matter of fact. There was a little back and forth but no real challenges.

I think it interesting that Genesis chapter 3 opens with its introduction of Satan that he is "more crafty than any beast." This is a prelude description of Satan's mindset entering the conversation with Eve. It is also interesting to observe that Satan chose to enter a conversation about God with Eve, whom God did not give the only command. Why do you think that Satan would choose Eve to set up this first temptation?

We get our clues for the answer to that question from the text about Eve's creation. In the creation of Eve, we observed that God puts a huge value on relationship. We saw that God noted Adam's relationship void of completion and declared it "not good for man to be alone." Eve was Adam's pairing in God's creation. Eve was Adam's helpmate. Eve had great influence over Adam. Satan was aware of her position and of her influence. Adam was the rule keeper. Who better to start with than the one who has the most influence over the rule keeper?

Satan's Conversation with Eve

Let's break down their conversation. Satan starts it. "And he said to the woman, 'Indeed, has God said, 'You shall not eat from any tree of the garden?'" Remember the text said that Satan was crafty. Satan's approach is to take the command God gave to Man: Adam in a general, broad sense and reverse it as a question. Innocent enough. Was Satan asking this question merely to clarify Eve's understanding of God's command to Adam? Of course not! It is a set-up with an evil agenda.

Eve replies to Satan, "The woman said to the serpent, 'From the fruit of the trees of the garden we may eat; but from the fruit of the tree, which is in the middle of the garden, God has said, 'You shall not eat from it or touch it, or you will die.'" In Eve's reply, she answers Satan's question of supposed clarity. She says, "From the fruit of the trees in the garden we may eat." Asked and answered. Eve replied further, "But from the fruit of the tree which is in the middle of the garden, God has said, 'You shall not eat from it or touch it, or you will die.'" Eve, in her complete reply, did restate the command God gave to Man: Adam and one that she was obligated to obey as Man: Eve.

God's command was clear. God said don't. Period. End of story. God did not need to slice and dice His definition of death. His Word was given to man to simply obey. "But from the fruit of the tree which is in the middle of the garden," God has said from Eve's recollection, "You shall not eat from it or touch it" Did you gloss over the phrase "or touch it?" To me, that is not only a "no" but a "NO." But that was not part of the original command. To not "touch it" was something that Eve added to the context of the command given to Adam. When we don't recall God's Word correctly, we often add more restrictions than what His Word actually shows.[12] This distortion reveals Eve's mindset of doubting God's goodness. This mindset played into Satan's temptation that God was holding something good back from Adam and Eve. This was Satan's first objective in planting a seed of doubt to bring into question the goodness of God's character as he mocks the concept of death.

But God never held anything good back from Adam and Eve. There is no evidence of this in any experience that they had with God. The entire context of chapters 1 and 2 showed that God provided every good thing. God did not need to explain what death meant. He clearly commanded man to "X" off that specific tree, period. The command was not optional from God's point of view. In the history of the garden, there was not any interaction between Adam and God where Adam questioned God. God's Word went forth and it was. Adam always heartily did and agreed.

Remember the text stated that Satan was "more crafty?" The word crafty was more about wisdom than evil. Satan's reply to Eve's restatement of God's command, "The serpent said to the woman, 'You surely will not die! For God knows that in the day you eat from it your eyes will be opened, and you will be like God, knowing good and evil.'" Satan plays on Eve's doubt of God's goodness and implies God is holding back something that is good for them. Here the crafty devil attacks the one unclear area of God's command, namely death. Satan's strategy is to question one obscure, undefined area of God's command, and by doing so, he brings into question the entire command, including the very clear part of the command. This is a familiar strategy that Satan uses in our lives, even to this day. Then using his "Garden

---

[12] Dr. Thomas L. Constable, *Notes on Genesis 2019 Edition*, (Plano: Self-published eBook), 78.

relationship" with Eve, Satan uses a concept that Eve is familiar with namely that the phrases "God said" and "His Word" are the same thing. Here Satan presents what he is craftily relating to her that "God knows," implying with the same authority as the command of God to Adam, telling her his own interpretation. Satan has set up the trap for Eve to venture out to add her own interpretation of God's Word. Or actually, to incorporate Satan's interpretation as her own and supplant God's clear, no-need-for-interpretation Word given to Eve through Adam.

The sad part of Satan's temptation was to get Eve to believe that she did not have something when she already had it in her possession. Eve was already "like" God in that she was made in His image (Genesis 1:26). As a creature of the Creator, as He designed her, she could possess no higher image. No other creature was formed by the Creator as Adam and Eve were formed.

But the temptation was much deeper than that. It is the same depth of disobedience (sin) that Satan committed. Satan desired to be God's equal. To be a god like Him. Here with Eve, that is also Satan's goal for her to disobey (sin) in order to put her thoughts above God's command. Her "Word" is put above God's Word.

What the serpent said about Eve being "as (like) God (or 'gods')" was a half-truth. Ironically, she was already "like God," having been made in His image (1:26). She did become like God, or divine beings (Hebrew: 'Elohim), in that she obtained a greater knowledge of good and evil by eating of the tree. However, she became less like God, because she was no longer innocent of sin. Her relationship with God suffered. Though she remained like God, she could no longer enjoy unhindered fellowship with God (3:24). The consequent separation from God (broken fellowship with God) is the essence of (spiritual) death (2:17)—ultimately eternal death, and permanent separation for the unsaved.

The first doctrine Satan denied in Scripture was that sin results in death (separation from God); on the negative side, the first false doctrine was that God will not punish sin. This is still the truth that Satan tries the hardest to get people to disbelieve.[13]

How Was God Loved?

In Adam and Eve's relationship with God, all they could do, all they ever knew was His love and their loving Him in return. How did they love Him in return? By merely being the people God created them to be in His vision for them, in their lives for Him, in their purpose He created them to be. It was an obedience that was natural, not even a conscious effort. An obedience that was not questioned. There was no other way of expression but love embodied in loving obedience to the Word, will, and work of God. That expression of love by the first couple in a natural flow of loving obedience to God the Father is the same loving expression we see in the life of Messiah Jesus, the Man, to God the Father. It was pure and natural, but for the first couple, it was unconfirmed. The first couple constantly made their choice to lovingly obey God the Father until they did not.

[13] Constable, Notes on Genesis 2019 Edition, 79.

3

All About God's Words

I t is all about God's Words with the first couple in the Garden of Eden. It has always been since His relationship with man. In this context, it is it specifically about the Words out of God's mouth to Adam and Eve. The interpersonal aspect of God and man has always been God's Word to man (us) and our response to His Word. From the Garden to the Cross to today, it has always been about God's Word. Messiah Jesus Himself is called the Word from this beginning! Wow![14]

> **John 1:1-5** — *1 In the beginning was the Word, and the Word was with God, and the Word was God. 2 He was in the beginning with God. 3 All things came into being through Him, and apart from Him nothing came into being that has come into being. 4 In Him was life, and the life was the Light of men. 5 The Light shines in the darkness, and the darkness did not comprehend it.*

---

[14] For a brief overview of Jesus Being the Word read this article: https://www.gotquestions.org/Jesus-Bible-Word-God.html and this article: https://www.gotquestions.org/Jesus-Word-God.html

Jesus was the "Inspired Word that revealed the Infinite Word that became the Incarnate Word to become the Indwelling Word."[15] It is truly all about God's Word to man (us).

First Encounter with Bad Interpretation

In this Genesis 3 conversation between Satan and Eve, where we have our first encounter with bad interpretation. Eve not only added to God's Word, but she also read meaning into them with Satan's words rather than accepting God's meaning. I often hear Christians whine about the use of theology and standard Biblical concepts. It is like an epidemic of non-reading and non-study that does not even approach the level of the definition of academic. There is an American conservative political commentator, Jesse Watters, who has a show called Watter's World. In one part of that show, Mr. Watters interviews college students and asks them very simple, dumbed down questions about well-known political figures of past and present. What stood out was how the college student's education had miserably failed them so that most interviewed had no clue of who these key people were. This same lack of education epidemic appears to not be only regulated to the college crowd but has come to rest in our society and sadly in our churches too.

Parroting

With the churches in particular, it may have its roots in how one views the authority of the Bible. What position does the Bible, God's Word, hold in your life? I can remember whenever I was 17 years old and a brand new believer in Christ, that I made this statement, "Oh yeah, the Bible is a good book, but it contains errors since it was written by man." I can hardly believe I had said those words today. I was merely a societal parrot speaking back a statement that I had heard over and

---

[15] The Four Words of God: Inspired, Infinite, Incarnate, Indwelling from Dr. Ken Boa, Friday Morning Men's Bible Study

over from my culture without any self-analysis or intelligent discovery of my own. Of course, while parroting it, I felt it made me appear in grasp of current thought and to be intelligent. But, in my current opinion, it is more a poor self-esteem issue than anything else.

Why do we do that? Why do we parrot what we hear? There are various motives attached. There can be devious and malicious motives for sure. Sometimes it is a matter of pride within the crowd in which we find ourselves. We are not willing to say a different thing. However, I believe, for the most part that the motive stems from a need to have a "whole" and not a "part." I think human nature likes a whole thought, idea, belief, a whole history and not parts. We stuff into a void something, in our opinion, that is the best thought, idea, or belief part for that assumed particular whole. It becomes a mental placeholder or bracket if you will. However, sometimes, that action of stuffing or filling the void of that part into the assumed whole is more closely scrutinized by us, but sadly, sometimes not at all. But to complete the whole story we are compelled. Of course, ever since that statement as a 17-year-old, I have long changed that part of my thinking about the Bible as the Words of God with the same authority as God Himself.

What Does the Bible Mean to Me?

There is a concept that is running rampant in the Christian church and has been for decades. It has gained a lot more ground today it seems. The concept is best expressed in what is actually said. It goes like this, "What that Bible verse (or verses or passage) means to me…" It is part of the umbrella statement of "What Does the Bible Mean to Me?" The problem with this statement is that it is putting our own perception as an overlay on the content of the Scriptures. I think if this idea were peeled back, we may find out that at its root is our concept of the authority of the Word of God.

Our discovery, our understanding of the Scripture's meaning is coming from the outside into the Word of God rather than from the Word of God out. It does not matter where that "outside" influence is coming from. It could be from within us. We have so many influencers buried in our minds that the origination has been lost. But no matter where we find the connection in our own mind or from some outside source, it is still an arbitrary overlay we place onto the Scripture. We will see later on that this was Eve's problem as well. She read meaning into the Words of God that the Author never intended. Instead, if we are serious about discovering what the Word of God actually says, we need to seek what was the original author's meaning to their original audience.

I believe that this can be done innocently, without malice, but it does have its roots, it seems to me, in what position of esteem and authority do you place the Word of God in your Christian life? The key phrase is "Word of God." This is foundational. Remember when I said as a 17-year-old that the Bible contained errors since it was written by man? If I had continued to hold that position of the Bible, it would be an escape door. I lessened the Bible's position of authority thereby lessening the position of God's authority over the practices in my life. Kind of crafty, huh? Well, where does that craftiness originate from? It seems that you and I are pretty much in the midst of the Garden every day, right there with the temptation put before Eve.

God's Word Authority or Not

The position in which you place the Bible's authority in your daily life will have an enormous effect on you and with whom you connect. Not only the people but their belief in God's Word and how that it affects their actions, interactions and influence in your life. This is true now and it was equally true with Adam and Eve in the Garden. It will have a foundational effect on how you view God and the quality of your relationship with Him. From your relationship with God emanates the quality of relationships with your mate, children, fellow Christians, neighbors, and unbelievers. Bible teachers maintain that God chose to superintend the human writers and was able to control what was being written without having to dictate. God used the individual writing style, personality, and life experiences of these authors but, by His superintendence, still produced word-for-word what He wanted to produce. This is called "inerrancy," meaning that when these original writings were composed, they were without error. Copies of the Scripture from that original did contain errors. But these copy errors were insignificant.

If you are interested in this, I would recommend the books by Josh and Sean McDowell, *Evidence Demands a Verdict* Volumes I and II. I used these texts extensively as resource documents when I was in my undergraduate studies. Their discoveries about the Bible and its reliability were an enormous faith builder for me personally in the cynical, aversive world of college academics.

So in your Garden as either an Adam or an Eve, if this was *actually* "the" Word of God to you, how different would you treat it? Would you make it the top priority for your reading, studying, and digging deeper academically? The use of theology in its simplest form is the packaging of God's aspects on a particular subject from His Word. Wouldn't one want to know all there is about God's love, hate, sovereignty, unchanging character, image, justice, creation, etc.? Of course, you would. So, theology is not a bad thing but a necessary thing if you are going to be serious about your discovery of God and all He is.

Correct Interpretation First Key Concept: Context

Interpretation is one of those standard Biblical concepts every Christian needs to know. While I won't go into everything about interpretation here, one concept is sorely important and is fundamentally basic to any correct interpretation. This one concept is yet a simple one, context. I love this concept because it is a very critical part of the foundation to the house of interpretation. I have often taught that if you keep this one simple rule of interpretation, it will keep you out of 90% of bad or inaccurate interpretations of the Bible. It is very simple. Every word has a context within the sentence in which it is found, that sentence within the paragraph, that paragraph within the chapter, that chapter within the book, and that book in the context of the other 66 books of the Bible. The words derive their meaning from their context.

There are several contexts to broaden your search for original meaning. There is the textual context where the word is found in the text, but there is also a grammatical, historical and cultural context of word(s) as well.

In the context we are currently reviewing, we know that man had access to God. We know that just after Adam's creation, the text states that

Genesis 2:15 — *Then the LORD God took the man and put him into the garden of Eden to cultivate it and keep it. 16 The LORD God commanded the man, saying, "From any tree of the garden you may eat freely; 17 but from the tree of the knowledge of good and evil you shall not eat, for in the day that you eat from it you will surely die."*

Key in on the phrase, "the Lord God took the man and put him into the garden of Eden." Look at the verbs "took" and "put." Add to that the phrase, "The Lord God commanded the man, saying." What do these phrases imply? It at least implies that Adam was in near proximity to the Lord God. That nearness and what the verbs imply is relationship and a positive one at that. The very next verse drives this concept home even further.

Genesis 2:18 — *Then the LORD God said, "It is not good for the man to be alone; I will make him a helper suitable for him."*

The God of the Universe sees that it is not good for Adam to be alone. Wow! Here Adam is in a relationship with the LORD God, and the LORD God said that was not enough. God said that He would make a helper suitable for Adam. That act alone should give us a key to how important the marriage relationship is to God. We often think if I were to be stranded on an island, just give me my Bible and Jesus. That is all I need. But God said, "No, you also need Eve!"

Another example of this closeness to the Lord God and Adam is in the naming of the living creatures.

> **Genesis 2:19** — *Out of the ground the LORD God formed every beast of the field and every bird of the sky and brought them to the man to see what he would call them; and whatever the man called a living creature, that was its name.*

Who brought the living creatures to Adam? The Lord God "brought them to the man to see what he would call them." Again, this closer interaction shouts relationship to us off the pages of the text.

I am driving home the point that in the context we observe that Adam and the Lord God were in a close relationship. But there is nothing from the text that we could conclude that Eve did not also have this same kind of access and closeness to the Lord God. We observe that the Lord God brought her to man after He had created her.

> **Genesis 2:21** — *So the LORD God caused a deep sleep to fall upon the man, and he slept; then He took one of his ribs and closed up the flesh at that place. 22 The LORD God fashioned into a woman the rib which He had taken from the man, and brought her to the man.*

Later in the Garden, we observe God addressing Eve personally. So, all of this discussion about Man's (both Adam and Eve) relationship with the Lord God is why I referred to Eve's consideration of what she understood as the Word from God given directly to them as a bad interpretation. She read into what she knew correctly of God's Word given directly to them an interpretation of Satan's influence.

Is It Reading into the Text of Scripture or Read Out from the Text of Scripture?

Wikipedia defines reading into the text as Eisegesis. Here is their definition:

> *Eisegesis is the process of interpreting a text or portion of text in such a way that the process introduces one's own presuppositions, agendas, or biases into and onto the text. This is commonly referred to as reading into the text. The act is often used to "prove" a pre-held point of concern to the reader and to provide him or her with confirmation bias in accordance with his or her pre-held agenda. Eisegesis is best understood when contrasted with exegesis. While exegesis is the process of drawing out the meaning from a text in accordance with the context and discoverable meaning of its author, eisegesis occurs when a reader imposes his or her interpretation into and onto the text. As a result, exegesis tends to be objective when employed effectively while eisegesis is regarded as highly subjective.*[16]

This goes back to our brief discussion about the use of theology and Biblical concepts. Eisegesis (into) and exegesis (out of) are tools used in Biblical interpretation. Many a mistake has been made with thousands of printed pages over centuries using eisegesis as part of the process of Biblical interpretation. How could this apply here to Eve? What does the definition of eisegesis state? It is "interpreting a text or portion of text in such a way that the process introduces one's own presuppositions, agendas, or biases into and onto the text. This is commonly referred to as reading into the text."

We have already established in our own observation of the context of the Scripture text that Eve, like Adam, was in a close relationship with God. It was also clear that she was in a close relationship with Adam. We observed that Eve clearly understood what God had said about the tree in the center of the Garden. By

---

[16] "Eisegesis," Wikipedia, https://en.wikipedia.org/wiki/Eisegesis. Accessed February 26, 2024.

replacing the clear, literal, objective interpretation of the Words of God with the subjective Satanic agenda imposed onto the Word of God, she committed a grave error in the interpretation of God's Word. This error was reading meaning into His Words rather than drawing its meaning out from the context of His Word.

Eve had no reason to substitute Satan's interpretation of God's command. The use of context goes further than just the language of the words in the text. There is also a cultural context. Within the cultural context of the Garden we observed that Eve had two close relationships, one with Adam and the other with God. She could have used these relationships to discover her error and not commit her bad interpretation. Eve could have gone to either Adam or to the Lord God for clarity. However, she did not. Even in the context of her relationship with God, when did God ever invite Eve or Adam to repeat back to Him what they thought He meant? There is never a recorded conversation where Eve or Adam misunderstood what God had said nor where they asked for clarification. She knew who God was in relationship to every other living thing. She knew that any word from Satan who tried to reclarify or restate God's Word should be suspect. She knew the importance of God's Word over any other word from any other creature, including Satan.

I like how Dr. Thomas Constable summed up the dynamics and purpose of the relationship of Adam and Eve and God in his commentary on Genesis:

> However, a main point of this unit (2:4-25) seems clearly to be that God made human beings "male and female," with a spiritual capacity, and mutually dependent. He did so that they might serve and obey Him, and so enjoy His creation. As with Adam and Eve, God later placed Israel in a place of blessing. The nation could enjoy His blessing by being obedient and trusting, with the assistance He had provided for them in marriage. Even today, serving and obeying

God is man's greatest privilege, and we find help to do this in the marriage relationship.[17]

It is amazing that man would use their power of choice in the way they did, given the personal knowledge they possessed of God and the experience they enjoyed with God. However, we do the same today. It really shows that we, too, have the same sinful (disobedient) nature that Adam and Eve had. So, sin as we defined as disobedience to God's Word goes deeper than that. It goes to our nature before we believe in how the Messiah has taken away our sins.

"This decision [of Adam and Eve] to disobey God introduced sin into the world. But of course it didn't end with just one sin. Their act of disobedience changed them. They now had a sin nature that has been passed on to their descendants—that is, every person who has ever existed or will exist, including you and me. (This is called original sin.) Thus, because of Adam's fall, each and every one of us has a sin nature, a proclivity toward sin, a bent toward self (Rom 5:12-21). Moreover, because of our natural inclinations, each and every one of us commits specific acts of disobedience against God."[18]

Today as Christians redeemed by the blood of Messiah's sacrifice and released from the power over our sin nature, we now have true freedom. This freedom is the true restored power of choice that Adam had in the Graden. We now have the power of choice to either obey or disobey God's Word and God Himself. Through the redeemed, restored relationship with God the Father through God the Son, we are back in the Garden every day. We can choose to obey God's Word or we can still choose to sin. Stop and think about that. It's like Bill Murray's *Groundhog's Day* but much more real and very positive (at least it is designed to be).

---

[17] Constable, Notes on Genesis 2019 Edition, 75.
[18] Jon, "What is Sin?" *What is Theology Series?*
   https://www.youtube.com/@biblicalnow6644/featured

The big difference between the original Garden experience and this current one for the restored believer is that eternal separation from God the Father is off the table. Messiah Jesus paid the Father's penalty for us. So, does that mean we can kick up our heels and disobey (sin) all the more? The Apostle Paul wrote about this in his letter to the Romans.

Romans 6:1-11 — *What shall we say then? Are we to continue in sin so that grace may increase? 2 May it never be! How shall we who died to sin still live in it? 3 Or do you not know that all of us who have been baptized into Christ Jesus have been baptized into His death? 4 Therefore we have been buried with Him through baptism into death, so that as Christ was raised from the dead through the glory of the Father, so we too might walk in newness of life.*

5 For if we have become united with Him in the likeness of His death, certainly we shall also be in the likeness of His resurrection, 6 knowing this, that our old self was crucified with Him, in order that our body of sin might be done away with, so that we would no longer be slaves to sin; 7 for he who has died is freed from sin.

8 Now if we have died with Christ, we believe that we shall also live with Him, 9 knowing that Christ, having been raised from the dead, is never to die again; death no longer is master over Him. 10 For the death that He died, He died to sin once for all; but the life that He lives, He lives to God. 11 Even so consider yourselves to be dead to sin, but alive to God in Christ Jesus.

4

The Hook Was Set Including Jesus

The Anatomy of Sin

After her encounter with Satan, Eve did not even reply to Satan's interpretation of God's Word. It was as if she went into a trance or auto-drive. But is that not what happens to you and me? Once we have committed that handshake with Satan's temptation designed specifically for us, we also go into this trance, this auto-drive. We can even be conscious that we are in the midst of this disobedience, yet it is as if we see obedience objectified "over there" and we are passing it by in this temptation trance toward completing this disobedience against God's Word. It is so eerie and weird for us. Yet we find ourselves in the midst of this same thing but hopefully less as we mature in Christ. This is how the text describes Eve.

> **Genesis 3:6a** — *When the woman saw that the tree was good for food, and that it was a delight to the eyes, and that the tree was desirable to make one wise, she took from its fruit and ate;*

Let's break this response down.

Anatomy of Sin	
Genesis 3:6a	**1 John 2:16**
saw the tree was good for food	lust of the flesh
it was a delight to the eyes	lust of the eyes
the tree was desirable to make one wise	boastful pride of life

1 John 2:16 — *For all that is in the world, the lust of the flesh and the lust of the eyes and the boastful pride of life, is not from the Father, but is from the world.*

Once Eve did not go to her established relationships, especially to God Himself to validate this new interpretation of His command, she was doomed. But because the command was given to Man: Adam, I believe that Eve's sin by itself would not have thrust all of mankind into sin. This is true if you only consider the birth of Jesus Himself.

Jesus was not born into sin or from the sin of the originator like you and me being sons and daughters of Adam. Note I wrote Adam and not Eve. Why would that be? As I explained, the commandment to not eat of the Tree of the Knowledge of Good and Evil was given to Adam and not Eve. Adam was the command keeper, not Eve. When Adam stood by and watched Eve commit her disobedience against God's Word to them in the Garden, he broke God's command. It was his act of disobedience that cursed all of humanity for all generations.

But Jesus born of a virgin, Whose Father is God through a miracle from the Holy Spirit, Jesus entered this world without sin (disobedience) attributed to Him. [19]

I think it interesting to align the progression of Eve's sin in Genesis 3 and see the correlation with the progression of sin that the Apostle John outlined in his epistle 1 John 2. The Bible speaks to three

[19] "What Is the Fall of Man? Genesis 3 Explained," Christianity Today, Revised February 28, 2022, https://www.christianity.com/wiki/bible/what-is-the-fall-of-man-genesis-3-explained.html.

temptation influencers over the Christian: the world, the flesh and the devil.

> **Ephesians 2:2-3a** — *"In which you formerly walked according to the course of this **world**, according to the **prince of the power of the air**, of the spirit that is now working in the sons of disobedience. 3 Among them we too all formerly lived in the lusts of our **flesh**."*

But whatever or whomever the influencer of our disobedience, the Apostle James lays the responsibility squarely at our own feet. This is why prayerful, faithful study of God's Word is so important for the follower of Christ, Messiah. It should be the next layer in your foundation after the layer of faith in Christ's resurrection.

> **James 1:13-18** — *Let no one say when he is tempted, "I am being tempted by God"; for God cannot be tempted by evil, and He Himself does not tempt anyone. **14 But each one is tempted when he is carried away and enticed by his own lust. 15 Then when lust has conceived, it gives birth to sin; and when sin is accomplished, it brings forth death.** 16 Do not be deceived, my beloved brethren. 17 Every good thing given and every perfect gift is from above, coming down from the Father of lights, with whom there is no variation or shifting shadow. 18 In the exercise of His will He brought us forth by the word of truth, so that we would be a kind of first fruits among His creatures.*

Temptation Is an Ominous Force

Temptation is an ominous force. Look at the angels of God. They were the first eternal holy beings created but their initial state of holiness was not yet confirmed. Where in the world did I get that from? Theology. Remember, I stated that the use of theology in its simplest form is the packaging of the concepts of God from His Word. But the last part of that sentence is the key "from the Word of God." I mentioned that observation is the first part of the process in accurate

Bible Study methods. Observation is the first step that sets up correct interpretation that leads to meaningful application of the truths of the text of Scripture to our lives. A meaningful application as an end product of that process is hosted in one's theology.

What?! Yes, I said the word "theology." The Church overall has promoted, it seems, over recent years, a distaste for theology (objective) and more for feelings (subjective). Granted, that distaste stemmed from a lot of bad theology that was rooted in man's opinion rather than in the Word of God, but that distaste, in my opinion, has resulted in the dumbing down of Christians overall. The pendulum has swung to feelings-oriented aspects of the Christian life: prayer, fellowship, music worship and guidance from the Holy Spirit. DO NOT GET ME WRONG. (Sorry for the caps, but even with that, I will still be misquoted.) ALL the feelings aspects of the Christian life are important but left apart from your faithful study and prayerful reading of the Word of God, those activities will result in an anemic, unhealthy, and imbalanced Christian lifestyle.

Let's say you engage in Bible study. You are interested in learning what the Bible says about salvation. You use a Bible dictionary, Bible concordance, and handbook, all endeavor to seek out exhaustively what the Bible states about the word or subject "salvation." Guess what you just participated in? *Theology!* Yep, you did it! Don't you see that theology is not only necessary but truly unavoidable if you are going to be a student of the Bible?

Neither theology nor doctrine are bad things. All Christians use theology and doctrine in their daily lives. I have held to a particular school of theology that has the label "dispensational." Dispensationalism is a theology within the world of Christendom. Don't stop reading and pitch the book. Set aside any previous criticisms of this you may have and give me a fair hearing. As with anything, theology surrounding the Bible has pros and cons associated with each. There are also promoters and dissenters associated with dispensational theology as well. I personally hold parts of the theology loosely where there is not as solid Biblical support as there are of other parts. However, I heartily support that theology as it is, in my opinion, the most comprehensive theology most broadly supported in the Biblical text. It is my goal to hold all my beliefs as closely aligned with the Biblical text in an interpretation that the original writers wanted to convey (author's intent). The reader should understand that there is no theological system or school of thought that has all their loose ends neatly tied up around absolute Biblical proof—my choice of theology included. Personally, I think this is designed by God. He is God and we are not. He is God and He is not to be "figured out" by us, His creatures, but only what He chooses us to discover or to be revealed.

I think that is a key truth that anyone's theology should hold at its core. Honesty. Honesty with oneself and with God about your theology. God has the authority to change our theology at any point in time. If we are truly in tune with the Holy Spirit, then I believe, as hard as it can be we are obligated to make a course correction in our theology. To do otherwise we risk the same fault of the Pharisees.

A quick note on theology in general. As I already mentioned, in many Christian circles today, just the mention of the words theology or doctrine causes people to curl their lips and tend to either distance themselves or change the subject. I always thought that odd.

Maybe it was my desire to be involved in apologetics in college. I wanted to make a difference for Christ in my studies and classes. I understood how when we put lenses in front of our eyes it changes the focus and even colors what we see. As an analogy that holds true for our minds as well and what truth we store in them. The term "worldview" was coined several years ago. The word means what truths, beliefs, opinions, and experiences that you have collectively gathered through your life become the lens through which you view (analyze, accept, reject, judge) the world around you. Whenever you go into this subject, you find out just how pervasive it is and how subtle. Sometimes how concrete. I found out that we all have a worldview. It is part of the human experience and no one can be without one. The discovery is just how solid and true your worldview is or is not. That answer will depend on how honest you will be with yourself.

Christianity is a worldview. That worldview is also made up of theology and doctrines whether you accept that or not. It just is.

Theology is a Greek compound word of God "Theo" and study "ology." So in its simplest sense it the study of God. As time marched on from the first century, educated men (and eventually women) would correlate subjects of life with Scripture. These packages of subjects correlated with Scripture began to be placed into a systematic order. This led to the term **Systematic Theology** which made for easy and quicker study. For instance, what does the Bible say about the subject of salvation? People who studied these subjects found that it opened the door to a whole host of questions and ultimately arguments, positive and negative. Of course, these arguments unresolved would cause the differing groups to collect off to themselves and eventually they would label "their" theology. There is nothing wrong with that as long as you are upfront and honest with your position or theology. Otherwise, it is kind of like having a conversation with someone operating with the same words as you but from a different dictionary with totally different meanings. So, with this study in theology as a whole and as a defined school of theology came out, in particular, a set of doctrines. A **doctrine** is a set of beliefs held and taught by a group of people (Church, political party, other groups). Over the centuries these differences produced several hundred denominations within the Christian Church as a collective whole. I realize that is a great simplification of hundreds of years of history, but the detail of that history is not my focus. The supernatural thing is that even with all of this diversity within the Church, the Spirit of God has used it all to the glory of God the Father.

The diversity of doctrine can be seen very early in the first century church. The Apostle Paul made note of this in writing to the Church at Corinth.

1 Corinthians 1:10-17, 29-31 — *Now I exhort you, brethren, by the name of our Lord Jesus Christ, that you all agree and that there be no divisions among you, but that you be made complete in the* *same mind and in the same judgment. 11 For I have been informed concerning you, my brethren, by Chloe's people, that there are quarrels among you. 12 Now I mean this, that each one of you is saying, "I am of Paul," and "I of Apollos," and "I of Cephas," and "I of Christ." 13 Has Christ been divided? Paul was not crucified for you, was he? Or were you baptized in the name of Paul? 14 I thank God that I baptized none of you except Crispus and Gaius, 15 so that no one would say you were baptized in my name. 16 Now I did baptize also the household of Stephanas; beyond that, I do not know whether I baptized any other. 17 For Christ did not send me to baptize, but to preach the gospel, not in cleverness of speech, so that the cross of Christ would not be made void.*

29 so that no man may boast before God. 30 But by His doing you are in Christ Jesus, who became to us wisdom from God, and righteousness and sanctification, and redemption, 31 so that, just as it is written, "Let him who boasts, boast in the Lord."

The bottom line for the Apostle Paul was Christ Jesus. Considering my theological disclosure, a quick note on dispensational theology would be warranted if you are unfamiliar. And if you are familiar and don't agree with its teaching don't chunk the book and walk away. Keep an open mind, my dear friend.

There are a number of different ways the Bible can be divided in order to understand the parts as well as the whole. One of the ways is by means of the dispensations, which are contained in the Scriptures.

On the one hand, the term dispensation refers to a specific way by which God administers His program and His will in the world, and on the other hand, it covers a period of time.

As to its content and meaning, a dispensation is a stewardship, a responsibility, or an administration. As to time, it is an age, because every dispensation covers a period of time. Within each dispensation,

God administers His economy, His rule, His authority, and His program in some different way than the previous dispensation.

Dispensations are separate periods of time in which God dispenses His will in a specific and unique way, based on a covenant upon which a particular dispensation is founded.[20]

It is through the lenses of dispensational theology that I used the concept of unconfirmed holiness; we discussed the holy state of the angels, and Adam and Eve, which helps us understand how the holy angels became unholy and, therefore, how holy man became unholy.

The specific test of the Dispensation of Innocence or Freedom was the test concerning the tree of the knowledge of good and evil. This was a test to see if Adam and Eve would obey the most minimal demand of the divine will. They had absolute authority over the entire planet. As far as the Garden of Eden itself was concerned, they had absolute authority over it and had the right to eat of every single tree in the garden, including the tree of life. So, the test was very minimal.

If Adam and Eve had passed the test, their state would have changed from unconfirmed creaturely holiness to confirmed creaturely holiness. This means that they would have passed from the ability to sin to the ability not to sin, or better, they would no longer have the ability to sin after their holiness was confirmed.

This was the same kind of test that all of the angels underwent when they were first created. All angels were created in unconfirmed creaturely holiness. Then came the test. Satan was the first to fail, and he was followed by one third of the entire angelic host. The one-third who failed the test are now totally corrupt. Two thirds of the angels did pass the test, changing their state from unconfirmed

---

[20] Dr. Arnold G. Fruchtenbaum, *The Dispensations of God* (Ariel Ministries, 2005), #041.

creaturely holiness to confirmed creaturely holiness. Now they are no longer able to sin whatsoever.

The same thing would have been true for Adam and Eve. Had they passed this test, they would have been confirmed in creaturely holiness just as the good angels and would not have been able to sin anymore.[21]

Temptation's Power Is an Amazing, Mysterious Power

Temptation's power is amazing and mysterious. But as James told us, it comes from within. After the cross, we are responsible since we are given power over disobedience (sin) through our salvation in the Messiah by His Spirit. After the cross our holiness is not up to us to be confirmed as did Adam. After the cross, our holiness is in the holiness of Messiah Jesus and His holiness is attributed to each of us as believers in Him. Slow down and let that soak into your soul. Messiah Jesus' holiness was *attributed* to you and me. That is a mindblower for me. You too?

But for Adam, Eve and the angels, they were created holy but unconfirmed. Adam and Eve were created in a state of 'unconfirmed creaturely holiness,' like the angels were, but they "were also given the power of contrary choice: the ability to choose contrary to their nature."[22]

They were perfect and holy, but they had the ability [like the angels] to make an unholy and imperfect choice. On their own, they must choose to love and obey God. Had they passed that one test, their holiness would have been confirmed without the ability to sin.[23]

Eve Did Not Cause Mankind to Fall...Adam Did.

Adam had a front row seat in silence.

---

[21] Fruchtenbaum, The Dispensations of God, 6.
[22] Fruchtenbaum, The Dispensations of God, 5.
[23] Fruchtenbaum, The Dispensations of God, 6.

Genesis 3:6 — *When the woman saw that the tree was good for food, and that it was a delight to the eyes, and that the tree was desirable to make one wise, she took from its fruit and ate; and she gave also to her husband with her, and he ate.*

We already know from the text that the woman Eve was a significant influencer on her husband Adam. After all, Eve was Adam's perfect match handmade by the God of everything! Recall that the command to not eat from the tree in the center of the Garden was given to Man: Adam not Man: Eve. Adam clearly knew God's Word of command to them. There was nothing arbitrary in God's command to Adam. There was nothing vague or left to chance. Adam knew exactly God's mind on the subject of the only one thing that God forbade him to do. The scene of the temptation and then the sin of disobedience is played out right in front of Adam. It was not like Eve took the fruit and had to go hunt Adam down and tell him what she did. The text tells us that Adam was front and present. He had a front row seat.

Genesis 3:6b — *And she gave also to her husband **with her**, and he ate.*

Did you observe his location? Adam was **with her**. Eve was doomed not only for her not questioning this new interpretation of God's Word, but she also had her spiritual leader at her side involved in real time. Nothing took Adam by surprise. Adam saw what Eve saw. Adam heard what Eve heard. Adam heard Eve's response. However, Eve could have stopped and not acted on her temptation. Eve could have turned to her spiritual leader and inquired of him if she was interpreting God's Word to them correctly. But she did not because evidently Adam was agreeing with her new interpretation of God's Word of command. Adam took Satan's bait as well.

It is my contention that had Adam said no to this new interpretation and he had gone to the Lord God to review, the original sin of disobedience would not have been committed. In the created order, Adam was Eve's spiritual leader; she was created after he was and purposed by God as his helpmate. The command to not eat of tree's fruit was given only to Adam by God Himself and not to Eve. So all of the Bible teachers and preachers who have placed this burden of the original sin of disobedience on the shoulders of women through Eve are absolutely wrong. Adam, even as men do today, abrogated his place of responsibility to God and to his wife.

Most Bible commentators would agree with this assertion. The editors of *The Moody Bible Commentary* cite a reference from the Book of Numbers that also bears this out in Jewish law, which surely has its model from this Genesis account.

> *In Numbers 30:6-12, a husband is held responsible for his wife's vows. In fact, if he hears his wife make a vow but does not speak up, he is responsible for her vow (Numbers 30:9-11). Similarly, Adam was responsible to speak his disapproval during the temptation and since he failed, is considered more culpable. Not only did the man fail to speak and stop the woman, but joining her folly, he also took the fruit, and he ate.* [24]

---

[24] Michael Rydelnik, Michael Vanlaningham, Bryaon O'Neal, Winfred Neely, Keving D. Zuber, James Coakley, John Jelinek, *et al*, *Moody Bible Commentary* (Chicago: The Moody Bible Institute of Chicago, 2014), 52.

5

Results When We Wanted to Be God

The Fracture...Its Result

What happened after they chose to disobey God's command? Or really, when *we* chose to be God?

Genesis 3:7 — *Then the eyes of both of them were opened, and they knew that they were naked; and they sewed fig leaves together and made themselves loin coverings.*

Everything Changed

Everything changed. The phrase "eyes...opened" is a Hebrew idiom that expresses acquiring new knowledge, not visual information.[25] Acquiring new knowledge is not a bad thing. In fact, it is implied by God in the total freedom He gave Adam and Eve in the garden and in their command to rule the world. But God's command to not eat of the Tree of Knowledge was dependent upon their relationship with God.

---

[25] Rydelnik et al., Moody Bible Commentary, 52.

The dependence on God is a key element in their relationship. It was in God's infinite wisdom and knowledge that God limited Man's knowledge. The text does not state it but the "knowledge of good and evil" is not the only limit on knowledge that God placed on man. After all this is comparing the infinite God with the finite man, but it was clear to man that God had named the limit of his knowledge to not include that of good and evil. That limitation was a test of Man's faithfulness to God's Word, His command. It was a test of their relationship of trust and love. Would man choose to remain dependent on God for all knowledge, or would man choose to become independent and seek his own knowledge?

This off-limit knowledge was also clearly no different in dependence on God alone especially with that body of knowledge fenced off surrounded by the command "no." I believe this knowledge dependence of Adam on God can be attributed to what some consider an odd question by God the Father with Adam after their Fall.

Genesis 3:8-11 — *They heard the sound of the Lord God walking in the garden in the cool of the day, and the man and his wife hid themselves from the presence of the Lord God among the trees of the garden. 9 Then the Lord God called to the man, and said to him, "Where are you?" 10 He said, "I heard the sound of You in the garden, and I was afraid because I was naked; so I hid myself." 11 And He said, "Who told you that you were naked? Have you eaten from the tree of which I commanded you not to eat?"*

In this divine hide-and-seek account, we notice God using concepts that are limited to man's being and intelligence. Did God know where Adam and Eve were located in the Garden? Of course. Did God know where Adam got the knowledge that they were naked? Of course, He is omniscient. So why was it written this way? I think the obvious conclusion is for Adam, Eve and us. It is about a relationship after all. God then and throughout the whole body of Scripture has limited Himself through His attributes for our benefit and at other times not but also for our benefit. I believe it is no different here in this context.

Adam and Eve Hid from God—How Do You Pull That Off?

Adam and Eve chose to hide from God for the first time in their lives. God obviously wanted to make that point in His question, "Where are you?" Had He ever had to ask that question of them? Of course not. Their relationship before this point was free, open and shameless.

Adam responded to God, "I heard You in the Garden, and I was afraid of You because I was naked and I hid myself." Adam is showing God that he gained knowledge apart from his designed dependence on the knowledge of God alone.

God leads them into confession through the next two questions.

Genesis 3:11 — *And He said, "Who told you that you were naked? Have you eaten from the tree of which I commanded you not to eat?"*

So again, God knew this already. He is omniscient. It seems obvious that God did this for Adam and Eve's benefit and ours. I believe the forbidden tree represents knowledge apart from a dependency on the knowledge of God or, put another way, the Word of God. Why would Adam and Eve need to know the knowledge of good and evil? They walked, worked, and loved openly and freely in the Garden. Their every need was fulfilled by the creation set forth by God the Father and sustained by His presence with them both every day of their lives. They wanted for nothing. Only one thing did God ever declare "not good" apart from God's relationship with Adam, and it was that Adam was alone. Therefore, in this innocent, dependent state Adam and Eve had no need for knowledge of good and evil. They lived everything "good" and didn't need to know the contrast, namely evil. They had not fallen. Only Satan and his angels had fallen from their original created state, not Adam and Eve.

We Have a Deep Attraction to All Things "NO"

Ever since God forbade man from eating of that tree, man has been deeply attracted by all things "no." I wonder if this is where we get our inbred tendencies to resist "no" from any authority from toddler age and up. It may be possible this is where we get the idea to "go it alone" and not listen to any knowledge from any authority. This is the internal mental battle that our way is better than anyone else's. That autonomous notion is at the core of pride. The effect on the relationships between Adam, Eve, God, and between the man and the woman was immediately obvious. This thought that God is holding out on us or holding back on us drove Eve nuts. It drives us nuts as well. We may have a flippant thought, "How dare God_____." Usually moved by a strong emotion, we say it and then feel sorry for it later. We are on a lifetime transformation. God's Spirit through His Word, prayer, fellowship of the believers and our relationship with Him is transforming us from our original sin (disobedience) of us wanting to be a god to us being totally dependent on God our Father.

Referring back to the verse, Genesis 3:7 is a great example of the need to use Bible Study Methods. We have discussed this before. But here if you don't go a little deeper into the context of the use of the language that this part of the Bible was written, you will not discover its intended meaning. Don't become worried about original Bible languages. You do not have to be a Bible scholar to appreciate the nuance of Hebrew in order to get closer to the original meaning intended by the author. If you have a good study Bible, the notes should be helpful here. There are some good, non-technical Bible commentaries that are also helpful.[26]

---

[26] Examples of commentaries: *The Moody Bible Commentary* by Michael Rydelnik and Michael Vanlandingham, General Editors. *Notes on Genesis 2019 Edition*, Dr. Thomas L. Constable – Dr. Constable has a "Notes on" commentary for every Bible book. Examples of study Bibles: Zondervan's *NASB Study Bible;* Crossway's *ESV Study Bible.* You can discover a wealth of Bible study helps at the web site of an adopted mentor of mine, Ken Boa. Dr. Boa's ministry website content covers most every book in the Bible: www.KenBoa.org.

I have a personal family story that illustrates the need to understand the nuance of a different language. I had a brother-in-law (I will identify as "Tony") who told the story of the first time he came to his then fiancé's (I will identify as "Barbie") house to call on her. Tony was British and had just moved to the USA. This was the first time that Tony had come to Barbie's house to call on her. Barbie's father answered the door. Tony enthusiastically greeted Barbie's father at the door, "Hello, I have come to knock up Barbie!" Tony was very happy and was very proud of his proclamation to Barbie's father. Barbie's father stood there stunned, anger started to swell and he was about to show Tony some aggressive American hospitality. Barbie rushed to intervene and explained to her father that Tony was from England and the term "to knock up" someone in England meant that you were going to call on them at their home. I am sure you can appreciate the awkward comedy in this story, but it does drive home the need to understand a language to fully understand its meaning. The Bible is no different.

In Genesis 3:7, we discovered that "eyes…opened" is a Hebrew idiom expressing acquiring new knowledge. This new knowledge allowed them to realize that "they were naked." Is that it? Or is it more than that?

Sometimes looking at the verse in different Bible translations can clarify the meaning. For instance, the NLT adds nuance to the meaning of "they knew they were naked."

Genesis 3:7, (NLT) — *At that moment their eyes were opened, and they suddenly felt shame at their nakedness.*

For the First Time, Adam and Eve Experience the Possibility of God's Displeasure

In looking at the Hebrew language, the term "naked" ('erummim), as used in this verse, does not mean being unclothed. The Hebrew word for naked in verse 2:25 does mean unclothed. However, here its use speaks to Adam and Eve's new knowledge of their shameful and guilty nakedness, exposure to God's punishment for sin or disobedience.

This new knowledge left them exposed to God's imminent punishment.[27] What did they do next because of this?

> **Genesis 3:7b** — *And they sewed fig leaves together and made themselves loin coverings.*

Their creation of "loin coverings" was more than covering their nakedness. Their new knowledge obtained through disobedience brought shame because of their separation from God. It brought shame because they lost their confirmation of holiness to the confirmation of their choice nature of sin or disobedience. They were like Satan.

Satan was not content with being the most beautiful creature that God created. He rebelled against God the Father and influenced a large number of angels to join him. Satan also chose in his pride to be a god in opposition to God the Father.

God's Meaning of Death Discovered

This was their attempt to also cover their shame and lessen their exposure to God's imminent punishment. They will learn that no covering they create can cover the shame that only God Himself can cover for them. Eve and Adam discovered that this "death" was not the cessation of physical life but the separation of their spiritual, relational life with the presence of God and also with each other.

> *This is consistent with the fundamental concept of "death" as noted in 2:17, as separation rather than cessation. In this case the "death" or "disjunction" was not in the fact of their relationship (the couple was still "married"), but in the ideally intended experience of that relationship, outwardly reflected in the barriers they set up between*

---

[27] Rydelnik et al., Moody Bible Commentary, 53

those parts of themselves that are most representative of physical intimacy.[28]

The result of the first couple's disobedience was starting its destructive path of wrecking all relationships in the Garden. Although God has not yet confronted Adam and Eve, there is no need as they already are experiencing the trauma of their act of disobedience. The path of disobedience and destruction starts with themselves.

Adam and Eve's disobedience echoes the Apostle James' words thousands of years later when he wrote, "When sin is accomplished, it brings forth death" (James 1:15). This death, for them as a couple, was the intimacy in their marriage. Before, they were free, innocent, and trusting with no barriers. The "loin coverings" symbolized all that changed between them.

They soon felt the pain of their separation and death in their relationship with God.

Genesis 3:8-13 — *They heard the sound of the Lord God walking in the garden in the cool of the day, and the man and his wife hid themselves from the presence of the Lord God among the trees of the garden. 9 Then the Lord God called to the man, and said to him, "Where are you?" 10 He said, "I heard the sound of You in the garden, and I was afraid because I was naked; so I hid myself." 11 And He said, "Who told you that you were naked? Have you eaten from the tree of which I commanded you not to eat?" 12 The man said, "The woman whom You gave to be with me, she gave me from the tree, and I ate." 13 Then the Lord God said to the woman, "What is this you have done?" And the woman said, "The serpent deceived me, and I ate."*

---

[28] Rydelnik et al., Moody Bible Commentary, 53

How Can We Hide from God?

I don't know about you, but I find how man's reaction (including my own) to God about sin and disobedience amazing. If you think about the Scriptures we have reviewed so far, think about what Adam and Eve knew about God. They knew Him as the Creator of all their reality and creatures. Had they ever known anything but love from Him? There was no contrast to love. That is an amazing state to be in if you can even get your head around it. They never knew a harsh word or action. They never knew to want for anything. There was no one with greater power and no one so close to them personally from their first breath until this scene in the Garden. But, after this incident with disobedience (sin) with all of their Garden experiential knowledge, "the man and his wife hid themselves from the presence of the Lord God among the trees of the garden." How can you hide from God? But we always try, don't we? It amazes me and always surprises me whenever I see it in others or in myself! We are truly children of Adam and Eve.

How can we hide from God? Short answer is no one can. If you think about it, it is self-defeating and useless. Adam and Eve tried to. Their hiding was apparently driven by all the emotions, feelings and thoughts that come out of an act of disobedience (sin) to God's Word. Remember God is Light. God is Life. God is the exact antithesis to all that disobedience (sin) is and contains. Disobedience (sin) is death, the absence of life.

God interacts with man through the Covenants He makes with us. I won't go into detail here on the Biblical Covenants, but they do affect all of our lives and are in place today. Our response to God when we have disobeyed Him will be different under the New Covenant today. Of course, that is if you have entered that New Covenant with the Messiah Jesus.

Ken Boa writes this about the benefit of being in the New Covenant, "Since God made us in his image and likeness, we have been created for community with him and with one another. The Bible is unique in its portrayal of God as a covenant maker and keeper. As we enter into the benefits of the new covenant through the blood of Christ (Jeremiah 31:31–33; Luke 22:20), we become members of a new community that is called to reflect the glory of the Godhead in its corporate unity (John 17:22–26). The two greatest commandments are to love God and our neighbor (Mark 12:30–31), and the clearest expression of our love for God is our love for others (1 John 4:7, 11, 20–21). In effect, our Lord tells us, 'If you love me, you will love the people I love.'"[29]

It is in this New Covenant, in this community of believers that makes it much harder to hide from God when we disobeyed. Not only do we have the witness of the Holy Spirit within us prompting the question "Where are you?" but we have a host of Messiah followers around us that will echo this question to us out of our community of believers. God won't let us hide. I had a long-ago acquaintance who related a family saying, "Your sins will find you out." I think that is true in the community of Christ, Messiah followers.

"They heard the sound of the Lord God walking in the garden in the cool of the day." If you look at several commentaries, you will get several nuances of what this picture would have looked like.[30] The fact that they "heard the sound of the Lord walking" depicts God here as more than Spirit. The scene brings up thoughts of a relaxed, casual visitation by the Lord God of the universe. But we know that God is Spirit (John 4:24), so Who could be creating the sounds of walking in the Garden?[31] A theophany is an appearance of God (Who is Spirit) in

---

[29] Kenneth Boa, Conformed to His Image, 245.

[30] Rydelnik et al., *The Moody Bible Commentary*, pg. 53.

NOTE: There are a host of other good commentaries on the market. I have chosen to use the Moody commentary, the *Bible Book Notes* by Dr. Constable, and the online resources at GotQuestions.com. I have referred to this group of resources as a mix of semi-technical to non-technical commentaries. This will give you what I hope is a broad exposure to different depths of Bible commentary.

[31] "What does it mean that God is spirit?" Got Questions Ministries, https://www.gotquestions.org/God-is-spirit.html. Accessed January 19, 2024.

a tangible, human form. I believe that in this Garden appearance it is the second Person of the Trinity, Jesus, God the Son. This idea fits Scripture with several references.[32]

We can safely project that prior to their decision to disobey God's Word, His sound in the garden would be greeted with delight and joyful anticipation. Instead, now we find Adam and Eve upon hearing "the sound of the Lord walking in the garden in the cool of the day" striking fear in their hearts, and they hide. That was the saddest day for humanity and the start of living under the curse for everyone and everything.

What do you think about God's first response to them? "Then the Lord God called to the man, and said to him, 'Where are you?'" (Genesis 3:9). This does not sound like a God of wrath, does it? God surely could have overwhelmed them with judgment. God's question was more of a gentle confrontation to invite them to come out of hiding and the distance they placed between themselves and Him. Disobedience impels a believer to respond the exact opposite of God's desire. After the act of disobedience, the believer will desire to hide from God. The shame is great, but just as this example of God in the Garden with Adam and Eve shows, it is the Spirit of God Who calls, "Where are you?"

Disobedience in our relationship with God will bring feelings that God is displeased. I can remember in my late teen years I took LSD on several occasions. Before I became a believer, these experiences were all fun and games. Once I became a believer, I was still around the same crowd. I found myself taking LSD again, but this time, there was no fun or games. The entire experience was all about God and Satan. I quickly learned that God no longer wanted me to experience any mind-altering experience apart from His Word and His Spirit. I learned the lesson that I had to walk away from a group that

[32] "Did God literally and visibly walk in the Garden (Genesis 3:8)?" Got Questions Ministries, https://www.gotquestions.org/God-walk-garden.html. Accessed January 19, 2024.

chose to continue destructive behavior and not have their influence over my choices and to be separate from them for the new calling of God in my life.

Disobedience (sin) brings forth death. For the unredeemed soul it brings forth eternal death. In the life of a believer an act of disobedience (sin) to God's Word brings forth a pause of something redeemable. Our active living relationship with the living God is the only redeemable part of our existence. Disobedience is death to that relationship. Therefore, disobedience for a believer is a pause of something redeemable. That pause, just as your initial submission to His calling you into faith is how long you chose to remain in that disobedience. I had a pause once that lasted two years. It was a sad, lonely, empty, spiritually dead time in my life. God was always there asking, "Where are you?" I am glad that I answered Him again.

Foreign Feelings in Their Relationship with God

Adam responded to God, "I heard the sound of You in the garden, and I was afraid because I was naked; so I hid myself" (Genesis 3:10). Never before in their relationship had this happened. God's presence strikes fear in man. The phrase "because I was naked" speaks about much more than just Adam and Eve's anatomy. As discussed, this was shame of their sin, disobedience that exposed them to God's punishment, His judgment, thus fear. Never before in their relationship with God had they experienced the concepts of punishment, judgment, or wrath. That moment of disobedience to God's Word fractures your relationship with God, too. Everything changes.

God furthers this gentle confrontation with His second question. "And He said, 'Who told you that you were naked? Have you eaten from the tree of which I commanded you not to eat?'" (Genesis 3:11). Pretty simple. Either someone gave you this new information or you acquired it from disobeying My command to you. We now await Adam's response to God's second question. It appears from the account that God is step by step moving Adam to discover how he had arrived at this place of shame, hiding, and distance from God.

Here Adam had a great opportunity to take ownership of his disobedience. But unfortunately, he did not. It is important to observe who God questioned first about this new knowledge. This reinforces that Adam was the leader and was the responsible one for keeping God's command to both Adam and Eve. Dr. Constable reminds us:

> *Adam, however, "was not...deceived" (1 Tim. 2:14). He sinned with his eyes wide open (v. 6b). Eve's was a sin of initiative, whereas Adam's was one of acquiescence. Too much aggressiveness in a woman, and too much passivity in a man, still are tendencies of the respective sexes. Death "passed unto all men" (Rom. 5:12) when Adam sinned—because Adam, not Eve, was the head of the human race under God's administration (cf. 3:18-23).[33]*

God intends for our feelings of disobedience to be foreign in our relationship to Him. For Adam and Eve it was in their face-to-face with God. For us as Messiah followers, our act of disobedience is to grieve the Holy Spirit which is a break in fellowship. That break should impact us in our inner being. Depending on the type of break in fellowship, that impact can extend outward from us into our community of believers.

> **Ephesians 4:30-31** — *Do not grieve the Holy Spirit of God, by whom you were sealed for the day of redemption. 31 Let all bitterness and wrath and anger and clamor and slander be put away from you, along with all malice.*

We are to operate our spiritual life on facts (Word of God), faith (choose to obey) and then feelings (what follows from the first two). But here in the context of this passage in Ephesians it is clear that any of these choices of disobedience (sin), we will grieve the Holy Spirit of

---

[33] Constable, Notes on Genesis 2019 Edition, 86.

God. As believers, if our heart is not hardened, we too will grieve and experience a godly sorrow that will lead to repentance.

Adam, the Creator of the Blame Game

Adam is the author of the blame game. While Adam's sin, as Dr. Constable put it, was one of acquiescence, his response to God's inquiry was one of blame shifting. I think it is fascinating to review this first initial account of humanity's disobedience. When we witness the same emotions and responses in ourselves as from the Scripture, we can truly see ourselves in the characters. We really don't need any commentary, do we? We have been in that same place so many times in our lives that we can visualize what were their inner thoughts, how they felt and what emotions were rumbling in their hearts.

> **Genesis 3:12** — *The man said, "The woman whom You gave to be with me, she gave me from the tree, and I ate."*

Wow! What a cowardly act. Adam did not man up. Adam is awarded the title of father of blame shifting. Break down his response. Not only did Adam blame shift to Eve, but he also blame shifted to God Himself! Adam answered God's inquiry as "the woman," Eve. Adam then added, "whom You gave to be with me." When an answer to a question when you are in trouble goes to the minute detail, you are gathering evidence to get yourself off the hook. This is exactly what Adam is doing here. Adam blames Eve and then reminds God that He gave her to him. So it is not only Eve's fault but Yours for giving her to me. Then God turns to Eve.

> **Genesis 3:13** — *Then the Lord God said to the woman, "What is this you have done?" And the woman said, "The serpent deceived me, and I ate."*

"Well, if blame shifting is good for my husband, then it is good for me too!" says Eve. Eve then blames the serpent for her deception about God's command and the reason she ate. Of course, she is not recalling that she repeated to the serpent in total accuracy God's command word for word. Oh, let's not let the details get in the way since we are in the midst of blame shifting.

Notice God's handling of Adam and Eve in the midst of their sin (disobedience). God was their Father, and God already knew. But God sought them out. He asked them questions to draw them into the truth and to confession. Notice that God does not argue with their version of the events nor their interpretation of them. Why? In my opinion it did not matter. God had given His Word to both Adam and Eve and they broke His command for them to obey His Word, so judgment was already pronounced. Their sentence was given. This was judgment. Forgiveness is to come later.

Adam, our Patriarch, was a master at playing the Blame Game. Eve and Satan followed suit. God calls us, as part of our active participation in the disciplines and habits of divine grace, to confess our sins to one another for the healing of our souls. God knows we are made with feet of clay and that sinful nature is not eradicated from our souls. The opposite of blame is ownership. I heard someone say that blame points the finger outward, whereas ownership points the finger at yourself. God wants us within the community of believers to take ownership for our disobedience (sin). In the Book of James, the Apostle gives us a great model.

James 5:16 — *Therefore, confess your sins to one another, and pray for one another so that you may be healed.*

It is hard to hide, hard to blame, and hard to put on a mask when you are openly confessing your sins to one another. Of course, follow wholesome social decorum. It is good for men to confess to other men and women to other women within the Body of Christ. Grace and discernment in mixed company is always a good rule.

God Rolls Out Judgment on All Garden Members

While we use the term judgment it may be better to use a different term for God's "punishment" of Satan as opposed to that of Adam and Eve. God's words to Adam and Eve are more like a Father and are characterized in the text as chastisement. A Father will still discipline but out of a heart of love with the goal of restoration. God does not appear, from the context, to have the same feelings for Satan. God rolls into an immediate judgment with a view of condemnation for Satan.

> **Genesis 3:14** — *The Lord God said to the serpent, "Because you have done this, Cursed are you more than all cattle, And more than every beast of the field; On your belly you will go, And dust you will eat All the days of your life; 15 And I will put enmity Between you and the woman, And between your seed and her seed; He shall bruise you on the head, And you shall bruise him on the heel."*

I am not going to slice and dice every word. My purpose is not to write a commentary. However, I thought it interesting that Satan's entrance into the Garden was through the form of a "cattle." Most commentaries will explain the word "cattle" used here in Hebrew as a domesticated animal. Of course, God gave all authority over all of creation, including cattle, to man: Adam and Eve. Man had the power over God's creation. Man's fall, his disobedience to God's Word, led to man's ownership position of God's creation being usurped by Satan. This transfer of ownership gave way for Satan to become **the prince of the power of the air** Ephesians 2:1-7) or **god of this world** (2 Corinthians 4:1-5). It will be this way until the first return of Christ Jesus. That is the start of the ownership transfer of God's creation removed from Satan. The Messiah, as the second Adam, fulfilled what the first Adam could not. The title deed of the world will fully transfer into the hands of Christ Jesus when He returns at His second coming, and Satan will be sent to the pit!

But as God rolls out His judgment of each Garden member, notice that it is specific to their role and to their particular disobedience (sin). Whatever the serpent's animal form, as a "cattle" or domesticated animal, the serpent now as part of the curse, judgment will crawl on its belly and eat dust. Note also that God cursed the serpent and the ground, but God did not curse Adam and Eve. Kenneth Matthews describes it this way.

> *"Curses are uttered against the serpent and the ground, but not against the man and woman, implying that the blessing has not been utterly lost. It is not until human murder, a transgression against the imago Dei, that a person (Cain) receives the divine curse."* [34]

Verse 15 is fascinating. In the Garden account, the Gospel of God's Messiah is predicted. All of this rests in the word "seed." God refers to the "seed" of the serpent and the "seed" of the woman.

Let's read this fifteenth verse of Gen three in the Amplified Bible.

Genesis 3:14 (AMP) — *"And I will put enmity (open hostility) Between you and the woman, And between your seed (offspring) and her Seed; He shall [fatally] bruise your head,*

And you shall [only] bruise His heel."

God said that He would put "enmity" or "open hostility" between you (Satan, serpent) and the woman (Eve). Further "open hostility" will remain between your seed (offspring) and her Seed. The prophecy comes into play here that He (the Seed of the woman) shall (fatally) bruise your (Satan, serpent) head, and you (Satan, serpent) shall (only) bruise His (the Seed of the woman) heel.

This part of the story focuses on the two seeds in which we will find God's redemption story of mankind. We will find this theme of "seed" that starts here throughout all Scripture. Derek Thomas, in his

---

[34] Kenneth A. Matthews, *Genesis 1—11:26. New American Commentary Series* (North Carolina: Broadman & Holman Publishers, 1996), 243.

article *The Significance of Genesis 3:15* for Ligonier Ministries made this point.

> *With the possible exception of John 3:16, no verse in the Bible is more crucial and definitive than Genesis 3:15: "I will put enmity between you and the woman, and between your offspring and her offspring; he shall bruise your head, and you shall bruise his heel." As Alec Motyer writes, "The whole of Scripture is not packed into every scripture, but we may allowably expect every scripture to prepare and make room for the whole. This is what happens in Genesis 3:15"* (Look to the Rock, IVP, p. 34).[35]

In theological circles, this passage is known as "protoevangelium" meaning simply the "first Gospel." It is clear that God is speaking to Satan who inhabits the serpent. God's curse to the serpent is that Satan will be forever at war with mankind. The seed is the key term to be traced all throughout the Old Testament and into the New Testament. This is why tracing the line or lineage of Biblical people was so important. It is this traceable lineage that leads us to the Person of the promised Messiah, Yeshua—Jesus.

The seed of Satan would be any entity, spiritual or human, who came against the seed of the woman, which is the lineage of and including the Messiah Himself.

The lack of the curse of Man: Adam, Eve is why I cited the quote from Kenneth Matthews earlier. God cursed Satan and the ground, but God did not curse Adam and Eve. The prophecy was that Satan's seed would only bruise the heel of the seed of the woman. But that the seed of the woman would crush a fatal blow to the head of the seed of the serpent.

The death of the Messiah was thought of by Satan as his victory, but it was only a bruising. The Messiah Jesus rose again on the third day to claim victory over death and pay for the sins of all mankind. It

---

[35] Derek Thomas, "The Significance of Genesis 3:15," Feb 23, 2018, https://www.ligonier.org/blog/significance-genesis-315/.

is in the resurrection that God the Father predicted the crushing of the head of Satan, all of his power, and redeem man and creation.

> **1 John 3:8** — *The one who practices sin is of the devil; for the devil has sinned from the beginning. The Son of God appeared for this purpose, to destroy the works of the devil.*

Messiah Jesus appeared for the purpose of destroying the works of the devil, Satan. The Messiah fulfilled the promise of God the Father to man. It is comforting to know that in our greatest failure to God the Father, He still had love in His heart for us, and at the moment of our sin (disobedience), God made a way of redemption and restoration. What amazing love!

Next, God pronounced His chastisement upon Eve.

> **Genesis 3:16** — *To the woman He said, "I will greatly multiply Your pain in childbirth, In pain you will bring forth children; Yet your desire will be for your husband, And he will rule over you."*

God said to Eve that He would "increase" her pain in childbirth. Evidently, there would have been some pain in childbirth had she had children before the Fall. Whatever that pain would have been, God promised to increase it greatly.

Eve would experience relationship pain as well. God said, "Your desire will be for your husband." There are several ways commentaries "could" go with this aspect "desire will be for your husband." But there is a more plausible explanation from the text, especially with the next connecting parallel phrase, "And He will rule over you."

> *"The 'curse' here describes the beginning of the battle of the sexes. After the Fall, the husband no longer rules easily; he must fight for his headship. The woman's desire is to control her husband (to usurp his divinely appointed headship), and he must master her, if he can. Sin had corrupted both the willing submission of the wife and the loving headship of the husband. And so the rule of love founded in*

paradise is replaced by struggle, tyranny, domination, and manipulation."[36]

The Fall has consequences for the inner created harmony with the relationship of Man: Adam and Eve. That consequence, characterized as the battle of the sexes, has been the subject of countless stage plays, books, radio dramas, television, movies, and any other media ever created.

God finishes His announced displeasure with Adam.

Genesis 3:17-19 — *Then to Adam He said, "Because you have listened to the voice of your wife, and have eaten from the tree about which I commanded you, saying, 'You shall not eat from it'; Cursed is the ground because of you; In toil you will eat of it All the days of your life. 18 "Both thorns and thistles it shall grow for you; And you will eat the plants of the field; 19 By the sweat of your face You will eat bread, Till you return to the ground, Because from it you were taken; For you are dust, And to dust you shall return."*

God's chastisement of Eve consisted of her role as mother and wife. Now, in a similar fashion, God's chastisement of Adam focuses on his work as steward over God's creation in every aspect, including Eve. Before the Fall, all of creation under the management of Adam including Eve, will now work against Adam and not be cooperative. Sure, Adam was tasked by God to work in the Garden, but from the context, it did not consist of strenuous toil. All aspects of creation were in harmony with Adam's rule. Now it will not be.

One would expect that God would have hammered Adam for his disobedience because God told Adam the rules clearly. Nothing in the text states that God stuttered or that Adam had a hearing problem. But instead of cursing Adam, God, as a Father, curses the ground (all creation), which is the work that God gave Adam to do.

---

[36] Susan T. Foh, "What Is the Woman's Desire?" *Westminster Theological Journal* 37:3 (Spring 1975):376-83. p. 69

What reason did God give to Adam as to why He was chastising him? God told Adam, "Because you listened to the voice of your wife" as opposed to God Himself. It was as if God was telling Adam in an eyeball-to-eyeball conversation about what to do and what not to do. "Adam, you and I were clear on this. You knew how important this was to Me. I knew the result of the outcome of your disobedience and was trying to protect you against it, but you listened to your wife's voice instead of mine. You chose her influence over Mine. You chose her word over My Word. You disobeyed My command. And now, because of that disobedience, all of creation is cursed and you will suffer to obtain a living where you never had to struggle before this. You were an immortal being, but because of your disobedience, you have allowed death to enter creation. You and Eve's days are limited."

While all of that looks bleak because it was not a curse of Adam and Eve themselves, there is hope because of the woman's seed in verse 15. He will crush Satan's power; there is hope of redemption and restoration for man.

Rest assured that God is not mocked and your sins will find you out.

Numbers 32:23 — *But if you will not do so, behold, you have sinned against the Lord, and be sure your sin will find you out.*

Galatians 6:7 — *Do not be deceived, God is not mocked; for whatever a man sows, this he will also reap.*

Of course, in their respective contexts, the above verses have specific applications to the audience intended, but their principles apply to us in general as believers. Rest assured that as a believer you cannot hide from the Holy Spirit of God and "your sin will find you out." Of course, do not be deceived, you reap what you sow, for God is not mocked. There is no hiding from God.

Adam and Eve's Response to God's Chastisement

Genesis 3:20-21 — *Now the man called his wife's name Eve, because she was the mother of all the living. 21 The Lord God made garments of skin for Adam and his wife, and clothed them.*

What do you think from the context? What is Adam and Eve's response to God? No anger appears here. No bitterness is apparent. Adam assumes his normal duty of naming. Adam names his wife Eve.

There is no rebellion here either. We can say then that Adam and Eve accepted God's chastisement for their disobedience. We can see this attitude in Adam's naming of the Woman—before, she was called "Woman" because she came out of Man. Now, Adam names her Eve, in Hebrew related verb means "to live." Adam still believed in God's command and promise to them to subdue the world and to multiply. Why wouldn't he? Nowhere in God's chastisement of neither Adam nor Eve did God rescind His blessing or His intended purpose for them to fulfil in His creation. We should take note of that since it is true in all of God's covenants He has made to mankind and to Israel.

This resulted in Adam changing the Woman's name to Eve. "Now the man called his wife's name Eve because she was the mother of all the living." Crowning her as the "mother of all the living" shows they embraced the blessing of the promise and purpose that God gave to them.

God shows Adam and Eve more grace in that the clothes they made themselves were inadequate for the new type of world they had to move into. "The Lord God made garments of skin for Adam and his wife and clothed them."

Finally, what is our response to God's chastisement whenever we have chosen to disobey Him?

What is disobedience (sin)? At the heart of it, it is rebellion against that object of authority. And what is at the heart of that rebellion? It must be one's autonomy. Whomever is requiring X of you and you are refusing X, then are you not placing your authority over theirs? It is a power struggle. A clash of sovereignty. That was the crux of it in the Garden between man and God.

To answer the above question, it is our hope that our response will be like Adam and Eve's: to yield, to submit our rebellious desire for sovereignty to the only true Sovereign Ruler, God.

Wait, God Is Holy?

There may be a question that arises at this point as to how our holy God can be in the presence of sinful man, Adam and Eve, or as we will next see in Gen 4, Cain and Abel. Good question. But it is really a reversal. It is not that God cannot be in the presence of sin and thus the limitation is upon God. It is really that sin cannot be in the presence of God because His holiness is an all-consuming fire. Thus, the limitation is upon the creature, not the Creator. Throughout man's close personal interaction with God, there have been limits placed within those meetings to protect the creature, man, from God Himself, specifically His glory, His Shekinah glory. Got Questions explains it this way in their article on this subject:

> *"Jesus was God in the flesh (John 1:1, 14) so when people saw Him, they were seeing God. So, yes, God can be 'seen' and many people have 'seen' God. At the same time, no one has ever seen God revealed in all His glory. In our fallen human condition, if God were to fully reveal Himself to us, we would be consumed and destroyed. Therefore, God veils Himself and appears in forms in which we can "see" Him. However, this is different than seeing God with all His glory and holiness displayed. People have seen visions of God, images of God, and appearances of God, but no one has ever seen God in all His fullness (Exodus 33:20)."[37]*

---

[37] "Has Anyone Ever Seen God?" Got Questions Ministries, https://www.gotquestions.org/seen-God.html. Accessed March 26, 2024.

Earlier, I discussed the "first Gospel" and the hope in the seed of the woman. It is in that traceable lineage of Eve's seed that leads us to the Person of the promised Messiah Yeshua, Christ Jesus. It is how the first Adam's office to rule creation (Theocratic Administrator) is restored through the messianic kingdom. Just as God the Father originally intended to indirectly govern the physical world through the first Adam, He will one day explicitly and in plain view govern the world through the Last Adam or God the Son, the Messiah Jesus.

1 Corinthians 15:44b-49 — *If there is a natural body, there is also a spiritual body. 45 So also it is written, "The first man, Adam, became a living soul." The last Adam became a life-giving spirit. 46 However, the spiritual is not first, but the natural; then the spiritual. 47 The first man is from the earth, earthy; the second man is from heaven. 48 As is the earthy, so also are those who are earthy; and as is the heavenly, so also are those who are heavenly. 49 Just as we have borne the image of the earthy, we will also bear the image of the heavenly.*

Romans 5:12, 15-21 — *Therefore, just as through one man sin entered into the world, and death through sin, and so death spread to all men, because all sinned…15 But the free gift is not like the transgression. For if by the transgression of the one the many died, much more did the grace of God and the gift by the grace of the one Man, Jesus Christ, abound to the many…18 So then as through one transgression there resulted condemnation to all men, even so through one act of righteousness there resulted justification of life to all men. 19 For as through the one man's disobedience the many were made*

NOTE: There are volumes written about this subject alone. As with any Biblical subject, one can go as deep into it as one desires. Check out these articles:

a. Michael Gleghorn, "How Can an Omnipresent God be Around Sin and Evil?" Probe Ministries, https://probe.org/how-can-an-omnipresent-god-be-around-sin-and-evil/

b. Dawn Wilson, "What Does 'Omnipresent' Mean?" Crosswalk, https://www.crosswalk.com/faith/bible-study/what-does-omnipresent-mean.html. Accessed March 26, 2024.

sinners, even so through the obedience of the One the many will be made righteous. 20 The Law came in so that the transgression would increase; but where sin increased, grace abounded all the more, 21 so that, as sin reigned in death, even so grace would reign through righteousness to eternal life through Jesus Christ our Lord.

How Was God loved?

How was God loved by Adam and Eve? Simple. Just as they always had shown their love to God before the Fall, they loved God by their submission to His authority, to His Sovereign rule, and to His Word. They found in obedience they loved God. It is in the outward displayed decisions of the heart that the inward non-coerced decisions are demonstrated. Obedience is God's love Language.

6

God Tosses Us Out; Not Abandoned

The First Couple and God Remain Connected

The first couple and God remain connected. The Adamic Covenant was still active and in force. The first children worshipped God, and we find God's sovereign rule in Cain and Abel's offering. In God's relationship, it is all about our hearts. God knows the motives of our hearts. The only power given to mankind is choice. Jesus, the Man, also had a choice.

Adam and Eve did follow God's command to be fruitful and multiply. Their first two children were named Cain and Abel. God was still connected to the first couple and now to their children. There was interaction between them and God. We will discover how the first children of the first couple loved God.

The First Children Worship God

Genesis 4 describes that the children had a different focus of labor concerning their day-to-day work. Cain was a "tiller of the ground" and Able was a "keeper of flocks." Both Cain and Abel brought an offering to worship the Lord.

Genesis 4:3-5a — *So it came about in the course of time that Cain brought an offering to the LORD of the fruit of the ground. 4 Abel, on his part also brought of the firstlings of his flock and of their fat portions. And the LORD had regard for Abel and for his offering; 5 but for Cain and for his offering He had no regard.*

This is not new. Is not the Lord God sovereign? Is not the Lord God, God? God was very present in the first children's life and worship. The same struggle that Cain's parents had with the Sovereignty of God was mirrored in Cain's response. It is still all about the creature's response to the Creator's sovereign rule. Of course, that is still the same for us all today. For us, it is about our response to life events. I encourage the Life Group I lead at my church to "Trust in the Who, not the what or how or when or why." God redeems what He allows. Trust the Father, abide in the Son, and walk by the Spirit.

Genesis 4:5b-8 — *So Cain became very angry and his countenance fell. 6 Then the LORD said to Cain, "Why are you angry? And why has your countenance fallen? 7 If you do well, will not your countenance be lifted up? And if you do not do well, sin is crouching at the door; and its desire is for you, but you must master it." 8 Cain told Abel his brother. And it came about when they were in the field, that Cain rose up against Abel his brother and killed him.*

We are not given details about how the conversation took place between Cain and the Lord, but that is not the focus. The relationships between Cain, Abel and God are the focus. We find through their interaction with one another the essence of those relationships.

There are several options given in commentaries as to how these first two sons of Adam would have known about offerings to God. Of course, all of it is speculation because the text simply does not say, but just as it was in our review of the Garden scene, what is not said also says a lot. The content jumps in Genesis 4 from Eve giving birth in verses 1-2a, to Cain and Abel having professions in verse 2b, to Cain and Abel "in the course of time" giving an offering to the Lord in verses 3-5. So, to expound a lot here even if you are digging nuggets out of the original languages, there is not a lot you can go into detail as to how or what they were instructed for the proper offering.

Dissecting Cain and Abel's Offering—Finding God's Sovereign Rule

From the context of the passage, however, we can observe several things. The text does not relate that Adam and Eve were taught anything about giving an offering to the Lord. Yet whenever it comes to their first children, "in the course of time," giving an offering to the Lord appears from the text as an established event. So, we can at least deduce from the text that presenting an offering to the Lord was not a foreign concept for either of Adam's sons.

Second, from the context, we can observe that there is no distinction as to their occupations, one being more accepted than another nor of the content of the offering itself. Cain was a farmer and Abel a shepherd. "Cain brought an offering to the Lord of the fruit of the ground…Abel, on his part also brought of the firstlings of his flock and of their fat portions." So, what do you think from our seats in the bleachers? Whose offering should be accepted? *Wrong.* Why? From our vantage point, both are acceptable. But that is the problem. It is "our" vantage point. We, nor the characters in this Bible story are *not* God. We don't have His vantage point. So, what does God say about the worthiness of these two offerings?

> **Genesis 4:4b-5a** — *And the Lord had regard for Abel and for his offering; 5 but for Cain and for his offering He had no regard.*

How so? The context again may give us a clue as to God's vantage point in His judgment concerning His acceptance of one offering over another.

> **Genesis 4:5b-7** — *So Cain became very angry and his countenance fell. 6 Then the Lord said to Cain, "Why are you angry? And why has your countenance fallen? 7 If you do well, will not your*

countenance be lifted up? And if you do not do well, sin is crouching at the door; and its desire is for you, but you must master it."

It is obvious from the text that the first family and God Himself had a living, daily interactive relationship. This relationship was under a covenant just as it was under a covenant in the Garden of Eden. Dr. Ken Boa wrote about God's covenants, "Since God made us in his image and likeness, we have been created for community with him and with one another. The Bible is unique in its portrayal of God as a covenant maker and keeper."[38] Theologians would point out that the first family and God are within a covenant, specifically the Adamic Covenant.[39]

In God's Relationship, It Is All About Your Heart – Every Aspect

God questions Cain in his angry response to His decision to accept Abel's offering over Cain's. Think about this for a moment. The subject here is the worship of God Himself through these offerings. The same goes for us. As with all worship, it is personal; it is intimate between you and God. Before you or I get too high up in our "vantage point," feeling at ease when God discusses motive, we too have motives in our worship of God.

How often has your mind wandered off during worship? Familiar song, thinking of lunch, how much work to get whatever done, some outing after church, some unwanted person is going to be there, or isn't she or he cute over there? It can spiral in all directions. Any thought during worship through the words you are singing that aren't prayerfully in confession, praise, or adoration of God, to me, is not worship. Some may say that this is too rigid, but that is where I

---

[38] Boa, Conformed to His Image, 245.
[39] "What is the Adamic covenant?" Got Questions Ministries, https://www.gotquestions.org/Adamic-covenant.html.
NOTE: For a short review of all the Biblical covenants review "What are the covenants in the Bible?" Got Questions Ministries, https://www.gotquestions.org/Bible-covenants.html.

have come to in my walk. You pray this before God and see what conclusion you come to.

The Lord says that we all have a heart condition and He is the only One Who can understand our hearts and motives.

> **Jeremiah 17:9-10** — *"The heart is more deceitful than all else And is desperately sick; Who can understand it? 10 "I, the Lord, search the heart, I test the mind, Even to give to each man according to his ways, According to the results of his deeds.*

The Lord reminded the prophet Samuel of His view of man's heart when He sent Samuel to Bethlehem to find a king for Israel that the Lord had selected.

> **I Samuel 16:5b-7** — *He also consecrated Jesse and his sons and invited them to the sacrifice. 6 When they entered, he looked at Eliab and thought, "Surely the LORD's anointed is before Him." 7 But the LORD said to Samuel, "Do not look at his appearance or at the height of his stature, because I have rejected him; for God sees not as man sees, for man looks at the outward appearance, but the LORD looks at the heart."*

God Knows the Motive of Our Hearts

Don't let that point slide by without taking note of it. Here is Samuel a prophet of God, who has had more intimate interaction with God than most of his contemporaries. When Samuel looked at Eliab, Jesse's son, Samuel thought, "Surely" (he was convinced) Eliab is the LORD's anointed," but God interrupted Samuel's thought. God, in essence, said, "Don't get too excited about how Eliab looks. I have rejected him, Samuel." God sees man differently than a man views a man. There are many examples of God viewing the motive of the heart of man. Think of the story of the widow's mite in the Gospels. Jesus is speaking to His disciples as to motive in giving. Motive of what? The heart. God has the only vantage point where motives of the heart can be judged. God is the only One Who can judge the human heart.

Mark 12:41-44 — *And He [Jesus] sat down opposite the treasury, and began observing how the people were putting money into the treasury; and many rich people were putting in large sums. 42 A poor widow came and put in two small copper coins, which amount to a cent. 43 Calling His disciples to Him, He said to them, "Truly I say to you, this poor widow put in more than all the contributors to the treasury; 44 for they all put in out of their surplus, but she, out of her poverty, put in all she owned, all she had to live on."*

Look at Jesus' comparison here. Jesus observed "how people were putting their money into the treasury." Jesus noticed that "many rich people were putting in large sums." But His focus came upon a widow. "A poor widow came and put in two small copper coins, which amount to a cent." Jesus called His disciples together and said to them, "Truly I say to you, this poor widow put in more than all the contributors to the treasury; for they all put in out of their surplus, but she, out of her poverty, put in all she owned, all she had to live on."

I like how The Message (MSG) renders verses 43-44.

Jesus called his disciples over and said, "The truth is that this poor widow gave more to the collection than all the others put together. All the others gave what they'll never miss; she gave extravagantly what she couldn't afford—she gave her all.

Jesus compared the sum amount of all the other contributors together to the amount of what this one poor widow offered to the Lord, and He chose her offering over all the others. Why? The motive of her heart rendered those two coins in pure worship.

Just as it was with that first observed recorded offering, the motive resulting from our hearts matters in our offerings today. We find this in the instruction about offerings given by the Apostle Matthew in his Gospel account.

Matthew 5:21-24 — *"You have heard that the ancients were told, 'You shall not commit murder' and 'Whoever commits murder shall be liable to the court.' 22 But I say to you that everyone who is angry* *with his brother shall be guilty before the court; and whoever says to his brother, 'You good-for-nothing,' shall be guilty before the supreme court; and whoever says, 'You fool,' shall be guilty enough to go into the fiery hell. 23 Therefore if you are presenting your offering at the altar, and there remember that your brother has something against you, 24 leave your offering there before the altar and go; first be reconciled to your brother, and then come and present your offering.*

In this small sampling of Scripture, it is obvious that God the Creator of the human heart is the only One qualified to judge the human heart. When it comes to your relationship with God through your worship, this last passage states that the condition of your heart is at the center of your worship.

Turning back to our story of the first family of man, God questions Cain. We established that God is the only One Who has the only vantage point to actually ask the question. He is the only One Who can judge the heart.

> **Genesis 4:4-7 (AMP)** — *But Abel brought [an offering of] the [finest] firstborn of his flock and the fat portions. And the Lord had respect (regard) for Abel and for his offering; 5 but for Cain and his offering He had no respect. So Cain became extremely angry (indignant), and he looked annoyed and hostile. 6 And the Lord said to Cain, "Why are you so angry? And why do you look annoyed? 7 If you do well [believing Me and doing what is acceptable and pleasing to Me], will you not be accepted? And if you do not do well [but ignore My instruction], sin crouches at your door; its desire is for you [to overpower you], but you must master it."*

God's Amazing Grace to Cain—Remember His Parents?

Even with Cain's murder, God offers Cain amazing grace, even with Cain's seemingly ungratefulness. It is obvious from Cain's response that his heart for the Lord is not right. Why? Who was the offering for? God. Who accepted or rejected the offering? God. Even so Cain may have been jealous of Abel, as we will see, but his issue is with God, but Cain took it out on Abel.

It appears from the text that Abel did that extra special touch with his offering. Not only did he give the teacher an apple, but he also made sure that the apple was perfect in every way and then he shined it up so that it would sparkle. Similar to our earlier discussion about the widow's heart motive by putting into her offering all that she possessed in money. That extra measure showed Abel's passionate heart for God, but Cain's action did not.

Even though Cain was ticked off, God, in His grace, warned Cain that sin crouched at his door and that its desire was to overpower him. God further tells Cain that he must master it. Apparently, in this Covenant relationship with God, **IF** Cain followed God's instructions, he could avoid the confrontation with sin. The same was true for Cain's parents. Had Adam followed God's instructions, the Fall of Man would not have taken place. They had been given the independent power and ability to obey or disobey God's Word and so did Cain.

The Greatest Power Given to Mankind: Choice

Just as the greatest power for a citizen in the Republic of the United States is to vote, the greatest power for an individual in a relationship with God is choice. Tracing relationships with God to the very first one, it is clear the power that God within His covenant grants each human being. The power of choice. That power was displayed, and we discussed it extensively in the Garden of Eden. It is not Shakespeare's "To be or not to be."[40] that is not the question of the times. It was the power of the Man: Adam to obey or not obey that was the real question. Adam held the power within his soul to choose to obey God's Word or not to obey. As we discussed it was not Eve's, but

---

[40] William Shakespeare, "Speech: 'To be or not to be, that is the question,'" from *Hamlet*, Poetry Foundation, https://www.poetryfoundation.org/poems/56965/speech-to-be-or-not-to-be-that-is-the-question. Accessed April 6, 2024.

Adam's choice that carried the weight of the decision because it was Adam to whom God alone gave the command.

It is the same choice that Cain is faced to make. God, as He always does for us, gave Cain a way out of his sinful choice.

Genesis 4:6-7 (AMP) — *And the Lord said to Cain, "Why are you so angry? And why do you look annoyed? 7 If you do well [believing Me and doing what is acceptable and pleasing to Me], will you not be accepted? And if you do not do well [but ignore My instruction], sin crouches at your door; its desire is for you [to overpower you], but you must master it."*

God told Cain, "If you believe Me, do what pleases Me, will you not be accepted? In other words, "Cain, this sacrifice is not an end-all deal-breaker between you and me. You have a choice here. Obey My instruction or disobey my instruction. There are blessings or consequences depending on the choice you make. This is reminiscent of the choice that was before Cain's parents.

The Apostle Paul tells us God provides for us as well in the midst of our temptations to disobey and sin against Him. In the context where this verse is found, Paul is instructing the church at Corinth to avoid Israel's mistakes. Paul did a short review of Israel in Egypt and the wilderness and then Paul tells the Corinthians in 1 Corinthians 10:6-14 that

"These things happened as examples for us, so that we would not crave evil things as they [Israel] also craved. 7 Do not be idolaters… 8 Nor let us act immorally… 9 Nor let us try the Lord… 10 Nor grumble…. 11 Now these things happened to them as an example, and they were written for our instruction, upon whom [you Corinthians] the ends of the ages have come. 12 Therefore, let him who thinks he stands take heed that he does not fall. 13 No temptation has overtaken you but such is common to man; and God is faithful, who will not allow you to be tempted beyond what you are able, but with that temptation will provide the way of escape also, so

that you will be able to endure it. 14 Therefore, my beloved, flee from idolatry."

Just as God offered Cain grace and mercy amid sin crouching at the door of his soul, Paul is telling us that God offers that same grace and mercy for us when temptation crouches at the door of our own soul. Our surrender to the sacrifice of Messiah Jesus to endure the punishment in our place has restored our relationship with God the Father. We have that Garden of Eden choice and all of its power restored to us. Just like Adam and Eve before their choice to disobey, they had the power to choose to obey or not.

After the Fall, they, like you and I, were slaves to the power of sin. However, Messiah Jesus' sacrifice has removed us from the power of sin just not its presence. You and I are no longer slaves to the taskmaster of temptation to obey its lusts. We are truly free to exercise our restored choice and choose the "way of escape," which is also powered by the Holy Spirit, that God has uniquely designed for us when temptation has crouched at our door.

The Bible speaks to three temptation influencers over the Christian: the **world**, the **flesh** and the **devil**.

Ephesians 2:2-3a — *"In which you formerly walked according to the course of this **world**, according to the **prince of the power of the air**, of the spirit that is now working in the sons of disobedience. 3 Among them we too all formerly lived in the lusts of our **flesh**."*

But whatever the influencer, the trigger emotion, event or person, the Apostle James lays the responsibility squarely at our own feet.

James 1:13-18 — *Let no one say when he is tempted, "I am being tempted by God"; for God cannot be tempted by evil, and He Himself does not tempt anyone. 14 But each one is tempted when he is carried away and enticed by his own lust. 15 Then when lust has conceived, it gives birth to sin; and* *when sin is accomplished, it brings forth death. 16 Do not be deceived, my beloved brethren. 17 Every good thing given and every perfect gift is from above, coming down from the Father of lights, with whom there is no variation or shifting shadow. 18 In the exercise of His will He brought us forth by the word of truth, so that we would be a kind of first fruits among His creatures.*

Temptation Is an Amazing and Mysterious Power

But as James told us, it comes from within. After the cross, we are responsible since we are given power over disobedience (sin) through our salvation in Messiah by the Spirit of Messiah. After the cross, our holiness is not up to us to be confirmed as with Adam. But after the cross, our holiness is in the holiness of Messiah Jesus and His holiness is attributed to each of us as believers in Him. Slow down and soak that into your soul. Messiah Jesus' holiness was *attributed* to you and me. That is a mindblower for me. You too?

The key verse in the Book of Galatians is 2:20:

"I have been crucified with Christ; and it is no longer I who live, but Christ lives in me; and the life which I now live in the flesh I live by faith in the Son of God, who loved me and gave Himself up for me." This is our mystery in the Book of Galatians! How does that work? What does that mean? "It is no longer I who live, but Christ lives in me."

I will address this later, but this is a Biblical mystery, that transformation where Christ lives in me. The transformation has to do with the Word of God used by the Spirit of God to transform us into the character qualities of Jesus through us as us.

The Bible speaks to our salvation in the Messiah Jesus as past, present and future.

#1 We Have Been Saved (2 Timothy 1:9)

- Was Saved from the Penalty of Sin
- Our Past Salvation—Positional Sanctification—through the Cross
- There is a sense in which God has already saved each and every Christian. In this sense, salvation is equated with the forgiveness of sins.

#2 We Are Being Saved (1 Corinthians 1:18)

- Being Saved from the Power of Sin
- Our Present Salvation—Progressive Sanctification—through our co-crucifixion
- There is a sense in which God is still saving each and every Christian. In this sense, salvation is equated with the Christian's growth and perseverance. We are freed from its power and can freely choose to obey God or not.

#3 We Shall Be Saved (Romans 5:9-10)

- Will Be Saved from the Presence of Sin
- Our Promised Salvation—Ultimate Sanctification—where our position will equal our practice
- There is a sense in which salvation is a future event. In this sense, salvation is equated with the second coming of Christ or when we see Him face to face.

Our choice that was lost in the Garden of Eden has truly been restored in our salvation *in Christ*.

Under the New Covenant, we are freed from the power of disobedience (sin) that has ruled over us and blinded us to His Word. The freedom of choice is restored to us. In the Garden, Adam and Eve had relational access to God the Father; their disobedience severed that access. It is the Messiah's sacrifice in our place that has been a propitiation (satisfied God's Wrath for Man. God is at peace with Man.) for our disobedience (sin) of His Word. That Garden relationship is restored to Man through Messiah Jesus and the giving of the Holy Spirit. In the midst of the temptation, God has uniquely designed a way of escape for us to not fall prey to sin crouching at our door. Man is no longer a slave to disobedience (sin). Satan will always be against us and will tempt us. Through the Messiah's sacrifice, man is free from the power of sin to rule us as a taskmaster but not from the presence of sin in this life.

How Was God loved?

The original sin (disobedience) becomes a generational sin of Adam and Eve passed to their children. Cain failed in his love response to God, but as believers with the promise of salvation *in Christ*, we are restored to our choice to lovingly obey the Father's Word.

7

God's Deep Grief Reveals His Deeper Compassion

God was deeply grieved that He made mankind. God's deeper compassion saves a remnant foretelling Jesus. Remember in the last chapter we saw the interaction between Cain and God? God graciously warned Cain of coming evil upon him in the form of a temptation. God told Cain he could overcome it but warned that temptation was anxiously ready to engage him. In fact, the evil was crouching at Cain's door.

> **Genesis 4:8-10** — *Cain told Abel his brother. And it came about when they were in the field, that Cain rose up against Abel his brother and killed him. 9 Then the Lord said to Cain, "Where is Abel your brother?" And he said, "I do not know. Am I my brother's keeper?" 10 He said, "What have you done? The voice of your brother's blood is crying to Me from the ground.*

Rage of Cain

Then there was only one. What jealousy, rage and envy that must have consumed Cain! Even in this unveiled relationship with the Living God, Cain still came back at God with an attitude. Of course, God knew what Cain had done. The conversation was for Cain and our benefit.

> **Genesis 4:11-16** — *Now you are cursed from the ground, which has opened its mouth to receive your brother's blood from your hand. 12 When you cultivate the ground, it will no longer yield its strength to you; you will be a vagrant and a wanderer on the earth." 13 Cain said to the Lord, "My punishment is too great to bear! 14 Behold, You have driven me this day from the face of the ground; and from Your face I will be hidden, and I will be a vagrant and a wanderer on the earth, and whoever finds me will kill me." 15 So the Lord said to him, "Therefore whoever kills Cain, vengeance will be taken on him sevenfold." And the Lord appointed a sign for Cain, so that no one finding him would slay him. 16 Then Cain went out from the presence of the Lord, and settled in the land of Nod, east of Eden.*

First Recorded Murder in Human History

God levied His punishment on Cain for the first recorded murder in human history. God upped Adam's curse upon Cain concerning the Earth's non-cooperation with his efforts to cultivate it.

So far mankind is not doing a good job at loving God with any excellence with a passionate heart. They definitely didn't have God in mind and were not seeking to obey God's Words.

Cain's Life Expands

Chapter 4:17-24 of Genesis depicts the expansion of Cain's family. No one knows what the mark was on Can's life, whether it was physical or spiritual, but nonetheless, Cain, in God's mercy, was allowed to thrive even as difficult as it was. Chapter 4 depicts that Cain "knew" his wife had sexual relations, with one of Adam's descendants.[41] The Mosaic

---

[41] Albertus Pieters, *Old Testament History. Vol. 1: Notes on Genesis* (Grand Rapids: Wm. B. Eerdmans Publishing Co., 1943), 104.

Law had not been given at this point and such sexual relations were permitted.

Cain's offspring are recorded as builders of cities (4:17), raisers of livestock (4:20), creators of music (4:21), artisans in bronze and iron, weapons for sure (4:22) and the spread of civilization. But the descendants of Cain all inherent his curse as well depicted in the last descendant of Cain, Lamech. Lamech was a murderer and a polygamist. Lamech's marriage of two women goes against the revealed will of God (2:24).

> *"By virtue of being Cain's descendants, the people named in the genealogy all inherit his curse. Thus the Cainite genealogy becomes part of the Yahwist's account of man's increasing sin."*[42]

Cain and Seth's Lineage a World Apart

The differences between Cain and Seth's lineage could not be more of a contrast. The family of Seth is recorded in Genesis 4:25-26.

> **Genesis 4:25-26** — *Adam knew [Eve as] his wife again; and she gave birth to a son, and named him Seth, for [she said], "God has granted another child for me in place of Abel, because Cain killed him." 26 To Seth, also, a son was born, whom he named Enosh (mortal man, mankind). At that [same] time men began to call on the name of the Lord [in worship through prayer, praise, and thanksgiving].*

It is with this third child given to Adam and Eve by God, named Seth, who replaced Abel, that we start to see through their lineage, worship, praise and thanksgiving will be offered to God.

From this point of the first family the corruption of mankind continues to spiral down. The spiral is so severe that God Himself is grieved in His heart for His creation of mankind.

---

[42] R. R. Wilson, *Genealogy and History in the Biblical World* (New Haven: Yale University Press, 1977) 155.

Genesis 6:5-10 — *Then the Lord saw that the wickedness of man was great on the earth, and that every intent of the thoughts of his heart was only evil continually. 6 The Lord was sorry that He had made man on the earth, and He was grieved in His heart. 7 The Lord said, "I will blot out man whom I have created from the face of the land, from man to animals to creeping things and to birds of the sky; for I am sorry that I have made them." 8 But Noah found favor in the eyes of the Lord. 9 These are the records of the generations of Noah. Noah was a righteous man, blameless in his time; Noah walked with God. 10 Noah became the father of three sons: Shem, Ham, and Japheth.*

God Was Deeply Grieved that He Made Mankind

Wow! God saw that the thoughts of mankind's "heart was only evil continually." Is that state of mind what we today call criminally insane? The Lord said He was "sorry that He had made man on the earth, and He was grieved in His heart." Think about that for a moment. Could you even imagine the sorrow of God's heart toward all He had made and provided? "From man to animals to creeping things and to birds of the sky; for I am sorry that I have made them." These people He made in His own image. He breathed life into man. God did not do that for any other created kind. The God of all creation was sorry that He had made man. He was disgusted with His work of art, His masterpiece. So much so that He wanted to destroy it all and not just mankind, but to blot out all of His creation down to the bugs! Now *that* is a broken heart on a cosmic level!

Then after that big reveal comes verse 8. "But Noah." If it was not for those two words, you nor I would have existed. We find out in Genesis 5 that Noah was in the line of Seth. Seth's line would carry forth the worship of God. God always has a remnant throughout history that will be faithful to Him. We can all definitely thank Noah's choices and the covenant that God made with Noah. Grace again; God's grace to His creation. In the midst of that grace, God still did destroy it all as He desired, but when you read about the story of Noah that God used him, what does that say about God? Noah was used as God's mouthpiece for 120 years to warn all mankind that God was going to destroy the world with a flood. Who says that God is not longsuffering, full of grace and mercy?

Often people characterize the God of the Old Testament as a God of Wrath and the God of the New Testament as a God of love. How can this be since the same God of the Old Testament is the same God of the New Testament? Of course it is ludicrous. We just witnessed the longsuffering of God in the Old Testament with mankind and that He was grieved that He ever made man, "But Noah...."

God Is Longsuffering

What is longsuffering? The editors at the Bible resource ministry GotQuestions had this to say about longsuffering:

> It has been said that longsuffering means "suffering long." That is a good answer, but a better definition is needed. The word longsuffering in the Bible is made up of two Greek words meaning "long" and "temper"; literally, "long-tempered." To be longsuffering, then, is to have self-restraint when one is stirred to anger. A longsuffering person does not immediately retaliate or punish; rather, he has a "long fuse" and patiently forbears. Longsuffering is associated with mercy (1 Peter 3:20) and hope (1 Thessalonians 1:3). It does not surrender to circumstances or succumb to trial.
>
> God is the source of longsuffering because it is part of His character (Exodus 34:6; Numbers 14:18–20; Psalm 86:15; Romans 2:4; 1 Peter 3:9; 2 Peter 3:15). He is patient with sinners. At the same time, God's longsuffering can come to an end, as seen in the destruction

of Sodom and Gomorrah (Genesis 18—19) and the sending of Israel into captivity (1 Kings 17:1–23; 2 Kings 24:17—25:30).[43]

God described part of His own character qualities to Moses as compassionate, gracious, slow to anger [longsuffering], abounding in lovingkindness and truth and forgiving of sin.

> **Exodus 34:6** — *Then the Lord passed by in front of him [Moses] and proclaimed, "The Lord, the Lord God, compassionate and gracious, slow to anger [longsuffering], and abounding in lovingkindness and truth; 7 who keeps lovingkindness for thousands, who forgives iniquity, transgression and sin;*

So this Old Testament God proves Himself to be the same God characterized by love in the New Testament. This same God graciously gave mankind a warning of His coming wrath through Noah for 120 years. Each and every day for 120 years. Do you know how many days of witness that is for Noah to present the warning of God to his disobedient generation? 43,800 days of warning. But no one listened to Noah until it was too late.

Noah Was a Righteous Man, Blameless for His Time

Noah was a righteous man, blameless for his time. Of all the people on the earth in the times of Noah, he alone was judged by God as a righteous man and would be saved from God's all-consuming judgment of the entire would. Noah and his household. What amazing blessing does a head of household bring to their family before God?

> **Genesis 6:13-14a; 22** — *Then God said to Noah, "The end of all flesh has come before Me; for the earth is filled with violence because of them; and behold, I am about to destroy them with the earth. 14*

---

[43] "Longsuffering," Got Questions Ministries, https://www.gotquestions.org/Bible-longsuffering.html. Accessed April 12, 2024.

Make for yourself an ark of gopher wood; 22 Thus Noah did; according to all that God had commanded him, so he did.

You will see a pattern. God said. Noah did. God's Word. Noah obeyed.

Genesis 7:1, 5 — *Then the Lord said to Noah, "Enter the ark, you and all your household, for you alone I have seen to be righteous before Me in this time. 5 Noah did according to all that the Lord had commanded him.*

Again, God said. Noah did. God's Word. Noah obeyed.

Genesis 7:6-16 — *Now Noah was six hundred years old when the flood of water came upon the earth. 7 Then Noah and his sons and his wife and his sons' wives with him entered the ark because of the water of the flood. 8 Of clean animals and animals that are not clean and birds and everything that creeps on the ground, 9 there went into the ark to Noah by twos, male and female, as God had commanded Noah. 10 It came about after the seven days, that the water of the flood came upon the earth.*

11 In the six hundredth year of Noah's life, in the second month, on the seventeenth day of the month, on the same day all the fountains of the great deep burst open, and the floodgates of the sky were opened. 12 The rain fell upon the earth for forty days and forty nights. 13 On the very same day Noah and Shem and Ham and Japheth, the sons of Noah, and Noah's wife and the three wives of his sons with them, entered the ark, 14 they and every beast after its kind, and all the cattle after their kind, and every creeping thing that creeps on the earth after its kind, and every bird after its kind, all sorts of birds.

15 So they went into the ark to Noah, by twos of all flesh in which was the breath of life. 16 Those that entered, male and female of all flesh, entered as God had commanded him; and the Lord closed it behind him.

God Saves a Remnant

God saves a remnant. If God is a Covenant Maker and Keeper, He is also a Remnant Maker and Keeper. All throughout the Scriptures, whenever God's Chosen go under the influence of evil, God will always have a faithful remnant loyal and obedient to Him who will carry out His will. Here God's chosen remnant was Noah and his family. God carries on the covenant with Adam (Adamic Covenant) with Noah (Noahic Covenant).

This was again God's great grace. God, Who breathed the breath of life into man's nostrils was redeeming a remnant of man for salvation. This idea of God's remnant will carry throughout Scripture like the thread of the "seed of the woman" versus the "seed of the serpent." God in His great grace was saving a remnant of man to carry God's own great desire where He stated in the community of the Trinity, Let Us make man in Our image" (Gen 1:26). God through Noah was not ready to give up on His great desire to create man and give him life to have a relationship with the living God.

> **Genesis 7:17-24** — *Then the flood came upon the earth for forty days, and the water increased and lifted up the ark, so that it rose above the earth. 18 The water prevailed and increased greatly upon the earth, and the ark floated on the surface of the water. 19 The water prevailed more and more upon the earth, so that all the high mountains everywhere under the heavens were covered. 20 The water prevailed fifteen cubits higher, and the mountains were covered.*
>
> *21 All flesh that moved on the earth perished, birds and cattle and beasts and every swarming thing that swarms upon the earth, and all mankind; 22 of all that was on the dry land, all in whose nostrils was the breath of the spirit of life, died.*
>
> *23 Thus He blotted out every living thing that was upon the face of the land, from man to animals to creeping things and to birds of the sky, and they were blotted out from the earth; and only Noah was*

left, together with those that were with him in the ark. 24 The water prevailed upon the earth one hundred and fifty days.

God's Word is Solid, True, Dependable, Without Fault; Trust It

As we investigate the record of Scripture, it always bears witness that God's Word is rock solid. It is quite interesting that if one were to just look at the history of archaeology, one would be astonished that archeology has never disproven the biblical record. Just the opposite has happened. Archeology has always proven the historical people, places and events detailed in Scripture.

Every time in God's Word, when God said it to be so, it was. When God said, it did. This is without fail. Every time. God may have altered some things here and there in mid-stream, but it came about as He desired without fail. It is recorded in Scripture for all of creation to view.

The Flood was no different. God told Noah the waters were coming. They came. God said that the Flood came and in verse 20 of chapter 7, "The water prevailed fifteen cubits higher, and the mountains were covered." Mt Everest, which stands at 8,850 meters (29,035 feet) above sea level, undeniably has the "highest altitude" in the world. Fifteen cubits would be approximately 26 feet above the peak of Mt. Everest. For 150 days or about 5 months, Noah and his family saw nothing but water.

Here the judgment of God upon the evil of mankind was just as He told Noah. Notice Noah never haggled with God. He merely obeyed God's command. What went into that obedience do you think? Noah is never recorded to show any doubt, nor did he question God. Can you even possibly imagine the long obedience that it took Noah for 120 years to faithfully build a dry land monster ship? By its dimensions, Noah's ark was about half the size of the *Queen Mary II* with itself being approximately 1100 feet long. The *Titanic* was 800 feet long and the Ark is only 300 feet shy of that. It was no small order by God in that day to build that size ship. Depending on where you land on the size of a Biblical cubit, the Ark dimensions were approximately 515 ft in length, 75 ft wide, and 51 ft high. Holding to those dimensions, the Ark's square footage would have been 3,046,187.

Noah's Story is Spoken of as History in the New Testament

Could you imagine the ridicule and mocking Noah and his family endured for that 120 years? I cannot even fathom building such a structure by hand given any amount of time let alone 120 years. All the New Testament writers treated the story of Noah as history, not fiction, nor allegory. The writers recorded that Messiah Jesus Himself pointed to the Noah story as historical fact and compared Noah's times to His own. The setting is Jesus talking to His disciples about His second coming.

> **Matthew 24:37-41** — *For the coming of the Son of Man will be just like the days of Noah. 38 For as in those days before the flood they were eating and drinking, marrying and giving in marriage, until the day that Noah entered the ark, 39 and they did not understand until the flood came and took them all away; so will the coming of the Son of Man be. 40 Then there will be two men in the field; one will be taken and one will be left. 41 Two women will be grinding at the mill; one will be taken and one will be left.*

How do you want to be found when the Messiah comes in the clouds to call you? When you are one of the two in the field or one of the two in the mill. When you are the taken one, how do you want the Messiah to find you?

God's Judgment upon Mankind Is Coming Again

God's Word is solid and sure. By His Word, just as He executed judgment upon mankind in Noah's day, God will send His Son Messiah Jesus a second time. This second time it will be for the final judgment of mankind. Judgment was not the mission of Messiah Jesus at His first coming.

John 3:16-18 — *"For God so loved the world, that He gave His only begotten Son, that whoever believes in Him shall not perish, but have eternal life. 17 For God did not send the Son into the world to judge the world, but that the world might be saved through Him. 18 He who believes in Him is not judged; he who does not believe has been judged already, because he has not believed in the name of the only begotten Son of God.*

God the Father sent the Son to pay the penalty for the disobedience of Adam. Messiah Jesus was destined to be the second Adam. Jesus was to redeem the world and take the title deed to the world out of the hands of the Ruler of this world, Satan, given to him by Adam's failure. By the sacrifice of the Messiah's life, His blood redeemed all mankind. Messiah Jesus, in His first coming, established our return to the Garden relationship with God the Father.

Genesis 7:21a-23a — *All flesh that moved on the earth perished...22 of all that was on the dry land, all in whose nostrils was the breath of the spirit of life, died. 23 Thus He blotted out every living thing that was upon the face of the land.*

Messiah Jesus could have pointed to any other days in the history of mankind to compare what the days will be like in His second coming, but Jesus chose the days of Noah. Why do you think?

What did we just point out what the days of Noah were like?

Genesis 6:5-10 — *Then the Lord saw that the wickedness of man was great on the earth, and that every intent of the thoughts of his heart was only evil continually. 6 The Lord was sorry that He had made man on the earth, and He was grieved in His heart. 7 The Lord said, "I will blot out man whom I have created from the face of the land, from man to animals to creeping things and to birds of the sky; for I am sorry that I have made them."*

God Will Grieve Deeply Over Man's Destruction Once Again

In our terms, that kind of sorrow and grief makes us deeply sick. This is that throw-up, can't-get-out-of-bed, I-don't-care-if-you-live kind of grief. I am not saying that God had that kind of human grief, but I am trying to put His grief and sorrow in human terms that we could grasp its emotional depth. I would say take our kind of deep, devastating grief and multiply it by a billion and you just might approach God's grief here. And by contrast, God's love for us.

Jesus said that the days in His second coming are going to be just like those days of Noah that brought God's great judgment upon mankind and His creation. So, we can also gather that God the Father will be within the same grief and sorrow over His creation then just as He was in the days of Noah. We can also gather that just as in the days of Noah with the flood, the Messiah Jesus' second coming is to be an event of God's judgment upon mankind.

Matthew warns us, "But of that day and hour [the Second Coming of the Messiah] no one knows, not even the angels of heaven, nor the Son, but the Father alone" (Matthew 24:36). A Biblical mystery that only the Father knows the day and hour of the Messiah Jesus' second coming not even God the Son knows when this will be.

Covenant of the Rainbow

We do know that the next worldwide judgment of God upon mankind will not come by water. God promised Noah and his descendants (us) that He would not destroy the world with water again. First God gave them the same command He gave to their first parents, Adam and Eve.

Genesis 9:1-3 — *And God blessed Noah and his sons and said to them, "Be fruitful and multiply, and fill the earth. 2 The fear of you and the terror of you will be on every beast of the earth and on every bird of the sky; with everything that creeps on the ground, and all the fish of the sea, into your hand they are given. 3 Every moving* *thing that is alive shall be food for you; I give all to you, as I gave the green plant.*

God told the new first family to be fruitful and multiply. He also told them to rule and subdue the earth, that all creation would be subject to them, and that He has given "every moving thing that is alive shall be food for [us] as I gave the green plant."

God is a covenant Maker and a covenant Keeper. Just after God's command to Noah and his sons, God made a covenant between Himself and Noah who now represents all mankind as Noah's patriarch Adam did.

Genesis 9:8-17 — *Then God spoke to Noah and to his sons with him, saying, 9 "Now behold, I Myself do establish My covenant with you, and with your descendants after you; 10 and with every living creature that is with you, the birds, the cattle, and every beast of the earth with you; of all that comes out of the ark, even every beast of the earth. 11 I establish My covenant with you; and all flesh shall never again be cut off by the water of the flood, neither shall there again be a flood to destroy the earth." 12 God said, "This is the sign of the covenant which I am making between Me and you and every living creature that is with you, for all successive generations; 13 I set My bow in the cloud, and it shall be for a sign of a covenant between Me and the earth. 14 It shall come about, when I bring a cloud over the earth, that the bow will be seen in the cloud, 15 and I will remember My covenant, which is between Me and you and every living creature of all flesh; and never again shall the water become a flood to destroy all flesh. 16 When the bow is in the cloud, then I will look upon it, to remember the everlasting covenant between God and every living creature of all flesh that is on the earth." 17 And God said to Noah, "This is the sign of the covenant which I have established between Me and all flesh that is on the earth."*

God promised all mankind that He would never destroy them and all creation again by water. The rainbow that most of us take for granted or have explained away in our scientific-induced minds, is a visual sign from God of His covenant to all of us. It is unique in all creation and an amazing visual to all who see it.

The next coming of Messiah Jesus is the coming of God's final judgment upon mankind and the creation. The Apostle John who wrote the vision of the Book of Revelation described the Messiah's second coming this way:

> **Revelation 19:11-16** — *And I saw heaven opened, and behold, a white horse, and He who sat on it is called Faithful and True, and in righteousness He judges and wages war. 12 His eyes are a flame of fire, and on His head are many diadems; and He has a name written on Him which no one knows except Himself. 13 He is clothed with a robe dipped in blood, and His name is called The Word of God. 14 And the armies which are in heaven, clothed in fine linen, white and clean, were following Him on white horses. 15 From His mouth comes a sharp sword, so that with it He may strike down the nations, and He will rule them with a rod of iron; and He treads the wine press of the fierce wrath of God, the Almighty. 16 And on His robe and on His thigh He has a name written, "KING OF KINGS, AND LORD OF LORDS."*

How Was God loved?

God was loved by a remnant. Here the remnant started as one solitary man, Noah. The remnant was extended to Noah's family. We have no way of knowing the extent of the world's population but at least it was in the thousands. The evil was so profound that it utterly made God sorry that He ever created mankind. We are all well aware of the evil that exists in our current day, but God has not destroyed us—yet. Can you even imagine what level of evil existed at that time to bring God to that conclusion? But God found one man, Noah. We read what God recorded about Noah.

Genesis 6:9-10 — *9 These are the records of the generations of Noah. Noah was a righteous man, blameless in his time; Noah walked with God. 10 Noah became the father of three sons: Shem, Ham, and Japheth.*

Noah was a "righteous man, blameless in his time; Noah walked with God." Of all the thousands of mankind, one man was righteous, blameless, and walked with God. How are we to understand this term "righteous" attributed to Noah by God? The relationship with God was not as defined for us at this point but it will be later. God chose Noah and called him righteous and blameless and he Noah walked with God. So whatever comprised of that relationship, it was the exact opposite of Noah's contemporaries who were not righteous, nor blameless, nor did they walk with God. In fact, God said of Noah's contemporaries "that every intent of the thoughts of his heart was only evil continually."

That evil we have discovered was disobedience to God. That disobedience can be as simple as placing your judgment above God's, or it can be as complex as allowing your mind to race with whatever evil acts or thoughts; those too would be disobedience. We would consider the latter as more disobedient and thus more deserving of God's wrath, but we did not find that in the Garden. The entire downward spiral of falling away from our Garden relationship all started with what we might consider simple disobedience of placing our judgment over God's. To God, that act of disobedience to Him was just as horrendous as whatever our imaginations went about the other.

So how was God loved? Amid one of the first and most grievous times for God our Creator, one man, Noah, loved God by being obedient to God's Word and to His desires. God considered Noah a righteous man.

Jesus will refer to the days of Noah, the total disregard for anything concerning God, and will be the same mindset for mankind before He returns to set up His earthly kingdom (Matthew 25:31-33).

8

Earth 2.0

The Garden shows itself as part of mankind's DNA. After the Flood, God's sovereign choices in the nations shape the story of His continued intimacy with mankind and ultimately, the story of Jesus.

From the text in Genesis 8 after the flood waters subsided, we find the Ark rested upon Mt. Ararat and the focus turns to the first family of God's second chance to humanity. Noah's family. We will trace the progressive movement of God and man from God's promise to Noah with the rainbow to the formation of God's promise to a nation.

Noah's First Act on Solid Ground

God called Noah a righteous man. Noah proved that with his first act after exiting the Ark.

> **Genesis 8:20-21** — *Then Noah built an altar to the Lord, and took of every clean animal and of every clean bird and offered burnt offerings on the altar. 21 The Lord smelled the soothing aroma; and the Lord said to Himself, "I will never again curse the ground on*

account of man, for the intent of man's heart is evil from his youth; and I will never again destroy every living thing, as I have done.

At the top of Genesis 9, God reiterates His blessing Gen 1 on Noah and his sons. God gives Noah and his sons the same command as He gave to the first couple, Adam and Eve.

Genesis 9:1-3— *And God blessed Noah and his sons and said to them, "Be fruitful and multiply, and fill the earth. 2 The fear of you and the terror of you will be on every beast of the earth and on every bird of the sky; with everything that creeps on the ground, and all the fish of the sea, into your hand they are given. 3 Every moving thing that is alive shall be food for you; I give all to you, as I gave the green plant.*

God expands the food chain from the "green plant" to "every moving thing that is alive." So it appears that God was against rare meat because in Genesis 9:4, with this expanded menu, God gives the first family 2.0 a restriction. God commands them, "Only you shall not eat flesh with its life, that is, its blood."

God further tells them the first civil law and reiterates the command that He originally gave to Adam and Eve.

Genesis 9:6-7 — "Whoever sheds man's blood, By man his blood shall be shed, For in the image of God He made man. 7 "As for you, be fruitful and multiply; Populate the earth abundantly and multiply in it."

God Initiates Capital Punishment

God initiates capital punishment citing that every human is made in the image of God. If a man destroyed another man, he was, in God's view, destroying God since man is made in God's image. From this first interaction with God and the new start of Earth/Humanity 2.0, God is very interactive.

God provided for the new family just as He did for Adam and Eve. Recall that God provided for Adam and Eve after the Fall, after their disobedience. That provision was in the form of God's covenant with Noah as it was with Adam. The commentators in the Moody Bible Commentary summed up man's post-flood disobedience this way:

> *"In this section (10:1-11:26) God concluded His "prosecution" of depraved humanity by presenting a concise description of the first and greatest collective expression of human depravity in the post-flood period. The point is that sin— even more fundamentally, indeed, the impulse to sin (i.e., depravity)—is here to stay. At the same time, however, this section also introduces the complementary idea—taken up and developed in the next thematic "half" of Genesis (11:27– 50:26)—that a pardon from sin is available to humanity and that humankind's attainment of the prefall ideal is both the active and inevitable goal of human history."*[44]

Earth 2.0

God used Noah's family to populate Earth 2.0 and the formation of all the nations. Out of all the nations, we will see that God chose one people to be His mouthpiece and to represent Him on the earth.

> **Genesis 9:18-19** — *Now the sons of Noah who came out of the ark were Shem and Ham and Japheth; and Ham was the father of Canaan. 19 These three were the sons of Noah, and from these the whole earth was populated.*

Nations of the World

Chapter 10 of Genesis is the record of the nations of the world that formed out of the lineage of the three sons of Noah.

---

[44] Rydelnik et al., The Moody Bible Commentary, 69

Genesis 10:1, 32 — *Now these are the records of the generations of Shem, Ham, and Japheth, the sons of Noah; and sons were born to them after the flood. 32 These are the families of the sons of Noah, according to their genealogies, by their nations; and out of these the nations were separated on the earth after the flood.*

"Genesis 10 lists a total of 70 original founders of the nations of the world or racial groups. They are all divided into 3 primary classifications: Shem, Ham, and Japheth. Although the subject of the classification of the nations and the origin of languages is highly controversial, ethnologists agree on one key point: that all of mankind can be divided into three basic groups."[45]

Another more detailed article discussing the formation of the nations of the world in Gen 10 is one found on bible.org by Steven J. Cole:

"And in spite of the pot shots of numerous critics in the past, most Bible scholars have become convinced of the accuracy of Genesis 10. William F. Albright (not a conservative) said that this chapter "stands absolutely alone in ancient literature, without a remote parallel, even among the Greeks, where we find the closest approach to a distribution of peoples in genealogical framework... The Table of Nations remains an astonishingly accurate document" (supplement to Robert Young, Analytical Concordance to the Bible [Eerdmans], p. 30). You can count the number of nations in Genesis 10 in different ways and come up with slightly different figures. Jewish scholars counted 70 (26 from Shem, 30 from Ham [not including the Philistines, mentioned in passing; 10:14], and 14 from Japheth)."[46]

---

[45] "Table of Nations," Bible History, https://www.bible-history.com/maps/2-table-of-nations.html. Accessed April 23, 2024.

[46] Steven J. Cole, "Lesson 22: The Roots of the Nations (Genesis 10:1-32)," Bible.org,
https://bible.org/seriespage/lesson-22-roots-nations-genesis-101-32 Accessed 4-3-2024

Recall that God re-established His covenant with Noah and thus his descendants as He did with Adam and Eve. One aspect of that covenant was to be fruitful and multiply; to populate the earth abundantly.

> **Genesis 9:7** — *"As for you, be fruitful and multiply; Populate the earth abundantly and multiply in it."*

The Garden Is Part of Mankind's DNA

Contrast Noah's first act on solid ground regarding worshipping God to that of mankind who did not worship the living, true only God Almighty. Instead of collecting in one place for one desire to reach God, they could have chosen to obey the instruction of God to populate the ends of the earth. Amazing that man once again turned their back on their Creator. They collectively attempted to reach God through the Tower of Babel. An attempt to be equal to God and, sadly, once again to be gods. The original disobedience (sin) of the Garden is alive and well in Earth 2.0. It would seem here showing themselves to be more independent and in competition with God Himself. God had a covenant promise with Noah to not destroy the world by water. So, God confused the languages of man, and in doing so, mankind dispersed throughout the world, creating 70 different nations from the three lineages of Noah's sons: Shem, Ham, and Japheth.

> **Genesis 11:1-4** — *Now the whole earth used the same language and the same words. 2 It came about as they journeyed east, that they found a plain in the land of Shinar and settled there. 3 They said to one another, "Come, let us make bricks and burn them thoroughly." And they used brick for stone, and they used tar for mortar. 4 They said, "Come, let us build for ourselves a city, and a tower whose top will reach into heaven, and let us make for ourselves a name, otherwise we will be scattered abroad over the face of the whole earth."*

God was not going to allow mankind to stay in one spot and allow mankind to think that he could arise to be His equal. God's covenant with Noah was for him and his descendants to populate all of the earth. God took mankind's desire to reach Him and be as His equal was totally confused by one simple act. God gave each descendant group of Noah a different language. That confusion of language destroyed the tower of mankind's collective power construction project.

Genesis 11:7-9 — *Come, let Us go down and there confuse their language, so that they will not understand one another's speech." 8 So the Lord scattered them abroad from there over the face of the whole earth; and they stopped building the city. 9 Therefore its name was called Babel, because there the Lord confused the language of the whole earth; and from there the Lord scattered them abroad over the face of the whole earth.*

The clue to the rebellion against God is in the leader, as is usually the case. Here in this part of mankind's story it is a man named Nimrod. Steven J. Cole had this to say about Nimrod.

"It's overwhelming to think of all these names and to realize that they represent whole groups of people, whole nations, who lived and died, for the most part, without God. Perhaps there was more knowledge of God than we are aware of, but what we know of these nations from later history would not indicate that any of them worshiped the one true God.

Nimrod is a case in point. Apparently, his name was proverbial in Moses' day, so that people compared a powerful man to Nimrod (10:9), much as we may say, "a dictator like Stalin." At first glance, you might think that Nimrod was a good guy, since he is called a mighty hunter "before the Lord." But the point is rather that Nimrod asserted himself against the Lord...many commentators suggest that when the text says that Nimrod was a mighty hunter, it should be taken to mean not that he was a hunter of game, but a hunter of men. The Hebrew word is used elsewhere in reference to "a violent invasion of the persons and rights of men" (George Bush, Notes on Genesis

[Klock & Klock] 1:171). Nimrod used his skill and force in warfare to build a kingdom for himself at others' expense. Josephus wrote, "[Nimrod] was a bold man, and of great strength of hand; and he gradually changed the government into tyranny, seeing no other way of turning men from the fear of God, but to bring them to a constant dependence on his own power" (cited by Bush, p. 172).

Thus when it says that Nimrod was a mighty hunter "before the Lord," the Hebrew is, "in the face of the Lord," or "against the Lord" (as the Septuagint translates it). Moses is reminding his readers that Nimrod's tyranny did not go unnoticed by God. His name itself comes from a word meaning "we will revolt." He established his kingdom in defiance of God.[47]

Mankind's Desires to Be His Own God

It is amazing to me how man continually seeks to take control and be his own god. But I can only be amazed whenever I am looking at this as a researcher or writer. If I look at this as myself—part of the human race in the story—when I look into the mirror of my mind, I find myself guilty of this as well. I have a daily struggle with both the original sin (disobedience to the Word of God) and its motive (to be or replace God). As a Christian, it is the struggle with "my" will verses "God's" will. Both are alive and well in my soul. The only reprieve. The only salvation from myself is through Messiah Jesus, just as the Apostle Paul concluded himself in Romans 7. Praise Messiah Jesus.

From all the nations of the world that were created after God confused the language, there is only one nation that God had chosen to make a covenant relationship with. Much like one son of Noah was favored spiritually over the other two. Whenever "choice" is mentioned in the same sentence with God, it is on some level a discussion of God's sovereignty. I can't help but see that any discussion we have about God and especially, God's choice, it is the

---

[47] Cole, "Lesson 22: The Roots of the Nations (Genesis 10:1-32),"

little gods in our own mind that are casting judgment on the only God. But that judgment is allowed by the only God in any discussion concerning Him. After all, how else are we left to grow and stretch in our understanding of the only God without wrestling with our questions? We will see that this is also part of God's sovereignty in allowing us to discuss His right to choose to exist within and among us in our relationships with Him. Our main part of that exercise is to read from Scripture what God says about it and, in faith, accept it and, in humility, be glad about what He has allowed through His Spirit— and that we can even understand it.

> **Isaiah 55:8-11** — *"For My thoughts are not your thoughts, Nor are your ways My ways," declares the Lord. 9 "For as the heavens are higher than the earth, So are My ways higher than your ways And My thoughts than your thoughts. 10 "For as the rain and the snow come down from heaven, And do not return there without watering the earth And making it bear and sprout, And furnishing seed to the sower and bread to the eater; 11 So will My word be which goes forth from My mouth; It will not return to Me empty, Without accomplishing what I desire, And without succeeding in the matter for which I sent it.*

God's Copout?

So do you think that this is God's copout? No, but it *is* part of His explanation to you. Remember, His Sovereign grace and mercy allow you to explore and question His Being, His motive, and His choices because it is the relationship with you that the Almighty God seeks. You nor I will *ever* be able to understand the ways and means of God. We will always be the creature and He will always be the Creator. Get this. In order to fully understand Him, you would have to be Him! And that was *the* sin of the Garden!

You and I need to give God the same latitude we give to any of our friends or family that we are seeking to understand. It is also a true statement that for us to be able to fully understand our mother, father, brother, sister, mate, etc., we would have to be them. That is impossible to do, and so it is with our relationship with God. The possible part is our response. All we can do is either accept or reject our family and friends once we think we have fully come to know them. God allows you and I to have our own sovereignty. We have full sovereignty over our response to anyone and any circumstance in our lives. We are also given complete sovereignty over our response to God.

God Gave Man Sovereignty in One Area: Choice

I have said this before that the complete sovereign choice our Creator has given His highest creation, man, is the greatest power He has given any living thing in His creation. God has even extended that power of choice to our response to Him. He has revealed Himself to us within His creation (natural revelation) and in His Word (special revelation). In that response to Him, we are without excuse. The Apostle Paul pointed this out to the Roman Church in his letter to them.

> **Romans 1:18-24** — *For the wrath of God is revealed from heaven against all ungodliness and unrighteousness of men who suppress the truth in unrighteousness, 19 because that which is known about God is evident within them; for God made it evident to them. 20 For since the creation of the world His invisible attributes, His eternal power and divine nature, have been clearly seen, being understood through what has been made, so that they are without excuse.*
>
> *21 For even though they knew God, they did not honor Him as God or give thanks, but they became futile in their speculations, and their foolish heart was darkened. 22 Professing to be wise, they became fools, 23 and exchanged the glory of the incorruptible God for an image in the form of corruptible man and of birds and four-footed animals and crawling creatures.*
>
> *24 Therefore God gave them over in the lusts of their hearts to impurity, so that their bodies would be dishonored among them. 25*

For they exchanged the truth of God for a lie, and worshiped and served the creature rather than the Creator, who is blessed forever. Amen.

There is a lot to ponder in those verses let alone that entire first chapter in the book of Romans. What God is saying through Paul is that since the beginning of the world, with what God has made and man has seen, man is without excuse to know God, to honor Him and to give thanks to Him. But man exchanged truth for a lie instead. So, if God says man is without excuse to know Him through the natural revelation of His creation, how much more damning is man for His rejection of God through His special revelation of Himself through His word?

The mystery of God's Sovereignty is right here at the crossroads of acknowledging, not understanding, God's sovereign choice of one nation over another, just as in His sovereign choice of one person over another. There is this back and forth between God's sovereignty and man's responsibility (choice). There is this aspect that God's choice undergirds man's choice, especially in exercising of faith (Eph 2:8-9).[48]

God Is Sovereign

I found a definition of God's sovereignty from a writer I am not familiar with but I like his definition.

The sovereignty of God means that as ruler of the Universe, God is free and has the right to do whatever he wants. He is not bound or limited by the dictates of his created beings. Further, he is in complete control over everything that happens here on Earth.[49]

I would add to Zavada's definition of God's Sovereignty that while God has "the right to do whatever he wants," that action is

---

[48] Kenneth Boa, *God, I Don't Understand* (Colorado Springs, Victor Cook Communications Ministries, 2007). Chapters 4 & 5

[49] Jack Zavada, "What Is the Sovereignty of God?" Learn Religions, February 8, 2021, learnreligions.com/what-is-gods-sovereignty-700697

totally commensurate with His character and attributes. God is holy and righteous in the core of His nature, and therefore, His actions are in concert with that revealed nature. That is true whether we have or will ever understand it.

The subject of God's Sovereignty is scattered throughout the Bible. The publisher of the ESV Bible, *Crossway*, has an article that reviews "10 Key Bible Verses on God's Sovereignty."[50]

I will cite them for you here. The short article is well worth your reading.

- Ephesians 1:11
- Romans 8:28
- Matthew 10:29–31
- Colossians 1:16–17
- Isaiah 45:7–9
- Proverbs 16:33
- Job 42:2
- Lamentations 3:37–39
- Acts 4:27–28
- Ephesians 1:4

Take Job 42:2. There is an entire revelation of God's sovereignty versus mankind's sovereignty throughout the book of Job. The *Crossway* article I referenced above and cited below gives a short commentary on that verse.

Job 42:2 — *"I know that You can do all things, And that no purpose of Yours can be thwarted."*

In his second speech, the Lord asks Job particularly about power in relation to himself and other creatures he has made (40:6–41:34). Job, directly aware of God as never before, responds by humbly

---

[50] "Ten Key Bible Verses on God's Sovereignty," November 4, 2020, Crossway, https://www.crossway.org/articles/10-key-bible-verses-on-gods-sovereignty/

submitting to God's sovereignty and penitently despising himself for his earlier wild words (42:1–6). While Job had rightly defended himself against his friends' accusations of sin and had defined his circumstances as being governed by God, he had drawn conclusions about what his affliction meant that did not account sufficiently for what was hidden in the knowledge and purposes of God.

The *Crossway* commentator noted that Job "had drawn conclusions about what his affliction meant that did not account sufficiently for what was hidden in the knowledge and purposes of God." Ah, the mystery of God Himself, His Word and His ways! This is exactly what we already discussed that the Prophet Isaiah was pointing to when he wrote,

> **Isaiah 55:8-9** — *"For My thoughts are not your thoughts, Nor are your ways My ways," declares the Lord. 9 "For as the heavens are higher than the earth, So are My ways higher than your ways And My thoughts than your thoughts.*

The Mysteries of God

Before we leave this short discussion on the sovereignty of God, I want to introduce you to this idea of the mysteries of God. While we can only scratch the surface of teachings or doctrine of God's Sovereignty, at the very bottom of it, we will have to remand it to the bookshelf labelled "Mysteries of God." Kenneth Boa has a great discussion of the mysteries of God in his book, *God, I Don't Understand.*

> *"When a human does something beyond an animal's comprehension, it must remain a mystery to that animal since it has no categories it can use to correlate this behavior. A dog can be taught to fetch the morning newspaper, but it is another matter to teach it how to read.*
>
> *The corresponding analogy between a human and God is valid as well. However, the gap is even greater because we must compare a human's finite mental capacity to the Lord's boundless capacity. Even so, God can still communicate real truth to men. As Francis Schaeffer*

pointed out, God has communicated truly, though not exhaustively to man. He can comprehend a myriad of things that we cannot grasp. Since the Bible is God's revelation to man, it should not be surprising that it implies or directly states some of these areas.

We need to find a name for such revealed incomprehensibles. The word paradox isn't the best choice, because it implies only an apparent contradiction... The word oxymoron is also inappropriate since it's simply a combination of two contradictory or incongruous words...

We need a word to describe the fact that God's revelation to man sometimes goes beyond the level of human reasoning and comprehension by stating the fact two things that men cannot reconcile. The word antinomy comes closer to describing these phenomena in God's Word...

This word's two parts — anti (against) and nomos (law) — simply means "against the law" of human reasoning...

In the original version of this book, I used antinomy throughout to describe the things in the Bible that go beyond or against human reasoning. However, a few found the term confusing... Things revealed in Scripture that seem incomprehensible to the human mind are fully comprehended by the divine mind. They are "superrational" not irrational.

To overcome this possible confusion, I've decided to substitute the word mystery for antinomy. Mystery comes from the Greek word mysterion, used in the New Testament for "secret" or "secret teaching."...

In this book, the word mystery will refer to those truths in Scripture that are beyond the boundary of human understanding."[51]

I first met Ken Boa when he was a senior at Dallas Theological Seminary (DTS). He and other DTS students came to a small "house

---

[51] Boa, *God, I Don't Understand*, 22-23.

church" named Emmanuel's Fellowship that met in the home of a Dallas dentist. They shared the pastoral and teaching ministry. Most of the makeup of this small church were teenagers. There were a few older people but not a lot. Everyone there was an "ex-something:" ex-prostitute, ex-homosexual, ex-drug user, ex-alcoholic. You get the picture. We met on Saturday nights since a lot of our parents went to what we viewed as "dead" traditional churches on Sunday morning compared to what we were learning from Scriptures at that Saturday night fellowship. All the teenagers wanted to witness to their parents, so they all still went to the Sunday services to avoid conflict.

I was seventeen years old at that time. I was one of the ex-drug users. Ken Boa made a lasting impression on my faith that has lasted to this day some 53 years later. He has always been one of my "adopted mentors." His books over the years have kept me solid in the Word, even whenever my lifestyle choices pushed me away from God. Ken's influence was one thing the Holy Spirit used to draw me to center faith. Ken's influence was also significant years later whenever I made a choice to attend Dallas Theological Seminary as a student myself.

Ken and I recently shared the memories of Emmanuel's Fellowship. Ken brought into focus how small a world God's community of believers is. Ken recalled, "I loved your description of your head shop and of Pat Booth. As you know, Pat and Dave Penny were two of the three people who kept me at DTS during the first two years when I wanted to leave."

When he wanted to leave DTS and most likely his future ministry? That statement blew my mind! The same fellow that God used to bring me the Gospel also helped redeem my friend's ministry choice which would be foundational in Ken's deep and wide ministry of discipleship. God has used Ken worldwide to strengthen and deepen the faith walk of thousands—both men and women. To grasp what the void would look like without Ken's ministry, take a quick look at Appendix B.

Ken's book that I referenced above is the first book I read of his. It was brilliant. I always had an inquisitive mind. That character trait really ticked off my dad. But as I grew in my faith, understanding and Biblical knowledge, I used this concept of Ken's. I did not have any issues or confusion with the term and its use. But to keep consistency and to help understand why Ken made the change, I will also use the term "mystery" to reference "those truths in Scripture that are beyond the boundary of human understanding."

I guess apologies are in order for this long diversion in discussing God's Sovereign right to choose, but the discussion was needed since we will see God will choose one person over another, and God will also choose one nation over another.

We learned earlier that in Genesis 10, the nations of the world that were formed out of the lineage of the three sons of Noah.

> **Genesis 10:1, 32** — *Now these are the records of the generations of Shem, Ham, and Japheth, the sons of Noah; and sons were born to them after the flood. 32 These are the families of the sons of Noah, according to their genealogies, by their nations; and out of these the nations were separated on the earth after the flood.*

God's Sovereign Choice in Choosing Shem

Out of the three sons of Noah in Earth 2.0, God blessed Shem above his other two brothers. The significance of blessings from father to son in the Old Testament is lost to us as modern readers.

> *"Noah blessed Shem above his brothers (Genesis 9:26–27), and it was through Shem that the promised seed destined to crush Satan came (Genesis 3:15). That seed is traced back to Adam's son Seth (Genesis 5:1–32), through Shem, and on to Abraham, Judah, and David, leading all the way to Christ (Luke 3:36)."* [52]

---

[52] "Who Were the Sons of Noah and What Happened to Them and Their Descendants?" Got Questions Ministries, https://www.gotquestions.org/sons-of-Noah.html

Genesis 9:26-27 — *He also said, "Blessed be the Lord, The God of Shem; And let Canaan be his servant. 27 "May God enlarge Japheth, And let him dwell in the tents of Shem; And let Canaan be his servant."*

I am not making excuses for God whenever we run into a "mystery" in the Bible. It is not a "punt" disengaging our brains. It is accurately describing something factually found in Scripture. When we accept the Bible as "The Word(s) Of God," what happens when we run into the unexplainable? Are you or I going to attempt to explain it? Really? If we attempt to do so, then we are right back in the Garden of Eden committing the original sin—to be a god. We are not. God is the ONLY God.

If we attempt to read into the mystery additional information to help resolve it, then we commit what Bible teachers call eisegesis.[53] This is when we read meaning into the Bible from outside of the Bible. So the best thing we can do is acknowledge the "mystery" and allow the text to stand as is. When we practice the opposite of eisegesis, we are practicing exegesis. Exegesis is to read *out* from the text. This practice is to allow the text itself to interpret itself. When we practice this method of interpretation, we properly find and conclude a Biblical "mystery" as is the discussion at hand. Many will get hung up on this and just can't stand to allow a mystery to be a mystery. Those who get caught up in this usually miss the 98 percent of the Bible that is clearly to be understood (and practiced) and is not mysterious.

Ray Steadman, one of the great Bible teachers of the twentieth century, had this to say about the progression of the three families of

---

[53] "Eisegesis," Wikipedia, https://en.wikipedia.org/wiki/Eisegesis. Accessed April 24, 2024.

Note: Eisegesis is the process of interpreting text in such a way as to introduce one's own presuppositions, agendas or biases. It is commonly referred to as reading into the text. It is often done to "prove" a pre-held point of concern, and to provide confirmation bias corresponding with the pre-held interpretation and any agendas supported by it.

mankind coming from Noah's sons and Shem fulfilling the prophecy from God in Gen 9.

> *"Here we have the three families of mankind. The family of Ham is represented by Canaan, although not limited to his descendants. In certain of the old versions, in these two verses referring to Canaan, the account reads, "Ham, the father of Canaan," which is probably the more accurate rendering. Now this is a most important passage. We can hardly overrate its importance in understanding the world of our day.*
>
> *Notice that Shem is given religious primacy among mankind. The Semitic people, the descendants of Shem, were responsible under God to meet the spiritual needs of mankind. That is their role in humanity. It is most striking, isn't it, that the three great religions of earth, which can properly be called religions, all come from the Semitic family: Judaism, Mohammedanism, and Christianity. There is much distortion of truth in these, granted, but the sense of mission by the Semitic families of earth is very evident. This family includes the Jews, the Arabs, certain ancient peoples, as well as other modern groups.*
>
> *It is also interesting that three groups are recorded in the New Testament as specifically coming to seek the Lord Jesus. They are the shepherds, the wise men, and the Greeks. Here you have again the order: Shem, Ham, and Japheth.*
>
> *The shepherds were Israelites, Semitic. Most Bible scholars feel that the Magi, the wise men from the East, were really not from the East (that was a general term) but from Arabia, and represent the Hamitic peoples. The Greeks are clearly Japhethites. So there again, always in the same order, we have Shem, Ham, and Japheth."*[54]

---

[54] Ray Stedman, "The Three Families of Man," Ray Stedman Ministries, https://www.raystedman.org/old-testament/genesis/the-three-families-of-man. Accessed April 24, 2024.

From Shem to Abraham to Israel

Out of the lineage of Shem, God chose Abraham to be a new nation apart from the pagan nations of the world. Given the idolatrous origin of these nations, God through Abram, later renamed Abraham, began a new nation independent of this universal impact at Babel. Abraham was a Semite, a descendant of Shem. Abraham is the first person in the Bible who is referred to as a "Hebrew" (Genesis 14:13) Those with Abraham, and after him, were called Hebrews.

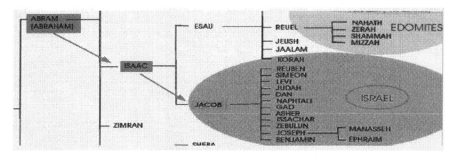

God's sovereign choice was to choose Shem's line through Abraham to Isaac to Jacob and the birth of Israel (Num 24:17). Israel would become His vehicle for exporting His messianic blessings, the message of mankind's redemption to the world (Gen 3:15; 12:3) and to be His mouthpiece to the entire world about Him, His will and His presence. God chose a relationship with the people of Israel to showcase to the world that He, Yahweh, the Great I AM, is the only God as opposed to all of the other false gods promoted by the other nations.

I mentioned earlier in this chapter that there are two types of revelation about God to mankind. One is natural revelation which is creation, and the second one is special revelation with the Holy Scriptures. Through the first one, God says to us that we are without excuse to know that He exists and He is the Creator. The second one is where He proclaimed for over 3,000 years to mankind through His chosen mouthpiece, the descendants of Shem, namely Israel and her prophets. This second revelation is categorized as special because you cannot get this detailed reveal of God anywhere else in creation. The Holy Scriptures we have today are the culmination of all of God's spoken revelation to mankind through His prophets and apostles and then transferred to His written Holy Scriptures.

The writer in Hebrews proclaims that God spoke "long ago to the fathers in the prophets in many portions and in many ways." The writer goes on to say to his mostly intended Hebrew audience that in "these last days [He] has spoken to us in His Son." The whole story of the Bible is about God creating man to have a relationship with Himself that man rejected. The story concludes with God, out of His great love, seeking to redeem us from our folly of disobedience. That is the story of the Bible in a nutshell.

> **Hebrews 1:1-4** — *God, after He spoke long ago to the fathers in the prophets in many portions and in many ways, 2 in these last days has spoken to us in His Son, whom He appointed heir of all things, through whom also He made the world. 3 And He is the radiance of His glory and the exact representation of His nature, and upholds all things by the word of His power. When He had made purification of sins, He sat down at the right hand of the Majesty on high, 4 having become as much better than the angels, as He has inherited a more excellent name than they.*

God, Man and Their Covenants

It is through this special revelation, God's Holy Scriptures, that God's relationship with man was and is never veiled in secrecy. God always defined the relationship. It is always amazing that God desired this relationship no matter how far away man ran from Him. This defined relationship was often explained to man in what the Bible calls covenants.

There are eight covenants detailed in the Bible between God and man. These eight covenants can be separated into two categories: conditional and unconditional. I will mention these covenants in the notes with a reference for your further study, but for our purposes, we will focus only on one, the covenant of God with Abraham (The Abrahamic Covenant).[55]

However, a quick note to place the Abrahamic Covenant in respect to the other covenants is worthwhile. Of the eight covenants two were conditional and six unconditional. The two conditional covenants were the one made with Adam in the Garden of Eden, referred to as the Edenic Covenant. The second one was the covenant made with Moses, referred to as the Mosaic Covenant. Dr. Arnold Fruchtenbaum explains why these two covenants are considered conditional.

> *A conditional covenant is a bilateral covenant in which a proposal of God to man is characterized by the formula: if you will, then I will, whereby God promises to grant special blessings to man providing man fulfills certain conditions contained in the covenant. Man's failure to do so often results in punishment. Thus one's response to the covenant agreement brings either blessings or cursings. The blessings are secured by obedience and man must meet his conditions before God will meet His.[56]*

In the Edenic Covenant the participants within that covenant were God and Adam. Adam was the representative head of the human race. The actions of Adam were attributed to all of humanity for all time since all humanity are direct descendants of Adam. The Edenic Covenant was the foundation for the Dispensation of Innocence, and

---

[55] Dr. Arnold G. Fruchtenbaum, "The Eight Covenants of the Bible,"(Ariel Ministries, https://www.ariel.org/resources/come-and-see/studies. Accessed April 24, 2024.

[56] "Bilateral," Merriam Webster Online Dictionary, https://www.merriam-webster.com/dictionary/bilateral = having or relating to two sides; involving two parties, especially countries

"Unilateral," Merriam-Webster Online Dictionary, https://www.merriam-webster.com/dictionary/unilateral = Unilateral = (of an action or decision) performed by or affecting only one person, group, or country involved in a particular situation, without the agreement of another or the others

the record of it being broken we discussed in detail in previous chapters. The record in Scripture is found in Genesis 3:1-8. The Edenic Covenant (innocence) as one part of the Adamic Covenant (grace). The Adamic Covenant can be found in Genesis 3:16-19. It was a result of Adam's sin and the curses that followed.

The second conditional covenant was the Mosaic Covenant. This covenant is very detailed, and Scriptural record of the covenant ranges from Exodus 20:1 to Deuteronomy 18:68. The participants of the Mosaic Covenant were God and Israel. While Moses acted as a representative of Israel the covenant included him as well as all Israel (Exodus 19:3-8). It should be noted that this covenant was made with Israel alone, not with the Gentiles or the Church. Revision Theology is running amuck in the Church today seeking to replace Israel with the Church. The covenant is with Israel alone and is clearly pointed out in Scripture (Deuteronomy 4:7-8, Psalm 147:19-20; and Malachi 4:4). The Law of Moses, as conditional, contained a total of 613 commandments. The Law provided blessings for obedience and curses for disobedience. It should be stated emphatically that the Law of Moses was never meant to be a means of salvation for mankind, That fact is born out in the writings of the Apostle Paul (Romans 3:20, 28; Galatians 2:16; 3:11, 21). The Law was given to reveal the holiness of God, a rule of conduct for Israel, individual and corporate worship, make the Jews a distinct people among all the nations, to be a wall of separation between Jew and Gentile, to reveal sin (disobedience), to show under the Law no one could attain righteousness, and finally to bring one to the Messiah for his salvation.[57]

The other six covenants are unconditional covenants. The six unconditional covenants include the covenant with Adam, Adamic Covenant; with Noah, Noahic Covenant; with Abraham, Abrahamic Covenant; the Palestinian or Land Covenant; with David, Davidic Covenant; and the New Covenant. Of these six covenants, four listed

---

[57] Fruchtenbaum, "The Eight Covenants of the Bible," https://www.ariel.org/resources/come-and-see/studies.

are made exclusively with Israel, and the two first ones in the list with all mankind. Again, I turn to Dr. Arnold Fruchtenbaum to explain why these six covenants are considered unconditional.

> *An unconditional covenant is a unilateral covenant and is a sovereign act of God whereby He unconditionally obligates Himself to pass definite blessings and conditions to the covenanted people. This covenant is characterized by the formula: I will which declares God's determination to do as He promises. Blessings are secured by the grace of God. There may be conditions in the covenant by which God requests the covenanted one to fulfill out of gratitude, but they are not themselves the basis of God's fulfilling His promises.[58]*

God's Covenant with Abraham Is Unconditional

God's covenant with Abraham, as described, is unconditional and was solely dependent upon God Himself to keep. It should be noted that once a covenant is sealed, its provisions do not necessarily go into effect right away. Some provisions may go into effect twenty years from then, one hundred years from then, or thousands of years later. As in the case of the Abrahamic Covenant, some provisions have not been fulfilled as of this writing!

As mentioned previously, it is God's choice to choose Abraham as the start of the nation of Israel in particular and, in general, many nations.

> **Genesis 12:1-3** — *Now the Lord said to Abram, "Go forth from your country, And from your relatives And from your father's house, To the land which I will show you; 2 And I will make you a great nation, And I will bless you, And make your name great; And so you shall be a blessing; 3 And I will bless those who bless you, And*

---

[58] Fruchtenbaum, "The Eight Covenants of the Bible,"
https://www.ariel.org/resources/come-and-see/studies.

the one who curses you I will curse. And in you all the families of the earth will be blessed."

Genesis 12:7 — *The Lord appeared to Abram and said, "To your descendants I will give this land." So he built an altar there to the Lord who had appeared to him.*

Genesis 13:14-17 — *The Lord said to Abram, after Lot had separated from him, "Now lift up your eyes and look from the place where you are, northward and southward and eastward and westward; 15 for all the land which you see, I will give it to you and to your descendants forever. 16 I will make your descendants as the dust of the earth, so that if anyone can number the dust of the earth, then your descendants can also be numbered. 17 Arise, walk about the land through its length and breadth; for I will give it to you."*

And again, in Genesis 15, the Lord speaks to Abram concerning the many descendants he will have, but it is Abram's response of belief acted on by his faith in God's Word that God counted this as righteousness.

Genesis 15:3-6 — *And Abram said, "Since You have given no offspring to me, one born in my house is my heir." 4 Then behold, the word of the Lord came to him, saying, "This man will not be your heir; but one who will come forth from your own body, he shall be your heir." 5 And He took him outside and said, "Now look toward the heavens, and count the stars, if you are able to count them." And He said to him, "So shall your descendants be." 6 Then he believed in the Lord; and He reckoned it to him as righteousness.*

Many of the provisions of this covenant are detailed in two other passages: Genesis 15:1-21 and Genesis 17:1-21. The sixth passage is in Gen 22, where God blesses Abraham for his obedience to not withhold his son from the Lord's command.

Genesis 22:15-18 — *Then the angel of the Lord called to Abraham a second time from heaven, 16 and said, "By Myself I* *have sworn, declares the Lord, because you have done this thing and have not withheld your son, your only son, 17 indeed I will greatly bless you, and I will greatly multiply your seed as the stars of the heavens and as the sand which is on the seashore; and your seed shall possess the gate of their enemies. 18 In your seed all the nations of the earth shall be blessed, because you have obeyed My voice."*

God Foretold Israel's Four Hundred Year Oppression

It was during the ceremony of God's unconditional covenant with Abraham that God foretold to Abraham that his "descendants will be strangers in a land not their own. They will be enslaved and oppressed for four hundred years." God told Abraham that He would judge that nation and "afterward they will come out with many possessions."

> **Genesis 15:12-16** — *Now when the sun was going down, a deep sleep fell upon Abram; and behold, terror and great darkness fell upon him. 13 God said to Abram, "Know for certain that your descendants will be strangers in a land that is not theirs, where they will be enslaved and oppressed four hundred years. 14 But I will also judge the nation whom they will serve, and afterward they will come out with many possessions. 15 As for you, you shall go to your fathers in peace; you will be buried at a good old age. 16 Then in the fourth generation they will return here, for the iniquity of the Amorite is not yet complete."*

It is amazing to witness God's sovereignty in Scripture. It is like that of the wind. Jesus used the wind to describe the Holy Spirit. I believe that is also a good description of God's Sovereignty which, if you think about it, is like that too. You don't know where it came from nor where it is going, and you may get a glimpse of what it does gentle or mighty. We are allowed a glimpse of God's sovereign choice of Abraham and the blessing of his lineage to be the mouthpiece for God to the world He created.

All of this interaction with God and Abraham is found in the book of Genesis. That book is one of five books that comprise what is called the Pentateuch. There is much evidence that the author of these books was Moses, but like anything else significant surrounding the Bible there is some controversy about it. This author accepts the Mosaic authorship of the Pentateuch.

"These books show a clear continuity of content, theme, purpose, and style point to a single author. They make up a unity, not a late and unreliable patchwork. Each book smoothly picks up where the previous book left off. There is a completeness about the Pentateuch not only in its connective history but also in its progressive spiritual development.

GENESIS: This book provides the foundation for the entire Bible in its history and its theology. Its first eleven chapters give a sweeping survey of primeval events: God's work of creation, the fall of man, the judgment of the Flood, and the spread of the nations. There is a sudden shift in chapter 12 as God singles out one man [Abraham] through whom He [God] would bring salvation and bless all nations. The remainder of Genesis traces the story of Abraham and his descendants Isaac, Jacob, and Joseph."[59]

Israel Is God's Chosen Mouthpiece to the World

The rest of the Old Testament is the detailed documentation of God's covenant with Abraham (and the other covenants). The corporate nature of Israel had a persona and reacted to God in either disobedience or obedience. The corporate makeup of Israel was comprised of the individual believer in Yahweh and their commitment to the covenants given to their patriarchs. So as the collective individual in Israel went so did the nation of Israel.

---

[59] Bruce Wilkinson and Kenneth Boa, *Talk Thru The Bible* (Nashville: Thomas Nelson Publishers, 2002), 3-4.

Born within those 39 books that make up the Old Testament are books of Israel's history, poetry, and messages from God to Israel through the major and minor prophets. The primary desire of Yahweh was/is to redeem the world from Satan. Yahweh would use Israel as His mouthpiece of blessings and judgments to the world. The promised Messiah would be a blessing of salvation and redemption not only for Israel but for the Gentiles (in Scripture considered the rest of humanity) who are grafted into the tree of Israel.

We will witness that the thread of God's redemption of humanity has always been through the shedding of a blood sacrifice to cover the sins (disobedience) of man. From God's first interaction with Adam and Eve over their sin (disobedience), we witnessed a blood sacrifice by God Himself. The penalty for breaking God's command was death, but God, in His mercy, chose to not kill Adam and Eve but instead brought a substitutionary death of an animal. I discussed in chapter six that after their sin against God, Adam made "loin coverings" out of leaves to cover their nakedness before God. God did not allow them that as a final solution for a "covering" of what their nakedness represented. Their solution was not good enough. Instead, God committed the first blood sacrifice for sin and used the skin of animals to be their "loin covering." People will have differing opinions as to whether this was a blood sacrifice but look at what it replaced. Adam and Eve used their "loin coverings" to cover their shame of disobeying the Word of God—they felt morally exposed in the presence of a holy God—what their nakedness really meant. It was not that their sexual body parts were sinful, but rather their state of awareness of their nakedness is a representation of the new knowledge they sought apart from trusting in God's Word. God obviously wanted them to trust in Him and His solution. What did God do? He replaced their solution with His by killing animals and providing their skin to provide the same covering for the same purpose.

Genesis 3:21 — *The Lord God made garments of skin for Adam and his wife, and clothed them.*

Blood sacrifices continued from this moment. I discussed the quality of the sacrifices of Abel and Cain back in chapter seven. It was discussed that while it appears that blood sacrifice, as an act of worship to the Lord God had been established, their sacrifices were the first ones recorded directed from man to God.

> **Genesis 4:4-5** — *Abel, on his part also brought of the firstlings of his flock and of their fat portions. And the Lord had regard for Abel and for his offering; 5 but for Cain and for his offering He had no regard. So Cain became very angry and his countenance fell.*

The writer of Hebrews shows the immense importance of the blood sacrifice God established by His grace and by the development of Israel.

> **Hebrews 9:18-23** — *Therefore even the first covenant was not inaugurated without blood. 19 For when every commandment had been spoken by Moses to all the people according to the Law, he took the blood of the calves and the goats, with water and scarlet wool and hyssop, and sprinkled both the book itself and all the people, 20 saying, "This is the blood of the covenant which God commanded you." 21 And in the same way he sprinkled both the tabernacle and all the vessels of the ministry with the blood. 22 And according to the Law, one may almost say, all things are cleansed with blood, and* **without shedding of blood there is no forgiveness.**

However, the writer of Hebrews warns us that the sacrifice of blood through animals is only temporary and not lasting.

> **Hebrews 10:1-4** — *For the Law, since it has only a shadow of the good things to come and not the very form of things, can never, by the same sacrifices which they offer continually year by year, make perfect those who draw near.*
>
> *2 Otherwise, would they not have ceased to be offered, because the worshipers, having once been cleansed, would no longer have had consciousness of sins? 3* ***But in those sacrifices there is a***

reminder of sins year by year. 4 For it is impossible for the blood of bulls and goats to take away sins.

The writer of Hebrews tells us the purpose of the Law is to show our need for forgiveness from our sins (disobedience) and to seek God's provided solution. Under the Law, God provided a temporary solution for Israel. However obedient one is to the Law, those sacrifices followed correctly would not "make perfect those who draw near." In fact, the writer emphatically stated that "it is impossible for the blood of bulls and goats to take away sins."

There is only One Who can "take away" the penalty for our disobedience. The transition from the Law to the Messiah is the transition from impossible to absolute. The Law could not take away the penalty of sin; it highlighted the inability of man to be holy. The Messiah literally took away the penalty for the sins of mankind. Here is John the Baptizer's testimony about "the One Who takes away the sins of the world."

*John 1:19-34 — This is the testimony of John, when the Jews sent to him priests and Levites from Jerusalem to ask him, "Who are you?" 20 And he confessed and did not deny, but confessed, "I am not the Christ." 21 They asked him, "What then? Are you Elijah?" And he said, "I am not." "Are you the Prophet?" And he answered, "No." 22 Then they said to him, "Who are you, so that we may give an answer to those who sent us? What do you say about yourself?" 23 He said, "I am a voice of one crying in the wilderness, 'Make straight the way of the Lord,' as Isaiah the prophet said." 24 Now they had been sent from the Pharisees. 25 They asked him, and said to him, "Why then are you baptizing, if you are not the Christ, nor Elijah, nor the Prophet?" 26 John answered them saying, "I baptize in water, but among you stands One whom you do not know. 27 It is He who comes after me, the thong of whose sandal I am not worthy to untie." 28 These things took place in Bethany beyond the Jordan, where John was baptizing. 29 **The next day he saw Jesus coming to him and said, "Behold, the Lamb of God*** *who takes away the sin of the world! 30 This is He on behalf of whom I said, 'After me comes a Man who has a higher rank than I, for He existed before me.' 31 I did not recognize Him, but so that He might be manifested to Israel, I came baptizing in water.'" 32 John testified saying, "I have seen the Spirit descending as a dove out of heaven, and He remained upon Him.*

33 I did not recognize Him, but He who sent me to baptize in water said to me, 'He upon whom you see the Spirit descending and remaining upon Him, this is the One who baptizes in the Holy Spirit.' 34 **I myself have seen, and have testified that this is the Son of God.**"'

Once again, appropriate:

Isaiah 55:8-9 — *"For My thoughts are not your thoughts, Nor are your ways My ways," declares the Lord. 9 "For as the heavens are higher than the earth, So are My ways higher than your ways And My thoughts than your thoughts."*

How Was God Loved?

I think God was loved in the response of obedience and worship from those He sovereignly chose to further His will and Word in setting apart Israel as His chosen nation, His mouthpiece to the world, and ultimately the line of the coming Messiah Jesus. Were they perfect in their love toward Him? No, not at all, but it in viewing this relationship between these chosen people and the only living true God is that we get to know Who He is. We get to witness His attributes, His Person, His character, and His heart. This relationship with Yahweh and Israel is His revelation of Himself to the world whom He has chosen to redeem and love.

9

Jesus Is God's Message

God's redemption of man from disobedience is by a loving God. Jesus is the fulfillment as God's redeemer. Throughout this book we have been looking at how man has loved God. I hope you have seen that the constant theme is that God has loved man far more than man has loved God. God is always faithful to faithless man. But God, our loving Father, never gives up. I can hear you say, "Wait a minute! God was so grieved that He ever made man and that man was so evil that God destroyed all mankind with the worldwide flood!" True, but even in Earth 1.0, God preserved a remnant through Noah. God made a way for Adam and Eve after their fall from their relationship with Him. He made a way for Adam and Eve's children. The lineage of their children can be traced from Noah to Abraham to Isaac to Jacob, keeping the continuity of not only the curse of sin but also the tracks to the Messiah as the Savior of mankind and the Holder of the key to God's ultimate salvation of man.

You cannot divorce the Old Testament from the New Testament; it is intertwined prophecy. In fact to clearly understand the New Testament, you must also include the Old Testament in your study.

If we limit our study to just the New Testament, then we lose a long, rich heritage of meaning and imagery to a less-than-surface understanding of the revelation contained in the New Testament. In fact, in the Book of Revelation, there are over 500 references to Old Testament passages. You will not correctly grasp the Book of Revelation without understanding those Old Testament references.

Salvation Was to the Jew First and Then to the Greek

God chose the Jews to be His messengers of His revelation to the world. But their failure to fulfill that mission did not stop God's timeline of presenting the Messiah, the Savior to the world. Salvation was to the Jew first and then to the Greek (Romans 1:16).

Ultimately, the prophetic office originated in God's purpose for Israel as a nation through which all nations could be blessed. When God gave Israel the Law, He promised them that if they would be obedient, they would become "[His] own possession" (special treasure) for the purpose of becoming a "kingdom of priests and a holy nation" among all the nations (Compare Exodus 19:5-6 with Deuteronomy 4:6-8).

This purpose could not happen, however, if they followed the beliefs and ways of the nations. In preparation for their entrance into the Promised Land just before the death of Moses, the illegitimate and demonic methods used by the nations to discern the future or the divine will, called divination, was thoroughly condemned by the Lord through Moses (Deuteronomy 18:9-14). So how, then, was God's will to be known? The true and legitimate means by which God's will would be delivered to His people is given in Deuteronomy 18:15-22.

Deuteronomy 18:15-22 — *"The Lord your God will raise up for you a prophet like me from among you, from your countrymen, you shall listen to him. 16 "This is according to all that you asked of the Lord your God in Horeb on the day of the assembly, saying, 'Let me not hear again the voice of the Lord my God, let me not see this great fire anymore, lest I die.' 17 "And the Lord said to me, 'They* *have spoken well. 18 'I will raise up a prophet from among their countrymen like you, and I will put My words in his mouth, and he shall speak to them all that I command him.*

19 'And it shall come about that whoever will not listen to My words which he shall speak in My name, I Myself will require it of him. 20 'But the prophet who shall speak a word presumptuously in My name which I have not commanded him to speak, or which he shall speak in the name of other gods, that prophet shall die.' 21 "And you may say in your heart, 'How shall we know the word which the Lord has not spoken?' 22 "When a prophet speaks in the name of the Lord, if the thing does not come about or come true, that is the thing which the Lord has not spoken. The prophet has spoken it presumptuously; you shall not be afraid of him.

God told Israel that He would speak to them through His prophets that He would send to Israel. However, the prophets of Israel did not just proclaim doom and gloom. They also proclaimed a message of salvation and coming glory.

In fact, salvation is the overall theme of the Bible: God's redemption of man from man's disobedience.

Ultimately, God's purposes would be fulfilled by the sovereign work of God in the lives of His people. Sometimes, these salvation messages were "crystal ball" like visions describing a particular event they had seen in a vision (Daniel 9). Other times they were just claiming and proclaiming the promises of God to Abraham and David as given in the Davidic Covenant of 2 Samuel 7:12-16.

God Is Fulfilling His Redemptive Plan Through Both Israel and the Church

God's redemptive plan is being fulfilled through Israel *and* the Church. Sad that many pastors and Bible teachers don't see it that way. The ones in this camp will see only two covenants of God: the Old Covenant given to the people of Israel at Mount Sinai and the New Covenant through the blood sacrifice of Messiah Jesus that replaced it.

The problem with this view is that it is too simplistic and turns a blind eye to a wealth of Scripture.

There are even those who say the Church has replaced Israel. Therefore, everything going forward that was prophesied for Israel now refers to the Church. Wow! I have no words. How can you tangle, turn, cut things out of Scripture and twist it into a pretzel and come out with that statement with a straight face?

By reviewing the focus and intensity that God placed into Israel over some three thousand plus years of recorded history in His Word warrants at least an argument with oneself about "God just dropping Israel in favor of the Church."

Covenants are the Building Blocks of God's Purposes

Remember we discussed briefly the Covenants God has made with mankind and Israel; those covenants detailed between Yahweh and mankind and/or Israel. God did not add any amendments. God did not stutter. These covenants are as solid and true as the Ten Commandments.

There is a ministry I have followed and loved for several years called "One for Israel." Since 1990, their ministry focus has been to bring both Jews and Arabs within Israel to a saving faith in Messiah Yeshua (Jesus). I like how David Herron, in an article on One for Israel's website positioned the Covenants of God.

"Covenants are the building blocks of God's purposes, and each one has a part to play in the unfolding of God's redemptive plan. Understanding the framework that God chose to hang this story upon is critical to understanding God and his story.

The framework he has chosen is Israel — four out of the five covenants are with the people of Israel, and the fifth was given within the people and land of Israel too. What many do not realize is that most of these covenants with Israel are still in action as God's plan continues to unfold.[60]

Did you catch the emphasis David Herron is placing on Israel? It is the same emphasis that God has placed on Israel in His Word. "Understanding the framework that God chose to hang this story upon is critical to understanding God and his story (unfolding of God's redemptive plan). The framework he has chosen is Israel."

In good crime detective work, the phrase "follow the money" is often used. In good Biblical detective work the phrase that should often be used is "follow Israel."

We mentioned before that there are eight covenants detailed in the Bible between God and man. If you recall, we separated these eight covenants into two categories: conditional and unconditional. Two of the eight were conditional and six were unconditional. Of the two conditional covenants, one is broken and one is fulfilled.

The covenant made between God and Adam in the Garden of Eden has been broken by Adam. While not specifically referred to as a covenant in Genesis, the prophet Hosea refers to it as a covenant.

Hosea 6:6-7 — *For I desire loyalty rather than sacrifice, And the knowledge of God rather than burnt offerings. 7 But like Adam they have violated the covenant; There they have dealt treacherously with Me.*

Hosea spoke for God and chastised the Northern and Southern Kingdoms of Israel and Judah. God said their loyalty was like the "morning cloud" and "dew which goes away early." God tells them through Hosea that He desired loyalty rather than sacrifice and knowledge of Him rather than burnt offerings. God desired their hearts, their faith, and their trust, not merely fulfilling their duty to Him

---

[60] David Herron, "Covenants: God's Building Blocks of Redemption," One for Israel, https://www.oneforisrael.org/bible-based-teaching-from-israel/covenants-gods-building-blocks-of-redemption/. Accessed February 18, 2021

under the Law. Hosea pronounces that they have violated the covenant just like Adam did. So what was the covenant that Adam violated? Adam broke the covenant God made with him in the Garden of Eden.

The other conditional covenant was the Mosaic covenant. The participants of the Mosaic Covenant were God and Israel. While Moses acted as a representative of Israel the covenant included him as well as all Israel (Exodus 19:3-8). This covenant made with the people of Israel at Mt. Sinai has been fulfilled. This covenant was superseded by Messiah Jesus in His first coming. How so? The Law was never God's fulfillment of man's redemption. The purpose of the Law was to show us how far short of God's standards we fall.

Messiah Jesus Superseded the Mosaic Covenant

The writer of Hebrews, using a prophecy out of the book of Jeremiah, explains this. The prophecy of the Messiah speaks to His office of Prophet, Priest, Servant and King.

Hebrews 7:23-28 — *The former priests, on the one hand, existed in greater numbers because they were prevented by death from continuing; 24 Jesus, on the other hand, because He continues forever, holds His priesthood permanently. 25 Therefore He is also able to save forever those who come to God through Him, since He always lives to make intercession for them. 26 For it was fitting for us to have such a high priest, holy, innocent, undefiled, separated from sinners, and exalted above the heavens; 27 who has no daily need, like those high priests, to offer up sacrifices, first for His own sins and then for the sins of the people, because He did this once for all time when He offered up Himself. 28 For the Law appoints men as high priests who are weak, but the word of the oath, which came after the Law, appoints a Son, who has been made perfect forever.*

The writer of Hebrews teaches us that the reason Israel had many priests was because they would continue to die. But Messiah Jesus has a permanent Priesthood that continues forever. This

Messiah, Jesus, is able to save all who come to God forever. This Messiah Jesus has no need to offer up sacrifices for Himself and of the people because "He did this once for all time when He offered up Himself." The Law (Mosaic Covenant) "appoints men who are weak" (subject to death, sinfulness), "but the word of the oath (PS 110:4 Messianic prophecy), which came after the Law, appoints a Son, who has been made perfect forever."

In chapter 8, the writer of Hebrews tells us that Jesus has obtained a more excellent ministry. He is a mediator of a better covenant (opposed to the Mosaic Covenant) and it is founded on better promises.

> **Hebrews 8:6** — *"But now He has obtained a more excellent ministry, to the extent that He is also the mediator of a better covenant, which has been enacted on better promises."*

> **Hebrews 8:7-13** — *For if that first covenant had been free of fault, no circumstances would have been sought for a second. (If the Mosaic Covenant had been free of fault – fulfilled its purpose = removal of sin continuously, then a second covenant would not have been sought). 8 For in finding fault with the people, He says (God found fault in the people under the Mosaic Covenant), "Behold, days are coming, says the Lord, When I will bring about a new covenant With the house of Israel and the house of Judah, 9 Not like the (Mosaic) covenant which I made with their fathers On the day I took them by the hand To bring them out of the land of Egypt; For they did not continue in My covenant, And I did not care about them, says the Lord.*

> *10 For this is the covenant which I will make with the house of Israel After those days, declares the Lord: I will put My laws into their minds, And write them on their hearts. And I will be their God, And they shall be My people. 11 And they will not teach, each one his fellow citizen, And each one his brother, saying, 'Know the Lord,' For they will all know Me, From the least to the greatest of them. 12*

For I will be merciful toward their wrongdoings, And their sins I will no longer remember."13 When He said, "A new covenant," He has made the first obsolete. But whatever is becoming obsolete and growing old is about to disappear.

Messiah Jesus High Priest of a New Covenant Replacing the Mosaic Covenant

This new covenant with Messiah Jesus as its High Priest has made the Mosaic Covenant "obsolete." The Apostle Paul told the Galatians that the Law is a Teacher to show our inability to live as God wants us and our great need for the salvation found in Messiah Jesus (Galatians 6:19).

Jesus Himself said, as recorded by the Apostle Matthew, that He did not come to abolish the Law and the Prophets, but He came to *fulfill* them (Matthew 5:17).

This new covenant does change how we view the continuation of the Mosaic Covenant, but it does not change the promises made in the covenants with Noah, Abraham and David.

My point in all of this is that God, in His sovereignty, chose Israel to be the revelation of His redemption to the nations of the world. God, Yahweh's redemption was through His Son, the Messiah of Israel, Whom the prophets proclaimed to the world for thousands of years.

The Messiah Was Given Numerous Titles Throughout the Old Testament

Besides the word Messiah, there are numerous titles of the eschatological King (relating to the death, judgment and final destiny of mankind). What follows is just a brief summary of the titles of Messiah found throughout the Old Testament.[61]

---

[61] Michael Rydelnik and Edwin Blum, *The Moody Handbook of Messianic Prophecy* (Moody Press, 2019), 33-38.

The Son of God

Psalm 2:1-2, 7 — *Why are the nations restless And the peoples plotting in vain? 2 The kings of the earth take their stand And the rulers conspire together Against the Lord and against His Anointed **[MESSIAH]** 7 "I will announce the decree of the Lord; He said to Me, 'You are My Son, Today I have fathered You.'"*

The Son of Man

Daniel 7:13-14 — *"I kept looking in the night visions, And behold, with the clouds of heaven One like a son of man was coming, And He came up to the Ancient of Days And was presented before Him. 14 And to Him was given dominion, Honor, and a kingdom, So that all the peoples, nations, and populations of all languages Might serve Him. His dominion is an everlasting dominion Which will not pass away; And His kingdom is one Which will not be destroyed.*

The Son of Man can be seen as the title Messiah Jesus identified for Himself throughout His ministry recorded in the Gospels.

"Therefore, when the High Priest asked Jesus to state plainly if He was 'the messiah, the Son of God' and Jesus responded by citing Daniel 7:13:14 in Matthew's Gospel, 'But I tell you, in the future you will see the Son of Man seated at the right hand of Power and coming in the clouds of heaven' (Mat 26:64), this was taken as Jesus affirming His full deity. The High Priest tore his garments and declared Jesus guilty of blasphemy (Mat 26:65). He clearly understood the title 'Son of Man' to mean full deity and not mere humanity. The title 'Son of Man' is an OT expression for the divine Messiah."[62]

---

[62] Rydelnik and Blum, The Moody Handbook of Messianic Prophecy, 34

The Son of David

2 Samuel 7:12, 16 — *When your days are finished and you lie down with your fathers, I will raise up your descendant [offspring, seed] after you, who will come from you, and I will establish his kingdom. 16 Your house and your kingdom shall endure before Me forever; your throne shall be established forever.*

The Teacher

Joel 2:23 — *So shout for joy, you sons of Zion, And rejoice in the Lord your God; For He has given you the early rain for your vindication [teacher of righteousness]. And He has brought down for you the rain, The early and latter rain as before.*

The Servant of the Lord

Isaiah 52:13-15 — *Behold, My Servant will prosper, He will be high and lifted up and greatly exalted. 14 Just as many were appalled at you, My people, So His appearance was marred beyond that of a man, And His form beyond the sons of mankind. 15 So He will sprinkle many nations, Kings will shut their mouths on account of Him; For what they had not been told, they will see, And what they had not heard, they will understand.*

The Prophet Like Moses

Deuteronomy 18:15-19 — *"The Lord your God will raise up for you a prophet like me from among you, from your countrymen; to him you shall listen. 16 This is in accordance with everything that you asked of the Lord your God at Horeb on the day of the assembly, saying, 'Do not let me hear the voice of the Lord my God again, and do not let me see this great fire anymore, or I will die!' 17 And the Lord said to me, 'They have spoken well. 18 I will raise up for them* *a prophet from among their countrymen like you, and I will put My words in his mouth, and he shall speak to them everything that I command him. 19 And it shall come about that whoever does not listen to My words which he speaks in My name, I Myself will require it of him.*

Immanuel

Isaiah 7:14 — *Therefore the Lord Himself will give you a sign: Behold, the virgin will conceive and give birth to a son, and she will name Him Immanuel.*

Wonderful Counselor, Mighty God, Eternal Father, Prince of Peace

Isaiah 9:6-7 — *For a Child will be born to us, a Son will be given to us; And the government will rest on His shoulders; And His name will be called Wonderful Counselor, Mighty God, Eternal Father, Prince of Peace. 7 There will be no end to the increase of His government or of peace On the throne of David and over his kingdom, To establish it and to uphold it with justice and righteousness From then on and forevermore. The zeal of the Lord of armies will accomplish this.*

The Branch of the Lord

Isaiah 4:2 — *On that day the Branch of the Lord will be beautiful and glorious, and the fruit of the earth will be the pride and the beauty of the survivors of Israel.*

The Lord (Yahweh) Our Righteousness

Jeremiah 23:5-6 — *"Behold, the days are coming," declares the Lord, "When I will raise up for David a righteous Branch; And He will reign as king and act wisely And do justice and righteousness in* *the land. 6 In His days Judah will be saved, And Israel will live securely; And this is His name by which He will be called, 'The Lord Our Righteousness.'"*

The One Shepherd

Ezekiel 34:11-16 — *For the Lord God says this: "Behold, I Myself will search for My sheep and look after them. 12 As a shepherd cares for his flock on a day when he is among his scattered sheep, so I will care for My sheep and will rescue them from all the places where they were scattered on a cloudy and gloomy day. 13 I will bring them out from the peoples and gather them from the countries and bring them to their own land; and I will feed them on the mountains of Israel, by the streams, and in all the inhabited places of the land. 14 I will feed them in a good pasture, and their grazing place will be on the mountain heights of Israel. There they will lie down in a good grazing place and feed in rich pasture on the mountains of Israel. 15 I Myself will feed My flock and I Myself will lead them to rest," declares the Lord God. 16 "I will seek the lost, bring back the scattered, bind up the broken, and strengthen the sick; but the fat and the strong I will eliminate. I will feed them with judgment.*

The Light to the Nations

Isaiah 49:5-6 — *And now says the Lord, who formed Me from the womb to be His Servant, To bring Jacob back to Him, so that Israel might be gathered to Him (For I am honored in the sight of the Lord, And My God is My strength), 6 He says, "It is too small a thing that You should be My Servant To raise up the tribes of Jacob and to restore the protected ones of Israel; I will also make You a light of the nations So that My salvation may reach to the end of the earth."*

The many titles the prophets of God have given to the Messiah illustrate that He is the final King over all Mankind.

Each of the Gospel Writers Had a Purpose to Their Writing

Each Gospel writer had a purpose to their writing, and it was not just being a stenographer of Messiah's history. With our current subject of Jesus as the promised Messiah, the Gospel writer to turn to is Matthew. Simply put, the Gospel of Matthew is written to Jews by a Jew about a Jew. And of course, not just any Jew but Jesus as the King of the Jews—the long-awaited Messiah—the Prophet, Priest, Servant, and King of Israel! The audience Matthew was addressing were his countrymen, his fellow Jews. Matthew has proclaimed the words and works of Jesus the Messiah, the Christ so that his readers could make an intelligent decision. Is Jesus Who He said He is, or is He Who the leadership of Israel, the Pharisees and Sadducees said He was?

Matthew's Gospel is written to the nation of Israel to proclaim that the Messiah has come. All that Jesus said and did is the culmination of promises delivered, as we have pointed out, by the prophets sent to Israel for a thousand years. After 400 years of prophetic silence from God, here is the Messiah!

According to Matthew's account, the Messiah began His ministry in chapter 4 of Matthew's Gospel. Later in chapter 9, Matthew summarized Messiah Jesus' ministry.

> **Matthew 9:35-38** — *Jesus was going through all the cities and villages, teaching in their synagogues and proclaiming the gospel of the kingdom, and healing every disease and every sickness. 36 Seeing the crowds, He felt compassion for them, because they were distressed and downcast, like sheep without a shepherd. 37 Then He *said to His disciples, "The harvest is plentiful, but the workers are few. 38 Therefore, plead with the Lord of the harvest to send out workers into His harvest."*

Jesus was proclaiming His Messiahship and preaching the Kingdom. Jesus was offering the kingdom of the Jewish prophets, but that kingdom was preconditioned by Israel's acceptance of Him. All of Jesus' miracles were to authenticate His Person and His message to the nation of Israel. The purpose was to force them to a decision about Him.

Then in chapter 12 of Matthew's Gospel, the purpose of Jesus' miracles and His whole ministry underwent a radical change. This is the key chapter where it all turns. I have always taught that *context* is the key element in Bible study to keep interpretation on track to what the author intended. An example of this is this key chapter 12 of Matthew. Many a Bible teacher, pastor and the like have guilted followers with a worry God never intended. The unpardonable sin cannot be committed by anyone other than the audience described in Matthew 12. How do I know? Context!

In chapter 12 of Matthew's Gospel we find that Jesus was miraculously healing and it infuriated the Pharisees. We saw that incident was fulfilling a prophecy out of Isaiah where the Gentiles (you and me) will have their hope in Him, Messiah Jesus.

Jesus was brought a demon-possessed man to heal. Jesus had cast out demons before this moment. He even cast out a demon from a man who was mute as well. But here, those who witnessed the miracle asked in disbelief that this man could not be the Son of David. We have just reviewed a summary of Messianic titles, and The Son of David is one of them. So the crowd of Jews witnessing this particular miracle attributed it to an act of the Messiah. The Pharisees' response, as Israel's leaders, was in the presence of Jesus and Israel.

Matthew 12:22-24 — *Then a demon-possessed man who was blind and unable to speak was brought to Jesus, and He healed him so that the man who was unable to speak talked and could see. 23 And all the crowds were amazed and were saying, "This man cannot be the Son of David, can he?" 24* **But when the Pharisees**

heard this, they said, "This man casts out demons only by Beelzebul the ruler of the demons."

Since we are over 2,000 years removed from this text, a little Jewish culture is needed. Like our commentaries today, Jews had their rabbinical commentaries. It was taught that if a demon possessed a host who was mute, then only the Messiah could exorcise that demon from them. You see, the Jews had a rite of exorcism but would only be successful if the person could speak and they could command the demon to give them its name.[63]

In fact, Jesus acknowledged that Jews could cast out demons in the next verses:

> **Matthew 12:25-28** — *And knowing their thoughts, Jesus said to them, "Every kingdom divided against itself is laid waste; and no city or house divided against itself will stand. 26 And if Satan is casting out Satan, he has become divided against himself; how then will his kingdom stand? 27 And if by Beelzebul I cast out the demons, by whom do* **your sons cast them out?** *Therefore, they will be your judges. 28 But if I cast out the demons by the Spirit of God, then the kingdom of God has come upon you.*

The Pharisees knew by what power He cast out demons and pronounced judgment on the nation of Israel for their rejection of Him and their sin against the Spirit of God:

> **Matthew 12:31-32** — *"Therefore I say to you, every sin and blasphemy shall be forgiven people, but blasphemy against the Spirit shall not be forgiven. 32 And whoever speaks a word against the Son of Man, it shall be forgiven him; but whoever speaks against the Holy*

---

[63] Dr. Arnold G. Fruchtenbaum, "Christology: The Doctrine of Messiah" http://www.messianicassociation.org/ezine48-af-three-messianic-miracles.htm#B._The_Casting_Out_of_a_Dumb_Demon_/. Accessed February 21, 2023

Spirit, it shall not be forgiven him, either in this age or in the age to come.

The leaders of Israel and the people present at this hearing of Messiah Jesus' words knew full well that Jesus was the Messiah. Since they knew the power that He had performed the miracle in was from God and not Satan, their proclamation that Jesus did it in the power of Satan pronounced judgment on them "in this age" and in the Messianic kingdom, "in the age to come." Their eternal fate was sealed then and there forever.

What does the context teach us? Jesus' judgment was for the leaders who represented Israel. That judgment of eternal doom was only for those present. Why? Because you would have to have witnessed Jesus perform the miracle and publicly attribute it to the power of Satan. Since no one past that time period could actually do that, this judgment was only for them and no one else. Therefore neither you nor I can commit the unpardonable sin and never be forgiven.

Blaspheming the Holy Spirit to incur eternal damnation that Messiah Jesus pronounced is impossible for either you or I to commit. The reason is that you nor I can be physically in the presence of Jesus, performing that miracle and then contributing its power to that of Satan rather than the Holy Spirit.

From this point forward we see the Messiah teaching in parables, increased attention to His disciples and the repeated statement that His death is near. Throughout chapters 13 through 23 of Matthew we see a progressive rejection of Jesus as King, a preparation of the disciples.

In chapter 23 of Matthew's Gospel, you will find the final words of the Messiah's public ministry. At the end of chapter 23 the Messiah gave the precondition of His return. Just as Israel's leaders rejected Jesus as Messiah, His second coming is when Israel's leaders accept Him as their Messiah.

Matthew 23:37 — *For I say to you, from now on you will not see Me until you say, 'Blessed is the One who comes in the name of the Lord!'"*

How Was God loved?

God has always had, throughout all ages, a faithful remnant who loved, trusted and were loyal to Him. We know that in Messiah Jesus' ministry He had the twelve disciples, but He also had the 120 disciples, including the twelve that also loved, trusted and were loyal to Him (after the shock of the trial and crucifixion) as they waited in the Upper Room as instructed by the Lord. You and I are part of God's faithful remnant in our time. Just as these disciples huddled in the Upper Room, we too should take stock of our own lives so that we do not break the heart of God. The Lord's salvation is a continuous action in our lives from our spiritual birth until our eternal home.

10

How Do I Not Break
the Heart of God?

Salvation is a continuous action. God's redemption has brought us peace with Him. We can discover our new identity daily as God the Father is now pleased with us. Our spiritual wealth is in the Person of Christ Jesus. To even believe in Him is grace given. We are set apart from all the world in Christ.

Because most of us have the innate ability to bend over and tie our own shoes, we extrapolate that experience to every other decision/capability aspect of our lives. The conclusion is that we are autonomous, intelligent, independent beings. Simple, but there's not a truer argument. That is exactly what happened in the Garden of Eden and every day since between man (you and me) and God. It broke His heart then, and it breaks His heart now.

We have witnessed the "I am god, not You" soul war within these pages in our very brief overview of mankind's history of that struggle through the Biblical lens from the Garden of Eden (Earth 1.0), Noah (Earth 2.0), and Israel out to the nations of the world. Finally, the promised Messiah comes on the stage of Israel to announce God's redemption of mankind and to model what God the Father defines as acceptable love for and to Him.

Acceptable love. How does that phrase strike you? Does judgment come to mind? Or haughtiness? Arrogance? Narrow? What about unloving, not open, exclusive or rigid? All of those responses strike "negative with a baseless purpose."

What if you turned one click on the emotional dial to hear responses like inclusive, private, privileged/unique, chosen? What about the words discerning or particular? Set apart or absolved? How about excused, spared, not responsible, or special?

Perspective

Perspective is everything. The most important thing about you is what you think about when you think of God.[64] Your perspective on that statement truly affects everything in your spiritual life. And really, knowingly or unknowingly, everything in your entire life before or after Christ met you personally. How you formulate that perspective has a direct effect on how you think, who you are "in Christ," and your view of the Word of God "over you." It affects how you read the Word, pray, and worship. It even changes how you view your role as a Christian: in your marriage, in your family, in your church, and at your job. How you think of God will direct your fulfillment in your relationship with God. How you think of God will define your entire Christian life, walk and purpose.

Given that, how you think of God is clearly the central most important concept to grasp deeply beyond your moment of entrance into the promised salvation that the Messiah freely bestowed upon you.

To be saved is of utmost importance for sure, but the church today as a whole, is one big nursery. People have come to Christ because they recognize their disobedience (sin) against a Holy God by the wooing of the Holy Spirit to receive His substitutional sacrifice. The Apostle Peter alluded to this baby-like immaturity among believers, "If you have tasted the kindness of the Lord."

---

[64] Kenneth Boa, "Session 1: A Growing Vision of God," (Conference, A Tale of Two Visions; Image and Identity in the World and Word, Atlanta, March 2022).

1 Peter 2:1-3 — *Therefore, putting aside all malice and all deceit and hypocrisy and envy and all slander, 2 like newborn babies, long for the pure milk of the word, so that by it you may grow in respect to salvation, 3 if you have tasted the kindness of the Lord.*

That passage into salvation is not only an entry point; it is the entire journey of faith, "grow in respect to salvation." Salvation is intertwined with several other concepts in the spiritual life that the Holy Spirit used the Apostle Paul to articulate. But leaving us in the state of "newborn babies" is not one of them.

Some members of the Church have come to assume that once you are saved that is it. In fact, they would think of salvation as a "once and done" event. That is untrue; the Apostle Paul did not teach salvation as "once and done." The three tenses of salvation are: We have been saved, we are being saved, and we will be saved. We went through this in a previous chapter but it is worth me repeating it here.

Salvation Is Not Once and Done

PAST — We have been saved: From the Penalty of Sin

2 Timothy 1:8b-9 — *The gospel according to the power of God, 9 **who has saved us** and called us with a holy calling, not according to our works, but according to His own purpose and grace which was granted us in Christ Jesus from all eternity,*

PRESENT — We are being saved: From the Power of Sin

1 Corinthians 1:18 — *For the word of the cross is foolishness to those who are perishing, but to us **who are being saved** it is the power of God. We are freed form its power and can freely choose to obey God or not.*

FUTURE — We shall be saved: From the Presence of Sin

Romans 5:9-10 — *Much more then, having now been justified by His blood, **we shall be saved** from the wrath of God through*

*Him. 10 For if while we were enemies we were reconciled to God through the death of His Son, much more, having been reconciled, **we shall be saved** by His life.*

As we can see, the concept of salvation through Messiah Jesus is an ongoing process that begins whenever we accept His gift throughout our everyday life and culminating whenever we see Jesus face to face.

Not to be irreverent here, but why is a relationship with God any different than any other human relationship we have? As you saw in our discussion about Adam in the Garden, the back and forth between him and God easily flowed. At least, that is what we gather from the text.

Through deduction, we know that sin had not entered the Garden yet. God made it clear to Adam that obedience to His Words was of the highest importance in their relationship. Up to the point of Adam's disobedience, and even after it, they still had a relationship. Granted, Adam's disobedience created a line of demarcation between God and man but there was still a relationship even if it changed dramatically.

Adam's Unfettered Access to God

Adam freely had unfettered access to the God of the Universe before his disobedience, walking in the Garden together, naming all the creatures of the earth, etc. After Adam's disobedience the entrance to the Garden was eternally blocked and while access to God was possible it was never again as easy and flowing.

But God, as our loving Father, would not leave His children in that state forever. Since God the Father is Creator, His Word, and His ways, are all that really matter. Psst, how did that sentence make you feel? Does it smack at your perceived autonomy? The control you exercise over your own life? Maybe you are experiencing a faint touch of the "I am god, not You" soul war? That soul war will always remain within you until the day it is totally eradicated when we meet Messiah

Jesus face to face. It is at that moment you will experience the future tense of the word salvation. You will be fully, totally saved. At that moment, you are saved from the presence of sin. It will be no more. Ultimate sanctification.

God's Redemption Brought Us Peace with Him

God the Father's loving plan of redemption brought God's peace between us and Him. We are no longer enemies of God. You were an enemy of God. Is that hard for you to believe? That was what God said of you prior to you being touched by the Holy Spirit. Here is how the authors Kenneth Boa and William Kruidenier put it in their commentary on the book of Romans, where the Apostle Paul delivers this message to the church at Rome.

> *"God cannot give us happiness and peace apart from himself, because it is not there. There is no such thing." —C.S. Lewis*
>
> *Having proven that justification before God comes only through faith, Paul now reveals the result of justification: peace with God. What the first Adam lost in the Garden of Eden, the second [last] Adam has restored. Now any who seek peace with God may have it.*
>
> *Peace: What the Gospel Produces*
>
> *There is one realm in which peace is available and attainable at any time, by any person, and that is peace in God's domain. Paul introduces Romans 5 with a revolutionary statement: "We have peace with God."*
>
> *Peace with God is what the gospel of Jesus Christ produces in the lives of those who embrace that gospel. And peace with God, Paul wants his readers to know, is the most fundamental peace there is. All other peace in the world has its basis in peace with God—which is the fundamental reason why peace will never be permanent in the human realm until all human beings embrace the rule of God. While the hippie and anti-war counter-culturists in the 1960s may have wanted*

us to "Give Peace a Chance," they would have been wiser to acknowledge that peace between people has little chance before peace with God is established. And the good news of the gospel message is that peace with God has been established! All that remains is for every person to enter the kingdom of God where peace is the norm.

Romans 5 will reveal that peace has blessings and a basis. In fact, the basis for peace is what Paul has been presenting in Romans through the end of chapter 4: peace with God is possible because the wrath of God has been deflected. God's wrath (Rom. 1:18) has been satisfied by the atoning sacrifice offered by his own Son, Jesus Christ (Rom. 3:25). His justice has been demonstrated and satisfied in the same event (Rom. 3:26), and he is at peace. All this is to say that peace with God depends on his being at peace with us, not our being at peace with him.

The idea that sinful humankind would find some fault in sinless God upon which to base hostility toward him is, of course, unthinkable. But the idea that sinless God has found fault in sinful humans, which fault has aroused his indignation, is thoroughly biblical, beginning in Genesis 3 and continuing in Romans 1 and 2. Therefore, it is God who needed to announce peace, which he has done.[65]

God has announced to all of mankind that we can have peace with Him through believing and accepting the Gospel of His Son Jesus.

The Process of Being Sanctified Is a Daily Process

This chapter title is "How Do I Not Break the Heart of God?" We will attempt to answer that question. First off, believe in God. Exercise your faith muscle every day of your life. Faith in God pleases Him. Be humble. Note that you will *never* "arrive" in the Christian Life. Faith

---

[65] Kenneth Boa and William Kruidenier, *Holman New Testament Commentary*, (Nashville: Holman Publishers, 2000), 94

and sanctification are daily walks, a living process, in walking through those three verb tenses of salvation: were, are being, and will be.

Seek the adventure of your salvation every day. Remember, because of Jesus' great sacrifice in your place, God has announced He is at peace with you. Apostle Paul said you are no longer enemies with God. Jesus' sacrifice has allowed us to start over with God. We now have that Garden of Eden relationship He desires and we longed for. God made it about Himself knowing there was nothing you could ever do to fix things. So God did it all for you. This is Love, pure and holy Love.

God the Father Is Pleased with You

I recently heard a young pastor at a men's conference put it this way, "God the Father is pleased with you." He made his point around that we not only receive salvation from the Lord Jesus but grace and mercy as well. He said that this all began at the baptism of Jesus and culminated on the cross of Jesus. As believers we are immersed in Jesus' death as well as His life. This young pastor pointed to the baptism of Jesus recorded in the Gospel of Matthew.[66]

> **Matthew 3:16-17** — *After being baptized, Jesus came up immediately from the water; and behold, the heavens were opened, and he [John] saw the Spirit of God descending as a dove and lighting on Him, 17 and behold, a voice out of the heavens said, "This is My beloved Son, in whom I am well-pleased."*

Can you entertain the thought that God the Father is "well-pleased" with you? If not, why do you think you can't? What is the first negative thought that comes to your mind that prevents the freedom to believe that truth? Note it and make it a matter of prayer. It is a lie to your soul from the father of lies.

---

[66] Pastor Ryan Visconti, "My Father is Pleased with Me," Men's 2022 Conference (Rockwall: Lakepointe Church, 2022).

Just before Jesus was baptized, He and John the Baptizer were discussing Jesus' need for baptism.

> **Matthew 3:13-15** — *Then Jesus arrived from Galilee at the Jordan coming to John, to be baptized by him. 14 But John tried to prevent Him, saying, "I have need to be baptized by You, and do You come to me?" 15 But Jesus answering said to him, "Permit it at this time; for in this way it is fitting for us to fulfill all righteousness." Then he [John] permitted Him.*

John the Baptizer was like, "Whoa, Jesus! I can't baptize You! I don't deserve the honor. I am not even fit to tie Your sandal!" Notice Jesus did not correct John's assessment of either himself or the situation. So acknowledging what John the Baptizer said to be true, Jesus commanded John to permit His baptism by John at this time. And why so? Jesus told John, "For in this way (baptizing Me) it is fitting for us to fulfill all righteousness."

Jesus' Righteousness Is Attributed to Us, His Followers

You and I, if we have entered the promised salvation, then we are one with Jesus. His righteousness is attributed to us. You and I started our journey in His righteousness at His baptism with the announcement that the Father is well-pleased with Him (and by virtue of His righteousness attributed to you and me).

The Apostle Paul, from his Roman "house arrest" prison, wrote to the Church at Ephesus. In this spectacular letter to all of us Christians over thousands of years he writes how *not* to break God's heart. I love the Bible. God is so good! We were His enemies, but God announced that we are no longer enemies. Not only this, but also that He is well-pleased with us in Christ Jesus, His Son, and as adopted sons and daughters, He has attributed Jesus' righteousness to us!

Our Spiritual Wealth

Now God the Father will use the Apostle Paul to teach us the truths of spiritual wealth that can be used as building blocks of faith to show our love to the Father! Did I say that I love the Bible? The Christians at Ephesus were exactly where you and I have been. They were spiritually rich but living as paupers or beggars. They were ignorant of their wealth and so regulated themselves to live as paupers. You and I need to understand the wealth that is in our spiritual bank account. Paul details for us that our spiritual bank account is fat: adoption, acceptance, redemption, forgiveness, wisdom, inheritance, the seal of the Holy Spirit, life, grace, citizenship—in short, every spiritual blessing. Ken Boa would agree with Paul about the great wealth we possess "IN" Christ Jesus.

> *"When the truths of who we are in Christ begin to define our self-image, they make us secure enough to love and serve others without seeking our own interests first. Because of our security and significance in Christ, we do not need to be controlled by the opinions and responses of others. We have nothing to prove because we know who and whose we are. Rather than trying to impress and manipulate people, we can do our work with excellence as unto the Lord (Colossians 3:23). The more we are concerned with what God thinks of us, the less we will be worried about what others think of us. And when we are no longer enslaved to people's opinions of us, we are free to love and serve them as Christ loves us—with no strings attached."*[67]
>
> **Colossians 3:23** — *Whatever you do, do your work heartily, as for the Lord rather than for men.*

---

[67]Kenneth Boa, *Conformed to His Image*, 32-33.

In Christ

Paul's most important phrase in writing Ephesians is the phrase "in Christ" (or its equivalent). This phrase in Ephesians appears about thirty-five times and is used more than any other New Testament book.

Paul starts off his letter to the Ephesians this way:

Ephesians 1:1-2 — *Paul, an apostle of Christ Jesus by the will of God, To the saints who are at Ephesus and who are faithful in Christ Jesus: 2 Grace to you and peace from God our Father and the Lord Jesus Christ.*

Paul moves from the greeting of the Ephesian believers who are *in Christ* to a blessing of God the Father.

Ephesians 1:3 — *Blessed be the God and Father of our Lord Jesus Christ, who has blessed us with every spiritual blessing in the heavenly places in Christ.*

Paul blesses the God and Father of our Lord Jesus Christ (Messiah). But Paul notes that God the Father has also blessed "us" (the Ephesian Christians at that time, the Apostle Paul but also you and me!). What did God the Father bless us with? "Every spiritual blessing in the heavenly places in Christ."

Don't discount this as some sort of religious Bible drivel double-speak. If you do it for this passage, then why not the passage for your salvation? Ouch! Remember God is good and the Bible is great! Let this sentence soak into your soul. Since you and I are in Christ, God the Father has taken *every* spiritual blessing found anywhere in the heavenly places that belong to Christ Jesus and has blessed you and me with them *all*.

That is a lot of spiritual wealth! We are deep and covered up! We are fat in spiritual wealth, but Paul wants us to truly know what that means.

Ephesians 1:4-6 — *just as He chose us **in Him** before the foundation of the world, that we would be holy and blameless before Him. In love 5 He predestined us to adoption as sons **through Jesus Christ** to Himself, according to the kind intention of His will, 6 to the praise of the glory of His grace, which He freely bestowed on us in the Beloved.*

Paul goes on to place you and me on rock solid ground. On granite! In verse 4, Paul tells us that He, God the Father, "chose us in Him" (Christ). When? "Before the foundation of the world." Why? "That we would be holy and blameless before Him" Who? God the Father.

The last two words of verse 4 belong at the beginning of verse 5. Don't worry; there's no error here. The chapter and verse division were added to the existing text 795 years ago. The original writings did not have any chapters or verse divisions.[68] But those last two words help verse 5 flow better. These words also speak to motive and they truly help soften the action they modify.

In love – don't miss that motive of God the Father! It was out of His love for you and me that:

5 He predestined us to be adopted as sons through Jesus Christ to Himself, according to the kind intention of His will, 6 to the praise of the glory of His grace, which He freely bestowed on us in the Beloved.

God the Father "predestined us." Why is that such a tough concept for us to accept? Remember, you and I are *not* God. Recall what was our state of being before God the Father redeemed us?

Romans 3:9b-18 — *"We have already charged that both Jews and Greeks are all under sin; 10 as it is written, 'There is none*

---

68 "Who divided the Bible into chapters and verses? Why and when was it done?" Got Questions Ministries, https://www.gotquestions.org/divided-Bible-chapters-verses. Accessed May 13, 2024.

righteous, not even one; 11 There is none who understands, There is none who seeks for God; 12 All have turned aside, together they have become useless; There is none who does good, There is not even one. 13 Their throat is an open grave, With their tongues they keep deceiving, The poison of asps is under their lips; 14 Whose mouth is full of cursing and bitterness; 15 Their feet are swift to shed blood, 16 Destruction and misery are in their paths, 17 And the path of peace they have not known. 18 There is no fear of God before their eyes.'"

God Chose Us in Christ

That was our state of being before God. But Paul tells us in verse 4 that God the Father *chose* us in Christ before the foundations of the world. So in verse 5, Paul is merely repeating the truth of verse 4. If God the Father "chose us in Christ before the foundation of the world," Paul further emphasizes that in love, God predestined – chose us – but how to be in Christ? God the Father predetermined us in love to be "adopted as sons." How? "Through Jesus Christ to Himself."

I think there's a pattern here. We were *not* righteous. None of us sought after God. We turned aside from Him and became useless. Not one of us did any good; our throats were open graves; our tongues could only deceive. Only poison extruded from our lips; our mouths were filled with curses and bitterness toward God. We were autonomous; we were our own god, and we ran to shed others' blood. Death and destruction were our only pathways. None of us ever knew the path of peace, and none of us feared God.

But God.

Before we lived Romans 3 out, and even before the world was created, out of His love, God predetermined that you and I would be redeemed from the *none* to the *one! Holy Father, we praise Your Name!* You can't figure this out (remember we are not God). You and I do not deserve this; you and I could not earn it.

Paul tells us not only out of God the Father's love but "according to the kind intention of His will." God, truly our Father in heaven, adopted us as sons through His only Son, Jesus Christ. God the Father adopted us to Himself from the state we were in as His enemies!

Grace Freely Bestowed

Paul says that all this is "to the praise of the glory of His grace." Yeah! *Right?* Paul says that grace was *freely* bestowed on us in His Beloved— Jesus Christ! That should put some shout into your worship; some step in your dance! Paul goes on to detail this lavish love and rich grace you and I have been immersed into.

> **Ephesians 1:7-14** — *In Him we have redemption through His blood, the forgiveness of our trespasses (Romans 3), according to the riches of His grace 8 which He lavished on us.*

Paul explains that our redemption was through the blood sacrifice of Jesus Christ, Messiah.

> *In all wisdom and insight 9 He [God the Father] made known to us the mystery of His [God the Father] will, according to His [God the Father] kind intention which He [God the Father] purposed in Him 10 with a view to an administration suitable to the fullness of the times, that is, the summing up of all things in Christ, things in the heavens and things on the earth. 11 In Him also we have obtained an inheritance, having been predestined according to His purpose who works all things after the counsel of His will, 12 to the end that we who were the first to hope in Christ would be to the praise of His glory. 13 In Him, you also, after listening to the message of truth, the gospel of your salvation—having also believed, you were sealed in Him with the Holy Spirit of promise, 14 who is given as a pledge of our inheritance, with a view to the redemption of God's own possession, to the praise of His glory.*

The Apostle Paul goes on after he gives this powerful introduction to the Ephesian Christians how God the Father has blessed them (and himself) in Christ, Paul turns on as personal note to them all.

> **Ephesians 1:15-16** — *For this reason I too, having heard of the faith in the Lord Jesus which exists among you and your love for all the saints, 16 do not cease giving thanks for you, while making mention of you in my prayers.*

The Eyes of Your Heart Enlightened

Paul tells these believers that he prays several specific things for them in light of what God the Father has done for them.

> **Ephesians 1:17-19a** — *That the God of our Lord Jesus Christ, the Father of glory, may give to you **a spirit of wisdom** and **of revelation in the knowledge of Him**. 18 I pray that **the eyes of your heart may be enlightened, so that you will know what is the hope of His calling**, what are the riches of the glory of **His inheritance in the saints**, 19a and what is the **surpassing greatness of His power** toward us who believe.*

Paul prays to God the Father for the Ephesian Christians and ultimately tells us that God the Father would give them a "spirit of wisdom" and "of revelation in the knowledge of Him (Jesus)." And the word "knowledge" used here is not just in knowledge "about" Jesus as some historical reference. This "knowledge" is to know Jesus intimately. Remember the Word of God for the New Covenant/Testament is being written and spoken through the Apostles as these letters were sent out to the churches. So Paul is praying that God would give these believers dynamically in real time these gifts of understanding and revelation about Jesus.

So That You May Know

From this request of the Father for this broader wisdom and knowledge, Paul gets specific in that he prays that "the eyes of their heart may be enlightened (see clearly)." Why? "So that you will know." Specifically, "what is the hope of His (Jesus) calling (mission and purpose as Messiah from God the Father). Further, that the Church at Ephesus would understand "what are the riches of the glory of His (Jesus) inheritance in the saints (those very same Ephesian Christians)."

Paul's prayer is asking the Father to enlighten the hearts of the Church (Ephesians then, us now) that they *never* deserved or earned anything to even be noticed by God the Father. But that out of His great endless love, God chose them before He formed the world to be an inheritance for His Son. Paul then asks the Father that the Church would understand "the surpassing greatness of His (Jesus) power toward us who believe."

Thankful Gratitude

Are you blown away yet? As I write this, I visualize myself with each sentence slowly moving from my chair to the floor and then stretched out on my back with my arms and hands raised toward heaven. I have no words but thankful gratitude and praise for all God the Father has done for me in Christ!

What about the "surpassing greatness of His power"?

Ephesians 1:19b-23 — *These are in accordance with the working of the strength of His might 20 which He brought about in Christ, when He raised Him from the dead and seated Him at His right hand in the heavenly places, 21 far above all rule and authority and power and dominion, and every name that is named, not only in this age but also in the one to come. 22 And He put all things in subjection under His feet, and gave Him as head over all things to* *the church, 23 which is His body, the fullness of Him who fills all in all.*

God's Heavenly Desires

God the Father gave us assurance of their delivery to us through His Son Jesus, in the "working out of the strength of His might" (v17-18). Paul tells us that working out of His might was brought about in Christ and details for us how and when.

- when He raised Him from the dead

- when God seated Him at His right hand in the heavenly places, far above all rule and authority and power and dominion,, and every name that is named, not only in this age but also in the one to come.

- How He put all things in subjection under His feet

- How He gave Him as head over all things to the church, which is His body, the fullness of Him who fills all in all.

Paul continues to tell the Ephesian Christians in what their true identity was when God opened their spiritual eyes.

> **Ephesians 2:1-3** — *And you were dead in your trespasses and sins, 2 in which you formerly walked according to the course of this world, according to the prince of the power of the air, of the spirit that is now working in the sons of disobedience. 3 Among them we too all formerly lived in the lusts of our flesh, indulging the desires of the flesh and of the mind, and were by nature children of wrath, even as the rest.*

DEAD

Paul tells them and us that we are dead. We were *dead* to all that Paul laid out in chapter one about the lavish love of God the Father. Until

He opened our eyes, we had no capacity to know anything of God. Just as a dead person can know nothing of the living—no sight, no hearing, no touch, no thought, no smell—simply nothing, so we were as to the things of God.

Paul tells us we were dead in our trespasses (committed an offense against the Word of God) and sins (disobedience to the Word of God). Paul explains that we all were in this state and formerly walked by a different power. We walked that dead existence "according to the prince of the power of the air, of the spirit that is now working in the sons of disobedience."

Paul tells them and us that he was in that state as well. "Among them, we, too, all formerly lived."

- lived in the lusts of our flesh
- indulging the desires of the flesh and the mind
- were by nature children of wrath, even as the rest.

To me, the greatest contrastive conjunction in the entire Bible comes in the next verse.

But God

God the Father chose to not leave them or us in that state of death!

Ephesians 2:4-9 — *But God, being rich in mercy, because of His great love with which He loved us, 5 even when we were dead in our transgressions, made us alive together with Christ (by grace you have been saved), 6 and raised us up with Him, and seated us with Him in the heavenly places in Christ Jesus, 7 so that in the ages to come He might show the surpassing riches of His grace in kindness toward us in Christ Jesus.*

This is such a mindblower! We may never fully know this side of heaven the depth to which God the Father loves us, but we surely, even knowing this, should spend our lives in loving gratitude and a life of obedience to the One Who loves us with such a great, grand love!

But God

- being rich in mercy
- because of His great love with which He loved us
- even when we were dead in our transgressions
- made us alive together with Christ (by grace you have been saved)
- raised us up with Him
- seated us with Him in the heavenly places in Christ Jesus

WHY?

"So that in the ages to come He might show the surpassing riches of His grace in kindness toward us in Christ Jesus."

This is the Bible too! You believed Jesus' message and mission for your salvation. You did it in faith. You believed! You need to also believe this: the rest of the Bible in that same faith. Faith is defined as belief with strong conviction, firm belief in something for which there may be no tangible proof, *complete* trust, confidence, reliance, or devotion. Faith is the opposite of fear or doubt. You could replace the word faith with trust; we are trusting the Father to keep His promise of salvation/redemption for us. These spiritual life concepts that Paul spelled out for us are just as real as our salvation and call for our faith/trust in this Word from God for us.

Pure Grace

Paul says that because of our previous dead state, God chose us and lavished His great love upon us as pure grace!

Ephesians 2:8-10 — *For by grace you have been saved through faith; and that not of yourselves, it is the gift of God; 9 not as a result of works, so that no one may boast. 10 For we are His workmanship,* *created in Christ Jesus for good works, which God prepared beforehand so that we would walk in them.*

Gift of His Grace to Even Believe

Paul tells us that the faith you were saved by was also a gift from God the Father as a gift of His grace in order for us to even believe. Just as centuries before when God made a covenant with Abraham and made him sleep so that He alone walked among the animal parts to secure the blood covenant, God has also ensured we, too, have nothing to do with His New Covenant with us! It is all a gift from God.

- not of yourselves
- it is the gift of God
- not as a result of works [our efforts]
- so that no one may boast
- For we are His workmanship
- created in Christ Jesus for good works
- which God prepared beforehand so that we would walk in them.

Set Apart from All Other Religions

This sets us apart from all religions to this day! Historic, first century Christianity is the only religion in which there is only God reaching out to mankind who has no ability to reach out to God. It is only God Who has forgiven and restored us to an intimate relationship with Himself as close as His own Son!

And can you ever wonder why we, as believers, sing a song such as "Amazing Grace?" That is the best we can do because our language fails us to rightly express our hearts for such a great, grand love that we never deserved!

The Apostle Paul says all of us are dead to God and then made alive by God the Father through His lavished love in Christ. The church at Ephesus was mainly Gentiles. It is good to note that for the first ten years of the Church's existence, it was mostly Jewish. Jews were in the leadership and they made up the congregations.

The prophet Isaiah proclaimed that the coming Servant of God would be a light to the nations.

> **Isaiah 42:1, 5-7** — *"Behold, My Servant, whom I uphold; My chosen one in whom My soul delights. I have put My Spirit upon Him; He will bring forth justice to the nations." 5 Thus says God the Lord, Who created the heavens and stretched them out, Who spread out the earth and its offspring, Who gives breath to the people on it And spirit to those who walk in it, 6 "I am the Lord, I have called You in righteousness, I will also hold You by the hand and watch over You, And I will appoint You as a covenant to the people, As a light to the nations, 7 To open blind eyes, To bring out prisoners from the dungeon And those who dwell in darkness from the prison."*

Messiah Replaced Israel to Be a Light of the Nations

Later in his prophecy, Isaiah proclaimed that His servant Israel, whom He had shown His glory, had failed. God said that He toiled with Israel in vain to basically be His mouthpiece to the nations of His redemption to the world. In place of Israel, God's Servant would fulfill that role by being "a light of the nations "so that [His] salvation may reach to the end of the earth."

> **Isaiah 49:3-6** — *He said to Me, "You are My Servant, Israel, In Whom I will show My glory." 4 But I said, "I have toiled in vain, I have spent My strength for nothing and vanity; Yet surely the justice due to Me is with the Lord, And My reward with My God." 5 And now says the Lord, who formed Me from the womb to be His Servant, To bring Jacob back to Him, so that Israel might be gathered to Him (For I am honored in the sight of the Lord, And My God is My strength), 6 He says, "It is too small a thing that You should be My Servant*

To raise up the tribes of Jacob and to restore the preserved ones of Israel; I will also make You a light of the nations So that My salvation may reach to the end of the earth."

Jews and Gentiles to Praise God's Holy Name

Paul desired unity among both the Jews and the Gentiles which is clearly seen in his letter to the Romans. Paul is calling for all believers, no matter our heritage or culture, to be of the same mind with one another regarding Jesus. He tells the Roman Christians whether they were found as a servant in the circumcision (a Jew) or as a Gentile, both are to bring glory to God for His great grace. Paul cites several passages from the Old Testament attesting to God's desire for both Jews and Gentiles to praise His Holy name.

> **Romans 15:5-12** — *Now may the God who gives perseverance and encouragement grant you to be of the same mind with one another according to Christ Jesus, 6 so that with one accord you may with one voice glorify the God and Father of our Lord Jesus Christ.*
>
> *7 Therefore, accept one another, just as Christ also accepted us to the glory of God. 8 For I say that Christ has become a servant to the circumcision on behalf of the truth of God to confirm the promises given to the fathers, 9 and for the Gentiles to glorify God for His mercy; as it is written, "Therefore I will give praise to You among the Gentiles, And I will sing to Your name" (2 Samuel 22:50; Psalms 18:49). 10 Again he says, "Rejoice, O Gentiles, with His people" (Deuteronomy 32:43). 11 And again, "Praise the Lord all you Gentiles, And let all the peoples praise Him" (Psalm 117:1). 12 Again Isaiah says, "There shall come the root of Jesse, And He who arises to rule over the Gentiles, In Him shall the Gentiles hope" (Isaiah 11:10).*

Paul goes on to tell the Roman Christians, both Jews and Gentiles, that God has appointed him a priest of the Gospel of Jesus Christ to the Gentile world.

Romans 15:15-16 — *But I have written very boldly to you on some points so as to remind you again, because of the grace that was given me from God, 16 to be a minister of Christ Jesus to the Gentiles, ministering as a priest the gospel of God, so that my offering of the Gentiles may become acceptable, sanctified by the Holy Spirit.*

It is with the calling that Paul speaks to the Ephesian Christians at the bottom of chapter two, whether Jew or Gentile, to recognize that they are BOTH ONE in Christ Jesus, their Messiah.

Ephesians 2:17-22 — *And He came and preached peace to you who were far away, and peace to those who were near; 18 for through Him we both have our access in one Spirit to the Father. 19 So then you are no longer strangers and aliens, but you are fellow citizens with the saints, and are of God's household, 20 having been built on the foundation of the apostles and prophets, Christ Jesus Himself being the corner stone, 21 in whom the whole building, being fitted together, is growing into a holy temple in the Lord, 22 in whom you also are being built together into a dwelling of God in the Spirit.*

Paul concludes his teaching that God has taken both Jews and Gentiles who were dead to Him and raised them up with the power He used to raise Jesus. Everything Paul stated in the first two chapters revealed to both the Gentiles and Jews a mystery that had never been revealed to mankind. Paul says that this mystery has been revealed to mankind by God's "holy apostles," who are the "prophets" of God "in the Spirit" to this age.

Ephesians 3:4-12 — *By referring to this, when you read you can understand my insight into the mystery of Christ, 5 which in other generations was not made known to mankind as it has now been revealed to His holy apostles and prophets in the Spirit;*

6 to be specific, that the Gentiles are fellow heirs and fellow members of the body, and fellow partakers of the promise in Christ Jesus through the gospel, 7 of which I was made a minister, according to the gift of God's grace which was given to me according to the working of His power. 8 To me, the very least of all saints, this grace was given, to preach to the Gentiles the unfathomable riches of Christ,

9 and to enlighten all people as to what the plan of the mystery which for ages has been hidden in God who created all things; 10 so that the multifaceted wisdom of God might now be made known through the church to the rulers and the authorities in the heavenly places. 11 This was in accordance with the eternal purpose which He carried out in Christ Jesus our Lord, 12 in whom we have boldness and confident access through faith in Him.

A Mystery of God Revealed

So this mystery of God that Paul, representing the Apostles, shows this generation that the "unfathomable riches of Christ" are being revealed to the Gentiles or the rest of the world. Paul says specifically "that the Gentiles are fellow heirs and fellow members of the body, and fellow partakers of the promise in Christ Jesus through the gospel." Paul tells us that this mystery was hidden in God the Father "so that the multifaceted wisdom of God might now be made known through the church to the rulers and the authorities in the heavenly places." Why? "This was in accordance with the eternal purpose which He [God the Father] carried out in Christ Jesus our Lord."

Bottomline: God the Father's "eternal purpose" also included that "in Christ Jesus...we have boldness and confident access through faith in Him."

You and I, whether a Jew or a Gentile (everyone else) have our access to God the Father restored through our faith in Messiah Jesus. That access is bold and confident.

The writers at Got Questions summed up this mystery of God well.

"God revealed His complete Word to His saints (Colossians 1:26) who have "heard and learned" the gospel (John 6:45; cf. Romans

10:17 and John 3:16-18), and it is they alone who fathom "the glorious riches of this mystery" (Colossians 1:27). In its fullest sense, the "mystery of God" is God's plan of salvation through Jesus. We would never have been able to comprehend the way to eternal life without the coming of Jesus, His death and resurrection."[69]

How Do I Not Break the Heart of God?

- **Rest.** Rest in what God has done for you!
- **Faith.** Believe what God has said He has done for you!
- **Walk.** Walk out your life before God as He said you have the power to do.
- **Proclaim.** Proclaim, in humility, with your life what God has done for you while you were dead to Him!

Trust the Father + abide in the Son + walk by the Spirit

Think these three action steps all moments of your day – daily walking thoughts.

Ask continually three questions often in your day:

1. What do you seek? (John 1:38) - right now more than anything else? That I may know You more clearly.
2. Who do you say That I am? (Matt. 16:15) - right now more than anyone else? May I love You more dearly.
3. Do you love Me more than these? (John 21:15) - are there "any" rivals in your life against Jesus? May I follow You more nearly.[70]

---

[69] "What is the mystery of God referred to in the Bible?" Got Questions Ministries, https://www.gotquestions.org/mystery-of-God.html. Accessed May 26, 2024.
[70] Saint Richard of Chichester, "Prayer of Saint Richard of Chichester," 1253. Spiritual Renewal Cards, Reflections Ministries, Trinity House Publishers.

How Was God Loved?

- **Rest.** Rest in what God has done for you!
- **Faith.** Believe what God has said He has done for you!
- **Walk.** Walk out your life before God as He said you have the power to do.
- **Proclaim.** Proclaim, in humility, with your life what God has done for you while you were dead to Him!

11

Mature Love, Look to the Man, Jesus

The driving focus of this book is man and his relationship with his Creator God. We have surveyed on a broad basis man's responsibility (ability to respond) to love God as God would define an acceptable love response to Him. What is that acceptable love response? It seems obvious. Obedience. Specifically, obedience to His Word. You may ask how God could define such a response. Why not? You and I do it all of the time. How else do you recognize or categorize various other human responses to yourself? You know the difference between a love or hate response, a kind, mean, gentle or harsh response. You get the idea. So why not to God from us?

In the previous chapters, we looked at how God was loved by the first couple Adam and Eve, the first family; we looked at the remnant God saved from evil mankind, Noah and his family, the nation of Israel, the Messenger of the nation, the Messiah, and the Messiah's remnant—His disciples. In this broad sweep, we have experienced a review of man's relationship with God and how man has loved God.

Where Have We Been?

We reviewed the beginnings, and the first relationships with Man: Adam and Eve. The first couple constantly made their choice to lovingly obey God the Father until they did not. The sad part of Satan's temptation was to get Eve to believe in something that she didn't have to believe. In fact, she already had God's truth in her possession. Eve was already "like" God in that she was made in His image (Genesis 1:26).

Sin, as we defined, is disobedience to God's Word, but it goes deeper than that. It goes as deep as our nature before our belief in how the Messiah took away our sins. As sons of Adam, we are now back in the "Garden of Eden" each day of our lives. We can choose to obey God's Word or we can still choose to sin or disobey God's Word to us. The difference with our faith in the Messiah's substitute death is that we are no longer separated in our relationship with God the Father and never will be again. Our relationship with God the Father is sealed permanently with the blood of Jesus and proven by the indwelling Holy Spirit as the Father's down payment.

Had Adam said no to this new interpretation of Eve and he himself had gone to the Lord God to review, then the original sin of disobedience would not have been committed. In the created order, Adam was Eve's spiritual leader; she was created after he was and purposed as his helpmate. The command to not eat the tree's fruit was given only to Adam by God Himself and not to Eve. Adam abrogated his place of responsibility to God and his wife.

How was God loved by Adam and Eve? Simple. Just as they always had shown their love to God since their creation in the Garden before the Fall, they loved God by their submission to His authority, to His Sovereign rule, and His Word. They found that in their obedience they loved God. It is in the outward displayed decisions of the heart that the inward non-coerced decisions of the will are demonstrated.

The original sin (disobedience) becomes a generational sin of Adam and Eve passed to their children. Cain, as the second generation, failed in his love response to God.

At one point early in human history, God was deeply grieved that He made mankind. God saw that the thoughts of mankind's hearts were "only evil continually" (Genesis 6:5). The God of all creation was sorry that He had made man. He was disgusted with His work of art, His masterpiece. So disgusted that He wanted to destroy it all—and not just mankind—but He also wanted to blot out all of His creation down to the bugs! Now, that is a broken heart on a cosmic level! It is hard to believe that our generation has not reached the level of evil that was in the human heart in the days of Noah!

However, God was loved by a remnant. Here, the remnant started as one solitary man, Noah. The remnant was extended to Noah's family. We have no way of knowing the extent of the world's population back then, but at least it was in the thousands. The evil was so profound that it utterly made God sorry that He ever created mankind. We are all well aware of the evil that exists in our current day, but God has not destroyed us like Noah's generation, yet. Can you even imagine what level of evil existed at that time to bring God to that conclusion? But God found one man, Noah.

Fast forward to Israel. I think God was loved in the response of obedience and worship from those He sovereignly chose to further His will and Word in setting apart Israel as His chosen nation to be His mouthpiece to the world and ultimately toward the coming Messiah Jesus. Were they perfect in their love toward Him? No, not at all. However, by viewing this relationship between these chosen people and the only living true God, we get to know who He is. We get to witness His attributes, His Person, His character, and His heart. This relationship with God, Yahweh and Israel is His revelation of Himself, His revealing of Himself to the world whom He has chosen to redeem and love. Later God would reveal Himself on an intimate level to mankind once again as He did to man in the Garden. This intimate reveal would be through the Person of Messiah Jesus. God is with us!

God always had a faithful remnant who loved, trusted and were loyal to Him. We know that in Messiah Jesus' ministry, He had the twelve disciples, but He also had the 120 disciples, including the twelve who also loved, trusted and were loyal to Him (after the shock of the trial and crucifixion as they waited in the Upper Room as instructed by the Lord).

It was from these same Apostles, these first century disciples that you and I have been soul touched by the Spirit of Messiah, His Holy Spirit. That Gospel became alive in their lives and passed like an eternal torch to all the generations of Messiah followers. That very same Gospel message through their spoken or written word had the Messiah's redemption and reconciliation landing in our hearts through that same power of the Holy Spirit as we came alive from death to being chosen by our God, King, Savior!

The Great Risk

We need to understand how great a risk God our Father took to reach each one of us with His salvation of love. Think about the review we swept through. All of the hundreds of times God the Father wrestled with His humans in covenant and out of covenant.

From the first sacrifice in the Garden God Himself committed to give coverings to Adam and Eve to all the sacrifices made by Israel to maintain their relationship with God's presence among them. None of them returned us to that sweet walk in the cool of the afternoon with God our Father amidst the Garden. None of those sacrifices had any true deep hope of lasting redemption.

But then Jesus! God the Son, the second member of the holy Trinity, took all the risk. But it was not just Him that took all the risk. It was all three, Father, Son, and Holy Spirit Who laid it all on the line for our redemption, our salvation.

The Father commanded. The Son obeyed. The Spirit sustained the Son as human Jesus. God took the risk to blow it all up for us to have a sustaining, everlasting relationship with Him. God loved us in the Garden and His desire was to restore His beloved to those cool afternoon walks.

God became one of us to live as we live. He came to see, hear, and taste as we do, to experience the limitations of being human. He also struggled with a fallen world under a curse, He felt the great human temptations to escape the pressure and the pain. We will see how Jesus, not diminished of His divinity, came to live, breathe, cry, and struggle with total dependence on the Holy Spirit to guide Him, and pray with Him in order to live a life of obedience to His Father without sin.

Who Was the Model Believer?

Who was their model, these first century believers, of how to love the Father God? Of course, it was the Man Jesus. In chapter five, we discussed how Adam, Eve and the angels "were created holy but unconfirmed." Adam and Eve were created in a state of "unconfirmed creaturely holiness," like the angels were, but they "were also given the power of contrary choice: the ability to choose contrary to their nature."[71] Then, if Jesus as a Man was the second or last Adam, He too, in His humanity was created in a state of "unconfirmed creaturely holiness." But Jesus' confirmation was His choice of perfect obedience to the Father's will all the way throughout His life to His death on the cross. Jesus' holiness was absolutely confirmed! His sinlessness is undeniably confirmed! It was confirmed in His final act of obedience as the Man Jesus with His death on the cross.

Jesus' mission from God was to redeem the world from Satan to God. As we discovered, whenever Adam failed in his obedience to God, he forfeited his position of ruler of God's world to that of Satan. Jesus, the second Adam or last Adam, became the Kinsman Redeemer to take possession of the title to the world from Satan. Jesus redeemed

---

[71] Fruchtenbaum, The Dispensations of God, 6.

the world by His obedience to the Father, even to the death as the Father commanded.

That redemption of our souls and the renewal of our spirits and hearts to the Father, has got to be the warmest, greatest sensation of love that we have ever experienced in our lives. If it is not, you need a blood checkup. We have a new identity that Jesus gave to us by dying in our place paying the penalty we deserved.

I want us to think about Jesus as Man for the next few moments to help endear His endeavor for us to have a restored relationship with Himself. He knew that just like with Abraham, His covenant with Himself had to be exclusively on His shoulders. To consider how Messiah Jesus humbled Himself to identify with us at every human level, yet without sin (disobedience), should move us to worship.

Discovering the Scriptures

Sometimes for us to believe all that God says we are in our new identity in Christ takes all the faith we can muster and even pray for. It helps to go through Scripture led by Holy Spirit and listen to what God the Father is revealing to you.

Pause and get your head around that one.

The Man Jesus had to have faith in His Father just like you and me. Jesus the Man was not a superman. God's love language is obedience to His Word. Jesus revealed in His life that there is great benefit of loving obedience in relationship with His Father.

I have a friend and brother in Christ, whom I shared in fellowship and worship many years ago whenever I lived in Central Florida. His name is Gerry Hodges. Gerry is a medical doctor of psychiatry and had a thriving practice many years ago. And still does, from what I have summarized. At the time I left that fellowship on my journey to attend Dallas Theological Seminary, Gerry was in the throes of finishing a writing project that took him through hundreds of Scriptures. He was fascinated with the Man Jesus.

As a believer, Gerry is committed to the absolute truth of the Scriptures and all that they proclaim about Jesus as God but also as Man. I believe Gerry's labor of love was to bring the humanness of Jesus closer to each one of us so that we could see our own potential as human Christ Followers. While at Dallas Seminary, I researched a quote for Gerry and was able to get one of my professors to read and review Gerry's book.

I mention this to share a couple of quotes from Gerry's book to have you slip into Jesus' sandals briefly to hear what this must have felt like for Him. Gerry's book, *Jesus, An Interview Across Time* gives us an idea of what that could be like. It is a fictional portrayal, and it is interesting to surmise how Jesus as a human discovered who He is from Scripture in faith and being full of the Holy Spirit for guidance.

Imagine standing around a group of people at a party. Someone is pointing out the guests and she says, 'The tall one, that's Bill. That's John on his right with the pipe. And the one next to him with the beard, that's God, and He goes by the name Jesus.'

It was hard to believe that I was to be alone on center stage, the one most important person in all of history! It took me a long time to get over being God. I felt so normal.

But the Scriptures took me even further. They told me that I had a 'previous life' with my Father for years, even before the earth was created. Listen to this: I had created the earth. You talk about having to have faith. Look at what I had to believe! I had to believe I had another life I couldn't remember and in it I was God. And this was long before I performed any miracles and had the use of all my Father's power.

It was at this profound moment that I began to realize how great an identity I had. My Father continued to use the great personalities of the Scriptures to confirm what was happening and had happened in my life. I was like He was saying, 'See it is all really true ....' I never ceased to be amazed at how rich the Scriptures were in their ability to communicate. It was like looking in a mirror."[72]

Faith Discovery in the Scriptures

Could you imagine the faith and trust it took to believe the Scriptures are talking to you and about you that you are the Messiah?

But God does call you and me to have that same faith in His Word. God the Father calls on you and me to put our faith and trust in Jesus Himself. Those same Scriptures tell us we deserved the death that Jesus died in our place. But by believing that Jesus took our place on the cross, you and I are reconciled to God the Father. We are completely forgiven, redeemed, and restored as God's adopted sons and daughters. We have total peace with God our Father. Relationship restored!

Those same Scriptures tell us about our new identity in Christ, Messiah. It tells us how God the Father now sees us through the covering of His Son. We are called to exercise faith to put on that new identity and engage in the relationship with God the Father that He so risked to give us.

It is all a mind-blowing WOW, is it not? Let's take another look at Gerry's book.

> *The more I began to understand who I was, the more I asked the same question. If I were truly God, then where was my power? Certainly, I didn't experience myself as someone who was omniscient.*
>
> *To my relief, the Scriptures answered that question too. They prophesied that the Messiah would have to learn. The seventh chapter of Isaiah speaks of the virgin born Messiah would have to learn right from wrong. Later the Scriptures report that the Messiah would teach*

---

[72] Andrew G. Hodges, Jesus, An Interview Across Time: A Psychiatrist Looks at HIS Humanity (Village House Publishers, 1986), 42-43.

Himself many things by his deeds. That's why the Gospel reporter, Luke, recorded about me:

'And Jesus grew in wisdom and in stature and in favor with God and man.'[73]

The Man Jesus Had to Have Faith In His Father

Just as the Man Jesus had to have faith in His Father and trust in the very same Scriptures to grow, learn and gain wisdom, our calling is no different. We truly have Jesus, Who demonstrated that He knew what it was like to be us! Jesus knew what it was like to have faith in those very same Scriptures to challenge us, grow us, impart wisdom to define who we are, and give us a mission to live pleasing to God the Father. Because the Scriptures did it for Him too. Gerry goes on further with this quote.

> *The Book of Hebrews underscores why my life as a man had so much value.*
>
> *'Only as a human being could he die and in dying break the power of the devil who had the power of death.'*
>
> *When I quoted Moses to Satan during the temptation in the wilderness, saying that 'man shall not live on bread alone, but on every word that proceeds out of the mouth of God.'*
>
> *Do you really think I didn't have to do that? Was my Father going to deny me the most precious experience a man can have — walking by faith in His words? The minute I had allowed immediate access to my full omniscience would have been precisely the moment that I wouldn't have needed the Scriptures and I wouldn't have had the faith. Then I would have had absolute certainty and that would have*

---

[73] Hodges, Jesus, An Interview Across Time: A Psychiatrist Looks at HIS Humanity, 45.

contradicted the Scriptures. Read Isaiah. He tells you that I had to trust when he quotes the Messiah as one day saying,

'I will put my trust in Him.'

To underscore the fact that Isaiah was describing me talking and stating that I had to have faith, the book of Hebrews in the New Testament quotes the identical verse.

The chosen self-limitation of becoming a man forced me into a mature, dependent relationship with my Father. God never intended for any person to have it any differently. My Father never let me get to the point of not having to walk by faith. To be tempted in all ways includes humanity's biggest temptation: not believing in God, doubting He's there. The first step in every sin is to think that God's not looking.[74]

Make My Joy Complete

The Apostle Paul, writing to the church at Philippi, asked them to make his joy complete.

Philippians 2:2 — *Make my joy complete by being of the same mind, maintaining the same love, united in spirit, intent on one purpose.*

Paul gives them a clear definition of what he meant by the "same mind," "the same love," "united in spirit," and being "intent on one purpose."

Philippians 2:3-4 — *Do nothing from selfishness or empty conceit, but with humility consider one another as more important than yourselves; 4 do not merely look out for your own personal interests, but also for the interests of others.*

---

[74] Hodges, Jesus, An Interview Across Time: A Psychiatrist Looks at HIS, 46.

Paul then exhorts the church at Philippi to have this same attitude in themselves. Why? Because this was the attitude that was modeled by the Messiah, Christ Jesus. It was the Man Jesus Who demonstrated this attitude for all the church at Philippi and all of us to follow and emulate. How did Jesus demonstrate this to us?

> **Philippians 2:5-8** — *Have this attitude in yourselves which was also in Christ Jesus, 6 who, as He already existed in the form of God, did not consider equality with God a thing to be grasped, 7 but emptied Himself by taking the form of a bond-servant, and being made in the likeness of men. 8 And being found in appearance as a man, He humbled Himself by becoming obedient to the point of death: death on a cross.*

The Apostle Paul describes this "kenosis" Greek for 'to empty." The term *kenosis* comes from the Greek word for the doctrine of Christ's self-emptying in His incarnation. The *kenosis* was a self-renunciation, not an emptying Himself of deity nor an exchange of deity for humanity. His Deity was never diminished in any way. Philippians 2:7 tells us that Jesus "emptied Himself, taking the form of a bondservant, and being made in the likeness of men."

Paul tells the church at Philippi what it looks like to have a "humility of mind," to "regard one another as more important than yourselves," and not to "look out for your own personal interests, but also for the interests of others?" Look no further than the Man Jesus!

Jesus the Man, Not a Superman

Jesus, the Man, was not a superman. How could we identify with a superman? How could we emulate the attitudes and actions of a superman? That would let us off the hook entirely. If that were truly the case, since Jesus was a Superman and we can never be, then we don't have to strive in our faith through dependence on the Word of God and the Spirit of God to obtain this high level of a loving obedient relationship with the Father. What's the point? Why try?

Gerry, in his fictional rendering, quoted above, Jesus said, "The chosen self-limitation of becoming a man forced me into a mature, dependent relationship with my Father." Here in his letter to the church at Philippi, Paul, in his non-fictional rendering, clearly shows the self-imposed limitations that Jesus placed upon Himself. And what was the culminating point that Paul says about Jesus' limitation? Paul says it was Jesus' humility demonstrated by His action. That action was His loving obedience to the Father. And to be more specific, it was His "becoming obedient to the point of death, even death on a cross."

Paul goes further to tell us that it was for this reason, His obedience to the Father "to the point of death, even death on a cross" that God the Father exalts Him.

> **Philippians 2:9-11** — *For this reason also God highly exalted Him, and bestowed on Him the name which is above every name, 10 so that at the name of Jesus EVERY KNEE WILL BOW, of those who are in heaven and on earth and under the earth, 11 and that every tongue will confess that Jesus Christ is Lord, to the glory of God the Father.*

Everyone Will Take a Knee

All humanity, who has ever lived will take a knee and bow to God the Father's Son, Jesus. And while doing so all humanity will confess that Jesus is Lord.

The Father proclaimed that Jesus' obedience to His Word and His will caused the Father to exalt Him. We will discover that Jesus told His disciples and us that it was obedience to Him and the Father that demonstrated our love truly for Him and His Father.

After Jesus told His disciples that He had to go away and prepare a place for them. Jesus told them that they knew the way He was going. This was Thomas's reply.

> **John 14:5-6** — *Thomas said to Him, "Lord, we do not know where You are going; how do we know the way?" 6 Jesus said to him,*

"I am the way, and the truth, and the life; no one comes to the Father but through Me."

Jesus told them that He was the way to the Father and that there was no other way. He told the disciples that to know Me is to know the Father!

John 14:7 — *If you had known Me, you would have known My Father also; from now on you know Him, and have seen Him."*

To that Philip says to Jesus

John 14:8 — *Philip said to Him, "Lord, show us the Father, and it is enough for us.*

Jesus is taken back by Philip's statement.

John 14:9-11 — *Jesus said to him, "Have I been so long with you, and yet you have not come to know Me, Philip? He who has seen Me has seen the Father; how can you say, 'Show us the Father'? 10 Do you not believe that I am in the Father, and the Father is in Me? The words that I say to you I do not speak on My own initiative, but the Father abiding in Me does His works. 11 Believe Me that I am in the Father and the Father is in Me; otherwise believe because of the works themselves.'"*

God's Love Language

Just after this lesson on oneness, how Jesus and the Father are intertwined, Jesus introduces the disciples to God's love language.

John 14:15 — *If you love Me, you will keep My commandments.*

That is not farfetched. Recall what Paul said of the Father's opinion of Jesus' obedience to His Word and will. Every knee of all humanity of all time periods will bow to Jesus for His obedience and proclaim Him Lord.

Love Equals Obedience

Throughout this dialogue with His disciples, Jesus will continue to drive home this concept of "love equals obedience." Jesus tells them that He is not leaving them as orphans but that He will ask His Father to send another Helper, the Spirit of Truth.

> **John 14:20-21** — *In that day you will know that I am in My Father, and you in Me, and I in you. 21 He who has My commandments and keeps them is the one who loves Me; and he who loves Me will be loved by My Father, and I will love him and will disclose Myself to him."*

Promises of Loving Obedience

Jesus promises a close, intimate relationship between anyone who demonstrates their love for Him and the Father by keeping and obeying His commandments. Jesus promises that this demonstration of love will be returned by love from the Father, love from Jesus, and that Jesus will disclose (reveal, making visible that which was previously hidden) Himself to them.

The disciple Judas, not Iscariot, pressed Jesus further about this disclosure of Himself to them. Jesus continues to emphasize the intersecting of love and obedience. One goes with the other. And to that reality, there is attached a heavenly benefit, the fellowship of the Father and the Son. Jesus tells them that this word you hear from Him is not His but is from the Father.

> **John 14:22-24** — *Judas (not Iscariot) said to Him, "Lord, what then has happened that You are going to disclose Yourself to us and not to the world?" 23 Jesus answered and said to him, "If anyone loves Me, he will keep My word; and My Father will love him, and We will come to him and make Our abode with him. 24 He who does not love Me does not keep My words; and the word which you hear is not Mine, but the Father's who sent Me.*

Just after this, Jesus is teaching about Himself being the vine and His followers the branches of that vine. Within that teaching, Jesus again speaks to this concept of love and obedience.

> **John 15:9-11** — *Just as the Father has loved Me, I have also loved you; abide in My love. 10 If you keep My commandments, you will abide in My love; just as I have kept My Father's commandments and abide in His love. 11 These things I have spoken to you so that My joy may be in you, and that your joy may be made full.*

Great Benefit of Loving Obedience

Jesus tells them of the great benefit of loving the Father and Him by obedience. Not only will they experience more intimacy with both the Father and Him, but they will also have their joy complete and full.

John illustrates that he got this lesson on love for the Father and Son, which is actually obedience to their Word in his first letter.

> **1 John 2:3-6** — *By this we know that we have come to know Him, if we keep His commandments. 4 The one who says, "I have come to know Him," and does not keep His commandments, is a liar, and the truth is not in him; 5 but whoever keeps His word, in him the love of God has truly been perfected. By this we know that we are in Him: 6 the one who says he abides in Him ought himself to walk in the same manner as He walked.*

And the Apostle John wraps this concept up neatly in his second letter.

> **2 John 6** — *And this is love, that we walk according to His commandments. This is the commandment, just as you have heard from the beginning, that you should walk in it.*

This loving obedience to His Word is not by my human power, of course. My natural talents wrapped in lessons of experience can only go so far before I hit my "ceiling of humanity." To go beyond the natural, it takes SUPERnatural. That is what the Last Adam, the Man

Jesus modeled for all men. While Jesus was *both* fully God and fully Man, Jesus willfully chose to lay aside His glory as God to become fully Man. Jesus is our manly model! (Philippians 2:5-11). He is the one to follow to depend on the same SUPERnatural power that He depended upon to effectively obtain beyond what our natural talents can obtain. And what is that, you may ask? Jesus, the Man, obeyed God the Father completely! Jesus, the Man, fully depended upon and trusted in the power of the Holy Spirit!

I understand fully that we are wrapped in Christ, by mercy and grace, in every aspect of His righteousness. We have discussed this fully. But just as the Man Jesus stood alone, full of the Holy Spirit in His obedience to the Father, let's see how that would look on you or me. Ask yourself ... how far will you go in obedience to God the Father? Obedience is God the Father's love language out of a willing and wanting heart, not out of compulsion. How far will your humility take you? What is God the Father going to say about you when the Holy Spirit writes, "FOR THIS REASON ALSO, GOD HIGHLY EXALTED [fill in my name]. What do you think about that? At this point, I know I would be ashamed. I am praying to change that daily! How about you?

We have come full circle. We started with the relationship of humanity's patriarchs with the first Adam in the Garden with God. We traced man's relationship with God through the nations, the covenants, and through Israel.

We drew close to the Messiah, the last Adam, and then focused on the Man Jesus. God's point with Jesus being fully man was to give us an eternal model that Man has the capacity to obey His Word. Adam did, but he chose not to obey. It did not have to be the way it was in the Garden. The Last Adam, Jesus the Man, proved that in His obedience throughout His entire life without sin! Jesus chose to submit His entire self to the will of the Father and be filled with the Holy Spirit. Jesus had to trust His Father, abide in His Word, and walk by the Spirit daily. Jesus proved it by obeying the Father's command for

Him to willingly go to the cross of death in our place to redeem our lives from the power of death!

Jesus the Man models for us that in Him we have all the gifts granted by the Father to obey Him and carry out His Word and ways in our daily missions for Him.

All of our excuses have been taken away from us. There is no one to blame. There is no reason to look around. It is only you and the Father.

Unique Biblical Mystery, God Reveals How

God the Father, as a good Father, has not left us without provision. We have discussed the concept of the Mysteries of God previously. However, this last discussion on Biblical Mysteries is one provision from our good Father that you can execute in your daily walk with Messiah Jesus. As Bible students, we can point out a Biblical Mystery. There are varying degrees of exposure to these mysteries. Some mysteries remain stoic and have no inkling of resolution. These types have two unresolved, exclusive, opposite positions, both totally treated as equally true in the Scriptures. Some mysteries go a bit further in filling out their definition and descriptions but still remain opposite and are treated equally true. It is quite rare, however, that when a Biblical Mystery is identified, its definition of why may be given, but the deeper insight as to how that mystery works is a rare occurrence indeed.

In the book of Galatians, the Apostle Paul was battling legalism and his enemies sought to redefine the Gospel of grace given to Paul by the Risen Christ as His message to preach to the Gentiles. It is in this context that Paul reveals to the Galatians the first theological foundation of their faith, justification.

> **Galatians 2:20** — *I have been crucified with Christ; and it is no longer I who live, but Christ lives in me; and the life which I now live in the flesh I live by faith in the Son of God, who loved me and gave Himself up for me.*

What does that mean? How does that work? God our Father, in His genius, has pulled back the curtain and given us the answer as to *how* this can take place in our lives. This is one of those rare occurrences where we can identify a mystery, but through God's sovereign wisdom, *how* this mystery works itself out is revealed to us.

It is reminiscent of Jesus' priestly prayer in John 17:23:

"I am in them, and you are in me. May they experience such perfect unity that the world will know that you sent me and that you love them as much as you love me."

Again, we are left with those two questions of what this means and how it works. The key to this is in understanding the four words of God.[75] Dr. Boa identifies that these four words of God fall into two categories: General Revelation and Special Revelation.

General Revelation

1. God's Infinite Word manifested throughout His universe from the macro to the micro.

   Romans 1:20 — *For since the creation of the world His invisible attributes, His eternal power and divine nature, have been clearly seen, being understood through what has been made, so that they are without excuse.*

Special Revelation

2. God's Inspired Word manifested through multiple agencies and most definitely in Yeshua HaMashiach (Jesus the Messiah).

   Hebrews 1:1-4 — *God, after He spoke long ago to the fathers in the prophets in many portions and in many ways, in these last days has spoken to us in His Son, whom He appointed heir of all things,*

---

[75] Dr. Kenneth Boa, *Four Words of God*

through whom also He made the world. And He is the radiance of His glory and the exact representation of His nature and upholds all things by the word of His power. When He had made purification of sins, He sat down at the right hand of the Majesty on high, having become as much better than the angels."

Special Revelation

3. God's Incarnate Word is the mystery of the kenosis (keh noh' ssihss), the act of Christ in emptying Himself of the form of God, taking on the form of a servant, and suffering death on a cross.

    Philippians 2:5-8 — *The Apostle Paul tells the Philippians, "Have this attitude in yourselves which was also in Christ Jesus, who, although He existed in the form of God, did not regard equality with God a thing to be grasped, but* **emptied Himself***, taking the form of a bondservant, and being made in the likeness of men. Being found in appearance as a man, He humbled Himself by becoming obedient to the point of death, even death on a cross."*

In Christian theology, the teaching of the incarnation is the preexistent divine person of **Jesus Christ, God the Son**, the second person of the Trinity, and the eternally begotten Logos (Koine Greek for "word"), took upon human nature and "was made flesh" by being conceived in the womb of a woman, the Virgin Mary. The teaching of the incarnation then entails that Jesus was at the same time both fully God and fully human—two natures in one person.

The Apostle John asserted the same concerning Christ's incarnation in John 1:14, "The Word was made flesh."

Special Revelation

4. God's Indwelling Word is Christ in us, the hope of glory, "you in Me, and I in you" (John 17:22-23). It unifies the inside and outside, the transcendent and immanent, divine

sovereignty and human responsibility, Thou and I, the eternal and temporal, and the one and many. We are graced with eternal agency in the providential nexus of space and time.

John 17:22-23 — *The glory which You have given Me I have given to them, that they may be one, just as We are one;* **I in them and You in Me**, *that they may be perfected in unity, so that the world may know that You sent Me, and loved them, even as You have loved Me.*

The interplay of God's latter three in the special revelation where we will find the *how* of our present mystery, which we address in Galatians, and *how* it works its way into us.

It is God's Inspired Word manifested through the Person of Jesus the Messiah, Who became God's Incarnate Word, that through our salvation becomes the interchange of God's Indwelling Word planted in us by the Holy Spirit!

This is how we abide in Christ. This is how the Indwelling Christ, the Word of God made flesh, becomes incarnate within us. As the Word of Christ dwells within us, He is in us, and we are in Him!

Through the Indwelling Word of Christ and by His Spirit, we can live the life of the age to come now in this world. We need to seek to serve an invisible audience of One instead of the visible audience of many. The audience to whom you play will shape what you believe and, therefore, how you live your life.

I pray the Word of God will take on a greater and deeper importance for each of us as we contemplate this mystery of abiding in Christ. It is truly our faith placed in His Word and then the mysterious interchange of His Word in us, transforming us to be more like Jesus' character. It truly then becomes Him in us and us in Him.

The spiritual blessings we have **in Christ** are from the heavenly places or realms. These are for our benefit in the here and now, not just the then and there. Through Jesus's sacrifice, He has restored us to our Garden relationship and the original power of choice. So, we are truly without excuses. The way forward has been cleared.

At the very beginning, I envisioned God's heart:

What Does God Want from Me?

The point I made is that God threw His all into Jesus the Man to fight the Father's battle over Satan's claim on the world. God risked His own self, His Holy Being to do it. But at the same time, God showed us that in our daily battle against evil, where He commands us to **stand firm**, we have that same assurance that the Father placed in the Son, He places in us. Why? Not because of us, but because the Father placed us **in Christ**. Jesus won by His dependence on the Father, the Word and the Holy Spirit's guidance, we can too. We can, in Christ, can fulfill the Father's command for us to **stand firm**.

Jesus is recorded in the Gospel of Luke 6:46, where He poses His great relationship question to you and me.

"Why do you call Me, 'Lord, Lord,' and do not do what I say?"

This is the only question that remains for you or me: Will we truly prove our love of the Father by obeying His Word?

Trust the Father – Abide in Christ – Walk by the Spirit [76]

My Prayer for Us All

Father in heaven, thank You for Your grace and mercy in choosing me to be Your child before You created the world. I love You, Sir, for declaring peace with me through Your Son's great sacrifice. I praise You for hiding me in Jesus' love and His claim to be His own. Jesus, I will never imagine the pain and agony You felt when the Father turned away from You for the first time in all eternity because my disobedience (sin) was upon You. You expressed that pain on the

---

[76] Taught consistently by my friend and mentor, Ken Boa.

cross. Thank You for the salvation You alone have placed me into. Holy Spirit, forgive me for grieving You. I pray that You will fill my life today with Your presence. Today, I pray I listen to Your Word You authored. May Your Word continue to transform me to conform to the image of Jesus and His life. Please interpret this prayer as I can't even know how to pray to the ears of the Father. I love you, Father. I love You, Jesus. I love You, Holy Spirit. In the name of Jesus, my Messiah, I pray.

AFTERWARD

This book focuses on our relationship with God the Father, Jesus the Son, and the Holy Spirit. Talking about the longsuffering of God. Wow. There is no truer statement. Remember, we are not gods. Only God is God. The entire Bible can be summed up in this sentence: God is God, and we are not. Therefore, we can only know about God and what He has allowed to be revealed. We will always be the creature and He will always be the Creator. I hope you have grasped that God has so loved us beyond John 3:16 in that at every conceivable intersection of our historical walk with Him throughout the ages, He has intervened and has supernaturally provided what we needed to be **in Christ** to win our race set before us.

We are engaged in a cosmic battle that far exceeds any intensity of physical war the world has ever or will experience. The enemy? Of course, Satan and his host of fallen angelic principalities and powers. But in all the cosmic battle and evil, God the Father is in sovereign control in some plan that not even, I suppose, Michael, the Archangel of God, has any comprehension of.

Our only part in the battle is to be faithful to the transforming process that God the Father through Jesus and the Holy Spirit started once we became aware of our faith in Jesus' work on the cross. Our part is to learn the wisdom of being faithful to that process and letting loose of the results. All opportunities that come into our lives are because of Divine Sovereignty. Our sole human responsibility is obedience to His Word and will in the opportunities. We are called to let loose of the results because the outcome of those opportunities is also in His Divine Sovereignty.

If you have not done so already, I desire that you will fall in love with your first love again, Jesus. To believe and see yourself so enveloped in Christ that you will see as He sees, feel as He feels, and love as He loves but through you and as you. It goes so far beyond religion and showing up at church on Sunday, dropping a few bucks in the "plate," memorizing some Scripture, and serving soup in a breadline. It is passion. Passion for wanting to please God because you love Him so much!

Falling in love with Jesus is desiring to know the Word so much—to know Him, His character, and His attributes so that you will be able to love Him more, praise Him more, and worship Him more on a personal basis and not just corporately in church. It is from this intimate knowledge that passion rises and desires fire up. Going to church, Scripture study, reading and memorizing, praying and fellowship with other believers are not a means to themselves but parts of an overall passion to love God more each day than the day before. It is to truly be in a loving obedient walk with Him in a thoughtful, breathing, walking daily relationship.

Our bodies could not accomplish much without our skeleton of bones to hold it up and allow for the thousands of maneuvers it allows us to make. Without our skeletons, we would all be worthless blobs. Structure is needed for anything. We need structure, in our daily Christian walk. We need the disciplines of Bible study, Bible reading, prayer, worship personal and corporate, the body of believers in a church setting, sharing our faith, and serving in multiple ways. All of that is our Christian structure, our skeleton, but all of that is a means to an end. That end is our relationship with God the Father, Jesus the Son, and the Holy Spirit.

Out of all of those passionate desires, obedience is not a have-to or a must. Obedience becomes the fulfillment of those passionate desires, the ultimate thanks to God the Father, the focal point of our love for God. We finally understand that obedience to God's desires is the love language He seeks from us and we are finally speaking it to Him daily.

There is no arrival point. You are either growing closer to God, plateauing, or falling away. I hope Appendix A and B will help you in your daily pursuit of loving God.

It has been my privilege to write this book about my journey, a sojourn that continues as I type these words. I pray that you have found it helpful in deepening your loving obedience to God our Father.

Blessings, Charlie Thrall

TRUST the FATHER + ABIDE in the SON + WALK by the SPIRIT

You can practice the sentence above until it becomes second nature to you. Pray it often throughout your day.

Psalm 147:11 (AMP) — *The Lord favors those who fear and worship Him [with awe-inspired reverence and obedience], Those who wait for His mercy and lovingkindness.*

Appendix A

Obedience Is More Than You Have Been Taught[77]

Lordship over every aspect of life. Practicing the presence of God – everything matters. What you are called to do at a moment of action. Do it well as to the Lord, because it is. We are commanded "Rejoice always – Pray without ceasing and then give thanks. To abide in Him, Walk by the Spirit, Set your minds on the things above." And on and on. There are multiple practices that are not hints but actual commands.

Everything then can be a process where we are to immerse ourselves in His manifest presence and welcome Him into the routine and ordinary. Take out the trash. Wash the dishes. Helping with supper preparations. Everything you do, do it unto the King. There is no sacred/secular dichotomy.

http://kenboa.org/tag/8-spiritual-essentials/

[77] Dr. Kenneth Boa, "Everything Matters," Lecture from *The Tale of Two Visions Conference,* Part 1 of 4 March 2022, https://kenboa.org/library/living-out-your-faith/

Jesus asked three questions during His ministry that similarly pierce at the heart of spiritual matters:

1. "What do you seek?" – right now more than anything else? (John 1:38; "What are you looking for?" in some translations)
2. "Who do you say that I am?" – right now more than anyone else? (Matt. 16:15)
3. "Do you love Me more than these?" – are there "any" rivals in your life against Jesus? (John 21:15)

How we answer any one of these questions is indicative of our true desires and affections. Do we really want to follow Jesus, or do we want to live for ourselves?

Whoever does not long for and love God will live a self-centered life. Only when our desires are turned away from ourselves and toward the living God will we be able to live the Christian life.

Even lifelong Christians, though, easily shift back and forth between Christ-centered and self-centered living every day. The eight "essentials" in this series, therefore, are meant to center or re-center your desires and affections on Christ in day-to-day life.

1 Corinthians 14:23 — *Therefore if the whole church assembles together and all speak in tongues, and ungifted men or unbelievers enter, will they not say that you are mad?*

Take "tongues" out and apply any other "so-called" physical manifestation of the Holy Spirit - same point.

"Living on borrowed time to accomplish unfinished business."[78]

---

[78] Dr. Kenneth Boa, "8 Spiritual Essentials," Reflections with Ken Boa, November 30, 2018,

Appendix B

Suggested Further Study

Books from Dr. Kenneth Boa

Visit Dr. Boa's website. There is a wealth of resources there to download and to purchase: www.kenboa.org.

Devotionals:

Passionate Living Series, Handbook to Leadership, Handbook to Prayer, A Guided Tour of the Bible.

For great personal encounters with Scripture to grow you in your spiritual formation, I encourage you to seek Ken's work: *A Journal of Sacred Readings.*

Eternal Perspective Trilogy:

- *Rewriting Your Broken Story: The Power of an Eternal Perspective*
- *Life in the Presence of God: Practices for Living in Light of Eternity: A Guide to Practicing God's Presence*
- *Shaped by Suffering: How Temporary Hardships Prepare Us for Our Eternal Home*

Want to Know How to Change Your Daily Attitude, Perspective on Life:

Recalibrate Your Life: Navigating Transitions with Purpose and Hope

Want to Know Jesus More Intimately?

Then this bundle is your serious choice:

Conformed to His Image, Revised Edition: book + Study Guide + DVD Video Study

Note: There are a host of other choices from Dr. Boa, but the above choices would be a solid foundational start.

A Tool to Help You Abide in Christ:

The Word Hand illustration, by the Navigators, is an easy-to-remember tool highlighting five methods of learning from the Bible. We encourage you to use it to spur your own spiritual growth and to inspire others.

MEDITATE in the Word Psalm 1:2-3
MEMORIZE the Word Psalm 119:9-11
STUDY the Word Acts 17:11
READ the Word Revelation 1:3
HEAR the Word Romans 10:17

To download a copy, visit:
https://www.navigators.org/resource/the-word-hand/

Good Bible Study Tools to Have in Your Library

- *Talk Thru the Bible*, Bruce Wilkerson and Kenneth Boa, Thomas Nelson

- The Tony Evans Bible Commentary, Holman Reference

- Tony Evans Theology You Can Count On, Moody

- Biblical Theology of the Old Testament, Zuck and Merrill, DTS

- Biblical Theology of the New Testament, Zuck and Bock, DTS

- The Bible Knowledge Commentary Old Testament, New Testament, Walvoord and Zuck, DTS

- *The Moody Bible Commentary*, Rydelnik and Vanlaningham editors, Moody

- *Dr. Constable's Expository (Bible Study) Notes*, Dr Thomas L. Constable, Chair of Bible Exposition, retired, Dallas Theological Seminary. Dr. Constable has commentary notes on every book of the Bible. The notes are updated yearly with any new studies, etc. They are in PDF format and can be downloaded from the following link:

https://planobiblechapel.org/constable-notes/

Of course, there are numerous other tools available. I consider the above tools to be a mid-range blend of non-technical text discussions but solid Biblical hermeneutics in their resulting commentary.

In-depth Study into Jesus as the Messiah:

Dr. Arnold Fruchtenbaum's ministry, Ariel Ministries, Bible teaching from a Messianic Jewish Perspective. All of his and his team's writings, video, audio works can be found at the link below:

https://www.ariel.org/

Learn from the best on how to study the Bible:

Living By The Book: The Art and Science of Reading the Bible, Howard G., and William D. Hendricks Book, Study Guide and DVD. Simply the best in Bible study methods.

Want to draw closer to the humanity of Jesus?

I do not know a better resource than Gerry Hodges book: *JESUS: An Interview Across Time*, Andrew G. Hodges, M.D. Understand that this is a fictional story. But Gerry did extensive research in the Scriptures before writing this book.

https://andrewghodges.com/publications/
jesus-an-interview-across-time

If You Struggle with a Poor Self-image...

This book was used greatly by God's Spirit in my life as a young man and for re-reads since:

You're Someone Special, Narramore

It is out of print. I have found copies at www.Thriftbooks.com.

Struggling with Guilt?

Guilt is a huge gun that Satan uses against us. I found this book also was greatly used by God's Spirit as a young man and for re-reads since:

Freedom From Guilt, Narramore and Counts

It is out of print, I have found copies at www.Thriftbooks.com.

I purchase both of the above books and offer them to my Life Group at Church freely.

Appendix C

Scripture References

In the order of their occurrence.

Chapter One: Jesus is God, but ….

- John 3:16
- John 10:10b
- Romans 3:23
- Romans 6:23a
- Romans 5:8
- 1 Corinthians 15:3-6
- John 14:6
- John 1:12
- Ephesians 2:8-9
- Revelations 3:20
- 1 John 5:11-13
- Galatians 3:11
- Acts 2:24
- John 5:21
- Romans 4:17
- John 6:47
- 1 Corinthians 6:14

Chapter Two: The First Relationships, Jesus's Honorable Mention

- Genesis 1:26-31
- Genesis 2:15-17
- Genesis 2:18-24
- Genesis 1:26-27
- Genesis 2:7
- Genesis 1:26
- Genesis 2:22-25
- Genesis 3:1
- 1 Peter 1:12
- Genesis 3:1-5

Chapter Three: All About God's Words

- John 1:1-5
- Genesis 2:15
- Genesis 2:18
- Genesis 2:19
- Genesis 2:21
- Romans 6:1-11
- Chapter Four: The Hook Was Set Including Jesus
- Genesis 3:6a
- 1 John 2:16
- Ephesians 2:2-3a
- James 1:13-18
- 1 Corinthians 1:10-17,29-31
- Genesis 3:6

Chapter Five: Results When We Wanted to be God

- Genesis 3:7
- Genesis 3:8-11
- Genesis 3:11
- Genesis 3:7
- Genesis 3:8-13

- Ephesians 4:30-31
- Genesis 3: 12
- Genesis 3: 13
- James 5:16
- Genesis 3:14
- 1 John 3:8
- Genesis 3:16
- Genesis 3:17-19
- Numbers 32:23
- Galatians 6:7
- Genesis 3:20-21
- 1 Corinthians 15:44b-49
- Romans 5:12, 15-21
- Galatians 6:7

Chapter Six: God Tosses Us Out, Not Abandoned

- Genesis 4:3-5a
- Genesis 4:5b-8
- Genesis 4:4b-5a
- Genesis 4:5b-7
- Jeremiah 17:9-10
- I Samuel 16:5b-7
- Mark 12:41-44
- Matthew 5:21-24
- Genesis 4:4-7
- Genesis 4:6-7
- Ephesians 2:2-3a

Chapter Seven: God's Deep Grief Reveals His Deeper Compassion

- Genesis 4:8-10
- Genesis. 4:11-16
- Genesis. 4:25-26
- Genesis. 6:5-10

- Exodus 34:6
- Genesis 6:13-14a; 22
- Genesis 7:1,5
- Genesis 7:6-16
- Genesis 7:17-24
- Matt 24:37-41
- John 3:16-18
- Genesis 7:21a-23a
- Genesis. 6:5-10
- Genesis 9:1-3
- Genesis 9:8-17
- Revelation 19:11-16
- Genesis 6:9-10

Chapter Eight: Earth 2.0

- Genesis 8:20-21
- Genesis. 9:1-3
- Genesis 9:6-7
- Genesis 9:18-19
- Genesis 10:1,32
- Genesis 9:7
- Genesis 11:1-4
- Genesis 11:7-9
- Isaiah 55:8-11
- Romans 1:18-24
- Job 42:2
- Isaiah 55:8-9
- Genesis 10:1,32
- Genesis 9:26-27
- Hebrews 1:1-4
- Genesis. 12:1-3
- Genesis 12:7
- Genesis 13:14-17
- Genesis 15:3-6

- Genesis 22:15-18
- Genesis 15:12-16
- Genesis 3:21
- Genesis 4:4-5
- Hebrews 9:18-23
- Hebrews 10:1-4
- John 1:19-34
- Isaiah 55:8-9

Chapter Nine: Jesus is God's Message

- Deuteronomy 18:15-22
- Hosea 6:6-7
- Hebrews 7:23-28
- Hebrews 8:6
- Hebrews 8:7-13
- Psalm 2:1-2,7
- Daniel 7:13-14
- 2 Samuel 7:12,16
- Joel 2:23
- Isaiah 52:13
- Deuteronomy 18:15-19
- Isaiah 7:14
- Isaiah 9:6-7
- Isaiah 4:2
- Jeremiah 23:5-6
- Ezekiel 34:11-16
- Isaiah 49:5-6
- Matthew 9:35-38
- Matthew 12:22-24
- Matthew 12: 25-28
- Matthew 12: 31-32
- Matthew 23:37

Chapter Ten: How Do I Not Break the Heart of God?

- 1 Peter 2:1-3
- 2 Timothy 1:8b-9
- 1 Corinthians 1:18
- Romans 5:9-10
- Matthew 3:16-17
- Matthew 3:13-15
- Colossians 3:23
- Ephesians 1:1-2
- Ephesians 1:3
- Ephesians 1:4-6
- Romans 3: 9:b-18
- Ephesians 1:7-14
- Ephesians 1:15-16
- Ephesians 1:17-19a
- Ephesians 1:19b-23
- Ephesians 2:1-3
- Ephesians 2:4-9
- Ephesians 2:8-10
- Isaiah 42:1, 5-7
- Isaiah 49:3-6
- Romans 15:5-12
- Romans 15:15-16
- Ephesians 2:17-22
- Ephesians 3:4-12

Chapter Eleven: Mature Love, Look to the Man, Jesus

- Philippians 2:2
- Philippians 2:3-4
- Philippians 2:5-8
- Philippians 2:9-11
- John 14:5-6
- John 14:7

- John 14:8
- John 14:9-11
- John 14:15
- John 14:20-21
- John 14:22-24
- John 15:9-11
- 1 John 2:3-6
- 2 John 6
- Galatians 2:20
- John 17:23

About the Author

Charles A Thrall, "Charlie," is Texas born and bred. Holds a BA in Philosophy from the University of Central Florida, 88 graduate level hours of study in the ThM program at Dallas Theological Seminary, and a Certificate of Biblical and Theological Studies from Dallas Theological Seminary. He has been an entrepreneur for most of his adult life in several computer-related businesses. He has served as an intern on a church's staff, as a staff pastor of adult ministries, as an adult Bible class teacher, and as a leader in several home-based Bible study groups and has preached a few times when given the opportunity. Married for over 29 years to his lovely bride, Shirley, with a blended family of three sons, one daughter, three daughters-in-law, and eight grandchildren.

The Crisis in Continental Philosophy

Continuum Studies in Continental Philosophy
Series Editor: James Fieser, University of Tennessee at Martin, USA

Continuum Studies in Continental Philosophy is a major monograph series from Continuum. The series features first-class scholarly research monographs across the field of Continental philosophy. Each work makes a major contribution to the field of philosophical research.

The Crisis in Continental Philosophy
History, Truth and the Hegelian Legacy

Robert Piercey

continuum

Continuum International Publishing Group

The Tower Building	80 Maiden Lane
11 York Road	Suite 704
London SE1 7NX	New York NY 10038

www.continuumbooks.com

British Library Cataloguing-in-Publication Data
A catalogue record for this book is available from the British Library.

ISBN-13: 978-1-4411-1804-2 (Paperback)

Library of Congress Cataloguing-in-Publication Data
Piercey, Robert.
  The crisis in continental philosophy : history, truth and the Hegelian legacy / Robert Piercey.
  p. cm.
  Includes bibliographical references.
ISBN 978-1-4411-1804-2
  1. Continental philosophy. I. Title.

B791.P54 2009
190–dc22   2008033783

Typeset by Newgen Imaging Systems Pvt Ltd, Chennai, India
Printed and bound in the UK by the MPG Books Group

Dedicated to my mother,
Louise Piercey,
and to the memory of my father,
Douglas Piercey

Contents

Acknowledgments

I began working on this book at the University of Notre Dame. The first debt I have to record is to Notre Dame for providing me with such an agreeable place to work. Notre Dame provided me with an environment that was humane as well as rigorous, challenging but not soul-crushing. This was largely because the people who worked with me there (Karl Ameriks, Gerald Bruns, Fred Dallmayr, Gary Gutting, and Steve Watson) are all remarkably decent people as well as remarkably accomplished scholars. Some other remarkably decent people took good care of me at Notre Dame as well: Montey Holloway, Coleen Hoover, Paul Weithman, and especially Ann Pouk. I'm grateful to all of them.

I also have some more official debts to acknowledge. My research for this book was funded by the Social Science and Humanities Research Council of Canada. I'm grateful for this assistance, and for the research grant from Campion College that helped me to revise the manuscript. Also at Campion, Benjamin Fiore, S. J. and Samira McCarthy deserve my thanks for their constant help and encouragement. I'd like to thank several journals for letting me reuse material that has already been published elsewhere. Some material from Chapter 1 originally appeared in *Idealistic Studies* 35. Part of Chapter 2 was first published in *International Studies in Philosophy* 36. An early version of Chapter 4 appeared in *Human Studies* 27. Finally, material from Chapters 2 and 5 appeared in *International Philosophical Quarterly* 43.

I'm indebted to Sarah Campbell and Thomas Crick at Continuum for their many helpful suggestions about the project, and to Jim Fieser for helping to bring the project to press. I'm indebted as well to my tireless research assistant Sarah Gray, who made the process of writing the book much easier. I'm always indebted to Anna, who gets to watch this process from a front row seat, and who probably wonders more often than she admits just what she's gotten herself into. Most of all, I'm indebted to my parents: my mother,

Louise Piercey, and my late father, Douglas Piercey. They supported me in every way imaginable as I started studying philosophy, and if they were disappointed that I didn't go to law school, they never showed it. Books meant a lot to my father. I think he would have liked this one.

Abbreviations

The following abbreviations are used to refer to frequently cited titles:

BT   *Martin Heidegger,* Being and Time, *trans. John Macquarrie and Edward Robinson. San Francisco: Harper Collins, 1962.*

EL   G. W. F. Hegel, *The Encyclopedia Logic*, trans. T. F. Geraets, W. A. Suchting, and H. S. Harris. Indianapolis: Hackett Publishing Company, 1991.

KRV   Immanuel Kant, *Critique of Pure Reason*, trans. Norman Kemp Smith. London: Macmillan, 1927.

LHP   G. W. F. Hegel, *Lectures on the History of Philosophy*, Volume One, trans. E. S. Haldane. Lincoln: University of Nebraska Press, 1995.

OG   Jacques Derrida, *Edmund Husserl's* Origin of Geometry*: An Introduction*, trans. John P. Leavey. Lincoln: University of Nebraska Press, 1978.

PS   G. W. F. Hegel, *Phenomenology of Spirit*, trans. A. V. Miller. Oxford: Oxford University Press, 1977.

TA   *Paul Ricoeur,* From Text to Action*, trans. Kathleen Blamey and John Thompson. Evanston: Northwestern University Press, 1991.*

TI   *Emmanuel Levinas,* Totality and Infinity, *trans. Alphonso Lingis. Pittsburgh: Duquesne University Press, 1969.*

TM   *Hans-Georg Gadamer,* Truth and Method, *2nd ed., trans. Joel Weinsheimer and Donald Marshall. New York: Crossroads, 1992.*

TN1   Paul Ricoeur, *Time and Narrative*, Volume One, trans. Kathleen McLaughlin and David Pellauer. Chicago: University of Chicago Press, 1984.

TN3   Paul Ricoeur, *Time and Narrative*, Volume Three, trans. Kathleen McLaughlin and David Pellauer. Chicago: University of Chicago Press, 1988.

Introduction

An inherently historical discipline?

Why do we study the history of philosophy? Why do we think it is important for philosophers to know something about the history of their discipline? Philosophy is, after all, a problem-solving enterprise. Philosophers set out to answer perennial questions about the good, the true, and the beautiful. And it is not clear why someone who wants to solve these problems needs to pay attention to the history of other attempts—generally *failed* attempts—to solve them. Mathematicians do not think they must study the history of mathematics if they are to solve the problems posed by their discipline. Chemists and physicists do not think they have to study the history of science in order to do their experiments properly. Yet many philosophers think they must be familiar with the history of their enterprise if they are to engage in it properly themselves. Why? Why is an acquaintance with past thought considered important in philosophy but not in other problem-solving disciplines?

The answer usually given is that studying the history of philosophy helps us to *do* philosophy. On this view, contemporary philosophers have questions they wish to answer, and the history of philosophy is a repository of possible answers to them. We read Aristotle on the virtues because *we* have questions about the virtues, and Aristotle's writings may contain the answers to them. Jonathan Bennett sums up this view quite well when he says that '[w]e study philosophy's past because it may lead us straight to philosophical truths.'[1] Bennett's work is a clear example of how one might study the history of philosophy in search of the answers to contemporary philosophical questions. And while Bennett's writings have been savagely attacked for misrepresenting the work of earlier thinkers,[2] such distortions are perfectly in keeping with his conception of the history of

philosophy. The historian's task, according to Bennett, is not to determine what Spinoza and Kant really thought, but to mine their work for
answers to contemporary questions. Whether our histories are good, bad,
or not really histories at all is beside the point. What matters is that we
exploit these thinkers in a way that advances our own philosophical projects. Studying the history of philosophy, in short, is subordinate to *doing*
philosophy.

Bennett's view of the history of philosophy is the most common one,
but there are subtler variations on it. Some argue that studying the history of philosophy is not a way of answering contemporary philosophical questions, but a precondition of posing those questions properly. On
this view, great historical texts need not lead us *straight* to philosophical truths. We cannot expect to open Plato's dialogues and find out, for
example, whether uncaused free action is possible or moral values objective. But if we are to pose these, or any, philosophical questions intelli-
gently, we must understand how they have been shaped by the history of
philosophical thought. Edwin Curley defends a view of this sort. Curley
argues that 'making progress towards solving philosophical problems
requires a good grasp of the range of possible solutions to those problems and of the arguments which motivate alternative positions, a grasp
we can only have if we understand well philosophy's past.'[3] Note that on
Curley's view—unlike Bennett's—it is important for us to be *good* historians. If we are to appreciate the range of alternatives open to us, then
we must not view Spinoza and Kant as mere resources to be mined. We
must try to understand them in their own terms and to get their philosophies right. Nevertheless, Curley agrees with Bennett that studying the
history of philosophy is subordinate to doing philosophy. We must study
this history properly, but the ultimate *reason* we study it is to advance our
contemporary agendas.

These views have something in common. Though Bennett and Curley
see the history of philosophy as important, they do not think it has any
intrinsic importance. For both, we study the history of philosophy because
it offers resources that we happen not to be able to get in other ways. But
our inability to get these resources in other ways is, finally, an accidental
fact about the kinds of creatures we are. Bennett argues that we must study
the history of philosophy because it may contain the answers to our own
philosophical questions. But we might ask: Is it truly *necessary* to find these

answers in the history of philosophy? Or could we arrive at them on our own, through ahistorical reflection? Perhaps *we* cannot; perhaps we are not smart enough or imaginative enough to answer our philosophical questions without consulting history. But this is a purely contingent fact about us, and there seems to be nothing preventing more clever thinkers from doing philosophy without studying its past. Similarly, Curley maintains that we must study the history of philosophy in order to appreciate the range of possible answers to our own philosophical questions. But again, is a study of the history of philosophy really *necessary* on this view? Would it not be possible to arrive at a proper understanding of our philosophical questions, if only we were clever enough or imaginative enough? In short, if we view the history of philosophy as a handmaiden to the doing of philosophy, then it can be important only *per accidens*, not *per se*. We seem forced to conclude that, as Louis Dupré puts it, the history of philosophy is 'devoid of any *intrinsic* philosophical significance.'⁴

For the last two centuries, however, a large subculture has seen matters differently. It has denied that the practice of philosophy and the study of its history are separate enterprises connected only accidentally. It has denied that philosophy is one thing, its history something else, and that the latter is simply an instrument that helps us with the former. This subculture has maintained that the attempt to separate philosophy and its past, and the desire to subordinate the latter to the former, is misguided in principle. As Lesley Cohen puts it, these philosophers maintain that 'philosophy is an *essentially* historical enterprise.'⁵ They argue not only that philosophers must study the history of their discipline, but that they must do so because of something internal to philosophy itself. This view is admittedly not common in Anglo-American philosophy, though it does have some distinguished Anglo-American proponents—Charles Taylor, Alasdair MacIntyre, and Louis Dupré, for example. It is more commonly associated with so-called 'continental' philosophers: with Derrida and Gadamer, with Dilthey and Heidegger, and above all with Hegel. Taylor has even given this view of philosophy a name: the 'historical thesis about philosophy.'⁶ Roughly, it is the view that '[p]hilosophy and the history of philosophy are one,' such that we 'cannot do the first without also doing the second.'⁷

Why would one think that the historical thesis is true? Why would one view philosophy as an inherently historical discipline? And how would one

go about *showing* that it is? Given the prevalence of the historical thesis in continental philosophy, one would expect the members of this tradition to have impressive resources for posing and answering these questions. But this is not the case. Despite widespread acceptance of the historical thesis, contemporary continental thought has done surprisingly little to clarify it. For one thing, there is a striking lack of explicit arguments for the historical thesis in contemporary continental philosophy. The importance of history is often taken as an article of faith, with few philosophers seeing the need to argue for it. Further, the arguments that have been advanced—or that can be reconstructed by sympathetic interpreters—are often not very good. Most troubling of all, there is no agreement about what kind of argument is appropriate here—that is, about what the historical thesis *means*. So while contemporary European philosophers tend to agree that there is a close relation between philosophy and its past, they are surprisingly silent about what this relation is and why it obtains. This is an odd situation, and one that cries out for explanation. As I will argue, it could be described as a 'crisis,' in Husserl's sense of the term. A certain view of the history of philosophy is taken for granted in a great deal of contemporary continental philosophy, but without being explicitly defended or adequately understood. How could this have happened? Why is continental thinking about the history of philosophy marked by a crisis, a consensus that masks a deep lack of understanding?

This book offers a diagnosis and critique of the crisis. It tries to explain how continental thinking about the history of philosophy became mired in confusion, and to show what the continental tradition must do to come to terms with this crisis. The book constructs a narrative about the development of the crisis—a narrative that explains how the crisis originated early in the history of the continental tradition, and was unwittingly transmitted to later thought. My central claim is that the crisis originates in Hegel's way of thinking about the relation between philosophy and its past. It persists because this Hegelian framework has remained in place in more recent philosophy, often despite appearances to the contrary. Specifically, I argue that the crisis originates in Hegel's incomplete break with Kant. Hegel rejects Kant's view of the history of philosophy while retaining the epistemological assumptions that give rise to it. The result is a deeply incoherent conception of the history of philosophy. I then show how this incoherent framework has been passed down to contemporary

philosophy through a line of thinkers influenced by Hegel. At each stage of this historical development, one of these thinkers tries to rearticulate a Hegelian understanding of the history of philosophy in the face of Kantian criticism. But at each stage, the rearticulation is unsuccessful, because it remains rooted in the framework that rendered Hegel's own account problematic. Thus my narrative exhibits a recurring pattern. First, a Kantian orthodoxy about the history of philosophy emerges. Then there is a Hegelian break with this orthodoxy, one that ultimately fails because of the hidden assumptions it shares with its Kantian opponent. As a result, a new Kantian orthodoxy replaces it. Then a new Hegelian view emerges, one that tries both to reject the Kantian picture of the history of philosophy and to solve the difficulties that plagued the last Hegelian account. This new Hegelian view in turn collapses because of *its* unrecognized affinities with Kant, and so the pattern continues. An attempt to defend the historical thesis about philosophy, therefore, typically emerges in dialogue with both external and internal difficulties. The external difficulties take the form of criticisms from Kantian and neo-Kantian thinkers who reject the historical thesis. The internal difficulties take the form of problems that made the last formulation of the historical thesis incoherent.

The book is divided into five chapters. In Chapter 1, I make a prima facie case for my claim that continental work on the history of philosophy is in crisis. The chapter surveys three prominent branches of continental philosophy that attach considerable importance to the history of philosophy: Derridean deconstruction, Gadamerian hermeneutics, and the ethical thought of Emmanuel Levinas. I explore why each of these schools sees philosophy as inherently historical, and I argue that each is confused in important respects about the relation between philosophy and its past. Finally, I claim that this widespread confusion should be understood as a crisis, in Husserl's sense. Like Husserl, I propose that the best way to make sense of this confusion is to tell the story of how it originated.

Chapter 2 begins this story. It describes the first major episode in the development of the historical thesis: the emergence of this thesis in Hegel's work. Chapter 2 argues that Hegel's approach to the history of philosophy is the source of the contemporary crisis. It tries to show that by setting the terms of the debate about the history of philosophy as he did, Hegel

helped guarantee that this history would be misunderstood by later thinkers. Hegel's version of the historical thesis seeks to realize two opposed
goals: first, to reject Kant's claim that the study of the history of philosophy
is not really part of philosophy; and second, to salvage the ultimate source
of Kant's claim, namely the Kantian view of mimesis. Hegel's attempt to
retain both is unsuccessful, and it gives rise to a deeply incoherent understanding of the relation between philosophy and its past.

Chapter 3 deals with the next important episode in the development of
the historical thesis: Heidegger's reappropriation of Hegel's approach to
the history of philosophy. In this chapter, I examine Heidegger's attempt
to articulate a version of the historical thesis about philosophy in the 1920s
and 1930s. I interpret Heidegger's work from this period as an attempt to
solve the problems that plagued Hegel's way of thinking about the history
of philosophy, while retaining Hegel's claim that philosophy is inherently
historical. I argue, however, that Heidegger's attempt to amend Hegel is
incomplete and ultimately unsuccessful. Heidegger remains trapped within
a Hegelian framework for thinking about the history of philosophy, but
does not recognize this fact. Whereas Hegel gives us an incoherent picture
of the relation between philosophy and its history, Heidegger transforms
this picture so that its incoherence is covered up.

Chapter 4 brings the story up to the present. It shows how the crisis
has persisted in more recent European philosophy, despite sophisticated
attempts to move beyond it. Specifically, it examines the work of Paul
Ricoeur, and argues that the disguised incoherence that Heidegger contributed to continental thinking about the history of philosophy dominates
Ricoeur's thought as well. Like Heidegger, Ricoeur thinks that philosophy
is an inherently historical enterprise. And like Heidegger, he thinks that
this is so for decidedly un-Hegelian reasons. But—again like Heidegger—
Ricoeur tries to amend Hegel's version of the historical thesis without
uprooting the Kantian premises that underlie it. Ricoeur therefore shows
how easy it is for contemporary philosophy to remain within the framework articulated by Hegel.

In Chapter 5, I criticize this framework. I show that the Kantian account
of mimesis—which, I argue, is the ultimate source of the crisis—is dubious.
Drawing on recent work in aesthetics, I argue that a different understanding of mimesis is preferable, and I sketch some of the criteria that such an

account would have to meet. Next, I claim that adopting this new view of mimesis forces us to rethink what it means for a history of philosophy to be true. It requires that we reinterpret truth as something that is genuinely *in* history. The chapter closes with some suggestions about how to do so.

Finally, in the book's conclusion, I return to the present, and ask whether this new account of historical knowledge is compatible with the major positions in contemporary continental thought. I argue that if we think truth can be genuinely in history, then Gadamerian hermeneutics is the most promising fellow traveler. It does, however, need to be modified in some ways. Thus my narrative does not just diagnose a problem in contemporary philosophy; it offers a way of adjudicating among rival contemporary positions.

This book is primarily critical. It examines earlier attempts to argue for the historical thesis, shows that they are confused, and explains how they became widely accepted despite this confusion. While I sketch some of the criteria that a successful argument for the historical thesis would have to meet, I do not give such an argument myself. This silence should not be taken as a suggestion that no good argument is possible. Perhaps such an argument is possible; perhaps not. I suspect it is best to remain neutral on the issue. After all, one of the lessons of this book is that philosophy's historical turn is *much* more complicated than has usually been realized. As a result, the task of formulating a new argument for the historical thesis is best left aside for now. Besides, a study of this sort need not provide a new argument to be valuable. As Stanley Rosen has pointed out, not all contributions to philosophy take the form of a solution to a problem. Sometimes we contribute to philosophy simply by clarifying a problem.[8] That is all I hope to do here.

Still, while I do not rule out the possibility of a successful argument for the historical thesis, I might encourage a certain skepticism about such arguments. I spend several hundred pages studying a great many arguments advanced by a great many philosophers, and I claim that none of them work. If Hegel, Heidegger, and Ricoeur cannot give a satisfactory argument for the historical thesis, then what chance does anyone else have? To paraphrase Alasdair MacIntyre, should we not think there is no good argument for the historical thesis for the same reason we think there are no unicorns—namely, that every attempt to prove that there *are*

unicorns has failed?⁹ Perhaps. Perhaps this study will encourage a certain skepticism about the project of arguing for the historical thesis. Perhaps it will be tempting to conclude that if Hegel, Heidegger, and Ricoeur cannot formulate good arguments for the historical thesis, then the prospects of anyone else doing so are bleak. I see no way to rule out this skeptical conclusion. But even if we do draw this conclusion, it does not follow that we have no good reason to see philosophy as an inherently historical enterprise. A failure to *argue* for the historical thesis is not the same thing as a failure to *justify* it. We endorse philosophical positions for all sorts of reasons, and the availability of a sound argument is only one. Another is a lack of alternatives. We sometimes endorse a position for which we lack sound arguments because its alternatives are obviously worse. Thus we might endorse the historical thesis in the absence of sound arguments because the attempt to define philosophy in *ahistorical* terms leads to problems more serious than those raised by the historical thesis itself.¹⁰ So even if we are skeptical about all arguments for the historical thesis, it does not follow that we have no good reason to accept it. It might just be that our reasons are not arguments, in any usual sense of the term. But if this is so, we must recognize that it is so. The real enemy is not a lack of arguments, but a lack of clarity.

This book covers a lot of ground. It discusses quite a few figures—Kant, Hegel, and Heidegger, to list just a few—whose work is complex and difficult. I have no illusions about doing justice to these figures. I am keenly aware of how sweeping my claims are, and of how little one can demonstrate in a book of this length. I do not claim to have said the last word about these figures. I do not even claim to have given a satisfactory treatment of their views of the history of philosophy. For that reason, I implore my readers not to see this book as a piece of Hegel or Heidegger scholarship—that is, as a balanced and comprehensive account of the details of their work. Instead, the book examines a *style of thinking*, a philosophical tendency that it both tempting and quite widespread. This is the tendency to think that history is important for reasons connected with something outside of history. It is the tendency to see the history of philosophy as a vehicle for teaching lessons about something distinct from it. This tendency is what I mean when I speak of the 'Hegelian legacy.' It is a tendency that I think really is at work in the figures I discuss, even though it is only one aspect of their thought. In short, what this book

offers is a *way of looking* at French and German thought of the past two centuries. It is certainly not the only way. But it is a way of looking that sheds new light on a wide range of figures and problems. If the book has a contribution to make, it lies not in what it adds to Hegel or Heidegger scholarship, but in what it *discloses*: what it helps us to see about the state of philosophy today.

Chapter 1

The Crisis in Contemporary Continental Philosophy

This chapter deals with contemporary continental philosophy. But the phrase 'continental philosophy' will make some readers suspicious, since it is often considered a dubious and unhelpful label. 'Continental philosophy' does not name a doctrine or a method. It is usually used to refer to French and German philosophy since Kant, and as Brian Leiter has pointed out, as many as nine distinct philosophical traditions coexist in France and Germany during this period.[1] Some of these traditions have little in common. German idealism, for example, seems to share little with Husserlian phenomenology, and even less with the traditions of structuralism and post-structuralism. But while the term 'continental philosophy' is problematic, it is well-established as a professional self-description. British and American universities offer courses in it; professional organizations devote themselves to the study of it. The term itself has a surprisingly long history, having been used at least since the time of John Stuart Mill.[2] More importantly, while there is probably no position endorsed by *every* so-called continental philosopher, there are themes that recur again and again in post-Kantian French and German thought. As different as Hegel is from the post-structuralist Michel Foucault, both share an abiding concern with 'the social dimension of knowledge'[3]—a concern that was rare among English-speaking philosophers until recently. Identifying these recurring themes is not only possible, but of great interest.

One of the most widespread of these themes concerns the importance of the history of philosophy. Nearly all of the French and German traditions since Kant contain figures who claim that philosophy and its history are intimately linked. Despite their differences, these figures agree that philosophy is an inherently historical discipline, and that we cannot do philosophy properly without studying its past. Consider Hegel's declaration that 'the

study of the history of philosophy is the study of philosophy itself' (*LHP*, 30). Consider Heidegger's claim, made a century later, that '[w]hatever and however we may try to think, we think within the sphere of tradition.'[4] Or consider Husserl's insistence near the end of his career that '[e]very-where the problems, the clarifying investigations, the insights of principle are *historical*.'[5] These figures belong to three distinct traditions: the traditions of German idealism, philosophical hermeneutics, and phenomenology respectively. Yet they seem to agree that the 'history of philosophy is not an arbitrary appendage to the business of teaching philosophy.'[6] If anything, agreement on this matter is even more widespread in recent French and German thought. When thinkers such as Derrida declare that metaphysics is 'closed,' and that 'every transgressive gesture reencloses us within the closure,'[7] they seem to be devising new names for an old idea. Like Hegel, Heidegger, and many other figures, they are insisting that philosophy cannot turn its back on its past, but must revisit its history again and again. In short, if we had to identify a single theme running through the various traditions of continental thought, we could do worse than to say, with Robert Bernasconi, that 'continental philosophy is defined by its readiness to face the challenge posed by the recognition of the historicity of philosophy.'[8]

A quick look at continental philosophy reveals something of a consensus about the importance of the history of philosophy. A closer look shows something different. Despite widespread acceptance of the historical thesis, continental thought tends to be quite muddled in its thinking about the history of philosophy. For one thing, there is a striking lack of arguments for the historical thesis. It is often taken as an article of faith, with few philosophers seeing the need to explain why they accept it. Those arguments that have been advanced in support of this thesis often appear quite bad. Above all, even the most distinguished continental philosophers seem to be unsure what claim they are defending when they say that philosophy is inherently historical. While these thinkers see the historical thesis as clearly true, neither they nor their readers seem to have a clear grasp of what it means. Their discussions of this topic tend to be so full of tensions, confusions, and inconsistencies that they verge on incoherence. As I have suggested, this state of affairs could be described as a *crisis*, in Husserl's sense of the term: a consensus that masks a deep lack of understanding.

This chapter makes a prima facie case for my claim that continental work on the history of philosophy is in crisis. I survey three prominent continental schools that attach great importance to the history of philosophy: Derridean deconstruction; Gadamerian hermeneutics; and the ethical thought of Emmanuel Levinas. I ask why these schools see philosophy as inherently historical, and I argue that each is confused in important ways about the link between philosophy and its past. But why these figures, and not others? First, I suspect they are as representative as any three thinkers could be. One would be hard pressed to find three other continental philosophers who are as widely discussed and as influential as Derrida, Gadamer, and Levinas. At the same time, one would be hard pressed to find a better cross-section of themes and concerns than the one provided by their work. Their thought deals with—to use some decidedly un-continental labels—epistemology, ethics, semantics, and the philosophy of religion, for example. A survey of these figures offers as comprehensive a picture of continental philosophy as it is possible to give in a short study. Second, Derrida, Gadamer, and Levinas are good examples of a style of thinking whose development I will trace in the chapters that follow. In these later chapters, I will argue that the historical thesis about philosophy is best understood as a way of thinking that originates in Hegel's work, is transmitted by Hegel to Heidegger and, through Heidegger, is passed along to more recent continental thought. Derrida, Gadamer, and Levinas fit into this historical development particularly well because they all take their beginnings from Heidegger. They are good subjects for a discussion of the historical thesis because their work draws attention to the evolution of this thesis. Derrida, Gadamer, and Levinas help to illustrate a line of development that extends from Hegel to the present.

All I am seeking here is a prima facie case for the claim that continental thought about the history of philosophy is in crisis. I cannot discuss all the figures and schools that fall under the label 'continental philosophy.' It may well be that other thinkers have more satisfactory approaches to the history of philosophy than the ones I examine here. Nor am I suggesting that the work of Derrida, Gadamer, and Levinas is hopelessly flawed and not worth reading. I am merely surveying their views on a single topic. My goal is to show that if we quickly survey what continental philosophy has to say about this topic, we will find enough signs of a crisis to warrant a closer

look into what has gone wrong. The closer look will come in Chapters 2, 3, and 4.

Derrida and the persistence of logocentrism

We might describe Derrida's project as a certain kind of critique of the philosophical tradition. Derrida's aim is to draw our attention to a way of thinking that he believes has dominated Western philosophy, and to undermine the pretensions of this way of thinking. Derrida refers to this way of thinking in a variety of ways, calling it 'logocentrism,' 'phallocentrism,' and 'phallogocentrism,' for instance. But Derrida's target is most usefully described as the *metaphysics of presence*. For Derrida, the metaphysics of presence is a set of unspoken ontological assumptions that identify what is with what can be made fully and unequivocally present to us. Derrida has in mind our tendency to assume that 'Being' means nothing more than the totality of entities that exist at the present moment; to think of the subject as a node of consciousness completely identical with itself; and to identify meaning with the intentions present in a speaker's mind. Derrida sides with the forces that would 'decenter' these ways of thinking.[9] He allies himself with 'the Heideggerian destruction of metaphysics, of onto-theology, of the determination of Being as presence;'[10] with Freud's unraveling of the subject's self-identity; and with Nietzsche's celebration of play, perspective, and a 'mobile army of metaphors.'[11] Of course, Derrida's project is not wholly negative. He also sets himself positive tasks, such as the development of a new vocabulary that will allow us to speak of that which exceeds metaphysical thinking. But it is clear that a certain kind of critique drives Derrida's project. Derrida's work is an attempt to show how philosophical thinking has been structured by ideals that cannot be sustained.

But Derrida does not simply turn his back on the tradition. He does not urge us, as Descartes does, 'to demolish everything completely and start again right from the foundations.'[12] Derrida's critique engages with the tradition. Instead of sweeping aside the tradition and beginning anew, Derrida goes to work '*within* the text of the history of philosophy.'[13] He develops his critique of the metaphysics of presence from inside the metaphysics of presence—by reading central texts of the metaphysical tradition and undermining their pretensions from within. Rather than arguing that the principles of logocentric thinking are false, Derrida points out ways in

which specific works fail to live up to these principles. For that reason, his work typically takes the form of commentaries on texts. Moreover, Derrida does not just happen to carry out his critique by engaging with the history of philosophy. He claims that he *must* engage with the tradition, since escaping the history of philosophy is impossible. 'There is,' he writes, 'no sense in doing without the concepts of metaphysics in order to shake metaphysics. We have no language—no syntax and no lexicon—which is foreign to this history.'[14] We cannot criticize the metaphysical tradition from an external vantage-point. All we can do is rattle it from within. As Derrida puts it, 'the passage beyond philosophy does not consist in turning the page of philosophy (which usually amounts to philosophizing badly), but in continuing to read philosophers *in a certain way*.'[15] So it is clear that Derrida accepts the historical thesis about philosophy. He thinks that his project requires him to confront the history of philosophy over and over again. Derrida's programmatic statements, as well as his practice of commenting on texts, make this clear. But why does Derrida think this? Answering this question is not easy, since Derrida nowhere advances an explicit historiography of philosophy. We should not expect Derrida to defend his view in so many words. But we can try to make explicit the conception of the history of the philosophy that is at work in Derrida's texts. Why, then, does Derrida see his work as enclosed within the history of the metaphysics of presence? What is it about his project that compels him to engage with the history of philosophy?

   The answer has to do with the ambitions of the metaphysics of presence. As I have suggested, Derrida claims that Western philosophy has been preoccupied with the *presence* of entities: with the alleged fact that beings are best understood as what is 'present' to us, in all senses of the word. It has been preoccupied with the ways in which beings are 'presented'— that is, made available to us, or placed before us as objects. Moreover, its way of doing so has privileged the present moment over the other temporal modalities, and identified the being of entities with their 'nowness.' The tradition, Derrida says, has thought of beings in terms of 'the absolute proximity of self-identity, the being-in-front of the object available for repetition, the maintenance [*maintenant*] of the temporal present.'[16] It has assigned itself the task of accounting for this presence, of explaining how beings are made present in the first place. This attempt is best embodied by the epistemological tradition, which has sought to account for our

'knowledge of the presence of the object.'[17] But Derrida also sees it in other projects. Implicit in this way of thinking is the assumption that objects *are* present to consciousness. In Derrida's view, Western philosophy has not adequately considered the possibility that objects are not fully present to consciousness—not fully available as objects, and not capable of being exhaustively understood in terms of 'nowness.' It has taken for granted that objects are present, and it has been content to try to explain how this presence is possible.

It is natural to bristle at the reductionism of this story. But surely a great many figures in the history of philosophy *have* considered it indisputable that beings are made present to us, and that the philosopher's task is to explain how this presence is possible. Consider Plato's invocation of the Forms in his early and middle dialogues. The Forms are posited to explain our ability to know intelligible, changeless entities when no such entities are encountered in sensible experience. Or consider Kant's transcendental conditions of possible cognition, which are posited to account for our ability to know things about physical events—for example, that they are causally connected—that are never actually perceived in them. It is not implausible to suggest that these projects have thought it more important to explain how the presence of entities is possible than to ask whether it is. According to Derrida, these projects embody a way of thinking that is rampant in the tradition. That is why he maintains that Western philosophy has been guided by the metaphysics of presence.

Derrida occasionally makes the same point in a slightly different way. He argues that Western philosophy has been preoccupied with *sense*: with the ability of beings to *mean* something for consciousness. It has repeatedly tried to account for the phenomenon of sense, and to explain how it is possible for entities to *be* something for us at all. More specifically, it has taken for granted the existence of univocal sense—sense that is fixed, unchanging, and so constantly 'present.' But to say that the tradition has been preoccupied with sense is to say that it has been concerned with the presence of beings to consciousness. It is to say that the tradition has tried to give an account of sense, an explanation of how entities come to be presented to us, or become meaningful for us. The tradition has tried to find the origin of sense and presence: that, whatever it is, that allows entities to mean something. And the tradition has found it easier to assume that there is sense than to ask whether there is.

In Derrida's view, the tradition's concern with presence and sense has led it to be suspicious of history. Most often, Western philosophy has looked for the origin of sense outside the empirical and outside history. It has insisted that what makes sense possible cannot be an event in history or a part of the empirical world. The tradition has tended to assume that the answers to its guiding questions lie outside history, outside the empirical world, rather than within it. Again, this is a sweeping claim, but it is not without plausibility. The philosophical tradition does have a strong ahistorical streak. It is littered with attempts to jump outside the contingencies of history and the empirical world, and to ground our access to objects on something altogether different. Consider Plato's Forms, or Kant's conditions of possible cognition, or Descartes's non-deceiving God, or any number of other such grounds. Regardless of the examples one chooses, the tradition has seemed to assume that sense, or the presence of objects, is not explicable in merely historical terms. It has maintained that the origin of sense is not within history. The metaphysics of presence has most often been a search for 'what—*although it has no truth in itself*—conditions the movement and concept of truth.'[18]

Moreover, Derrida thinks the tradition has been *right* to try to turn its back on history in this way. It has been right to try to account for sense in terms that are not purely historical or empirical. No condition that is merely historical can do what the tradition has asked. No merely empirical condition can account for the ability of beings to be present to us. If we are to account for the possibility of sense, we must seek a transcendental condition instead. We must look for an origin of sense that is outside history, because no merely historical condition can guarantee univocity of sense. History is full of 'sediment.'[19] Meanings that are generated through history are for that reason not fixed or stable. A sense that arises purely through a historical process is mutable, because it is transmitted through history, passed from one thinker to another over time. This transmission invariably leads to equivocity of sense: changes or additions to the meanings that are built up over history. For Derrida, history and historical sedimentation just *are* the sphere of equivocity: 'The equivocity of expression is the chosen field of sedimentary deposits' (*OG*, 100). And Derrida insists that '[e]quivocity is the path of all philosophical aberration' (*OG*, 100).

Derrida finds a particularly instructive example in Husserl's later work. Husserl's *Origin of Geometry* is an attempt to account for the sense of geometrical claims. It tries to explain how geometrical entities can be made

present to us—how we can grasp the *meaning* of geometrical claims. It does so by seeking the 'origin' of geometry, the source of geometrical thinking. It therefore tries to 'reactivate' the meanings of geometrical claims—that is, to recapture the presence of geometrical objects—by unearthing their origins. But while this study looks like a straightforward empirical history, it is not. It is not an inquiry into the factual or historical origin of geometry. The origin Husserl seeks is not a historical event. Husserl is adamant that the origin he seeks is not 'some undiscoverable Thales of geometry.'[20] He does not wish to reconstruct the thoughts of the first person to stumble upon certain geometrical truths, or to show how geometrical meanings originated in some event that actually took place. Reconstructing a historical origin is not necessary, because '[t]he sense of the first demonstration can be rigorously grasped, even though we know nothing of the first geometer' (*OG*, 39). More importantly, the sense of a geometrical entity is not reducible to any merely historical event. The objects of geometry are ideal. And no empirical event can furnish the sense of an ideal object. Empirical considerations tell us only that the angles of a triangle *do* add up to 180 degrees, not that they always or necessarily do. But this universality and necessity belong to the triangle's sense. Husserl's project, then, is a 'regression towards the nonempirical origins' (*OG*, 39) of geometry. It can only be a search for transcendental conditions. Since Husserl's inquiry embodies a tendency that runs through the entire metaphysics of presence, Derrida claims that it has 'exemplary significance' (*OG*, 153).

Derrida maintains that the problem with Husserl's project—and, by extension, with the rest of the metaphysics of presence—is that what it seeks can never be found. Its attempt to find the origin of sense is doomed to failure. The source of presence can never itself be made present. Derrida's project consists in showing how the origin of presence cannot be made present, in specific cases—showing how particular texts from the tradition gesture toward an origin of sense that retreats from our attempts to make it present. Again, Husserl's *Origin of Geometry* is of exemplary significance here. The *Origin of Geometry* delves into the history of geometry to discover how ideal objects can be made present to us. But it finds that no episode in that history can be a genuine origin of geometrical thinking, since no empirical or historical event can possibly underwrite the sense of ideal objects. The *Origin of Geometry* therefore draws an ambivalent conclusion. It shows that we can make no sense of geometrical thinking unless we posit an origin for it, but

it shows as well that in principle, this 'origin' is one that can never be discovered. Derrida draws an equally ambivalent conclusion about other major projects from the metaphysics of presence. He tries to show that these projects are, and must be, attempts to find transcendental conditions for the possibility of sense. Despite their intentions, however, these projects show that the transcendental conditions in question cannot account for themselves. As the supposed source of presence, they cannot themselves become present. Though the existence of sense cries out for them, they can never be made fully present. They are, to use a Derridean expression, endlessly delayed.

Derrida therefore concludes that the ahistorical ambitions of the metaphysics of presence cannot be realized. Its attempt to secure the univocity of sense *via* transcendental conditions cannot succeed. 'Sense,' Derrida claims 'is never simply present.'[21] Pure univocity eludes us. In its absence, all we can do is show how the ahistorical project fails to deliver what it promises, and fails on its own terms. All we can do is deflate the ambitions of the metaphysics of presence from within—show how it is committed to transcendental conditions of the possibility of sense that can never be made present. This is why Derrida's critique goes to work within the metaphysics of presence. His aim is not to criticize the ahistoricist project from without. Rather, his aim is to demonstrate how different texts fail in different ways to realize the goal to which they are committed. His aim is to deconstruct the metaphysics of presence from the inside and on its own terms. This does not mean that Derrida abandons all talk of origins. He does not. Nor does he see the search for the origin of sense as a simple mistake that could have been avoided. Derrida, no less than Husserl, argues that sense cries out for an origin and that presence must be accounted for. He does, however, rethink the nature of this origin. Accounting for sense 'cannot mean grasping it in its identity, its purity, or its origin, for it has none.'[22] Entities are not simply present, but are caught in a play of presence and absence. The origin of sense can never simply be present, but is always 'already engaged in the "movement" of the trace.'[23] The origin of sense, in short, is an origin that is 'present only in being deferred-delayed (*différant*) without respite' (*OG*, 153). This 'deferring' and 'delaying' origin—which Derrida calls *différance*—is the closest thing we can find to what the tradition has sought. He writes:

> The primordial Difference of the absolute Origin, which can and indefinitely must both retain and announce its pure concrete form with *a*

priori security: i.e., the beyond or the this-side which gives sense to all empirical genius and all factual profusion, that is perhaps what has always been thought under the concept of 'transcendental.' (*OG*, 153)

Difference is a condition that makes presence possible while destroying it—or, better, *by* destroying it. 'Difference,' then, 'would be transcendental' (*OG*, 153).

Why, then, does Derrida see his project as inseparable from the history of philosophy? Simply because it is a critique of the metaphysics of presence, a critique of the attempt to account for the presence of objects by jumping outside of history. Derrida wants to show that attempts to do this are inevitably incoherent. He wants to show that the very philosophical projects that seek to escape the equivocity of history end up unable to extricate themselves from it. And he does so through an internal critique. He goes to work within the metaphysics of presence, and tries to show how particular versions of it fail to transcend history despite their best efforts. It is, in short, a deconstruction of the ahistoricist project. Of course such a project will be intimately bound up with the history of philosophy. Its purpose is to draw attention to the inescapability of this history, even when the tradition is at its most ahistorical. As Derrida might say, its aim is to show that the history of logocentric theorizing is 'closed,' and that every attempt to escape it only reaffirms our enclosure within it. A critique of the metaphysics of presence is a critique of how thinking has tried to escape history and failed. It shows how the history of philosophy inhabits our philosophical thinking, despite our attempts to banish it. Derrida's critique of logocentrism is a critique of an ahistoricism that is ambivalent and incomplete.

At the same time, Derrida's criticism of this break is also ambivalent and incomplete. His critique of logocentrism does not simply condemn it; his criticism of the metaphysics of presence does not simply repudiate it. Derrida's attitude toward logocentrism is more complex. On the one hand, Derrida accepts the motives that gave rise to the ahistoricist project. He thinks that the metaphysics of presence had good reason to want to escape history and to secure the univocity of sense by means of transcendental conditions. History is a field of sediment and equivocity. Husserl was right to claim that a mere historical event cannot guarantee univocity of sense, and that whatever allows objects to be present cannot be an empirical, historical thing. We are driven to ahistoricism to escape utter

equivocity—which Derrida, like Husserl, sees as 'the path of all philosophical aberration' (*OG*, 100). But Derrida differs from Husserl in believing
that this project to which we are driven can never be completed. We must
seek the origin of presence, even as we recognize that there is no final origin to be found. We must seek transcendental conditions of the possibility
of sense, though we know that no such condition can justify itself. So there
is a tension in Derrida's project. We cannot bring the ahistoricist project
to fruition, but neither can we abandon it. We cannot dispense with the
history of philosophy, but neither can we take it too seriously. We cannot
overlook the aberrant equivocity that made us want to escape history in the
first place. Derrida cannot fully endorse either history or ahistoricism. He
is torn uncomfortably between the two.

  This discomfort is evident at several points in Derrida's work. One is
an interview with Julia Kristeva, where Derrida expresses mixed emotions about the impossibility of doing philosophy ahistorically. On the one
hand, Derrida is adamant that we cannot simply leave the metaphysical
tradition behind and start afresh. But on the other hand, he seems disappointed at this. He says: '[S]upposing, which I do not believe, that someday
it will be possible *simply* to escape metaphysics, the concept of the sign will
have marked, in this sense, a simultaneous impediment and progress.'[24]
Derrida's words betray a certain disappointment about the insufficiency
of this 'progress,' a desire to escape the tradition and a frustration at the
impossibility of doing so. Another example of Derrida's ambivalence is the
famous discussion of Joyce in his commentary on *The Origin of Geometry*.
This discussion tries to articulate a conception of sense that steers between
two pitfalls. The first—which Derrida identifies with Husserl—is a naive
ahistoricism that equates sense with pure univocity. The other—which he
identifies with Joyce—is an equally naive historicism that reduces sense to
pure equivocity. Neither approach is satisfactory. Sense cannot be purely
univocal, because pure univocity would require that we step outside history
altogether, and as we have seen, that is impossible. 'Husserl,' as Derrida
has argued, 'had to admit an irreducible, enriching, and always renascent
equivocity into pure historicity' (*OG*, 103). On the other hand, we cannot
understand sense simply as the equivocity of historical sediment either.
Pure equivocity is as unsustainable as pure univocity. 'Joyce's project,'
Derrida claims, 'could only succeed by allotting its share to univocity . . .
Otherwise, the very text of its repetition would have been unintelligible;

at least it would have remained so forever and for everyone' (*OG*, 103). We cannot dispense with the idea of an origin of sense, despite our recognition that there is no final origin. We must rather conceive of the origin of sense as indefinitely withdrawn, indefinitely delayed. We must understand it as a *différant* origin.

Thus there is a serious tension in Derrida's conception of the history of philosophy. He thinks that the pretensions of logocentrism need to be deflated, and that philosophy's attempt to leave its history behind is doomed to failure. Yet he also thinks that a naively historicist conception of philosophy is doomed to failure as well. The metaphysics of presence was right to try to step outside history, though its attempt to do so cannot succeed. In Derrida's view, we must accept the goals of an ahistorical approach to philosophy, while recognizing that these goals are unattainable. All we can do is attempt the ahistoricist project again and again and show from within how it collapses. All we can do is endlessly deconstruct ahistoricism. So while Derrida recognizes the impossibility of stepping outside the history of philosophy, his commitment to univocity prevents him from taking that history seriously. He cannot give a wholehearted endorsement to either a richly historical philosophy or an utterly ahistorical one. He accepts the historical thesis about philosophy, but in a decidedly ambivalent way.

Gadamer and the persistence of tradition

Let us now turn to someone who is also ambivalent about history: Hans-Georg Gadamer. History is obviously central to Gadamer's work. His project might be described as an epistemic rehabilitation of history: an attempt to show that being situated in history is not an obstacle in the search for truth, but is required by it. So it is not surprising that Gadamer describes philosophy as an inherently historical discipline. In *Truth and Method*, he claims that philosophical thinking 'is not its own master but remains constantly dependent on the given circumstances in which it operates' (*TM*, 276). He insists that 'we are always situated within traditions' (*TM*, 282) and that the 'continuity of custom and tradition' (*TM*, 297) helps make philosophy possible. Gadamer also says that his writings continue the work of Hegel and Heidegger, calling *Truth and Method* a Hegelian 'reconstruction' of the past (*TM*, 164). Hegel's project—and Gadamer says that he follows Hegel in this (*TM*, 173)—'consists not in the restoration of the past but in *thoughtful*

mediation with contemporary life' (*TM*, 169). Similarly, Gadamer describes his work as a continuation of Heidegger's thought. 'The hermeneutics I developed,' he says, 'was also based upon finitude and the historical character of Dasein,' and its aim is to 'carry forward' Heidegger's philosophy.[25] Since Hegel and Heidegger both think philosophy is inherently historical, and Gadamer says he is continuing their work, it seems clear that Gadamer sees philosophy as inherently historical as well. Above all, Gadamer *does* philosophy in a way that is historically informed. His work is in constant dialogue with earlier figures in the tradition, and he repeatedly describes his work in relation to theirs. *Truth and Method*, for instance, narrates a long and detailed history of the hermeneutic movement, a history that has the aim of justifying Gadamer's own standpoint. Gadamer philosophizes exactly as one would expect a proponent of the historical thesis to do. It is clear that he sees an important link between philosophy and its past. But *why* does Gadamer view philosophy as inherently historical? As with Derrida, we must look beyond Gadamer's explicit pronouncements on the history of philosophy, and place this topic in the context of some more general features of his work. For reasons that will become clear, Gadamer's historical conception of philosophy is best seen as a consequence of his discussion of *tradition*. Specifically, it is best seen as a consequence of the role that tradition plays in human understanding. And like much of the rest of his thought, Gadamer's discussion of tradition has its roots in Heidegger's *Being and Time*.

Truth and Method builds on Heidegger's claim that our manner of understanding the world is rooted in, and limited by, our way of being in the world. Heidegger's phenomenology of human existence—his *Daseinanalytik*—discovers that our being is not that of a purely rational subject capable of detaching itself from the world by objectifying it. I am not, in Hegel's words, 'a completely abstract "I" in which all concrete limitation and reality are negated and invalidated.'[26] Dasein, the type of being that we ourselves are, is *being in the world*. It is always already engaged with the world, carrying out projects involving future potentialities of its own being. And as Gadamer puts it, 'no freely chosen relation towards one's own being can get behind the facticity of this being. Everything that makes possible and limits Dasein's projection ineluctably precedes it' (*TM*, 264). This is true even of Dasein's theorizing about an objective world. Understanding the world does not involve gaining a God's eye view of this world, but is rather

'a founded mode' of being *in* the world (*BT*, 86). Since this is so, under-standing cannot involve escaping the limitations of one's point in space and time. It cannot require one to put aside all beliefs that are susceptible to doubt. Understanding must rather take advantage of the ways in which it is situated in space and time. It must make use of the biases one always has in virtue of being in the world. In particular, it must make use of the preju-dices [*Vorurteilen*] one inherits from one's age and one's culture. Gadamer maintains that 'presuppositions are always at work in our understanding.'[27] That is why understanding involves a hermeneutic circle. Gadamer writes:

> A person who is trying to understand is exposed to distraction from fore-meanings that are not borne out by the things themselves. Working out appropriate projections, anticipatory in nature, to be confirmed 'by the things' themselves, is the constant task of understanding. The only 'objectivity' here is the confirmation of a fore-meaning in its being worked out. (*TM*, 267)

Understanding is an interplay between the insights one brings to an inquiry and those one takes away from it, an interplay in which the two rely on and modify one another. For instance, it would be impossible to read a text if one's mind were a *tabula rasa*. We need preconceptions about what the text will be like: that it will be unified, that it will resemble other texts we have read in important respects, and so on. These preconceptions are not always borne out. Sometimes we are 'pulled up short by the text' (*TM*, 268) and forced to modify our expectations. If there were no expectations to modify, however, understanding would be impossible. Thus the hermeneu-tic circle 'is not to be reduced to the level of a vicious circle, or even of a circle which is merely tolerated. In the circle is hidden a positive possibility of the most primordial kind of knowing' (*BT*, 195).

Understanding therefore requires preconceptions—the beliefs and biases one acquires before theoretical inquiry begins. But where do we get them? Heidegger cryptically suggests that we must 'make the scientific theme secure by working out these fore-structures in terms of the things themselves' (*BT*, 195). Gadamer's answer, by contrast, involves the notion of tradition (*Überlieferung*). Dasein does not understand the world on its own. Certain ways in which others have understood have always already been handed down (*überliefert*) to it. We find ourselves situated in intellectual

traditions—'processes of handing down,' historically given and accretive ways of thinking about the world. These traditions give us the fore-conceptions we bring to the event of understanding. This does not mean that we are slaves to tradition. Acknowledging its importance is not the same as endorsing a romantic 'traditionalism' that glorifies prejudice for its own sake. But 'being situated within an event of tradition, a process of handing down, is a prior condition of understanding' (*BT*, 309).

What is true of understanding in general is also true of philosophical understanding in particular.[28] Just as there are broad traditions that cut across many branches of inquiry—the 'humanist tradition,' for example—there are narrower traditions within particular branches of inquiry. In particular, there are philosophical traditions—the phenomenological tradition, the idealist tradition, and so on. And just as understanding in general always takes place at some particular point in space and time, the philosopher always finds herself situated in some historical tradition of philosophizing. Gadamer says the following about the way in which the hermeneutic circle manifests itself in philosophy:

> Philosophy must incorporate within itself that anticipation of the whole which makes our desire to know go round, that anticipation of the whole which lies embedded in language as the totality of our access to the world. And in its thought philosophy must give an account of that anticipated whole.[29]

Philosophy emerges from a history and cannot be understood apart from that history. A philosophy is part of a dialectical conversation extended through time. '[O]ne only "understands" a statement when one understands it as an answer to a question;'[30] similarly, one only understands a philosophical position when one grasps it as a response to some earlier stage in the history of philosophy. Doing and understanding philosophy are inseparable from the history of philosophy. Understanding, then, is an event in which we take up beliefs and biases from the past and modify them as inquiry proceeds. Philosophical understanding is no different in this respect. To practice philosophy is to adopt projects and preoccupations from the history of philosophy and either continue them, modify them, or react against them. One engages in philosophy to the extent that one takes part in this event, this historical process of handing down. In short,

Gadamer thinks philosophy is inherently historical because 'com[ing] into the circle in the right way' (*BT*, 195) demands that we take our beginnings from tradition. The history of philosophy need not have the last word, but it always has the first word.

What should we make of Gadamer's view? It is not an implausible one. The problem is that a very different but equally compelling view is advanced elsewhere in Gadamer's work. Gadamer puts forth two views of the history of philosophy, and there is considerable tension between them. Worse, there does not seem to be any way of choosing one over the other and proclaiming it Gadamer's real view. There is an antinomy in Gadamer's thought about the relation between philosophy and its history: two incompatible but equally plausible views about the same topic. Let me explain why this is so.

Gadamer follows Heidegger in viewing tradition as an *Überlieferung*, a 'process of handing down' (*TM*, 309). Tradition is an extended event in which we receive beliefs and biases from the past, alter them, and hand them down to others. Belonging to tradition therefore involves considerable continuity among past, present, and future. We must be open to what tradition has to say to us. We need not endorse everything that tradition passes down. But we must begin with it if we are to get into the hermeneutic circle in the first place, and we cannot reject it all at once. We can criticize particular elements of our tradition, but we cannot repudiate it *tout court*. After all, if Gadamer's account of understanding is right, then the motives that might lead us to break with tradition would themselves have to come from tradition. The idea of a radical break with the past is therefore self-defeating. Yet there are other parts of Gadamer's work that not only allow for radical breaks with the past, but demand them. Gadamer frequently suggests that such a repudiation of the tradition not only could occur, but has occurred. Consider his discussion of 'historical consciousness' (*TM*, 283). Gadamer uses this term to refer to the transformations that took place in philosophy and the other *Geisteswissenschaften* in the nineteenth century. The rise of historical consciousness corresponds to the appearance of what I have been calling the historical thesis about philosophy. It is the recognition by Hegel and his followers that there is an intimate relation between philosophy and its past. It is the becoming-self-conscious of the philosophical tradition. Before the emergence of historical consciousness, as Joseph Flay puts it, 'the tradition did not exist as *the* tradition.'[31] After this emergence, a certain conception of philosophy—that it is the

search for eternal, immutable truths—was swept away. The appearance of historical consciousness marks a decisive break with the philosophical tradition. It is not just the discovery of history, but the awareness that after this discovery, things can never be the same again.

Truth and Method is full of suggestions that with the appearance of historical consciousness, Western philosophy experienced a decisive break with the past—precisely the sort of break that should not be possible, on Gadamer's view. Consider the following passage, from the book's introduction:

> However important and fundamental were the transformations that took place with the Latinization of Greek concepts and the translation of Latin conceptual language into the modern languages, the emergence of historical consciousness over the last few centuries is a much more radical rupture. Since then, the continuity of the Western philosophical tradition has been effective only in a fragmentary way. We have lost that naive innocence with which traditional concepts were made to serve one's thinking. (*TM*, xxiv)

Gadamer goes on to argue that a 'new critical consciousness must now accompany all responsible philosophizing' (*TM*, xxv). It is hard to imagine how this new critical consciousness can be at once beyond the 'naive innocence' of philosophy's past and still continuous with it. Consider as well Gadamer's discussion of the classical. *Truth and Method* goes to great lengths to develop a new theory of the classical, a theory that sees it neither as a timeless ideal nor as one historical style among others. Gadamer redefines the classical as 'a notable mode of being historical: the historical process of preservation that, through constantly preserving itself, allows something true to come into being' (*TM*, 109). But why does Gadamer see the need for a new theory of the classical? Simply because the rise of historical consciousness has rendered older theories useless. 'The historicization of the concept,' he argues, 'involves its uprooting, and that is why when historical consciousness started to engage in self-criticism, it reinstated the normative element in the concept of the classical as well as the historical uniqueness of its fulfillment' (*TM*, 289). This reinstatement, in Gadamer's view, is hardly positive. It marks an undesirable break with the history of the *Geisteswissenschaften* and should be resisted. So does the way in which 'historical consciousness has altered the orientation of the critic,' causing

him to '[give] up the claim that his texts have a normative validity for him' (*TM*, 337). Here too, Gadamer suggests that the nineteenth century did not merely take up and modify what the tradition had transmitted to it. It turned its back on much of what had defined the tradition, seemingly leaping out of the hermeneutic circle and severing its links to the past.

We might dismiss Gadamer's discussion of historical consciousness out of hand, since it seems inconsistent with other parts of his thought. We might conclude that Gadamer cannot mean what he says in this discussion, and insist that his other treatments of tradition—the ones that portray it as continuous—constitute his real view on the matter. In other words, we could resolve the antinomy in Gadamer's discussion by rejecting one of his views and embracing the other. But there are two problems with this strategy. The first is that it is arbitrary and ad hoc. If we are to ignore passages that Gadamer allowed to be published, we will need some compelling evidence that he did not mean what he says in them—not just that he *could not* have meant them, because to do so would be inconsistent with other things he says. We cannot ignore parts of an author's work because we do not know how to make sense of them. In the absence of independent reasons to dismiss Gadamer's discussion of historical consciousness, we have no choice but to make sense of it. The second problem with ignoring this discussion is that it does not just happen to appear in Gadamer's work. It belongs there. Given the nature of Gadamer's work, we should expect him to advance two incompatible views of the history of philosophy. And we should expect there to be no way of choosing between these views. Let me explain why.

Gadamer describes his work as 'an analysis of the hermeneutic experience that has become reflectively aware of itself.'[32] This analysis has two parts. The first is a description of the 'hermeneutic experience,' an account of what Gadamer calls the event of understanding. This is an account of how historical traditions make understanding possible. It describes how tradition acts on us by transmitting its contents to us, contents we in turn act upon and pass on to others. It is an account of how intellectual traditions develop over time according to a dialectic of question and answer, with each stage acting as the answer to a question posed by an earlier one. But Gadamer is not content to describe the hermeneutic experience. He also wants to describe a hermeneutic experience that has become self-conscious, or 'reflectively aware of itself.' He wants to account for not

just the development of the tradition, but also one specific stage in this development: its discovery of history in the nineteenth century. This is why Gadamer is drawn to a dialectical account of tradition. Dialectic is a way of explaining the transition from consciousness to self-consciousness, from the hermeneutic experience to this experience's recognition of itself. Thus he says, waxing Hegelian, that 'intercourse with the philosophic tradition becomes meaningful only when reason is recognized in it.'[33] But while Gadamer sees the evolution of tradition as dialectical, this evolution is markedly different from a Hegelian dialectic. Gadamer's dialectic is an 'open dialectic' that is 'based upon finitude.'[34] Shunning the idea of final resolutions and higher syntheses, it insists that '[t]he very idea of a definitive interpretation seems to be intrinsically contradictory.'[35] It is, in short, a dialectic without *Aufhebungen.*

The problem is that a dialectic without *Aufhebungen* risks being little more than a series of contradictions. To accomplish the first part of his task—to describe the hermeneutic experience as such—Gadamer makes room for the first moment of Hegel's dialectic. He makes room for immediacy, for the moment of continuity in tradition's development. To accomplish the second part—to explain how the tradition ruptured by becoming self-conscious—he makes room for negation as well. This allows him to explain how the nineteenth century broke with tradition by recognizing it *as* tradition. But because of his commitment to Dasein's finitude, Gadamer does not make room for the higher syntheses that come about through the negations of negations. Accordingly, he has no resources for reincorporating negativity back into the dialectic. He has no way to make the transition to a higher standpoint at which the tension between continuity and discontinuity is resolved. Perhaps he does not want to resolve this tension. Perhaps resolving it would be out of place in a hermeneutics that sees '[t]he very idea of a definitive interpretation [as] intrinsically contradictory.'[36] But in the absence of such a resolution, we should expect Gadamer to say two incompatible things about the relation between philosophy and its past. We should expect him to say that the philosophy of today both is and is not firmly tied to the philosophy of the past. And we should not expect him to have any way of choosing between these incompatible claims. Both follow from his view of tradition as a dialectic without higher syntheses. This view necessarily gives rise to contradictions. But Gadamer has no way of resolving them.

So it is not that Gadamer advances two different conceptions of the history of philosophy and fails to say which is his real view. The problem is more serious. In principle, there does not seem to be any way of adjudicating between these views. Gadamer's thought is unclear, and *necessarily* unclear, about the link between philosophy and its past.

Levinas and the persistence of ontology

The last position I will discuss is the ethical thought of Emmanuel Levinas.[37] At first, it might seem absurd to say that Levinas considers the history of philosophy important.[38] Like Derrida, he is best known as a critic of the philosophical tradition: someone who sees this tradition as fundamentally misguided, or at least incapable of accomplishing what it intends. Indeed, Levinas's critique of the tradition is considerably more ambitious than Derrida's. While Derrida would have us supplement logo-centric theorizing with a new view of theory—or more accurately, a new orientation *within* theory—Levinas's critique is directed at theory as such. He does not just claim that the West has philosophized naively and should do so differently. He insists that there is something objectionable about the philosophical enterprise as such. This enterprise involves an unacceptable way of relating to beings, and it should be criticized for ethical reasons. That said, Levinas still attaches a great deal of importance to the history of philosophy. He sees his ethical work—regardless of whether he would call it 'philosophy'—as firmly situated within the closure of metaphysics. Levinas concedes that his critique of the history of philosophy can only be an internal critique. It can proceed only by engaging with the history of philosophy—though he does not always seem happy about this fact. To that extent, even Levinas accepts the historical thesis about philosophy. To see why this is so, we must know something about Levinas's critique of the tradition.

Perhaps the best way to understand Levinas's critique is through his distinction between *ontology* and *metaphysics*. Levinas uses these terms in the course of giving a phenomenological description of ethical experience—that is, a description of how the I finds itself relating to other beings.[39] According to Levinas, the I's dealings with entities are marked by a drive toward transcendence. Transcendence is an encounter with alterity, a movement 'from an "at home" which we inhabit, toward an alien outside-of-oneself, toward

a yonder' (*TI*, 33). The I, in other words, is defined by its need to relate to what is different from itself. Unlike the Fichtean or Hegelian I, however, it does not encounter the other as its own other, something inseparable from its own activity. It 'tends toward *something else entirely*, toward the *absolutely other*' (*TI*, 33). Levinas calls this the Other (*Autrui*): 'The absolutely other (*autre*) is the Other (*Autrui*)' (*TI*, 39). In its desire for transcendence, the I finds that it must adopt one of two stances toward the other. The first, which Levinas calls the metaphysical stance, seeks to preserve the other's alterity. Preserving this alterity is something I find myself obliged to do. In encountering the other, I recognize that I am responsible to him, and that he issues a command to me: 'you shall not commit murder' (*TI*, 199). This command is immediate and nonnegotiable. It is not something I discover through reasoning, or something I decide to accept because it serves my interests. My responsibility to the other is, as Gary Gutting puts it, 'a simple assertion of the inviolability of this person before me, of my responsibility to respect this person's presence.'[10] Thus for Levinas, the metaphysical relation is an ethical one. Metaphysics is 'concretely produced as ethics,' and it involves a 'calling into question of my spontaneity by the presence of the other' (*TI*, 43).

Metaphysics must be sharply distinguished from another way of relating to beings, which Levinas calls *ontology*. When the I adopts an ontological stance toward the other, it does not have its spontaneity checked. It seeks to reduce the other to itself. Ontology is the attempt to cancel alterity by appropriating and comprehending the other. Levinas associates it with the theoretical stance, since theory deals with objects existing for a subject—that is, with entities in so far as they can be objectified by the I. The objects I confront in the theoretical stance are always *my* objects, objects given as meaningful *to me*. This is why Levinas's critique applies to theory as such, not just one version of it. 'Theory,' for Levinas, 'designates comprehension—the logos of being—that is, a way of approaching the known being such that its alterity with regard to the knowing being vanishes' (*TI*, 42). Philosophy is a particularly problematic form of theory. 'Western philosophy,' Levinas claims, 'has most often been an ontology: a reduction of the other to the same by interposition of a middle and neutral term that ensures the comprehension of being' (*TI*, 43). As examples, he cites Berkeley's claim that the qualities of objects are identical with my ideas of them, as well as the phenomenological thesis that the truth of beings consists in their being

disclosed to me. All of these positions ignore what is individual about the other, and in that way do violence to it. Violence, however, 'does not consist so much in injuring and annihilating persons as in interrupting their continuity, making them play roles in which they no longer recognize themselves' (*TI*, 21).

Levinas sometimes describes the ontological and metaphysical stances by identifying them with the notions of *totality* and *infinity*, respectively. Ontology totalizes entities. It ignores individual others *qua* individuals, reducing them 'to being bearers of forces that command them unbeknown to themselves' (*TI*, 21). Ontology maintains that the other is nothing more than the totality of meanings attached to it by the I. It sees an individual person as nothing more than her race, or class, or gender, for example. For the ontological stance, the 'meaning of individuals (invisible outside of this totality) is derived from the totality' (*TI*, 22). The metaphysical stance, by contrast, acknowledges the I's inability to master the other. It recognizes the ways in which the alterity of the other resists my attempts to reduce it to a product of my activity. It acknowledges the *infinity* of the other. Levinas therefore uses the term 'infinity' to denote the other's 'transcendence with regard to totality' (*TI*, 23). But to avoid totalizing the other is not to adopt some new theory about the other. It is the theoretical stance as such—the very attempt to turn others into objects for a subject—that is the target of Levinas's critique. Thus an ethically acceptable relation with others cannot take place within philosophy, or within any theoretical discourse. Instead of replacing a faulty theory with a better one, Levinas's work addresses the failings of theory as such. His project is to get behind theory—'to proceed from the experience of totality back to a situation where totality breaks up, a situation that conditions this totality itself. Such a situation is the gleam of exteriority or of transcendence in the face of the Other' (*TI*, 24).

This project is germane to a discussion of the history of philosophy because Levinas associates history in general, and the history of philosophy in particular, with totality and ontology. A few exceptions aside—such as Descartes's God and Plato's Good beyond being—Levinas sees the history of philosophy as the history of a thinking that totalizes the other. There are two reasons for this. First, as we have seen, Levinas thinks that a theoretical stance is always an objectifying stance, and that to turn the other into an object is precisely not to preserve its alterity. Since these objects

are the philosopher's stock in trade, there is something necessarily totalizing about the attempt to think philosophically. Second, there is something particularly totalizing about historical thinking. To view the other as a constituent in historical events—as historians do—is inevitably to totalize. To see something as a historical event *just is* to reduce it to a mere part of some larger structure, and to ignore what is individual about it. This is why Levinas says that historical events 'are the visible *par excellence*; their truth is produced in evidence. This visible forms, or tends to form, a totality' (*TI*, 243). Ethics commands us to resist understanding things historically. Thus Levinas says that the 'judgment at which subjectivity is to remain apologetically present has to be made against the evidence of history (and against philosophy, if philosophy coincides with the evidence of history)' (*TI*, 243). The historian of philosophy is doubly blameworthy: first because she is a philosopher and therefore an objectifier, and second because she is a historian.

So for Levinas, there is a sense in which we must escape the history of philosophy. He announces that he has 'broken with' what he calls the 'neuter philosophers:' 'with the Heideggerian Being of the evident whose impersonal neutrality the critical work of Blanchot has so much contributed to bring out, with Hegel's impersonal reason, which shows to the personal consciousness only its ruses' (*TI*, 298). The choice of Hegel and Heidegger is significant. Levinas singles out these most historical of philosophers for special scorn: as both philosophers and historians, they have let themselves be governed by 'impersonal reason,' exalting 'an obedience which no face commands' (*TI*, 298). To the totalizations of philosophical and historical thought, Levinas opposes a more eschatological way of thinking. Eschatology orients itself toward a 'messianic peace' (*TI*, 22) that never fully appears in historical time but is always still to come. Similarly, Levinas asks us to think in ways that cannot be fully captured by the discourses of philosophy and history, precisely because they point out the weaknesses of these ways of thinking. Eschatology 'cannot mean the passage of the invisible to the status of the visible; it does not lead back to evidence' (*TI*, 243). Likewise, the ethical failings of philosophical and historical thinking cannot be fixed by further theory. Ethics commands us to break with theory, particularly the style of thinking embodied by the history of philosophy. It demands 'a relation with being *beyond the totality* or beyond history' (*TI*, 22).

This break, however, is not simply a repudiation. It would be wrong to see Levinas as turning away from the history of philosophy altogether, as though he had forgotten the past and begun anew. Levinas does not think such repudiation is possible. The break with tradition that he seeks is partial, tenuous, and ambivalent. Like Derrida, he claims that it is impossible to leap out of the history of philosophy and criticize it from outside. And this is precisely what one would expect from a critic of the theoretical stance. Levinas is, after all, pointing out the ethical failings of theory by means of theory. He is carrying out an ethical critique of philosophy by writing a piece of philosophy. Levinas's work reveals itself to be less a repudiation of the tradition than a tension-filled continuation of it. The clearest indication of this comes in *Otherwise Than Being*, where Levinas again takes up the 'philosophers of the neuter,' Hegel and Heidegger. Hegel, he says, has taught us to be suspicious of works that begin with prefaces, and Heidegger has taught us to be leery of those who claim to have escaped the hermeneutic circle and begun from first principles. 'Should we not,' Levinas asks, 'think with as much precaution of the possibility of a conclusion or a closure of the philosophical discourse? Is not its interruption its only possible end?'[41] Levinas's claim here is that it is impossible to turn one's back on the history of past thinking and begin anew. A critique of this history is not simply the end of one enterprise and a beginning of another. The critique of philosophy must take place within the 'closure' of philosophy. It is possible only as an internal 'interruption' of the tradition, or as

> a drama between philosophers and an intersubjective movement which does not resemble the dialogue of teamworkers in science, nor even the Platonic dialogue which is the reminiscence of a drama rather than the drama itself. It is sketched out in a different structure; empirically it is realized as the history of philosophy in which new interlocutors always enter who have to restate, but in which the former ones take up the floor to answer in the interpretations they arouse.[42]

Levinas's own work is just such an interruption. It is a critique of the tradition, to be sure—but an *immanent* critique that is deeply continuous with what it criticizes.

While this view is stated most clearly in *Otherwise Than Being*, it appears in *Totality and Infinity* as well. A superficial reading of this book might

suggest that Levinas wishes to abandon the ontological stance altogether and replace it with a purely metaphysical one. A closer reading shows that the relation between totality and infinity is much less tidy. Levinas concedes that whatever lies beyond totalizing ways of thinking 'is, however, not to be described in a purely negative fashion. It is reflected *within* the totality and history, *within* experience' (*TI*, 23). Levinas's critique of the theoretical stance is not a step beyond theory, but a gesture within theory. Robert Bernasconi is surely right when he says that 'the terms of the title *Totality and Infinity* are not related to each other antithetically,' because our only access to the infinite is by way of totality.[13] For that reason, Levinas's critique of historical thinking does not pretend to escape history. Rather, 'Levinas's strategy is to question totality and history so as to show that they themselves refer to the beyond.'[14] To be sure, Levinas does not always seem happy that our attempts to go beyond totality themselves take place within a totalizing framework. In his essay 'God and Philosophy,' for example, he bristles at what he sees as an overly hasty attempt to re-enclose his work within metaphysics.[15] At the end of the day, however, Levinas concedes that his work is so enclosed. He grants—reluctantly—that his critique of the history of philosophy is itself a totalizing continuation of that history.

It should now be clear why Levinas belongs in a discussion of the historical thesis about philosophy. He believes that his project is intimately bound up with the history of philosophy, and that it may not turn its back on this history. Levinas's reasons for accepting this thesis are ultimately ethical. On the one hand, Levinas insists on the need for a critique of totalizing ways of thinking. Such ways of thinking do violence to the other, and we find ourselves under an immediate ethical obligation not to do so. The history of philosophy embodies a particularly odious way of totalizing the other. But a critique of the history of philosophy can only be an immanent critique. The more we try to escape this history, the more we remain under its sway. We have to be within the tradition in order to gesture toward that which exceeds it. Perversely, the only way of meeting our ethical obligation to criticize the tradition is to remain enclosed within it. Levinas's critical project is therefore unavoidably historical.

What should we make of Levinas's discussion? Like those of Derrida and Gadamer, it faces serious difficulties. Some of these difficulties concern

the sorts of evidence Levinas offers to support his position. As I have suggested, Levinas's view of the history of philosophy rests on a phenomenological description of ethical experience. He claims that engaging with the tradition is the only way to criticize that tradition's totalizing tendencies. Criticizing this totalization is in turn necessary because we have a pretheoretical obligation not to do violence to the other. Levinas claims to know these things on the basis of a phenomenological description of ethical experience. But is his description compelling? Of course, criticizing a phenomenological description is a complicated business. The only really decisive criticism is a further description—one that is, for example, richer or deeper than the original description, or that shows that what the original description took to be evident is really not. I will not try to give such a criticism of Levinas here. But it is always legitimate to ask whether a phenomenological description is as purely descriptive as it claims to be. If a description claims to have bracketed certain theoretical assumptions and reached a pretheoretical level, then it is always legitimate to point out ways in which it seems not to have done so. This does not necessarily destroy the description. But it does show that the claims arising from the description are not as evident as they purport to be.

There is good reason to doubt that Levinas is giving a purely descriptive, pretheoretical account of ethical experience. There is compelling evidence that Levinas's theoretical commitments—commitments that are not at all self-evident—sneak into his phenomenological description. Consider Levinas's claim that historical thinking is inevitably totalizing—that it 'forms, or tends to form, a totality' (*TI*, 243). Levinas presents this claim, and a series of related claims about politics and community, as results of his phenomenological description of the ethical, results that are valid because they have been made evident to intuition. Yet to a suspicious reader, they look less like facts manifest to intuition than consequences of what Stephen Watson calls Levinas's 'Hobbesian blinders—resulting from lingering (false) antinomies between "theory" and "ethics," desire and recognition, self and other, egoism and respect, power as violence and knowledge as calculation.'[46] Why should we assume that historical thinking is inevitably totalizing, or that politics is inevitably warlike? These claims are far from self-evident. To a suspicious reader, they seem more like unspoken theoretical commitments that sneak into Levinas's phenomenology

than evident consequences of it. Consider as well Levinas's claim that theory inevitably totalizes. Levinas presents this claim as a discovery made by his phenomenological investigation. To be an object of theoretical inquiry is to be an object made evident to a subject, and this process inevitably totalizes. Why should we assume this? Should we accept Levinas's claim that it is supported by a purely descriptive account of the I's relation with others? Or should we suspect that it has another source: namely, the 'lingering (false) antinomies' to which Levinas remains bound? Levinas seems to assume that theory always objectifies and totalizes. He does not seem to entertain the idea that certain kinds of theory might not, or that his highly subjectivist understanding of theory is not the only one possible. But in light of Levinas's tendency to mistake optional theoretical commitments for the self-evident results of phenomenological description, we should be suspicious of this view of theory. Of course, it does not follow that Levinas's claims about theory are false. Clearly, though, Levinas does not do as much as he could to demonstrate that they are true. Thus it is not clear why we should accept them.

So the phenomenological basis of Levinas's view of history looks suspect. But there are deeper problems. The most troubling is the discrepancy between what Levinas *says* about the history of philosophy and what he *does* with it. Philosophers who accept the historical thesis typically work in a way that reflects their commitment to it. Derrida and Gadamer clearly do so. Derrida's work almost always takes the form of commentaries on traditional texts, while Gadamer's preferred way of defending his philosophical standpoint is to reconstruct the history from which it has emerged. We would expect Levinas to do something similar. If he really believes that the history of philosophy is a 'drama between philosophers . . . in which new interlocutors always enter who have to restate, but in which the former ones take up the floor to answer,'[17] then there should be signs of this in the way he works. We would expect Levinas to argue for the historical thesis in a way that makes clear his commitment to it. But Levinas does not philosophize in the historically informed ways that Derrida and Gadamer do. His ethical work does not take the form of commentaries on texts, and he does not support his positions by tracing their histories. On the contrary, Levinas's way of proceeding seems strangely ahistorical, and thus strangely at odds with his commitment to the historical thesis. Let me give some examples.

First, consider the type of phenomenology that Levinas practices. As we have seen, Levinas's claim that we must criticize the tradition from the inside rests on a piece of phenomenological description. This description reveals me to be under an immediate obligation to the Other; it shows that the face of the Other 'expresses the first word: "you shall not commit murder"' (*TI*, 199). But there are two types of phenomenological description: *static* and *genetic*. Static phenomenology describes an experience that it treats as an accomplished fact. It describes what is involved in, for example, hearing a melody or judging a proposition to be true. It does not ask where the objects encountered in such an experience come from, or how they came to acquire the meanings they have. It simply describes the experience as it is. Genetic phenomenology, on the other hand, describes the *origins* of the meanings these objects possess. It describes how certain meaning structures are built up over time through successive cognitive acts, successive processes of sedimentation. Phenomenologists who are interested in history usually engage in genetic phenomenology. Husserl's *Origin of Geometry*, for example, traces the genesis of the meanings of ideal objects such as mathematical entities. It is not a mere factual or empirical history, of course, but it is concerned with development all the same. Given Levinas's commitment to the historical thesis, we might expect his phenomenology of ethical experience to be genetic as well. But it is not; it is static. It describes ethical experience as we happen to find it, and it does not inquire into the genesis of that experience. On the contrary, ethical experience as Levinas understands it is not the sort of thing that can *have* a genesis. *Totality and Infinity* argues that the ethical relation to the Other is presupposed by a wide range of phenomena and helps make these phenomena possible. Ethical experience is the ultimate origin of reason as a search for impersonal truth (*TI*, 201–204), language as 'a system of signs' (*TI*, 205), and many other phenomena. But if the ethical relation is as basic as Levinas claims, then there would seem to be nothing in terms of which its genesis could be explained.[48] The result is that for Levinas, the ethical relation can only be an 'epiphany' (*TI*, 197) that is radically discontinuous with the rest of experience. He cannot describe this relation genetically; he has no choice but to engage in static phenomenology. His understanding of ethics forces him to work in a decidedly ahistorical way.

Consider as well the sort of sort of I, the sort of subject, whose experiences Levinas describes. This subject is not embedded in history or

culture in any obvious way. Levinas's I does not seem to owe its identity or
its self-understanding to larger historical forces. The setting in which it
initially finds itself is an 'earthly paradise,' as Adriann Peperzak puts it.[49]
Levinas describes this setting as a sort of Eden that does not resemble any
historical community or any particular time or place. The I that resides
there gives itself over to the pleasures of nourishing itself and appropriating things—activities more like the ones performed by non-human animals than those of concrete historical agents. If the setting in which the
I finds itself seems cut off from history, then its ethical obligations seem
even more so. Levinas understands my responsibility toward the other as
absolute and non-negotiable. No particular feature of my being gives me
this responsibility. I do not respect the other because doing so advances
my interests, or because my sentiments make me feel empathy for him, or
because the practices and values of my community incline me to do so. My
responsibility must transcend all of these so that there can be *no* considerations, 'not even that of my own death, that can in any way limit my obligation to the other.'[50] This obligation overrides every particular feature of
my being. In short, the subject that is responsible to the other is a 'subject
without qualities,' to use Rudolf Bernet's phrase.[51] It is a subject that has
been stripped of all the particularities that accrue to agents embedded
in culture and history. In this way as well, Levinas's way of philosophizing
seems strangely ahistorical. It is not the method one would expect from a
defender of the historical thesis.

So there is a puzzling discrepancy between what Levinas says about the
history of philosophy and what he does with it. He says that this history
casts an inescapably long shadow, and that the metaphysical tradition is
closed. But the way he carries out his project is quite ahistorical, and this
fact raises serious questions about how he really sees the history of philosophy. In pointing this out, I am not advancing an *ad hominem* argument.
I am not claiming that Levinas's view of the history of philosophy should
be rejected because he does not act in accordance with it. I am making a
claim about conceptual linkages. Someone genuinely committed to the
historical thesis would philosophize in ways that make this commitment
clear. Levinas does not, and this suggests that his view of the historical thesis is much more conflicted than we might initially think. Like Derrida and
Gadamer, he views the history of philosophy in a way that is full of curious
and troubling tensions.

Toward a critique of the crisis

This brief survey suggests that there is quite a bit of ambivalence about the history of philosophy in contemporary continental thought. Each of the schools discussed claims to accept the historical thesis about philosophy. But each seems confused about what this thesis means, why one might hold it, and what it requires of us. Derrida's version of the historical thesis founders on a tension: the tension between Derrida's sympathy for the goals of ahistoricism and his pessimism about whether these goals can be attained. A similar tension is at work in Gadamer's thought, leading him to say that philosophy both is and is not inherently historical. And Levinas's discussion of the history of philosophy is both undermined by some dubious phenomenology and threatened by a tension of its own—a tension between what Levinas says about the history of philosophy and what he does with it. Again, I am not suggesting that the projects of Derrida, Gadamer, and Levinas are philosophically worthless. But the discussions of the history of philosophy found in their work are fraught with tensions. This should give us pause. Three of the most prominent and influential schools of contemporary continental thought endorse the historical thesis, but without giving a good reason to accept it, or even a satisfactory explanation of what it means. This is a curious fact, and one that cries out for explanation. But how should we explain it?

One strategy would be to give a different explanation for each of the philosophers in question. We could argue that Derrida, Gadamer, and Levinas each have their own reasons—biographical reasons, for instance—for accepting the historical thesis without being able to explain why they do. We might say that Derrida is a pedantic French scholar who has been taught that philosophy amounts to nothing more than commenting on the canon of great philosophers. It would not be surprising for such a person to assume that philosophy is identical with its history. In Gadamer's case, we could say that *Truth and Method* is an inconsistent patchwork assembled over several decades, and that it is not surprising that such a book contains incompatible or even contradictory views of the history of philosophy. As for Levinas, we might say that he is less a philosopher than an ethical activist, and that it is not surprising for such a person to insist that studying the history of philosophy is above all a way of advancing a certain moral agenda. And if we find these explanations unsatisfactory, we could look for ones that are equally case-specific.

There are two problems with explanations of this sort. First, they are unphilosophical. The phenomenon to be explained here—the confusion about history in continental thought—is a philosophical one. But the explanations we have just considered are concerned with extraneous biographical matters. We should look for a more philosophical explanation first. This is not to say that biography has no bearing on philosophy, or that we should never explain a thinker's views with reference to her time or her circumstances. But we should look for explanations outside philosophy only when the search for one within philosophy has failed. If we think we can account for Derrida's, Gadamer's, and Levinas's positions in terms of the logic of those positions, then we should try to do so first. Unphilosophical explanations should come later, if at all.[52] The second problem is that this strategy rules out some explanations in advance. More specifically, it rules out the possibility that the confusions in the work of Derrida, Gadamer, and Levinas are all symptoms of the same problem. It prevents us from asking whether there is a common source for the tensions in Derrida's, Gadamer's, and Levinas's work on the history of philosophy. But perhaps these tensions do have a common source. It seems foolish to rule out this possibility. So whatever explanation we accept, it will have to take seriously the possibility that the confusions in these philosophers's reflections on history are all manifestations of the same problem. What kind of explanation should we look for?

The phenomenon to be explained here is a widespread confusion about the history of philosophy: a situation in which a certain view of this history is taken as incontestably true, yet not adequately argued for or fully understood. In the 1930s, Husserl found himself in a similar position with respect to the exact sciences. He claimed that these sciences had lost sight of the ways in which their fundamental concepts originate in pretheoretical experience. They took for granted that nature was a 'mathematical manifold' capable of being exhaustively described in the language of geometry.[53] They gradually forgot that the mathematical view of nature had been constructed over centuries, and that it was not the only possible way of viewing the world. Husserl called this situation a *crisis* of the exact sciences. It had arisen because the scientific world view had been built up gradually through a process of passive sedimentation. 'Greater and greater segments' of this world view, he wrote, 'lapse into a kind of talking and reading that is dominated purely by association; and often enough, in

respect to the validities arrived at in this way, it is disappointed by subsequent experience.'[54]

Husserl's response to this crisis was to carry out a *Rückfrage*, a 'return inquiry.' By studying the origins of the scientific worldview, Husserl sought to reconstruct it—to explain how it had grown out of pretheoretical experience and, eventually, how that origin had been forgotten. A *Rückfrage* has two aims. First, because it traces a science in crisis back to a point before the crisis occurred, it identifies the point where things went wrong. It reveals when the science began to be dominated by passive sedimentation, and it thereby isolates the wrong turn that was taken. It shows where a remedy needs to be applied. Second, and more important, the *Rückfrage* serves as this very remedy. The *Rückfrage* actively reconstructs a history dominated by passive sedimentation. As Husserl would put it, it 'reactivates' meanings that have become dead. Since a crisis is a forgetfulness of origins, to explain how it came about is to remedy this forgetfulness. By investigating how the crisis set in, a *Rückfrage* helps overcome it. It is both a diagnosis and a treatment.

If what I have said in this chapter is right, there is a crisis in contemporary continental philosophy that displays many of the same symptoms as Husserl's crisis of the European sciences. Like Husserl's crisis, the crisis in history consists in a certain view being widely accepted but not adequately defended. The historical thesis about philosophy, no less than the mathematical view of nature, is taken as incontestably true but not understood. And like the mathematical view of nature, this thesis has a definite historical origin. It is not, however, recognized as having this origin. Instead, it seems to have been passed down through the tradition by a process of passive sedimentation. We need to retrace the path back to this origin: to explain the crisis by carrying out a *Rückfrage* into how the historical thesis has been passed down. Like Husserl's, this inquiry has two goals. The first is the diagnostic goal of identifying where the crisis set in. If we can determine when continental thinking about the history of philosophy became confused, then we may discover where a remedy is needed. Second, the *Rückfrage* will itself help serve as this remedy. The problem to be solved is a lack of understanding about the history of philosophy. To explain how this lack of understanding came about is to replace it with a new understanding. Explaining how a crisis in origins came about is one way to remedy it.

The result of this inquiry will be a narrative. It will be a wide-ranging story about the development of a way of thinking. It must be judged according to the standards we apply to all narratives: comprehensiveness, coherence, and so forth. Its adequacy or inadequacy will not be apparent until the end of the story. With these caveats in mind, let us turn to the narrative.

Hegel's Mixed Message to Historians of Philosophy

This chapter describes the first episode in the development of the historical thesis about philosophy: the emergence of this thesis in Hegel's work. It tries to show that Hegel's account of the history of philosophy is the source of the contemporary crisis. Hegel, I claim, sends a mixed message about the history of philosophy. He *says* that philosophy is inherently historical, but he tacitly accepts a view of historical thinking that is incompatible with this claim. By approaching the subject in this way, by setting the terms of the debate as he does, Hegel helps ensure that later thinkers will misunderstand the significance of the history of philosophy.

Chapter 2 falls into five parts. The first discusses the background to Hegel's work on the history of philosophy: Kant's call for a critical history of philosophy. The next section shows how Hegel tries to break with this approach by articulating an anti-Kantian historiography of philosophy in the *Phenomenology of Spirit*. Sections 3 and 4 describe Hegel's later attempts to distance himself from this historiography in the *Lectures on the History of Philosophy* and the *Encyclopedia*. In the fifth and final section, I ask *why* Hegel assigns less and less importance to the history of philosophy as his career progresses. The later Hegel's hostility to the history of philosophy, I argue, is a natural outcome of the way he thinks about history.

Kant's legacy: critical history of philosophy

Kant is often thought to be uninterested in the history of philosophy. Conventional wisdom has it that philosophy discovered the importance of its past in the nineteenth century, not the eighteenth. R. G. Collingwood has argued that the history of philosophy is at best peripheral to Kant's

interests,[1] while Heinrich Srbik claims that Kant's remarks on the history of philosophy are tacked on to his work as an afterthought.[2] It is easy to understand why Kant has been read in this way. Kant's critical project seems to assume that a great deal of past thought is radically misguided. We would hardly expect someone who thinks that speculative metaphysics is impossible to have much use for the history of metaphysics, for example. Moreover, while Kant did publish essays on historical topics—essays such as 'Idea for a Universal History With a Cosmopolitan Purpose,' for instance—they are written in a popular style that seems to suggest that Kant did not view them as serious philosophy.[3] Finally, Kant's work on history relies so heavily on Whiggish notions of progress and enlightenment that they appear less interested in studying the past than in escaping it. It is hard to imagine that the author of these works attached any philosophical importance to the history of philosophy. So it is no surprise that Kant is remembered as the thinker who declared that one can only learn to philosophize, not philosophy itself—a thinker who sees the tradition as of interest only to historians, not to practitioners of the critical philosophy.

This reading of Kant, however, is mistaken. Kant actually assigns an important task to historians of philosophy—an important *philosophical* task. Far from being peripheral to the critical philosophy, this task is required by it. Kant makes these claims about the history of philosophy in a brief discussion near the end of the first *Critique*. In the *Transcendental Doctrine of Method*, Kant claims that once the critical philosophy has determined the limits of reason, four tasks remain. The first is the development of a discipline of pure reason: a set of norms that will correct the faculty's 'constant tendency to disobey certain rules' (*KRV*, A709/B737). Next comes a canon of a priori principles to govern reason's correct employment. Third is the development of an architectonic of pure reason, or a systematic unity of our knowledge 'in view of the affinity of its parts and of their derivation from a single supreme and inner end' (*KRV*, A834/B862). Finally, critical philosophers will have to construct a history of pure reason, one that discusses earlier philosophies from a critical standpoint. This last task might seem out of place. And to be fair, the *Critique of Pure Reason* devotes only three pages to the history of pure reason. Kant is content to sketch its general structure and to leave its completion to 'future workers' (*KRV*, A852/B880). But the appearance of the history of pure reason in the *Doctrine of Method* suggests that Kant does not view the

history of philosophy as a mere appendix to philosophy. It, no less than the project of keeping reason within its proper limits, is demanded by the critical project itself.

Why does critique require a confrontation with the history of philosophy? Kant's view seems to be that a history of pure reason helps satisfy reason's need for systematicity. After all, the three other tasks left to critical philosophy all have to do with satisfying reason's demands. A discipline of pure reason specifies in general terms what the faculty must *not* do; a canon specifies in equally general terms what it *ought* to do; and an architectonic 'makes a system out of a mere aggregate of knowledge'(*KRV,* A832/B860). The fourth task seems to fit this pattern by transforming existing philosophies—one specific kind of 'ordinary knowledge'—from a mere aggregate into a system. A sign that Kant has something of this sort in mind appears in the *Architectonic of Pure Reason,* where he suggests that the task of making ordinary knowledge systematic requires a familiarity with its history. He writes:

> Systems seem to be formed in the manner of lowly organisms, through a *generatio aequivoca* from the mere confluence of assembled concepts, at first imperfect, and only gradually attaining to completeness, although they one and all have had their schema, as the original germ, in the sheer self-development of reason. (*KRV,* A835/B863)

The history of pure reason will help our knowledge of past philosophies attain systematic completeness. We know that our philosophical knowledge *can* take this form because 'not only is each system articulated in accordance with an idea, but they are one and all organically united in a system of human knowledge' (*KRV,* A835/B863). Presumably, reason systematizes the history of philosophy by identifying the ideas underlying the various stages of this history, and then combining these ideas into a whole. And despite 'the great amount of material that has been collected, or which can be obtained from the ruins of ancient systems,' a systematic history of philosophy 'is not only possible, but would not indeed be difficult' (*KRV,* A835/B863). So Kant does not see the history of philosophy as a mere appendix to the critical project. On the contrary, he shows how we can reinvigorate the study of the history of philosophy: by making this study critical.

What would a critical history of philosophy look like? Kant's *Lectures on Metaphysics* offer an answer. In these lectures, Kant actually does what the *Critique of Pure Reason* says historians of philosophy ought to do. He provides histories of philosophy that satisfy the demands of reason by transforming previous philosophy into a systematic unity. The most detailed of these histories appears in *Metaphysik Mrongovius*. Here, Kant narrates a brief history of philosophy that does three things. First, it isolates several important stages in the history of philosophy; second, it argues that each of these stages embodies a certain philosophical principle; and finally, it argues that this principle anticipates one of the major insights of the critical philosophy. Kant's history has only three stages: the Eleatics, the Athenians, and the moderns. Eleatic thought is based on the distinction between *sensibilia* and *intelligibilia*, and it advances the thesis that '[t]here is no truth in the senses.'[4] This distinction anticipates the first *Critique*'s claim that 'our cognition is twofold (first intellectual and second sensitive).'[5] Unfortunately, Kant tells us, the Eleatics articulated this insight poorly. They 'should not have divided philosophy in terms of objects,' but rather in terms of cognitive faculties.

Kant does something similar with the other two stages of his history. Athenian philosophy, he maintains, introduced a further distinction between *kinds* of intellectual things. Plato argued for the existence of 'mystical intellectual things,' or self-subsistent Forms. Aristotle claimed that there are only 'logical intellectual things' that 'arise through the reflection of the understanding.'[6] Each philosopher expressed part of the truth, for as the critical philosophy has taught us, 'all concepts are acquired, only not all from the senses; we also have many through the pure use of reason.'[7] The philosophers of the modern era advanced this discussion by applying the insights of Plato and Aristotle to a debate over the relation between concepts and objects. According to Kant, 'Locke adheres to Aristotle and maintains that concepts arise from experience through acts of reflection. Leibniz adheres to Plato, and says that the concepts of the understanding are prior to acquaintance with sensible objects.'[8] Again, each expressed part of the truth. Locke discovered that all cognition begins with experience, while Leibniz saw that it was not all *about* experience. Needless to say, Kant's history is rather paltry. It contains only three stages, omitting the medieval period entirely.[9] Moreover, it is exclusively a history of metaphysics and epistemology, and says nothing about

other branches of philosophy.[10] But it is a useful illustration of the sort of history that Kant thinks philosophers ought to write. It is a *systematic* history that unifies past thought by grasping it as the expression of a handful of basic epistemological principles. In Lucien Braun's words, it is a 'philosophical history of reason,' and as such it is 'a part of the system of pure reason itself.'[11]

In the decades following the appearance of the *Critique of Pure Reason*, a generation of German historians of philosophy took up Kant's call for critical history. The most famous was surely Reinhold, whose seminal essay 'Über den Begriff der Geschichte der Philosophie' served as a sort of manifesto for the Kantian historians of philosophy.[12] Other prominent critical historians were Tennemann, Heydenreich, Goess, Fülleborn, and Grohmann. Each of these thinkers tried to transform knowledge of the history of philosophy into a systematic totality by means of cues taken from the *Critique of Pure Reason*. Like Kant, they argued that a philosophy is invariably based on one of a small number of 'principles,' 'ideas,' or 'forms.' These principles were generally ones that had been better articulated in the first *Critique*: that sensation and intellect are distinct, that acquired concepts are different from a priori concepts, and so on. The Kantian historians then categorized earlier philosophical positions by showing how they embodied one of these few basic forms.[13] The point is that the widespread view that philosophy became concerned with its own past only in the nineteenth century is false. Well before the end of the eighteenth century, a sophisticated conception of the history of philosophy was in place in Germany. Kant and his followers did what Hegel and his followers are commonly thought to have done for the first time: take the history of philosophy seriously for philosophical reasons. They argued that doing a certain kind of history of philosophy is central to the philosophical enterprise itself. However original Hegel's approach to the history of philosophy was, then, it was *not* original in claiming that philosophers must come to terms with the history of their discipline, and for philosophical reasons. This view had been defended and popularized by the Kantian historians long before the beginning of Hegel's career. So what *was* novel about Hegel's approach to the history of philosophy?

The answer has to do with the *relation* between philosophy and its history. Hegel does not part with Kant by claiming *that* these enterprises are connected. He does so through his views on *how* they are connected. Hegel

differs from Kant in his conception of what we might call the chain of command between philosophy and its history. For Kant, this chain of command
is one-way: it proceeds from philosophy to its history, but not in the other
direction. The insights we gain from philosophy influence our view of philosophy's past, and they compel us to write our histories of philosophy in a
certain way. In other words, the history of philosophy must answer to philosophy. Philosophy gives the history of philosophy its goals, its methods,
and its reason for being. The reverse, however, is not true. For Kant, philosophy in no way needs to answer to the history of philosophy. The insights
we take away from the study of past thought can in no way shape the way we
philosophize now, or compel us to adopt one philosophical position rather
than another. Nothing we might learn from Plato or Aristotle could lead
us to abandon the transcendental deduction, or to carry it out in one way
rather than another. Although the philosopher needs to study the history
of philosophy eventually, she need not and should not consult it while constructing her philosophical system. Matters are the other way around. She
turns to the history of philosophy after completing her philosophy, and on
the basis of her philosophy, she sees that history aright. We might call this
view the *top-down* thesis about the history of philosophy. It is the view that
while philosophy needs its history, it directs this history rather than being
directed by it.

Describing Kant's approach to the history of philosophy as a top-down
one is the best way of accounting for a curious tension in it. While Kant
argues that critical history is an important part of the system of pure reason,
he derides philosophers who pay history too much attention, or the wrong
kinds of attention. In particular, he heaps scorn on those who think they
can acquire philosophical knowledge simply by reading the philosophers
of the past. He mocks those who approach philosophy solely through its
history. In the *Logic*, Kant ridicules the '*littérateur*' who 'learns the product
of the reason of others' but never learns to think for himself.[14] Likewise, in
the *Prolegomena*, he derides those 'scholarly men who think that the history
of philosophy (both ancient and modern) is philosophy itself.'[15] In Kant's
view, the thinker who tries to philosophize by mastering extant philosophies is 'merely a plaster cast of a living man' (*KRV*, A836/B854). Such a
thinker simply apes his predecessors, and doing so is not philosophy. He
may stumble on views that are true, but his knowledge of these views 'has
not in him arisen *out* of reason,' and so it is 'merely historical' (*KRV*, A836/

B854). Kant's criticism is based on his distinction between rational and historical knowledge. Rational knowledge is knowledge through principles, '*cognitio ex principii*' (*KRV*, A836/B854). It arises through the activity of pure reason. Historical knowledge, on the other hand, is '*cognitio ex datis*' (*KRV*, A836/B854), or knowledge derived from extant data.[16] Whatever its ultimate origin, it is, 'in relation to the person who possesses it, simply historical, if he knows only so much of it as he has been given from the outside (and this in the form in which it has been given to him)' (*KRV*, A836/B854). Learning a system of philosophy is therefore inferior to generating the same system out of principles through the use of pure reason.

For Kant, it seems, genuinely philosophical knowledge must be active. It must be produced by reason. Knowledge of the history of philosophy, on the other hand, seems decidedly passive. When I appropriate a position that has been handed down through the history of philosophy, I clearly am not producing it. I am taking up a content external to me, a content with respect to which I am not active. And as far as Kant is concerned, it does not matter whether the position I appropriate is rational, justified, or even true. It 'has not in [me] arisen *out* of reason, and although, objectively considered, it is indeed knowledge due to reason, it is yet, in its subjective character, merely historical' (*KRV*, A836/B854). To put the point differently, my knowledge of the history of philosophy is *imitative* or *mimetic*. Taking up an earlier position in the history of thought requires me to represent it, to mimic a content transmitted from without. Kant insists, however, that 'the imitative faculty is not itself productive' (*KRV*, A836/B854).[17] To imitate someone else's philosophy is precisely not to produce it or exert my spontaneity over it. Imitative knowledge is not philosophical knowledge. And since knowledge of the history of philosophy always involves imitation, it is not itself philosophical. So while Kant thinks that philosophers must confront the history of philosophy, and for philosophical reasons, he sees this confrontation as a matter posterior to philosophy itself. It is not a part of philosophy. Nor can it be, since it embodies a cognitive stance that has no place in the philosophical enterprise. The philosopher as such is active with respect to her subject matter; the historian of philosophy as such is passive with respect to hers. For this reason, Kant concludes: 'He then that desires to become, properly speaking, a philosopher, must exercise himself in making a free use of his reason, not a mere imitative and, so to speak, mechanical use.'[18]

It is on this point that Hegel breaks with Kant. Hegel does not distinguish himself from Kant by attaching philosophical importance to the history of philosophy. He does so by rejecting the top-down thesis. Hegel does not think that the chain of command between philosophy and its history is entirely one-way. He agrees with Kant that our philosophical views should influence our approach to the history of philosophy. But he further argues that our understanding of that history must inform the way we do philosophy. He suggests that a certain kind of history of philosophy is not just a necessary footnote to the philosophical enterprise, but a part of that enterprise. It is in this respect that Hegel's approach to the history of philosophy breaks with Kant's.

Hegel's work is full of attacks on the view that philosophy is distinct from its past and that the latter in no way shapes the former. Hegel typically argues that if the top-down thesis were true—that is, if philosophy were not informed by its history from the start—then the philosopher's enterprise would be futile. In other words, the attempt to understand philosophy in ahistorical terms is fruitless, or incoherent, or silly. Consider the following passage, from the *Lectures on the History of Philosophy*:

> If the history of philosophy merely represented various opinions in array, whether they be of God or of natural and spiritual things existent, it would be a most superfluous and tiresome science, no matter what might be brought forward as derived from such thought-activity and learning. What can be more useless than to learn a string of bald opinions, and what more unimportant? (*LHP*, 12)

This passage might be read as a criticism of philosophers who pay too much attention to the history of philosophy—of those who equate philosophy with 'a string of bald opinions.' But it is better understood as an attack on an excessively ahistorical conception of philosophy, and more specifically, on the top-down view of the history of philosophy associated with the critical enterprise. Philosophers, Hegel suggests, like to think of their discipline as aimed at the simple discovery of truth, at the uncovering of a *philosophia perrennis*. But according to Hegel, if this were the aim of philosophy, then philosophy would be fruitless. After all,

> the most various thoughts arise in numerous philosophies, each of which opposes, contradicts, and refutes the other. This fact, which cannot be

denied, seems to contain the justification, indeed the necessity for applying to philosophy the words of Christ: 'Let the dead bury their dead;
arise, and follow me.' The whole history of philosophy becomes a battle-
field covered with the bones of the dead; it is a kingdom not merely
formed of dead and lifeless individuals, but of refuted and spiritually
dead systems, since each has killed and buried the other. (*LHP*, 17)

Philosophy cannot be a search for timeless truth, because this search is
doomed to failure. Our astonishing lack of success at finding a *philosophia
perennis* should lead us to think that there is none to be found. We must
instead understand philosophy's mission in some other way. Whatever the
correct conception of philosophy is, it will be one that does not, in the light
of historical diversity, make philosophy look silly.

In making these claims, Hegel is advancing a radically anti-Kantian
approach to philosophy's past. He is claiming that philosophers must take
account of the lessons of the history of philosophy *while doing philosophy*,
and even while coming to understand what philosophy is. The conception of philosophy they eventually adopt must take the historical diversity of philosophies seriously. It will have to show that this diversity does
not undermine the project of philosophy, but is consistent with it, perhaps
even demanded by it. This is a sharp rebuff to those, such as Kant, who
think philosophy can deal with its history in a purely top-down manner.
According to Hegel, we cannot construct a philosophical system first and
see the history of philosophy aright only later. We cannot even begin to
philosophize until we have learned certain key lessons from philosophy's
past. Philosophy and the history of philosophy must mutually shape and
influence one another. This view is, in effect, a rejection of Kant's top-
down approach to the history of philosophy.

Yet Hegel does not have just one view about the relation between philosophy and its history. Over the course of his career, he advances no fewer
than three different views on this matter. Let me begin with the first: the
view advanced in the *Phenomenology of Spirit*.

The historical thesis in the *Phenomenology of Spirit*

The *Phenomenology* advances a particularly strong version of the historical thesis. It claims that philosophy and the history of philosophy are

identical, and that at bottom, philosophy just *is* the process of coming to terms with the history of philosophy. This view is articulated most clearly in the *Phenomenology*'s treatment of 'science' [*Wissenschaft*]. Hegel's discussion of 'scientific' knowledge is a sustained critique of the view that one can think philosophically without taking the history of philosophy seriously. Far from being 'unscientific,' Hegel argues, an interest in the history of thought is demanded by the nature of science. Hegel claims that the goal of the *Phenomenology* is to 'bring philosophy closer to the form of Science, to the goal where it can lay aside the title "*love* of knowing" and be *actual* knowing' (*PS*, 3). There are two pitfalls to avoid here. One is the assumption that a scientific philosophy is impossible. 'To lay down that the true shape of truth is scientific,' he writes, 'seems, I know, to contradict a view which is in our time as prevalent as it is pretentious' (*PS*, 4). Hegel's target here is the intuitionistic philosophies of feeling, especially Jacobi's, that maintain that 'the True exists only in what, or better *as* what, is sometimes called intuition, sometimes immediate knowledge of the Absolute' (*PS*, 4). The philosophers of feeling are hostile to science because they see reason as an improper medium for representing the Absolute. But their 'fear of error,' Hegel charges, 'reveals itself rather as fear of the truth' (*PS*, 47). The other pitfall is an imprudent haste in our search for the Absolute. To assume that science is a straightforward business is as dangerous as assuming that it is impossible. Hegel has in mind here a naive enthusiasm for the goals of scientific philosophy—the temptation to proceed immediately to the construction of a *philosophia perennis* without first reflecting on what science demands. He calls this temptation 'the rapturous enthusiasm which, like a shot from a pistol, begins straight away with absolute knowledge, and makes short work of other standpoints by declaring that it takes no notice of them' (*PS*, 16). Hegel argues that it is naive and dangerous to make short work of philosophical standpoints besides one's own. In particular, it is unwise to regard the history of philosophy as a series of failed searches for timeless truths. Philosophical knowledge 'is essentially a *result*' (*PS*, 11). It is to be understood organically, as inseparable from the historical process that produced it and as intelligible only in light of that process. Accordingly, the very attempt to articulate a *philosophia perennis* is flawed. Scientific philosophy cannot consist merely of a series of propositions about reality, since 'a so-called basic proposition or principle of philosophy, if true, is also false, just because it is *only* a principle' (*PS*, 13). The true

is not to be located solely in a philosopher's conclusions; it is 'the whole' (*PS*, 11). This organic whole, which includes the history of philosophy, 'can only be expounded . . . as *system*' (*PS*, 13). Only such a system deserves the name 'science.'

Why does Hegel think that a scientific philosophy must take the history of philosophy seriously from the beginning? The *Phenomenology* suggests that it is because of his conception of philosophy's subject matter—his understanding of what philosophy is *about*. Hegel is adamant that philosophy *has* a specific subject matter. He mocks the Kantian dictum that one cannot learn philosophy, but only to philosophize. Instead, he wants philosophy 'to lay aside the title "*love* of knowing" and be *actual* knowing' (*PS*, 3). Further, he maintains that the nature of this subject matter places restrictions on how we study it. We may not approach it unscientifically, by means of feeling or intuition, or with the 'rapturous enthusiasm' that treats it as though it were a shot from a pistol. The *Phenomenology* variously refers to philosophy's subject matter as 'spirit,' 'the True,' and 'the Absolute.'[19] There is, of course, a great deal more to be said about what spirit, the True, and the Absolute are. At a minimum, these terms refer to what Frederick Beiser calls 'thought'—that is, '[t]he art, religion, constitution, traditions, manners, and language of a people.'[20] Others read a great deal more into these terms. Charles Taylor, for example, takes them to be names for a 'cosmic subjectivity,'[21] an 'independent spiritual reality'[22] of which human beings are merely 'vehicles.'[23] A detailed discussion of these interpretations would take us too far afield, and is unnecessary for our purposes. The crucial point is that whatever spirit is, Hegel describes it as essentially developmental. Spirit is not static, or a mere in-itself. It is 'purposive activity' (*PS*, 12) and as such 'is actual only in so far as it is the movement of positing itself' (*PS*, 10). Philosophers must study spirit in a way that does justice to this developmental character. They cannot view philosophy as the mere study of what spirit *is*, once and for all. Spirit is nothing apart from its development.

This development has a definite goal. The goal is what Hegel calls absolute knowledge: spirit's recognition of itself *as* spirit. Spirit 'must be an *object* to itself, . . . a sublated [*Aufgehoben*] object reflected into itself' (*PS*, 14). It 'has to express itself outwardly and become *for itself*, and this means simply that it has to posit self-consciousness as one with itself' (*PS*, 15). Spirit's development is therefore not a mere conceptual development. It is not a progress discernible from the philosopher's armchair but nowhere else. It

is a development that can be observed in human cultural and intellectual life. Seen in this light, the history of spirit is inseparable from the history of certain human institutions. It is 'a *conscious, self-mediating* process—spirit emptied out into time' (*PS*, 492). But while spirit's evolution toward absolute knowledge can be observed in many areas of human culture—in art and religion, for example—it takes place fully in just one of them: philosophy. Spirit can recognize itself as spirit in many different media, but in philosophy alone is this recognition effected 'not only *implicitly* or in a universal sense, but *explicitly* or in a developed and differentiated way' (*PS*, 483). Spirit's recognition of itself through philosophy is the richest and deepest recognition possible, and ultimately the only real recognition spirit has. The philosopher's task is to study the development of spirit—that is, the *history* of spirit—as it is manifest in the institution of philosophy.

What is Hegel arguing here? He has claimed that philosophy is the study of spirit. Spirit alone is philosophy's proper subject matter, even though most philosophers are unaware of this fact. Spirit is essentially developmental—it *is* nothing apart from the movement of its self-positing. So philosophy turns out to be the study of the development of spirit. Since this development necessarily takes place in time—since, that is, time is the form of spirit's development—we can further say that philosophy is the study of the *history* of spirit. Spirit is embodied in many human institutions, so the history of spirit is to be found in the history of art, the history of religion, and so forth. Ultimately, however, it is in philosophy and no other area of culture that spirit's development takes place fully. The true history of spirit turns out to be the history of philosophy. But philosophy just *is* the study of the history of spirit. It follows that philosophy is identical with the history of philosophy. Properly understood, philosophy is identical with the process of coming to terms with the history of philosophical thought. The philosopher as such must study the history of her discipline, because philosophy is precisely this study.

The *Phenomenology of Spirit*, then, advances an especially strong version of the historical thesis. It does so on the basis of considerations involving the nature of spirit, which is the one proper subject matter of philosophical thinking. For this reason, I will call Hegel's defense of the historical thesis here a *content-based* defense: an argument that is based on a conception of what philosophy is *about*. No doubt it is misleading to call this reconstruction an argument, because it is not an argument that Hegel advances in so

many words. Hegel does not take himself to be giving an explicit argument
for the historical thesis in the *Phenomenology*. Clearly, though, he *does* take
himself to be describing his 'scientific' project, and to be advancing a particular conception of philosophy. The historical thesis about philosophy
is intimately connected with his description. To reconstruct Hegel's argument for the historical thesis, as I have done, is merely to make explicit a
view that is implicit in the *Phenomenology*.[24]

In 1807, then, Hegel articulates a richly historical approach to philosophy. It is no surprise that he is seen as the most historically minded of all
philosophers. The author of the *Phenomenology of Spirit* surely *is* the most
historically-minded of all philosophers. But Hegel does not endorse the
standpoint of the *Phenomenology* for his entire career. His later works—
specifically the *Lectures on the History of Philosophy* and the *Encyclopedia*—say
very different things about the history of philosophy.

History and its rival:
the *Lectures on the History of Philosophy*

At first glance, the *Lectures on the History of Philosophy* might seem perfectly
consistent with the *Phenomenology*. Hegel famously says in these lectures
that 'the study of the history of philosophy is the study of philosophy itself'
(*LHP*, 30). This looks like a restatement of the *Phenomenology*'s claim that
philosophy and its past are one and the same. Nevertheless, the *Lectures on
the History of Philosophy* mark a significant break with the *Phenomenology*. The
Phenomenology argues that philosophy and its history are identical, and that
to study one just is to study the other. The *Lectures on the History of Philosophy*,
by contrast, argue that the two are merely 'similar' (*LHP*, 30). The *Lectures*
abandon a central premise of the *Phenomenology*: that spirit just *is* its historical development, so that the *only* way to understand spirit is to see how it
develops through the history of philosophy. Hegel now argues that spirit
may be understood in two different ways, ways that are merely parallel, not
identical. While Hegel continues to see philosophy and its past as closely
related, he no longer claims that one *must* study the philosophical tradition
in order to understand the development of spirit. At least in principle, one
can understand spirit in an ahistorical manner. Before we can see this,
however, some background is in order.

Hegel describes the *Lectures on the History of Philosophy* as an attempt to resolve a contradiction. He begins these lectures by noting that there is a tension between the nature of philosophical truth on the one hand, and the actual state of philosophy on the other. There is an apparent contradiction between what 'the instinct of reason' (*LHP*, 117) says philosophy ought to be, and what, as a matter of fact, it is. Philosophy 'aims at understanding what is unchangeable, eternal, in and for itself: its end is truth' (*LHP*, 7–8). The philosopher seeks a systematic account of what there is, an account not dependent on any particular perspective or relative to any particular time. 'Eternal' and 'unchangeable' turn out to be important characteristics of such an account, since 'true, necessary thought—and it is only with such that we have to do—is capable of no change' (*LHP*, 5). But of course, philosophy as actually practiced *is* capable of change. Philosophical schools rise and fall. In so far as philosophers insist that the true is the whole, they seem unable to explain 'the spectacle of ever-recurring changes in the whole' (*LHP*, 10). One might think that this diversity is incompatible with philosophy's goal, as Hegel conceives it. One might even conclude that this goal cannot be achieved and should be abandoned. Philosophical practice, in short, seems to founder on a contradiction.

Not surprisingly, Hegel insists that this apparent contradiction is really no contradiction at all. He argues that the historical diversity of philosophies, far from compromising philosophy's mission, is required by it. He does so by repeating a point made in the *Phenomenology*: that philosophy is essentially developmental. Philosophy's subject matter—which Hegel now calls the idea[25]—is 'the objective *truth*, or the *truth as such*.'[26] Considered in itself, the idea is eternal and unchangeable, and the truth that 'a thing possesses . . . in so far as it is idea'[27] is likewise eternal and unchangeable. At the same time, 'it is essentially in the nature of the idea to develop' (*LHP*, 20). The subject matter of philosophy 'internally bestirs and develops itself,' and is 'an organic system and a totality which contains a multitude of stages and of moments in development' (*LHP*, 27). What spirit is in its essence does not change. But this essence expresses itself by evolving. The stages of this evolution not only do display change, but must. To understand philosophy's subject matter as development allows one to claim both that this subject matter 'contains a multitude of stages' and that it is 'eternal and unchangeable.'

So far, the *Lectures on the History of Philosophy* look a great deal like the *Phenomenology*. The difference is that in the *Lectures*, Hegel distinguishes two different ways of understanding spirit's development. For obvious reasons, I will call them the *historical* and the *logical*. What distinguishes them is the notion of *necessity*. According to Hegel, the most salient feature of spirit's development is that it is a necessary development. It 'a progression impelled by an inherent necessity, and one which is implicitly rational and *a priori* determined through its Idea' (*LHP*, 36). This necessity, however, may or may not be present in the philosopher's understanding of this development. To recognize this development as necessary is, as Hegel puts it, to grasp it with 'consciousness of necessity' (*LHP*, 29). To fail to recognize this necessity is to grasp it without consciousness of necessity. Hegel writes:

[A] difference with respect to the possible modes of manifestation must first be pointed out. That is to say, the progression of the various stages in the advance of Thought may occur with the consciousness of necessity, in which case each in succession deduces itself, and this form and this determination can alone emerge. Or else it may come about without the consciousness as does a natural and apparently accidental process, so that while inwardly, indeed, the Notion [*Begriff*] brings about its result consistently, this consistency is not made manifest. (*LHP*, 29)

In other words, the development of spirit may be represented either through the 'order of concepts,' by which Hegel seems to mean unaided philosophical reflection, or through 'the order of time,' by which he means the history of philosophy. To understand spirit through the order of concepts is to understand it logically; to grasp it through philosophy's past is to understand it historically.

What does it mean to grasp spirit's development without a consciousness of necessity? Hegel's point seems to be that while one can find spirit at work in history, to do so is to see spirit's development as 'a natural and apparently accidental process' (*LHP*, 29). For the historian, Hume just happens to follow Berkeley, and Berkeley Locke. Although the order of these instantiations is necessary, the necessity is not immediately apparent to the historian who reflects on them. It becomes apparent only in retrospect, when we reflect philosophically on the historian's work. To

understand spirit historically is therefore to grasp it without the conscious-ness of necessity. To grasp spirit's self-development *with* the consciousness of necessity, by contrast, is to recognize that its stages not only do occur in a certain order, but must occur in that order. This is something we can-not learn from the historical development as such. Thus when we grasp spirit 'logically,' we do not learn the succession of forms from any histori-cal process. Rather, as Hegel puts it, 'the succession deduces itself' (*LHP*, 29). Whatever this means, Hegel presumably thinks that pure philosoph-ical thought does not depend on its history. We can at least conceive of a philosopher discovering the stages of spirit's self-development without consulting its historical development. Moreover, we can see that such a 'self-deduction' is not merely another way of learning the same lessons we can learn from the history of philosophy. After all, it allows one to see the *necessity* of the various stages in spirit's development, while a grasp of the historical development does not. So Hegel's 'self-deduction' is in some sense richer than a merely historical understanding of spirit.

There are, of course, unanswered questions here. What exactly is the relation between spirit's logical and historical developments? To say they are parallel and leave it at that seems to raise more questions than it answers. And how likely is it that spirit's development in the order of ideas will exactly mirror its development in time? Hegel himself seems to detect problems here: in the *Philosophy of Right*, he warns that we should not expect the order of concepts to be exactly the same as the order of their manifestations in history.[28] Finally, even if the order of concepts were parallel to stages of the history of philosophy, it is unclear how one would go about deducing them. It might be the case that while an ideal spectator could deduce the stages of spirit's development a priori, flesh and blood philosophers probably cannot. A knowledge of how spirit has developed in history might prove invaluable in determining how it must develop in thought. But even on this less ambitious reading, the history of philoso-phy still turns out to be merely a heuristic device—a tool for discovering things we happen not to be able to discover on our own. Human beings happen not to be clever enough to deduce the stages in spirit's develop-ment entirely a priori. We happen not to be able to do philosophy without also doing history of philosophy. But this is a purely contingent fact about us, and perhaps more clever creatures could. Nothing forces the philoso-pher to come to terms with the history of philosophy. In principle, one can

do the former without doing the latter. Despite being closely connected, the two are no longer identical. The *Lectures on the History of Philosophy* therefore mark a significant departure from the *Phenomenology*.

History supplanted: the *Encyclopedia*

In an 1822 letter to von Altenstein, while discussing the subjects to be taught in the *Gymnasium*, Hegel says the following:

> I should like first expressly to exclude the *history of philosophy*, although it is just as frequently presented as immediately suitable for this purpose. But the history of philosophy, when it does not presuppose the specula- tive idea, usually becomes nothing but a narration of accidental idea opinions, and easily leads—indeed at times one might view such an effect as its aim, the very purpose of its recommendation—to a derogatory, contemptuous opinion of philosophy. It encourages in particular the representation that all has been mere vain endeavor in this science, and that it would be a still more vain endeavor for academically minded youth to occupy itself with it.[29]

It might be surprising to see Hegel question the value of studying the his- tory of philosophy—or at least the value of a certain approach to the his- tory of philosophy. Is this the same Hegel who, fifteen years earlier, argued that philosophy and its past are one and the same? The letter to von Altenstein seems to express a quite un-Hegelian sentiment. Nevertheless, the suspicion of philosophy's past that is evident in this letter is not at all out of character. It is, rather, quite representative of the later Hegel's work. If Hegel's thought is inseparable from the history of philosophy in 1807, and ambivalent toward it a decade later, then the Hegel of the 1820s and 1830s seems almost hostile to the history of philosophy. He argues that philosophy and its history have little to do with one another, and that the philosopher as such should pay little attention to her discipline's past. This hostility is nowhere more apparent than in the centerpiece of Hegel's later work: the *Encyclopedia of the Philosophical Sciences*.

Even at a casual glance, the *Encyclopedia* seems to attach far less impor- tance to the history of philosophy than Hegel's earlier works. While the system of the *Encyclopedia* reserves a niche for every discipline from

contract law to phrenology, it assigns no explicit role to the history of philosophy. This is a curious fact, to say the least. Consider as well that although the *Encyclopedia* contains its own version of the phenomenology of spirit, this phenomenology has been reduced to one brief stage in the development of subjective spirit. It also ends with the first appearance of reason: gone entirely is the rich history of the West found in the *Phenomenology*'s section on spirit. Granted, the history of spirit is concerned with cultural and intellectual history, not about the history of philosophy considered more narrowly. But the absence of a history of spirit shows that historical matters are further from Hegel's mind than in his other works, and it suggests that his conception of philosophy is now less closely linked with the history of philosophy. Consider as well the way Hegel describes philosophy in Part 3 of the *Encyclopedia*. The *Philosophy of Spirit* defines philosophy as 'a cognition of the necessity of the content in the absolute picture idea.'[30] What distinguishes philosophy from art and religion is its recognition that spirit necessarily comes to understand itself in a certain way. Compare this conception of philosophy to that found in Hegel's 1816 *Lectures*. There, philosophy was defined as a grasp of spirit's development that might or might not be accompanied by the consciousness of necessity. It was a grasp of a development that might or might not be understood historically. Now, there seems to be no room for this development to be understood historically. After all, Hegel identifies the historical with the seemingly accidental. To understand a succession historically is precisely *not* to understand it as necessary. But now, in the *Encyclopedia*, Hegel defines philosophy as a grasp *of the necessity* in spirit's development. The philosopher can no longer grasp her subject matter without being conscious of the necessity in its development. This necessity has now become her object of study. To the extent that she does not recognize it, she is not a philosopher. So there is good reason to suspect that the *Encyclopedia* attaches less importance to the history of philosophy than do Hegel's earlier works. The centerpiece of Hegel's later period certainly seems less historically informed than either the *Phenomenology* or the *Lectures on the History of Philosophy*. But what about my stronger claim—that Hegel now sanctions the 'rejection' (*EL*, 37) of the history of philosophy? This claim can best be supported by a look at the *Encyclopedia Logic*.

Near the beginning of the *Encyclopedia Logic*, Hegel distinguishes 'the history of philosophy' from 'philosophy itself' (*EL*, 38). He does this while repeating a point made in the *Phenomenology* and the *Lectures on the History of Philosophy*: namely, that all philosophies are attempts to understand spirit. Every stage in the history of philosophy, every particular philosophical position, is an attempt to grasp spirit's self-development, whether it recognizes itself as such or not. Thus Hegel says that '[t]he same development of thinking that is presented in the history of philosophy is presented in philosophy itself' (*EL*, 38). What distinguishes the history of philosophy from philosophy itself is their manner of grasping this development. Particular positions from the history of philosophy are all philosophies of the 'particular' (*EL*, 38). They identify spirit with just one of the stages of its development. Eleatic philosophy, for example, is a philosophy of the particular, because it 'apprehends the Absolute as being' (*EL*, 138). Aristotle's philosophy grasps the Absolute as *'energeia'* (*EL*, 215). Much like Kant, Hegel now argues that each position from philosophy's past manifests a principle, and that it is the historian's task to identify these principles.

Unlike Kant, however, Hegel does not think this exhausts the historian's task. Every philosophy of the particular has a shortcoming. It fails to see 'that the particular *principles* on which each system is grounded one by one are only *branches* of one and the same whole' (*EL*, 38). No particular stage of the history of philosophy can grasp spirit adequately, since each identifies it with a single 'principle.' A principle of this sort necessarily misleads, because it is only a principle. No particular principle can capture the whole of spirit's development. The correct way to understand spirit is as the totality of these principles, or, better, as a movement in which particular principles are posited, recognized as inadequate, and then *aufgehoben*. This is the standpoint of 'philosophy itself,' or what Hegel calls 'a philosophy whose principle is the universal' (*EL*, 38). Philosophy itself does not identify spirit with being, or with *energeia*, or with any other finite principle. It grasps spirit as something that must be grasped first as being, then as something more than mere being, then as something richer still, and so on. It understands spirit as the unity of its finite manifestations.

The crucial point here is that a philosophy of the universal—'philosophy itself'—is different in kind from a philosophy of the particular. The two are

radically different enterprises, and must not be seen as attempts to do the same thing. 'When we are faced with so many *diverse* philosophies,' Hegel says, 'the *universal* must be distinguished from the *particular* according to its proper determination' (*EL*, 38). To fail to do so results in absurdities:

> Taken formally, and put *side by side* with the particular, the universal itself becomes something particular too. In dealing with the objects of ordinary life, this juxtaposition would automatically strike us as inappropriate and awkward; as if someone who wants fruit, for instance, were to reject cherries, pears, raisins, etc., because they are cherries, pears, raisins, but *not* fruit. But in the case of philosophy we allow ourselves to justify the rejection of it by pointing out that philosophies are so diverse, and that each of them is only *one* philosophy, not *the* philosophy. (*EL*, 38)

The absurdity here consists in identifying fruit with a particular kind of fruit, instead of recognizing it as a category that comprehends every particular kind of fruit. Similarly, it is absurd to treat the attempt to grasp spirit as a development of finite principles as the same as the attempt to equate spirit with one such principle. To understand spirit as a synthesis of principles is not to identify it with one principle among others. It is to do something entirely different. This is what distinguishes philosophy from the history of philosophy. The history of philosophy consists of attempts to think spirit as being, *or* as *energeia*, *or* as something else. 'Philosophy itself' transcends every one of these attempts. It grasps spirit as the totality of principles manifest in the history of philosophy. Accordingly, *it is not itself part of the history of philosophy*. The kind of thinking that synthesizes all the moments of the history of philosophy is not itself another moment in that history. It is something quite different, in some sense beyond the history of philosophy altogether. To fail to recognize this is as ridiculous as treating fruit as a particular kind of fruit, or 'light and darkness [as] just two *diverse* kinds of light' (*EL*, 38).

There is no doubt that Hegel sees his own work as a philosophy of the universal. As early as the *Phenomenology*, Hegel argues that the principles of particular philosophies are really branches of the same totality. 'The true,' after all, 'is the whole' (*PS*, 11). From its inception, Hegel's thought seeks to preserve the truth of all stages of the history of philosophy—to grasp the flower as shoot *and* bud *and* bloom. But the *Encyclopedia* does so

by asserting that the sort of thinking that grasps the flower as a whole is different in kind from the sort that equates it with any one of the stages in its development. Hegel secures his universal perspective on the development of spirit by arguing that a philosophy of the universal is utterly separate from all philosophies of the particular. The philosophy that guards the insights of all positions in the history of philosophy is itself not in the history of philosophy. Hegel's 'philosophy itself'—'and it is only with such that we have to do' (*LHP*, 5)—is distinct from the history of philosophy.

The *Encyclopedia* therefore culminates Hegel's movement away from the history of philosophy. In the *Phenomenology*, Hegel argues that it is impossible to do philosophy without coming to terms with the history of philosophy. The very idea of an ahistorical philosophy is incoherent. The *Lectures on the History of Philosophy*, by contrast, argue that it is possible to do philosophy by coming to terms with its history, but that this is not the only way of doing philosophy—and perhaps not the best way. Now, in the *Encyclopedia*, Hegel argues that philosophy—understood as 'philosophy itself'—*must* turn its back on the history of philosophy. Seen in this light, even the passages from the *Encyclopedia* that look similar to passages in his earlier work must be reinterpreted. Consider the *Zusatz* to Section 86 of the *Logic*. Here, Hegel seems to repeat a point made in the *Lectures on the History of Philosophy*: that spirit's development can be understood either logically or historically. He writes:

> We find the various stages of the logical idea in the history of philosophy in the shape of emerging philosophical systems, each of which has a particular definition of the absolute as its foundation. Just as the unfolding of the logical idea proves to be an advance from the abstract to the concrete, so the earliest systems in the history of philosophy are the most abstract and therefore at the same time the poorest. But the relationship of the earlier to the later philosophical systems is in general the same as the earlier to the later stages of the logical idea. (*EL*, 138)

We might read this passage as a restatement of the main thesis of the *Lectures*: that one can understand spirit either logically or historically. Just as each stage in 'the unfolding of the logical idea' is richer than its predecessor, so each position in the history of philosophy is a more complete grasp of the nature of spirit. And just as the earliest, most abstract

characterizations of 'the logical idea' eventually give rise to the standpoint of absolute knowledge, so do the various stages in the history of philosophy give rise to a system that grasps it fully.

Hegel's distinction between the universal and the particular, however, renders this reading insupportable. There is now a crucial asymmetry between spirit's logical and historical developments. The final stage in 'the unfolding of the logical idea' is itself part of the unfolding. It is a stage—the last stage, but still a stage—of spirit's logical development. *There is no corresponding stage in the history of philosophy*. Each stage in that history identifies spirit with a merely finite principle—being, *energeia*, and so on. *No* finite principle grasps spirit completely. The standpoint that does grasp spirit completely is different in kind from all positions in the history of philosophy. It is a philosophy of the universal, not of the particular, and it differs from them as much as cherries differ from fruit. In short, Hegel does not and cannot understand his own thought as part of the history of philosophy. It must be seen as outside history, 'after' history, because it does something no merely historical position can do. But if this is the case, then Hegel's *Encyclopedia* leaves little room for philosophy to be understood historically. Philosophy itself cannot see its task as inseparable from its past. The philosopher's first task is to break with the history of philosophy.

That the history of philosophy is distinct from 'philosophy itself' does not make it worthless. Perhaps it has the same sort of status as art and religion: a way of understanding spirit, but not the richest way possible. However important art and religion are, however, they are not philosophy. The same must be true of the history of philosophy. Hegel's movement away from the historical thesis is now complete.

Kant's revenge

The three texts I have discussed show a development in Hegel's thought. They show him gradually distancing himself from the historical thesis, gradually moving away from the claim that philosophy and its past are inseparable. For the Hegel of the *Phenomenology*, philosophy is identical with the history of philosophy. The suggestion that one might do philosophy ahistorically is incoherent. Nine years later, in the *Lectures on the History*

of Philosophy, Hegel apparently thinks it is possible to do philosophy by coming to terms with its history, but that—at least in principle—there is a way of doing it ahistorically as well. And by 1830, Hegel seems to have abandoned the idea that philosophy is inseparable from its past. The task of studying the development of spirit is now reserved for the 'philosophy of the universal' articulated by the *Encyclopedia*, and is explicitly forbidden to historians. In short, Hegel attaches less and less importance to the history of philosophy as his thought matures. He spends the beginning of his career developing a sophisticated approach to the history of philosophy, and the next 23 years taking it back.

What should we make of this development? Is it nothing more than an example of a philosopher changing his mind? If it were, then it would not be very interesting. But Hegel does more than change his mind about the history of philosophy as his thought matures. He does not merely come to believe that a view he had taken to be true is in fact false. When Hegel distances himself from the history of philosophy, he is drawing out the consequences of his early approach to the topic—an approach that, despite appearances, remains constant throughout his career. Hegel thinks about the history of philosophy in the same general way in each of the texts I have discussed. He approaches it in a way that, properly understood, makes it dispensable and philosophically unimportant. Hegel does not initially see this. He does not realize that the approach to the history of philosophy articulated in the *Phenomenology*, and tacitly accepted in the rest of his work, entails that this history is dispensable. He does not initially see that his way of thinking about philosophy's past is incompatible with the historical thesis. He comes to see this only gradually. Hegel's movement from the *Phenomenology* to the *Encyclopedia* is his way of making explicit a view that is implicit in his work all along. But what view?

In the works I have discussed, Hegel gives what we might call *content-based* arguments for the historical thesis about philosophy. He argues that history is important because it tells us something about the content or the subject matter of philosophical thinking.[31] More specifically, Hegel claims that philosophy has spirit as its object. Spirit is essentially developmental. And our primary medium for observing its development is the history of philosophy. In effect, the history of philosophy is a means of representing a content that is external to it. In the *Phenomenology*, for example, Hegel

argues that philosophy is inherently historical because it is the study of
how spirit comes to self-consciousness through the history of philosophy.
In the *Lectures on the History of Philosophy*, he argues the same thing, adding
the qualification that spirit's development is not just identical with the history of philosophy. Spirit can be grasped as a logical development as well
as a historical one, and these two developments are merely parallel. Even
in the *Encyclopedia*, Hegel occasionally lapses into the content-based view
of the history of philosophy. The *Encyclopedia Logic* claims that '[w]e find
the various stages of the logical idea in the history of philosophy' (*EL*, 138).
Of course, we cannot read this as a mere restatement of the apparently
similar claims made in the *Phenomenology* and the *Lectures on the History
of Philosophy*. For the author of the *Encyclopedia*, the various stages of the
history of philosophy are mere philosophies of the particular, while 'philosophy itself' is concerned with the universal—with spirit understood as a
logical development. But Hegel's willingness to draw parallels between the
history of philosophy and 'the various stages of the logical idea' shows how
tempted he is to think of the history of philosophy as a medium for representing spirit's development, or as a tool for learning about philosophy's
subject matter. Hegel finds it natural to think of history as a privileged
expression of philosophy's content. Even in the *Encyclopedia*, he is reluctant
to abandon this way of thinking.

There are two things to note about these content-based arguments. First,
there is something un-Hegelian about them. Hegel is known for attack-
ing the assumption that cognition is an 'instrument' or a 'medium' for
representing the absolute (*PS*, 47). Yet these texts show him making very
similar claims about the history of philosophy. Hegel argues, in effect,
that the history of philosophy is important because it is an instrument or
a medium that represents philosophy's subject matter. Philosophy's past
represents the development of spirit in much the same way that, for the
critical philosophy, cognition allegedly represents reality. This is a surprising move, and one that is in deep tension with Hegel's attack on representational epistemology. Second, and more importantly, there is good
reason to doubt that this sort of strategy will work. There is good reason to
be leery of the strategy of giving content-based arguments for the historical thesis about philosophy. If history is seen as a means of representing
a content external to it, then it is bound to seem dispensable and philosophically unimportant. After all, what is a content? It is something that

can be cast into many different forms, many different media, precisely because it is distinct from them. By definition, a content can be represented through more than one form. That is what makes it a content. So how could anyone successfully argue that one particular form—say, the history of philosophy—is the only way of representing a certain content— say, spirit? A content that is essentially tied to just one form would not be a content at all. If the history of philosophy is merely a form for representing a content external to it, then that history is separable from the content and ultimately dispensable. If philosophy's subject matter is distinct from its history, then it is capable of being represented by means other than that history. We do not really *need* the history of philosophy.

Hegel's progression from the *Phenomenology of Spirit* to the *Encyclopedia* is his way of learning this lesson. First he argues that the history of philosophy is the only way of representing philosophy's subject matter; then he argues that it is one of two ways; and finally he abandons history altogether in favor of his 'philosophy of the universal.' But when Hegel distances himself from the history of philosophy in this way, he is not changing his mind. He is merely owning up to the consequences of his old approach—an approach that, as I have argued, remains constant throughout his career. The hostility to history that is made explicit in the *Encyclopedia* is implicit in the *Phenomenology*. To conceive of the history of philosophy as an instrument for representing a content is to see it as dispensable. It may have taken Hegel two decades to draw this conclusion, but the crucial premises were in place all along.

Hegel's move away from the history of philosophy, then, is a natural consequence of his approach to it. Throughout his career, Hegel thinks of the history of philosophy as a medium for representing philosophy's content. He gives content-based arguments for the historical thesis about philosophy. But if the historical thesis is interpreted as a thesis about philosophy's subject matter, then there seems little reason to think it is true. If, like Hegel, we see the history of philosophy as a tool for teaching lessons about something external to it, then we should accept Hegel's conclusion: this history is unnecessary. Conversely, if we accept the historical thesis, it will have to be for reasons different from Hegel's. It will be because of something other than a theory about philosophy's subject matter. In other words, we will not be able to give a 'content-based' argument for the historical thesis about philosophy. This is an important lesson.

But there is a deeper question here. I have argued that Hegel abandons the history of philosophy because he thinks of it as an instrument for representing a content external to it. But why does Hegel think about history in this way to begin with? Why does he view the history of philosophy as a medium for representing the development of spirit? The answer, I think, is that there is an unquestioned Kantian assumption at work in Hegel's thought. Like Kant, Hegel assumes that the imitative faculty is unproductive and therefore unphilosophical. He assumes that mimesis is passive, and that to imitate a philosophical position that one has learnt historically is inferior to generating the same position through principles. So despite everything Hegel says about the close connection between philosophy and its past, he ultimately cannot view historical reflection as an essential moment of the philosophical enterprise. His assumptions about mimesis will not let him.

Hegel's distrust of mimesis is a recurring theme in his work. At many points, and in many different contexts, Hegel displays a low opinion of mimesis—a suspicion of all cognitive stances in which the knower imitates or represents something external. Let me give three examples. First, consider the discussion of psychological representation in the *Philosophy of Mind*. Here, Hegel characterizes imitative thinking as inferior to non-imitative, saying that '[p]ure thinking knows that it alone, *and not feeling or representation*, is capable of grasping the truth of things.'[32] The problem with representation is that it is not free. In representing, I rely on something external to me—a content handed to me from without. Doing so is inferior to all cognitive stances in which the knower is free, or productive of its own contents and not reliant on external ones. Mimetic knowing is an early and crude stage in the development of *Geist*, and it is *aufgehoben* by forms of knowing in which mind *is* free.

A second example—also from the *Philosophy of Mind*—is Hegel's discussion of childhood education [*Bildung*]. Here, Hegel describes childhood as a time in which one relates to the world by imitating what one sees in it. Education is the process through which the child outgrows this reliance on imitation and comes to know the world in richer ways. According to Hegel, when children become intellectually aware—when they pass 'from play to the seriousness of learning'[33]—their first impulse is to mimic adults. They are moved by 'the awakening feeling in them that as yet they *are* not what

they *ought* to be, and the active desire to become like the adults in whose surroundings they are living.'[34] But this mimicry is soon outgrown, and it is inferior to the standpoint of the tortured adolescent who 'feels that both his ideal and his own personality are not recognized by the world, and . . . is no longer at peace with the world.'[35] Imitating the world is cognitively lower than rebelling against it. Something similar can be seen when a child learns the alphabet. Now able to live within an 'airy element, at once sensuous and non-sensuous,'[36] the child leaves behind mere '*picture-thinking*,' in which 'the world is only for his representational thinking.'[37] Language enriches the child's grasp of the world because it allows him to think abstractly, and to overcome his reliance on images and imitation. Hegel's point is clear: grasping the world mimetically is inferior to grasping it nonmimetically.

A third example is Hegel's treatment of symbolic art in the *Lectures on Aesthetics*. Hegel sees symbolic art as the lowest and least interesting form of art—lower than both classical and romantic art. Art that expresses the idea by means of symbolism is the most primitive form of art possible. The reason is that symbolic art is mimetic, or imitative. Symbolic art represents a content external to it—it 'finds itself confronted by what is external to itself, external things in nature and human affairs.'[38] In imitating these things, symbolic art 'corrupts and falsifies the shapes that it finds confronting it. This is because it can grasp them only arbitrarily, and therefore, instead of coming to a complete identification, it comes only to an accord, and even to a still abstract harmony, between meaning and shape.'[39] In symbolic art, there is no 'identification' between meaning and shape, between what is depicted and the manner of its depiction. There is only symbolic depiction, a standing-in for what is absent. The form of the symbolic artwork is not adequate to its content. Thus symbolic art is sharply opposed to classical art, in which there is 'an entirely harmonious unity between content and form.'[40] In classical art, content and form coincide; in symbolic art, form merely gestures toward content, and gestures poorly at that. It is a reliance on imitation that makes symbolic art inferior. Hegel's low opinion of symbolism results from his low opinion of imitation.

No doubt we could find other examples of Hegel's distrust of mimesis. We could read the *Phenomenology of Spirit* as the story of the overcoming

of imitative knowledge—as the gradual recognition that the mind does not merely represent an 'external world,' that all consciousness is *self-consciousness*, and that spirit stands in relation to another that is purely its own. But these examples will suffice. In many different texts, from many different stages of his career, Hegel reveals himself to be suspicious of mimesis. He sees philosophy as the overcoming of alterity, as the *Aufhebung* of mind's dependence on external contents. And like Kant, he believes that to imitate these external contents is passive, unproductive, and therefore unphilosophical. Obviously, someone who understands mimesis in this way will find it difficult to see historical knowledge as philosophical. Historical knowledge is mimetic knowledge par excellence. When I study a position in the history of philosophy, I imitate it. I represent positions handed to me from without, positions with respect to which I am not free. I do something that Kant and Hegel see as incompatible with philosophical knowing. Hegel's work on the history of philosophy, then, consists of two opposed tendencies. On the one hand, Hegel thinks that Kant's 'top-down' approach to the history of philosophy is shallow and misguided. He refuses to believe that the chain of command between philosophy and its history is entirely one-way. He is convinced that philosophers must learn certain lessons from history before they even begin to philosophize. On the other hand, Hegel believes that all historical knowledge is imitative, that all imitative knowledge is passive and unfree, and that as a result, knowledge of the history of philosophy is unphilosophical. Hegel sets himself an impossible task: to reject Kant's theory of the history of philosophy while accepting the assumptions that give rise to it. We should not be surprised that he is unsuccessful.

Nevertheless, Hegel does an impressive job of trying to reconcile these conflicting goals. To accomplish the first part of this task—that is, to repudiate the top-down thesis—he asserts that 'the study of the history of philosophy is the study of philosophy itself' (*LHP*, 30). He rejects Kant's claim that the history of philosophy is a mere handmaiden to philosophy. To accomplish the second part of his task—that is, to salvage his Kantian assumptions about the cognitive inferiority of mimesis—he denies that historical knowledge is *really* part of philosophy, though it is in some sense indispensable to it. And he argues that this is so because the history of philosophy teaches us about philosophy's subject matter. The history of philosophy is an instrument or a medium for representing the development of

spirit, for teaching us things about philosophy's content. But what it represents is a content separate from the history. Philosophy's subject matter is not in history. It is merely represented by history. If the truth about spirit were literally *in* the history of philosophy, then one could do philosophy simply by imitating particular positions from the history of philosophy. One could do philosophy mimetically. Hegel finds this suggestion repugnant. He does not want to dismiss history, but neither does he want to grant that historical knowledge is truly philosophical. Making the history of philosophy a medium for the representation of spirit is an attempt to have it both ways.

What else are we to make of the *Phenomenology*'s holistic view of truth? Even here, in Hegel's most historical work, he argues that the true is the whole. Whatever truth we find in history has to be identified with the *whole* of history understood as an organic unity, not with any particular part of that unity. If my reading is right, Hegel has to identify the true with the whole because he cannot identify it with the part. For if the true were found *in* history—*in* the concrete, *in* the ontic—then one could represent the true by imitating the particular. One could reach truth through mimesis. And Hegel, like Kant, finds this suggestion repugnant. His solution is to separate the particular stages of history from the whole of history, and to identify the true with the latter. Strictly speaking, the true is no longer *in* the concrete. It is beyond the concrete. In separating the true from the ontic, Hegel has turned it into a content or subject matter separate from history. He then tries to argue that something about this content forces the philosopher to know it historically. But as we have seen, this strategy is bound to fail. There will always be other, and perhaps better, ways of representing the same content. In viewing mimesis as unproductive, in banishing the true from the concrete, Hegel has made the history of philosophy dispensable.

I claimed at the beginning of this chapter that Hegel sees his approach to the history of philosophy as anti-Kantian. He thinks of himself as repudiating a 'top-down' approach to this history—the view that history needs philosophy but not *vice versa*. It now appears, however, that Hegel's disagreement with Kant is only skin deep. Granted, Hegel rejects Kant's explicitly stated views about the history of philosophy. But he does not reject the assumptions that give rise to them. He accepts a suspicion of mimesis that is incompatible with the historical thesis. As a result, Kant's hostility to the

history of philosophy sneaks back into Hegel's thought over the course of his career. By 1830, Hegel's work is no more historical than the critical philosophy had been, and Kant's revenge is complete. Hegel often presents his thought as a break with Kant. But with respect to the history of philosophy, he remains a Kantian *malgré lui*.

Chapter 3

Heidegger and the Myth of the Primordial

Chapter 2 discussed the first episode in the development of the historical thesis: the emergence of this thesis in Hegel's work. Chapter 3 deals with the next important episode. It discusses Martin Heidegger's reappropriation of Hegel's approach to the history of philosophy in the 1920s and 1930s. I interpret Heidegger's work from this period as a 'reciprocal rejoinder' (*BT*, 438) to Hegel—an attempt to break with Hegel's way of thinking about the history of philosophy, while salvaging his claim that philosophy is inherently historical. This break, however, is incomplete and ultimately unsuccessful. I argue that Heidegger remains trapped in a Hegelian framework for thinking about the history of philosophy, a framework that makes his rejoinder deeply problematic. He is left with an approach to the history of philosophy that is not adequately distinguished from Hegel's, but whose Hegelian roots Heidegger does not recognize. Chapter 3 is therefore central to my overall argument. Chapter 2 explained how a Hegelian way of thinking about the history of philosophy was put in place. Chapter 3 explains how it *stayed* in place, despite sophisticated attempts to move beyond it. So in Chapter 3, we see the emergence of a genuine crisis. Hegel gave us an incoherent view of the relation between philosophy and its history. Heidegger, I argue, transforms this picture so that its incoherence is covered up.

Chapter 3 consists of four parts. The first puts Heidegger's discussion of the history of philosophy into context. It describes Heidegger's defense of the historical thesis in the 1920s, and it contrasts his approach with the neo-Kantian philosophy dominant in Germany at the time. The next two sections describe Heidegger's approach as a reaction to Hegel—that is, as an attempt to solve certain problems with Hegel's way of thinking about the history of philosophy. Whereas Hegel argues that an engagement with the history of philosophy is required by philosophy's *content*, Heidegger

thinks it is required by philosophy's *form*. This is a significant break with Hegel, and one that shows some promise. In the fourth and final section, however, I argue that Heidegger does not succeed in breaking with Hegel. Heidegger does not separate philosophy's form and its content in the way his project requires. His hesitations leave the door open for a content-based approach to sneak back in.

This chapter deals only with Heidegger's work from the twenties and thirties. It does not discuss his later work in any detail. This is not because Heidegger's later work is unconcerned with the history of philosophy. Rather, it is because doing justice to the later work would take us too far afield. I should add that when I say that Heidegger's approach to the history of philosophy can be read as a break with Hegel's, I do not mean that Heidegger *intended* it as such or *understood* it as such. My claim is that Hegel and Heidegger can be fruitfully understood as taking part in a conversation about the history of philosophy. Heidegger may or may not have recognized this fact.

From Hegel to Heidegger

It is hard to overestimate Hegel's influence on later discussions of the history of philosophy. In the second half of the nineteenth century, there emerged something of a consensus in French and German thought: Hegel had discovered something essential about philosophy's past. This was obviously the case with Hegel's more historically minded followers, such as Cieszkowski and Feuerbach. But even philosophers unsympathetic to Hegel came to believe that he had discovered something crucial about their discipline. Dilthey, who often dismissed Hegel's project as an incoherent secularized Christianity, came to believe that philosophy and the rest of the *Geisteswissenschaften* were inseparable from their histories. So did the members of the 'Historical School,' who maintained that 'historical growth is the source of all spiritual [*Geistige*] facts.'[1] Even Comte, who claimed never to have read Hegel,[2] insisted that positivism was obliged to retrace its historical origins.[3] Of course, several of these thinkers incorrectly assumed that Hegel had been the first to maintain that philosophers must be historians as well. Many seemed unaware that Kant had already argued much the same thing. Still, they embraced what they took to be Hegel's discovery: philosophy is an inherently historical discipline, and it is

impossible to practice it well without studying its history. In that sense, they were all Hegel's children.

Toward the end of the nineteenth century, however, there was a backlash to this consensus. A new view of the history of philosophy became prominent in Germany with the rise of neo-Kantianism. Neo-Kantian historians did not simply turn their backs on Hegel. For the most part, they considered his work on the history of philosophy important. But they tried to pull its philosophical teeth. They wanted to show that one could grant many of Hegel's premises about the history of philosophy without concluding that philosophy is *essentially* historical. Like Kant himself, they argued that the history of philosophy is important, but is not identical with philosophy. The neo-Kantian to argue most forcefully for this view was no doubt Wilhelm Windelband. Windelband defines the history of philosophy as 'the process in which European humanity has embodied in scientific conceptions its views of the world and its judgments of life.'[4] Like art, religion, and politics, philosophy expresses an age's *Weltanschauung*. It differs from them, however, in that it embodies its age's worldview in 'scientific conceptions.' As cultures evolve, so do their ways of embodying their views of the world. The Baroque world view, for example, evolved out of the Renaissance *Weltanschauung*. The same holds at levels of greater specificity: Baroque art, for example, had antecedents in Renaissance art, and evolved as a reaction to it. Philosophy is no different in this respect. Its way of embodying the European *Weltanschauung* through scientific conceptions has evolved over time in response to specific historical conditions. Thus for Windelband, if we are to understand what eighteenth century philosophy reveals about the European world view, we should know something about its debt to seventeenth century philosophy and the world view it embodies. Understanding the logic of Leibniz's thought is crucial to understanding the logic of Kant's, and knowing how Leibniz embodies the European world view is a prerequisite for knowing how Kant does so. For Windelband, then, understanding the history of philosophical thought is a crucial part of understanding philosophy. It turns out that 'the *history* of philosophy . . ., as Hegel first recognized, must be regarded in this sense as an integral part of philosophy itself.'[5]

Windelband claims, however, that we can recognize the history of philosophy as an integral part of philosophy without seeing it as identical

with philosophy. According to Windelband, Hegel was right to see the history of philosophy as one of the things that allows us to understand a philosophical position—allows us, that is, to understand how a philosophical position embodies the European world view. But he was wrong to see it as the *only* such thing. Hegel, in Windelband's view, thought that to understand a philosophical view, it is sufficient to understand how this view has emerged from its history. All other factors are to be excluded.[6] But while Windelband thinks it is necessary to understand a philosophy by understanding its history, it is by no means sufficient. We cannot understand a philosophical position simply by viewing it as a response to earlier ones. We must take account of other factors as well: broader cultural and intellectual factors, 'the personality of its founder,'[7] and so on. Windelband writes:

> The mistake of Hegel's mentioned above, consists, then, only in his wishing to make of a factor which is effective within certain limits, the only, or at least the principal, factor. It would be the opposite error to deny absolutely the 'reason in history' and to see in the successive doctrines of philosophy only confused chance-thoughts of individuals.[8]

According to Windelband, Hegel was right to understand philosophy as the product of a conceptual development emptied out into time. But he was wrong to see it as *merely* the product of such a development. Doing so attaches too much weight to a philosophical position's internal logic and not enough to contingency, biography, and broader cultural factors. Understanding the history of philosophy is an indispensable part of understanding philosophy itself. But it is only a part. The two are not as closely connected as Hegel believed.

Windelband's criticisms amount to a neo-Kantian backlash to the Hegelian orthodoxy. Hegel had declared that philosophy and its history are one and the same, and while he later distanced himself from this claim, several generations of philosophers took it at close to face value. Windelband, however, insists that we can see philosophy and its past as closely related without seeing them as identical. He is advancing much the same view *after* Hegel that Kant had advanced *before* Hegel. To be sure, Windelband's understanding of the history of philosophy is different from Kant's. Kant held that there was a 'top-down' relation between

philosophy and its history, and that we turn to history only after getting our philosophy right. Windelband, by contrast, thinks we cannot make sense of philosophy until we get our history right—and not just the history of philosophy, but cultural and intellectual history as well. Yet there is a Kantian spirit common to the claims of both thinkers. Kant and Windelband both think we can accept the contributions of historians of philosophy while denying that the task of philosophy *just is* to make sense of these contributions.

Heidegger's work from the 1920s and 1930s should be read in the context of this neo-Kantian backlash. Windelband would have us retain much of Hegel's account of the history of philosophy while rejecting the historical thesis itself. Heidegger, on the other hand, wants to resurrect the historical thesis against the objections of its neo-Kantian critics. Just as Hegel had defined his version of the historical thesis in opposition to Kant, Heidegger defines his version in opposition to the neo-Kantianism of his day. Moreover, as we will see, Heidegger resurrects the historical thesis in a way that holds out some promise of avoiding the problems that had undermined Hegel's version. To see how it does so, we should turn to Heidegger's most important work from this period: *Being and Time*.

The primordial as content

At first glance, the historical thesis might seem incompatible with *Being and Time*. Heidegger's project in this book is to 'raise anew *the question of the meaning of Being*' (*BT*, 19), and he describes the history of philosophy as an obstacle to this questioning. According to Heidegger, philosophy has traditionally encouraged us to neglect the question of Being. It has led us to think that inquiring into the meaning of Being is fruitless and unnecessary. That it has done so is no accident. Heidegger tells us that a tradition (*Überlieferung*) always distorts what it transmits (*überliefert*). A tradition makes certain things appear self-evident, such that 'what it "transmits" is made so inaccessible . . . that it rather becomes concealed' (*BT*, 43). This is what has happened to the understanding of Being we have inherited from the Greeks. The tradition has passed down a certain way of thinking about Being, one that makes the meaning of Being appear self-evident and obvious to all. Seen in this light, the history of philosophy is the history of the forgetting of Being, the history of the decline and

distortion of the real business of philosophy. But it does not follow that we can turn our backs on the tradition and pose the question of the meaning of Being in an entirely new way. On the contrary, it is *because* tradition covers up the real business of philosophy that we must engage with it. Far from authorizing a break with the past, the nature of tradition demands that we confront it.

Heidegger calls this confrontation a *destruction* of the history of philosophy. It seeks to recover 'the soil from which the basic ontological concepts developed' (*BT*, 22), and so to reappropriate what the Greeks 'wrested with the utmost intellectual effort from the phenomena' (*BT*, 21). It does so by examining the ways in which later philosophy distorts the initial contributions of the Greeks. Destruction studies the ways in which tradition has misunderstood Being, in the hope of recovering a more primordial understanding that has become lost. Heidegger explains:

> When tradition thus becomes master, it does so in such a way that what it transmits is made so inaccessible, proximally and for the most part, that it rather becomes concealed. Tradition . . . blocks our access to those primordial 'sources' from which the categories and concepts handed down to us have been in the past quite genuinely drawn. Indeed, it makes us forget that they have had such origins. (*BT*, 43)

This is why a destruction of the history of philosophy is necessary. Tradition has covered up the sources of ontological thinking, making them inaccessible. If they are to become accessible once more, then

> this hardened tradition must be loosened up, and the concealments which it has brought about must be dissolved . . . [T]aking the *question of Being as our clue*, we are to *destroy* the traditional content of ancient ontology until we arrive at those primordial experiences in which we achieved our first ways of determining the nature of Being—the ways which have guided us ever since. (*BT*, 45)

To 'destroy' the tradition in this way is not to dismiss it as worthless, or to leave it behind altogether. It is to 'stake out the positive possibilities of that tradition' (*BT*, 45), and to ask whether a new understanding of Being might be erected on its basis.

But what exactly does destruction involve? *Being and Time* characterizes it as a *repetition* (*Wiederholung*) of the tradition. Repeating a tradition means '*handing [it] down explicitly*' (*BT*, 437). Repetition is an active and self-conscious return to decisive moments in the tradition. Thus it involves a break with Dasein's habitual way of dealing with its past. To repeat the history of philosophy, however, is not to adopt doctrines from the past. Repeating Descartes' philosophy, for example, does not require that we become Cartesians. Repetition seeks to 'loosen up' the tradition through active reappropriation. As Heidegger puts it in 1925's *History of the Concept of Time*, 'genuine repetition of a traditional question lets its external character as a tradition fade away,'[9] leaving us with the 'primordial experiences' that tradition has covered up. Repetition allows Dasein to '*choose* and *find* the possibility of its existence' (*BT*, 435), rather than encountering this possibility 'by accident' (*BT*, 435). 'Possibility' is a crucial word here. Repetition seeks to uncover possibilities from the past—that is, to revisit what was thought so that we may recover what it left unthought. Repetition 'does not let itself be persuaded of something by what is "past," just in order that this . . . may recur. Rather, the repetition makes a reciprocal rejoinder to the possibility of existence that has been there' (*BT*, 438). An inquiry into the meaning of Being must take the form of a reciprocal rejoinder to the history of philosophy. It cannot simply endorse past understandings of Being. But it must repeat them in order to uncover what the tradition has closed off.

Why, then, does Heidegger's project require him to engage with the history of philosophy? Because our ontological concepts, our ways of understanding Being, have been systematically distorted by tradition. The process that has handed them down has concealed something important. To combat this concealment, we must destroy the history of philosophy and so trace our ontological concepts back to their sources. What will remain at the end of this process are the 'primordial experiences' (*BT*, 44) of Being, the 'primordial "sources"' (*BT*, 43) in which our ontological concepts originated. Whatever these 'experiences' and 'sources' are, they are something from which tradition has separated us. For Heidegger, then, we must confront the history of philosophy in order to retrieve something: 'the primordial.'

But what *is* the primordial? We must find some clarity on this matter, because it is easy to misunderstand what Heidegger is doing. It might appear that Heidegger, like Hegel, wants us to study the history of philosophy in

order to learn something about philosophy's subject matter. Heidegger does, of course, disagree with Hegel about the nature of this subject matter. For Hegel, it is spirit; for Heidegger, it is Being, and more specifically, the 'primordial experiences' of Being that have been distorted by the tradition. Heidegger might seem to be saying that there is some body of information about Being to which the Greeks had access and that we can recover by destroying the tradition. In other words, he might seem to be claiming that there is some *content* about which the history of philosophy can teach us lessons. If that were the case, Heidegger's discussion of the history of philosophy would be a very unoriginal repetition of Hegel's indeed. But as I will argue, this is not what Heidegger means by 'the primordial.' His primordial experiences of Being are not a content or a body of information. Retrieving the primordial experiences of Being does not involve discovering facts about Being that the Greeks knew but that we have forgotten. Unlike Hegel, Heidegger does not see the history of philosophy as a tool for representing philosophy's subject matter. He understands it quite differently, and as a result, his conception of the history of philosophy should be read as an alternative to Hegel's, not a mere continuation of it. In order to see this, however, we must look more closely at the claims he makes about the primordial.

When Heidegger says that repeating the history of philosophy is a way to access the primordial experiences of Being that have been distorted by tradition, some of his readers take these words quite literally. They take him as saying that there is some body of information about Being that lurks behind the tradition, waiting to be uncovered. On this view, to gain access to the primordial experiences of Being is to unearth a forgotten doctrine and embrace it anew. Gail Soffer calls this interpretation the 'literal retrieval thesis.'[10] One reader of Heidegger who seems to endorse it is Charles Guignon. Guignon describes Heideggerian destruction as a two-step process that both 'diagnoses the misconceptions and confusions that run through the tradition' and then 'brings to light the underlying conception of time which is concealed by the tradition.'[11] According to Guignon, destruction unearths an object—namely, an underlying conception of time. Once we have removed the distortions of tradition, Guignon suggests, we will have access to this underlying conception as it was before the distortions began. The literal retrieval thesis has some evidence in its favor. It seems to be supported by Heidegger's talk of primordial 'sources'

and 'experiences,' as well as by his claim that repetition 'goes back *prior* to the questions which were posed in history,' such that 'the questions raised by the past are once again originally appropriated.'[12] It is also supported by Heidegger's tendency to criticize other philosophers for getting Greek ontology wrong—for not doing justice to the proper understanding of Being that lurks behind the obfuscations of tradition.[13] All of these considerations suggest that Heidegger wants 'to penetrate the distortions of the tradition and retrieve early Greek experience in its primordiality, "as it really was." '[14]

Other readers of Heidegger reject the literal retrieval thesis, but accept what Soffer calls 'a more palatable revision along Gadamerian lines.'[15] According to this reading, historians of philosophy might *like* to retrieve the early Greek experience of Being as it really was. But they recognize that they can never do so. They realize that all historical research 'is conditioned by the existential fore-structures, and hence the particular cares and projects of the historian, as influenced by his cultural milieu.'[16] The destruction of the history of philosophy is no exception, and 'even where the historian aims at an accurate reconstruction of the past, the result will never be an identical, repeatable recreation.'[17] The best we can hope for is an imperfect reconstruction that recognizes the limits of our understanding. This interpretation is clearly less ambitious than the literal retrieval thesis. Reconstructing Greek ontology within the limits of one's historical situation is a more modest goal than recreating Greek ontology as it really was. Like the literal retrieval thesis, however, this Gadamerian revision still conceives of the primordial experiences of Being as a *content*: a thing or a doctrine to be reconstructed. It grants that reconstruction of this sort can never be more than partially successful. But it still assumes that there is something to retrieve, however incomplete our attempts to do so. And it maintains that the historian of philosophy should *try* to recover this content as it really was, even as she recognizes that she is bound to fail. In short, both the literal retrieval thesis and its Gadamerian revision assume that Heidegger's primordial experiences of Being are things or contents. But a close reading of *Being and Time* shows that this assumption is wrong. Uncovering primordial experiences of Being cannot be a matter of retrieving a doctrine or finding a body of information, no matter how sophisticated we are about the hermeneutics of this retrieval. Heidegger's primordial experiences are not candidates for retrieval of this sort,

because they are not things or contents at all. For Heidegger, in this sense, the primordial is a myth. There are several reasons for this.

One reason has to do with Heidegger's characterization of repetition. The destruction of the history of philosophy is a repetition of decisive moments in this history. To destroy the history of philosophy is to reappropriate these episodes actively and hand them down explicitly, thus allowing their external character to fall away. But the episodes to be repeated are not actual events from the history of philosophy. Nor are they positions or doctrines that have actually been held during that history. They are *possibilities*—'possibilities of the Dasein that has-been-there' (*BT*, 437). Repetition does not result in the recurrence of past doctrines. It is a response, a reciprocal rejoinder, to earlier *possibilities* of thinking. It follows that what results from repetition cannot be any sort of doctrine or content. If it were—if repetition resulted in the recovery of lost theses, such as Guignon's 'underlying conception of time'—then it would yield something actual. It would result in the recurrence of a position that was once actual and that will be actual again. But while Heidegger is not entirely clear about what results from a repetition, he is adamant that nothing actual does. Thus his primordial experiences of Being cannot be contents or things in Guignon's sense.

Furthermore, if Heidegger's primordial experiences of Being were contents to be retrieved, then the need for repetition could eventually *end*. At some point, the goals of repetition would be achieved, once and for all. The historian of philosophy would succeed in getting behind the distortions of tradition, at least to the extent that her historical situation allows. Under those circumstances, she would be in possession of Heidegger's priomordial experiences of Being, and she would no longer need to keep repeating the past. But Heidegger insists that this could never happen. Repetition is an endless task. Heidegger is not merely skeptical that philosophers will ever achieve the goals of repetition—because they are not clever enough, for example. The need for repetition will never vanish, no matter how successful we are at philosophizing. *Being and Time* makes clear that there is a close link between the existential structures of Dasein and the essentially historical character of philosophy. We need to repeat the history of philosophy because we need to understand how tradition has distorted our ways of thinking about Being. But tradition's tendency

to distort the primordial is an expression of a more general phenomenon: Dasein's fallenness. Dasein is a fallen entity—or better, a *falling* entity—in that it tends to accept uncritically what others think and say. This reliance on others lulls Dasein into 'the tranquillized supposition that it possesses everything, or that everything is within its reach' (*BT*, 223). Dasein's tendency to fall is what turns its ways of thinking into traditions that we fail to investigate. Dasein tends to assume that if a way of thinking is widespread, it is entirely self-evident, and we no longer need to reflect on it. As a result,

> everything that is primordial gets glossed over as something that has long been well understood. Everything gained by a struggle becomes just something to be manipulated. Every secret loses its force. This case of averageness reveals in turn an essential tendency of Dasein which we call the 'leveling down' of all possibilities. (*BT*, 165)

The formation of traditions therefore manifests 'a basic kind of Being which belongs to everydayness: we call this the "falling" of Dasein' (*BT*, 219). Falling is a general phenomenon. It takes place not just in some traditions, but in traditions as such, and in the philosophical tradition in particular. Indeed, this is what we would expect, given that the attempt to know the world philosophically is a 'founded mode of Being-in-the-world' (*BT*, 86).

The point is that Dasein's falling does not end. We must, Heidegger says, not 'take the fallenness of Dasein as a "fall" from a purer and higher "primal status"' (*BT*, 220). It is 'a definite existential characteristic of Dasein itself' (*BT*, 220). Accordingly, Dasein cannot overcome its tendency to fall. The best it can hope is to gain 'mastery' over it 'just "for that moment"' (*BT*, 422). We 'can never extinguish it' (*BT*, 422). By extension, we can never extinguish the tendency to form traditions and thereby distort what is 'primordial.' As soon as we interpret something, we begin to distort it. So there will never come a point in the history of philosophy when we have freed ourselves completely of the distortions of tradition, or the misunderstandings of the primordial experiences of Being. There will never come a time when we no longer need to repeat the history of philosophy and loosen up its sedimentations. Since the need for repetition will never end,

Heidegger's primordial experiences of Being cannot be the sort of thing that one recovers, either wholly or partially. They cannot, in short, be contents of any sort.

So what are they? What does it mean to reappropriate the primordial experiences of Being? Let me offer a different answer to these questions— one that interprets the primordial not in terms of content, but in terms of form.

The primordial as form

Whereas Hegel gives a content-based argument for the historical thesis, Heidegger gives a *form-based* argument for it. According to this argument, an engagement with philosophy's past is required by philosophy's *method*, or by the *manner* in which it proceeds. Destroying the history of philosophy in search of primordial experiences of Being does not involve representing some content beyond that history. Rather, it involves adopting a certain method, a particular style of thinking. This method can and should be characterized independently of the contents to which it happens to be applied. The destruction of the history of philosophy is required not by philosophy's *what*, but by its *how*—not by its content, but by its form. Moreover, this form is to be privileged over its content. As a result, Heidegger's approach to the historical thesis can be seen as a sharp break with Hegel's. Let me explain why.

According to Heidegger, the task of destroying the history of philosophy does not stand alone. It is part of a larger project: fundamental ontology. The task of dismantling the history of philosophy cannot be separated from the larger task of posing and clarifying the question of the meaning of Being. Though it is not completely clear from the discussion of destruction in Section Six of *Being and Time*, posing the *Seinsfrage* and destroying the tradition are two aspects of one and the same project. Indications of this appear throughout *Being and Time*. For example, when Heidegger describes the histories of philosophy that are to appear in Part 2 of this work—histories he did not finish—he speaks of them as explications of the results of Part 1. He does not just claim that he will dismantle the history of philosophy in Part 2; he claims that he will dismantle it by means of 'clues' from Part 1. He says, for example, that the destruction of the

history of philosophy must proceed 'by taking *the question of Being as our clue*' (*BT*, 44). He says the same thing about particular figures from the tradition. He describes his destructive reading of Kant, for example, as a working-out of claims made in his discussion of ecstatic temporality (*BT*, 45). Granted, Heidegger says that posing the *Seinsfrage* and destroying the tradition are 'two distinct tasks' (*BT*, 69). But he also says that these tasks make up a single project—the 'treatment of the question of Being'—which 'branches out' into two mutually dependent sides (*BT*, 69). Destruction is made possible by the clues that originate in Heidegger's treatment of the *Seinsfrage*, but the working-out of these clues in Part 2 sheds new light on Part 1. These tasks are two sides of the same project.

Now, fundamental ontology is above all an interrogation of Dasein. It is 'sought in the *existential analytic of Dasein*' (*BT*, 33–34): a study of Dasein in its everydayness, an inquiry into how Dasein exists, proximally and for the most part. No other strategy is available. We cannot, for example, pose the question of the meaning of Being by giving a neutral description of our intuitions about Being. These intuitions are unreliable, since 'the *Being* of entities' does not manifest itself as other phenomena do, but 'shows itself only "*in disguise*"' (*BT*, 59). More importantly, the need to interrogate Dasein results from the 'formal structure' of the question of Being (*BT*, 24). Every question, Heidegger maintains, is guided by three structural items—'that which is asked about' [*Gefragte*], 'that which is to be found out by the asking' [*Erfragte*], and 'that which is interrogated' [*Befragte*] (*BT*, 24). In the case of the *Seinsfrage*, that which is asked about is Being. That which is to be found out by the asking is the meaning of Being. But what is to be interrogated? There seem to be indefinitely many candidates, since 'there are many things which we designate as "being" [*Seiend*], and we do so in various senses' (*BT*, 26). Being 'lies in the fact that something is, and in its being as it is; in Reality [*Realität*]; in presence-at-hand; in subsistence; in validity; in Dasein; in the "there is"' (*BT*, 26); and perhaps in indefinitely many other senses as well. But these different senses are all ways in which Being is 'looked at,' ways in which the meaning of Being is 'understood and conceptually grasped' (*BT*, 26). The different senses of Being are all ways of *conceiving* of Being, and as such, they are 'modes of Being for those particular entities which we, the inquirers, are ourselves' (*BT*, 26–27). In short, there are many things we might interrogate in posing the question of Being, but all are, at bottom, modes of Being for Dasein. They are all

ways in which Dasein is. To interrogate any of them, or all of them, is to interrogate Dasein's Being. If we are to work out the question of the meaning of Being, we must interrogate Dasein—or, better, we must interrogate the ways in which Dasein interrogates Being in its daily life. Fundamental ontology turns out to be a questioning of Dasein's everyday questioning of Being.

Heidegger calls this inquiry an *Auslegung*, an *interpretation* of Dasein's being.[18] To interrogate Dasein's Being is to conduct a phenomenological description of Dasein. It is to 'exhibit' Dasein's Being 'as it shows itself in itself' (*BT*, 59). But 'the meaning of phenomenological description as a method lies in *interpretation*' (*BT*, 61). Phenomenological method is interpretive, and a phenomenology of Dasein is necessarily an interpretation of Dasein's Being. Heidegger defines interpretation as the 'development of the understanding' (*BT*, 188), or a 'working-out of possibilities projected in understanding' (*BT*, 189). To interpret something is to make explicit the ways in which we understand it—or more accurately, the ways in which we have *been* understanding it, perhaps without recognizing this fact. Understanding does not arise from interpretation, but precedes it. Whenever we encounter a thing, 'the thing in question already has an involvement which is disclosed in our understanding of the world' (*BT*, 190–191). Interpretation makes these involvements explicit. Accordingly, interpretation is usually directed at something ready-to-hand, such as a tool that one uses for some practical end. In fundamental ontology, however, it is directed at Dasein itself. Fundamental ontology, then, is a phenomenology of Dasein. And '[t]he phenomenology of Dasein is a *hermeneutic* in the primordial signification of this word, where it designates this business of interpreting' (*BT*, 62).[19]

Heidegger insists that to call fundamental ontology a phenomenological enterprise, or an interpretive enterprise, is to characterize it in purely formal terms. It is not to say anything about what this enterprise studies. Phenomenology is a method. It has to do with *how* an inquiry proceeds. And Heidegger insists again and again that this method can be characterized independently of its subject matter. He says, for example, that '[t]he expression "phenomenology" signifies primarily a *methodological conception*. This characterization does not express the *what* of the objects of philosophical research as subject-matter, but rather the *how* of that research' (*BT*, 50). He also says that ' "[p]henomenology" neither designates the object of

its researches, nor characterizes the subject-matter thus comprised. The word merely informs us of the "*how*" with which "*what*" is to be treated in this science gets exhibited' (*BT*, 59). Similarly, he claims that '*any* exhibiting of an entity as it shows itself in itself, may be called "phenomenology" with formal justification' (*BT*, 59). He makes the same claim in other texts of this period. In 1927's *The Basic Problems of Phenomenology*, he says that to call an inquiry phenomenological is to say something purely formal. It is 'precluded from the start that phenomenology should advance any theses about Being which have specific content.'[20] After all, if phenomenology *did* advance theses about Being that had specific content, it would be an ontic inquiry, not an ontological one. Heidegger's project demands that phenomenology be simply a form of inquiry, and that it not be attached to any particular subject matter. This does not mean that phenomenological interpretation has no object. Phenomenology's first discovery is that all consciousness is intentional, or consciousness *of* something. But a phenomenological interpretation's subject matter is not what makes it phenomenological. What makes an inquiry phenomenological is that it grasps its objects '*in such a way*' (*BT*, 59).

The point of all this is that Heidegger's destruction of the history of philosophy is part of fundamental ontology. It is part of the task of interrogating Dasein, part of the project of questioning Dasein's questioning of Being. Fundamental ontology is a phenomenological inquiry. It is an interpretation of Dasein, one that proceeds according to phenomenological method. Phenomenological method can and must be understood in purely formal terms. What makes an inquiry phenomenological is how it proceeds, not what it studies. Phenomenology is simply a method, and it is defined independently of the subject matter to which it happens to be applied. It follows that the destruction of the history of philosophy is not an inquiry into the nature of some content. It is not a description of some subject matter, such as a forgotten theory of Being. The destruction of the history of philosophy is a part of the process of questioning Dasein's everyday questioning of Being. It is an account of how an understanding of the meaning of Being can be won—and can *only* be won—through a phenomenological interpretation of Dasein. In short, the destruction of the history of philosophy is not an account of *what* philosophy studies. It is an account of how the only access to philosophy's *what* proceeds through its *how*. It does not describe philosophy's content; rather, it describes how our only

access to this content is through philosophy's form. And it is an account that insists that this form can be characterized independently of the contents to which it happens to be applied. In short, Heidegger's remarks about the destruction of the history of philosophy do not constitute a content-based argument for the historical thesis about philosophy. Instead, they constitute a *form-based* argument for it. Coming to terms with the history of philosophy is not a matter of representing some subject matter correctly. It is a matter of approaching one's subject matter with the appropriate method. So for Heidegger, there is an asymmetry between philosophy's content and its form. We have no access to the former except through the latter, but the latter is capable of being understood in abstraction from the former. To that extent, fundamental ontology privileges form over content.

It should now be clear why I want to read Heidegger's discussion of the history of philosophy as a reciprocal rejoinder to Hegel's. Hegel's approach to the historical thesis is content-based. His view of the history of philosophy is grounded in considerations involving philosophy's content, or its subject matter. For Hegel, philosophy's subject matter is spirit. The history of philosophy is the only medium through which we can learn certain important things about the nature of spirit. If the philosopher wants to come to terms with her discipline's subject matter, she has to study the history of philosophy. As I have argued, however, this strategy is problematic. No content can force us to learn about it through any particular medium. By definition, a content can be represented though many different media, precisely because it is separate from them. If philosophy's subject matter is a content to be represented through the medium of the history of philosophy, then this history cannot be indispensable. Hegel seems to learn this lesson over the course of his career, since he eventually argues that the history of philosophy is *not* the only way to learn about spirit. A content-based approach seems bound to fail. If the history of philosophy really is inseparable from philosophy, it cannot be because of philosophy's content.

Heidegger is important in this context because he proposes a different way of thinking about the history of philosophy. He proposes a new way of understanding the claim that one cannot do philosophy without coming to terms with its history. This strategy seems to overcome some of the difficulties that plague Hegel's approach. Heidegger does not claim that we must come to terms with the history of philosophy in order to learn

about philosophy's subject matter. Granted, he seems to; he seems to say that we must dismantle the history of philosophy in order to uncover a forgotten theory of Being. But as we have seen, this appearance is misleading. It is ultimately philosophy's form and not its content that makes the history of philosophy indispensable. Unlike Hegel, then, Heidegger apparently need not face difficult questions about the shortcomings of a content-based approach. His view of the history of philosophy can therefore be seen as an alternative to Hegel's, and an alternative that avoids many of the difficulties inherent in Hegel's approach. Again, I am not suggesting that Heidegger intended it as such, or even recognized it as such. Nor am I claiming that what *motivates* Heidegger is a dissatisfaction with Hegel's view of the history of philosophy and a desire to develop an alternative. Heidegger's reasons for understanding the history of philosophy as he does are complex and deeply entangled with other parts of his project. But Heidegger *does* deny that the history of philosophy is a medium for representing a content. He does think that a confrontation with the history of philosophy is required by the form—the 'how'—of philosophical thinking. Heidegger may not have been trying to respond to Hegel's discussion of the history of philosophy, but his thought amounts to a response to it just the same. And his response looks promising. It seems to sidestep certain difficulties in Hegel's theory, and to offer a new way of thinking about the importance of philosophy's past.

So Heidegger is an important figure in the narrative I have been constructing. He articulates an approach to the historical thesis that looks different from Hegel's. He opens up a new way of thinking about the relation between philosophy and its history, and one that appears to hold some promise.

Distinguishing form and content: Kant's revenge, part two

That said, it would be a mistake to see Heidegger's approach to the historical thesis as a clean break with Hegel's. Despite its promise, Heidegger's form-based approach does not simply leave Hegel's approach behind. Heidegger does not manage to avoid all the problems that a content-based approach raises, because he never adequately distinguishes philosophy's

content from its form. As a result, he never shows that his position is a genuine alternative to Hegel's, and he never rules out the possibility that a problematic conception of philosophy's subject matter may sneak back into his account. In this respect, Heidegger's work on the history of philosophy may leave us no better off than Hegel's. In fact, in one way, it leaves us *worse* off. Hegel's approach to the historical thesis is plagued by incoherence, but this incoherence is not disguised. Heidegger's approach flirts with the same incoherence, but *looks* like an alternative to Hegel's. Heidegger's approach to the history of philosophy is not just incoherent; it is an approach whose incoherence is covered up. But why is this the case?

If we want to advance a form-based argument for the historical thesis, we must be able to distinguish philosophy's form from its content. And if we want to use Heidegger as the basis for an argument of this sort, we must be able to draw such a distinction in the context of his work. Otherwise, the very idea of advancing a form-based argument makes no sense. So if we want to use Heidegger's thought as the basis for a form-based argument, it must be possible for Heidegger to distinguish philosophy's form from its content—its 'how' from its 'what.' Heidegger need not do so himself. But it must be possible to do so in the context of his work. Among other things, this means that Heidegger's thought must allow us to define philosophy's form and its content independently of one another. Form and content cannot simply be the same thing. Heidegger clearly *wants* to draw such a distinction. It is implied by his claim that philosophy's method—phenomenology—is purely formal, and can be defined without reference to the contents to which it is applied. If Heidegger's form-based approach is to work, then he must be able to make good on this claim. He must have the resources to distinguish the object of phenomenological interpretation from the way in which that object is grasped. If he does not, then his approach to the history of philosophy will not be the alternative to Hegel's that it appears to be.

But it is not clear that Heidegger can distinguish phenomenological interpretation and its object in this way. There is an important asymmetry between Heidegger's discussion of interpretation in *Being and Time* and the uses to which he puts this concept in fundamental ontology. The discussion of *Auslegung* in *Being and Time* focuses entirely on the interpretation of entities that are ready-to-hand. It describes what is involved in seeing an entity *as* something. This is what Heidegger has in mind when he describes

interpretation as the process through which 'the ready-to-hand comes *explicitly* into the sight that understands' (*BT*, 189). Similarly, the *kinds* of interpretation he describes are all concerned with ready-to-hand entities: taking apart a piece of equipment 'with regard to its "in-order-to,"' viewing it 'in accordance with what has become visible through this process,' and so on (*BT*, 189). The *objects* of interpretation that he lists in this section— doors and houses, for instance (*BT*, 190)—are also ready-to-hand. It is easy to distinguish the 'what' and the 'how' of interpretation in this case. In interpretations of this sort, the object that Dasein understands is a door, or a house, or some other ready-to-hand entity. But the way in which it is understood, the procedure through which Dasein grasps it, is something quite different. In this case, the object or the content to be understood is a piece of equipment. The form, by contrast, is an act of interpretation performed by Dasein. And Dasein is radically different from all ready-to-hand entities. In interpretation of this sort, Heidegger can sharply distinguish interpretation's form and its content.

But matters are different in the case of fundamental ontology. Fundamental ontology is a ciphering of Dasein's existence. This is not the sort of interpretation [*Auslegung*] we perform when we make sense of a piece of equipment. It is an Interpretation [*Interpretation*] *of Dasein*, an Interpretation that Dasein directs at itself. In fundamental ontology, therefore, form and content are one and the same. Dasein's existence is at once philosophy's form and its content. Heidegger does not tell us how it is possible to distinguish form and content in the case of an Interpretation directed at Dasein. Heidegger does discuss the notion of Interpretation in Section 32 of *Being and Time*. But this discussion is of little help here, because it deals with Interpretation primarily in the sense of textual Interpretation. It does not explore what is involved in a specifically ontological Interpretation. It does not explain what is unique about an Interpretation of Dasein, or how we might distinguish Interpretation's form and content in this case. If Heidegger's approach to the historical thesis is to be a viable alternative to Hegel's, more needs to be said here. We need a more rigorous account of how Interpretation proceeds in the case of fundamental ontology. We need to see that it is possible to distinguish the form and the content of fundamental ontology, given that Dasein is at once the subject and the object of this Interpretive process. And we need an account of *how* it is possible.

Is there any way to give such an account? One strategy would be to distinguish two different kinds of Interpretation. We might distinguish Interpretation in general from *good* Interpretation—that is, from Interpretation that understands Dasein's Being correctly. On this view, the form of philosophical thinking would be the first kind of Interpretation, or the activity of Interpretation in general. Philosophy's content, on the other hand, would be identified with the *right* account of Dasein's Being. Clearly, there is a difference between Interpretation in general and correct Interpretation, since not every Interpretation of Dasein will be right. Interestingly, this is the strategy that Heidegger seems to adopt in some of his later texts. Consider the *Parmenides* lectures, for example. Here, Heidegger seems to be working with just the sort of distinction I have described: the distinction between the procedure of Interpretation in general and an Interpretation that gets its subject matter right. Specifically, while discussing the role that *aletheia* plays in Parmenides's thought, Heidegger considers the possibility that he is reading into Parmenides things that are not really there. He writes:

> It will necessarily appear that we are now more than ever Interpreting back into the essence of the Greek *aletheia* something that does not reside in it. Measured against the barriers of the horizon of historiography [*Historie*], and of what is historiographically ascertainable, and of the 'facts,' everywhere so cherished, what is said here about *aletheia* is 'in fact' an Interpretation read into it.[21]

In this passage, Heidegger is asking whether his Interpretation of Parmenides is a bad one because it does not do justice to the 'facts' as academic history understands them. But he goes on to reject this possibility. He says that there *is* a distinction between good and bad Interpretation, but that it is not based on correspondence to the 'facts.' Heidegger claims that

> if we do not force on history [*Geschichte*] historiographical [*historische*] horizons and cover it with them, if we rather let the beginning be the beginning it is, then another law holds. According to this law, we cannot read enough into the beginning, or, better said, we cannot Interpret enough out of it, so long as we merely pay heed to this beginning in the rigor of its essence and do not get caught up in our own arbitrariness.[22]

On this view, a good Interpretation is not one that represents the past correctly. It is one that does justice to this other 'law.' An inquiry governed by this other law does not try to discover 'what was once meant or was not meant. That could only be a *preparation* for the essential truth, which . . . concerns man's historical destiny, because this essence has come to presence for us already now long ago.'[23]

These passages show one way to distinguish good Interpretations from bad ones. A good reading of Parmenides is not one that gets his text right, in the sense of corresponding to its author's intentions. It is one that does justice to the 'essential truth' of which Heidegger speaks, the one that is 'a *preparation* for the essential truth.' It is necessary to prepare for this essential truth because it 'concerns man's historical destiny.' It is humanity's destiny that certain essential truths 'come to presence.' Though we might not recognize it, we have a destiny that is bound up with the history of Being—with Being's sending of itself in various epochs. An appropriation of the tradition is correct to the extent that it prepares for this presencing. What makes an Interpretation of a text good or bad is the extent to which it is in keeping with the destiny of humanity and the sending of Being. Of course, we must be careful when comparing Heidegger's later texts with *Being and Time*. I do not wish to suggest that Heidegger's later account of Interpretation—let alone his later account of destiny—is identical with the one advanced in *Being and Time*.[24] But the *Parmenides* lectures offer a useful illustration of what *kind* of view seems to be needed if we are to flesh out the discussion of Interpretation in *Being and Time*. The account in the *Parmenides* lectures is based on a distinction between Interpretation in general and correct Interpretation—that is, between any Interpretation that Dasein might perform, and one that is right. The correct Interpretation is the one that studies something 'in the rigor of its essence,' and that in so doing, does justice to the 'essential truth' that 'concerns man's historical destiny.'[25] Perhaps we can use this distinction to separate philosophy's content from its form. Perhaps we can say that philosophy's form is the process of Interpretation in general, while its content is an Interpretation that is in keeping with the 'essential truth' of which Heidegger speaks. In short, the *Parmenides*'s account of Interpretation serves as an example of how we might distinguish philosophy's form and content in the context of Heidegger's thought. Invoking an account like this would be one way

of separating form and content in *Being and Time*. It would be one way of clearing the way for a form-based argument for the historical thesis about philosophy.

But there is a problem here. Heidegger's talk of the 'presencing' of an 'essential truth' has curious Hegelian overtones. One might even suggest that in the *Parmenides* lectures, the role played by Being is quite similar to the role played by spirit in Hegel's discussion of the history of philosophy. For Hegel, the history of philosophy is the history of spirit's development. Similarly, for the Heidegger of the *Parmenides*, Being seems to display signs of agency. The aim of philosophy is to encounter its destiny in the right way—to prepare for an 'essential truth' that is bound up with Being's sending of itself. Suppose someone objected that the account of correct Interpretation in the *Parmenides* lectures looks a great deal like Hegel's account of the self-development of spirit. Suppose someone argued that Heidegger's later account of Interpretation is inseparable from a metaphysical story about the self-development of an impersonal agency—not spirit, but Being. And suppose she objected that this fact makes Heidegger's account of the history of philosophy just as content-based, and therefore just as problematic, as Hegel's. Does Heidegger have the resources to respond to this objection?

It is not clear that he does. It is not clear that Heidegger has the resources to distinguish the account of good Interpretation in the *Parmenides* lectures from this more metaphysical, Hegelian account of the self-development of spirit. Heidegger's account is simply too vague. It does not explicitly say what he means when he speaks of presencing and essential truths. Nor does it explain how these notions differ from Hegel's account of the self-development of spirit. Nor, finally, does Heidegger explain just how the role played by Being in his account differs from the role played by spirit in Hegel's. Heidegger may not explicitly endorse this reading of his account of Interpretation. But he does not rule it out. Accordingly, he does not dispel the worry that his accounts of presencing and essential truths may be content-based in the same way as Hegel's discussion of spirit. His suggestive language raises a worry and does not address it. But if we are to see Heidegger's approach to the history of philosophy as an alternative to Hegel's, then he *must* rule out this reading. He must show that his distinction between Interpretation in general and correct Interpretation—that is, between form and content—does not presuppose a speculative story

about the self-development of philosophy's subject matter. If he does not, then we cannot be sure that his distinction between form and content does not rest on an account of philosophy's subject matter that is just as problematic as Hegel's. If we cannot be sure of this, then the prospects of using Heidegger to remedy the problems with Hegel's position look bleak.

We seem to face a dilemma. On the one hand, the account of phenomenological method offered in *Being and Time* is just too vague. It does not explain how philosophy's form can possibly be separated from its content. In order for this account to be useful for our purposes, it would have to be supplemented with an account of *how* form and content may be distinguished—an account of the sort that Heidegger gives in his later texts. But if we supplement *Being and Time* with an account like the one in the *Parmenides*, we risk moving too close to a content-based approach. Such accounts separate form and content by distinguishing Interpretation in general from Interpretations that are in keeping with the presencing of Being. They raise the worry that Heidegger's account of the presencing of Being makes implausible metaphysical assumptions, assumptions not easily distinguishable from the ones made by Hegel's account of spirit. They are vulnerable to the charge that Heidegger's Being is inadequately distinguished from Hegel's spirit, and that Heidegger, like Hegel, sees the history of philosophy as a medium for teaching lessons about a content separate from it. And as we have seen, a content-based argument for the historical thesis is a non-starter. If the philosophical tradition is merely a medium for teaching lessons about a content outside it, then there is no reason to think it is indispensable. The dilemma is that the early Heidegger is too vague, while the later Heidegger risks being too close to Hegel. The former simply does not distinguish form and content. But the latter distinguishes them by means of an account of the presencing of Being that may rest on problematic claims about philosophy's content. Neither option is satisfactory. The first option fails to distinguish form and content at all, while the second distinguishes them only by means of a story that may ultimately be as content-based as Hegel's. Heidegger's reciprocal rejoinder to Hegel is therefore deeply problematic. It initially looks like a promising alternative to Hegel's content-based approach. But it does not succeed in demonstrating that philosophy's form really is separate from its content. It does not dispel the worry that

a problematic conception of philosophy's subject matter may sneak back into Heidegger's thought through the back door.

Heidegger therefore plays a curious role in the development of the historical thesis. He suggests that history's importance follows from philosophy's form, not its content. He thus points toward a different strategy for understanding the historical thesis, and a different way of explaining why it is true. On the other hand, Heidegger does not execute this strategy successfully. He does not do the one thing his strategy requires: show that philosophy's form really is distinct from its content. So while Heidegger points in the direction of an alternative to Hegel, he does not adequately develop this alternative himself. His reciprocal rejoinder to Hegel turns out to be a simple reversal, one that chooses form where Hegel had chosen content. This is bad enough. But matters are exacerbated by the fact that Heidegger's approach *looks* like an alternative to Hegel's. After all, Heidegger *says* that philosophy's form is independent of its content—that phenomenology 'does not express the *what* of the objects of philosophical research as subject-matter, but rather the *how* of that research' (*BT*, 50). Though Heidegger does not distance himself adequately from a problematic account of philosophy's subject matter, this fact is not immediately apparent, and it is contradicted by Heidegger's own pronouncements on method. Heidegger encourages us to think we have broken with Hegel's conception of the history of philosophy when we have not. He leads us to think we have overcome the problems with Hegel's account, when all we have done is push them under the surface.

So with Heidegger, we see the emergence of a true crisis in continental thinking about the history of philosophy. A crisis is a forgetfulness of meaning, one that arises when a discipline stops reflecting on its most fundamental concepts and theses. Practitioners of the discipline assume they know the meanings of these concepts and theses. But they are blind to the problems that lurk under a surface of self-evidence. Galileo encourages this sort of blindness in the natural sciences. Heidegger encourages it in the history of philosophy. His discussion of the history of philosophy presents itself as radically different from Hegel's. His characterization of phenomenological method encourages us to think he has left Hegel behind. But he has simply hidden his similarities with Hegel. Heidegger's legacy to the tradition is an incoherent conception of the history of philosophy whose incoherence has been covered up. We should not be surprised,

then, that contemporary thinking about the history of philosophy exhibits signs of a crisis. We should not be surprised that Heidegger's contemporary followers endorse problematic views of the history of philosophy without recognizing that they are problematic. This is precisely what we would expect. A field that builds on Hegel's and Heidegger's work on this topic is a field that we would expect to be in crisis.

Chapter 4

Ricoeur's Entanglements in the Aporias of Tradition

The last two chapters traced the crisis in the historical thesis up to the middle of the twentieth century. Chapter 4 brings this story up to the present. It shows how the crisis has stayed in place, despite sophisticated attempts to move beyond it. Specifically, it examines the work of Paul Ricoeur, and argues that the disguised incoherence that Heidegger injects into continental thought pervades Ricoeur's work as well. Like Heidegger, Ricoeur thinks philosophy is an inherently historical enterprise. Like Heidegger, he claims that this is so for reasons connected with philosophy's form. But—again like Heidegger—Ricoeur advances a form-based argument for the historical thesis without questioning the view of historical knowledge that underlies it. Like Hegel and Heidegger, Ricoeur assumes that historical knowledge is unphilosophical, and that truth cannot genuinely be *in* history. As a result, his conception of the history of philosophy suffers from the same problems as theirs. Ricoeur therefore shows how persistent the crisis is. He shows how easy it is for recent philosophers to remain under its spell, even as they strive to move beyond it. To that extent, Ricoeur embodies a widespread tendency in contemporary philosophy, a tendency that is deeply problematic but hard to avoid.

This chapter is divided into four parts. In the first two, I explain how Ricoeur's view of the history of philosophy emerges from a collision between two earlier approaches to the topic: the Heideggerian account of tradition discussed in Chapter 3, and the subsequent neo-Kantian backlash to it. I do so by interpreting the Gadamer-Habermas debate as the latest installment in a longstanding argument between Kant and Hegel, and then outlining Ricoeur's position against the background of this debate. In the next section, I show how Ricoeur's 'hermeneutics of historical consciousness' (*TN3*, 207) may be read as a response to this argument—that is, as an attempt to solve the problems in Hegel's and Heidegger's approaches to the historical thesis.

In the final section, I argue that Ricoeur's attempted break with this way of thinking is incomplete and unsuccessful. Ricoeur does not succeed in freeing himself from a Hegelian-Heideggerian picture of the history of philosophy. He does not free himself from the assumption that truth cannot be in history. With Ricoeur, the crisis is updated, but not overcome.

I have claimed that Ricoeur's treatment of the history of philosophy is representative of a widespread tendency in contemporary thought. Why single out Ricoeur in this way? The answer is that he is an unusually good example of this tendency, for three reasons. First, Ricoeur is an unapologetic member of the philosophical tradition whose development I have been tracing— the tradition of post-Kantian philosophy that stretches from Hegel though Heidegger to contemporary hermeneutical philosophy. Ricoeur has never hesitated to identify himself as a member of this tradition; he speaks freely of his indebtedness to the 'hermeneutical tradition to which I belong' (*TA*, 1). Ricoeur's willingness to situate himself in this tradition makes him an easier case study than philosophers who are less frank about their influences. Second, Ricoeur is an unusually synthetic thinker. His work has always brought together multiple influences. As Bernard Dauenhauer says, Ricoeur is 'the exponent of the "both-and," and the opponent of the "either-or," ' one who 'finds instruction not only in both Kant and Hegel but also in both Plato and Aristotle, Augustine and Benedict de Spinoza, and Karl Marx and Freud.'[1] The synthetic character of Ricoeur's work makes him as good a representative of recent European philosophy as we are likely to find. Finally, and most importantly, Ricoeur explicitly argues that philosophy's historical character results from the form of philosophical understanding, not its content. He endorses the way of thinking about the history of philosophy that originates in Heidegger's break with Hegel. Ricoeur is therefore an obvious heir to the way of thinking whose development I have been tracing. If anyone belongs in a narrative about the persistence of this way of thinking, he does.

Hermeneutics or critique: the Gadamer-Habermas debate

If European philosophers of the second half of the nineteenth century were Hegel's children, then those of the second half of the twentieth century

were Heidegger's. Just as Hegel's treatment of the history of philosophy was embraced by philosophers from Dilthey to Comte, Heidegger's treatment of the history of philosophy was embraced by a wide range of thinkers who came after him. Heidegger is constantly in the background of many discussions of this topic since the 1950s. When philosophers of this period talk about the importance of the history of philosophy, they tend to do so in explicitly Heideggerian terms. Heideggerian themes appear again and again in philosophy from this period. One such theme is a concern with tradition: a tendency to understand the history of philosophy as an *Überlieferung*, a process of handing down. Another is an insistence on the need to reappropriate this tradition critically, in order to loosen up its distortions. A third is a denial that such reappropriation can ever end, a denial that we will ever be able to stop engaging with the history of philosophy. In short, when recent continental thought discusses the importance of the history of philosophy—as it does often—it tends to let Heidegger set the terms of the debate.

Indeed, Heidegger's influence can be seen in each of the figures discussed in Chapter 1. Derrida, Gadamer, and Levinas all discuss the history of philosophy in Heideggerian terms. Recall Derrida's characterization of the tradition as a 'metaphysics of presence,' or a process through which problematic ontological assumptions have been sedimented over time. The link between Being and presence is a well-known Heideggerian theme. Recall as well Derrida's claim that we must 'decenter' this tradition in order to come to terms with it, as well as the way he compares this decentering with 'the Heideggerian destruction of metaphysics.'[2] Finally, recall Derrida's insistence that this decentering will never end, since there is 'no sense in doing without the concepts of metaphysics.'[3] Or consider Levinas's equally Heideggerian discussion of the history of philosophy. Consider the way he describes this history as 'a drama between philosophers'[4] that unfolds over centuries. Consider his claim that 'new interlocutors always enter who have to restate'[5] earlier moments in the drama—who must, that is, explicitly hand down the tradition. Finally, consider his insistence that it is 'naive' to expect 'a conclusion or a closure to this discourse,' and the way he invokes Hegel and Heidegger to justify this claim.[6] Levinas and Derrida both discuss the history of philosophy in ways that owe a great deal to Heidegger. This is not to say that Heidegger, Derrida and Levinas always see eye to eye on the topic. But the differences among them are differences within a shared framework.

The same is obviously true of Gadamer. Gadamer describes his account of tradition as a continuation of Heidegger's thought.[7] As we have seen,

Gadamer's analysis of the inescapability of tradition is rooted in the *Daseinanalytik* of *Being and Time*. Since Dasein is an essentially worldly entity, understanding cannot involve leaping out of one's historical and social situation. It must take its beginnings from what tradition [*Überlieferung*] has transmitted [*überliefert*] to it. This transmission is a circular movement in which we take up and modify prejudices from a tradition and, in doing so, shape that very tradition. This is so of all branches of inquiry, including philosophy. Hermeneutics, Gadamer says, is universal in scope.[8] So for Gadamer, philosophy is historical because understanding takes place by means of the hermeneutic circle. It is possible only on the basis of 'fore-meanings' (*TM*, 269) that come from tradition. We may, of course, criticize tradition. But criticism is a *reinterpretation* of tradition and thus another way of belonging to it. So like Derrida and Levinas, Gadamer agrees with Heidegger about the importance of philosophy's past. Just as a Hegelian consensus on this topic reigned for much of the nineteenth century, a Heideggerian consensus reigned for much of the twentieth.

But just as the Hegelian consensus gave way to a neo-Kantian backlash in the late nineteenth century, the Heideggerian consensus was followed by another Kantian backlash in the twentieth. Thinkers with Kantian sympathies attacked the Heideggerian consensus on tradition in much the same way that Windelband and his cohorts had attacked Hegel a century earlier. The best known of these Kantian thinkers was Jürgen Habermas. Habermas attacked Gadamer's understanding of tradition—and, by extension, the Hegelian-Heideggerian style of thinking that had given rise to it—for being philosophically reckless and ethically retrograde. Habermas granted that Heidegger and his followers had made an important discovery: that 'knowledge is rooted in actual tradition' and 'remains bound to contingent conditions.'[9] But he argued that philosophy can concede this fact while retaining a Kantian view of the link between tradition and reason. He insisted that philosophical reflection 'does not wear itself out on the facticity of traditional norms.'[10] On the contrary, an important part of philosophy is the impulse to break with tradition and expose the manipulative power relations at work in it. To that extent, philosophy can detach itself from its history and pass judgment on it. It can deal with its history in a top-down manner; it can set this history straight rather than being set straight by it.

Habermas's view of history is based on his theory of interests. According to this theory, all intellectual inquiry is directed by interests, which

Habermas defines as 'basic orientations rooted in specific fundamental conditions of the possible reproduction and self-constitution of the species.'[11] To say that inquiry is driven by interests is to deny that it is ever purely theoretical. Seemingly disinterested standpoints are in fact attempts to realize practical goals. Furthermore, the role played by practical considerations in inquiry is often concealed or rationalized away and so not seen. Inquiry, in short, is *ideological*. Habermas claims that there are three basic interests, each of which governs a distinct sphere of inquiry. The first is the *technical* interest that governs the empirical sciences. These sciences are driven by the desire to exert 'technical control over natural forces,'[12] or to subordinate nature to human ends. Next is the *practical* interest that governs the humanities. These disciplines seek *understanding*. They study the meanings of symbolic structures in the cultural world, particularly as these meanings have been transmitted by tradition. Finally, the disciplines that Habermas calls the critical social sciences are governed by an *emancipatory* interest. Rather than seeking to control nature or understand a cultural heritage, they unearth the interests at work in the other branches of inquiry. They seek to expose 'violently distorted communication,'[13] and to bring to light the ideologies that govern supposedly disinterested theoretical standpoints. They criticize the ideological bases of other branches of inquiry in the hope of liberating humanity from them.

Because of his theory of interests, Habermas denies that hermeneutics is universal in scope. He rejects Gadamer's claim that all inquiry is mediated by interpretation. Not all forms of inquiry take up and modify the fore-meanings handed down by tradition. According to Habermas, this orientation toward tradition appears only in the second sphere of inquiry. Only the humanities pursue an interpretive understanding of the contents of tradition. The other spheres do not. In fact, critical social science is hostile to this attitude toward tradition. Its aim is to expose the ideological element at work in tradition, to criticize and remedy the violently distorted communication that the past has transmitted to us. In short, the task of this sphere is to carry out a *critique of ideology*. And the critique of ideology, Habermas argues, is incompatible with a Gadamerian insistence on the universality of hermeneutics. He claims that 'Gadamer's prejudice in favor of the legitimacy of prejudices (or prejudgments) validated by tradition is in conflict with the power of reflection, which proves itself in its ability to reject the claim of traditions . . . Authority and knowledge do not

converge.'[14] From this perspective, Gadamer's insistence on the universality of hermeneutics is both theoretically dubious and ethically problematic. Far from making our link to tradition a universal condition of understanding, 'reflection requires that the hermeneutic approach limit itself.'[15]

What does the Gadamer-Habermas debate have to do with the history of philosophy? Habermas's critique of Gadamer amounts to a Kantian backlash to the Heideggerian consensus about the history of philosophy in much recent European thought. The Gadamer-Habermas debate is the latest version of the argument between Kant and Hegel that I have traced over the last several chapters. Like Heidegger and Hegel, Gadamer argues that it is impossible to do philosophy without coming to terms with its history. This is an endorsement of the historical thesis about philosophy. And Habermas, like Windelband and Kant, argues that we can grant that the history of philosophy is important while denying that philosophy just *is* the activity of coming to terms with it. Habermas concedes that 'knowledge is rooted in actual traditions,' and claims that we have Hegel to thank for pointing this out.[16] But this insight is compatible with a Kantian, top-down understanding of the relation between philosophy and its past. For Habermas, tradition is a repository for ideology. To fall under its sway is to risk giving in to violently distorted communication. Contemporary philosophy must criticize the past, in the sense of exposing its ideological elements and trying to remedy them. Philosophy is essentially critical and disruptive, and it is fundamentally opposed to the attitude toward tradition found in the humanities. Habermas's demand for critique is not so different from Kant's claim that we cannot embrace the history of philosophy until we have criticized it from the standpoint of the present. Like Kant and Windelband, Habermas sees the history of philosophy as a valuable resource, but one we turn to only after using critique to see it aright. The past must answer to the critical scrutiny of the present, but the present need not answer to the past. In this respect, Habermas's work is the latest installment in a recurring argument between Kant and Hegel.

Ricoeur's interventions in the debate

Ricoeur's thought should be seen against the backdrop of this Kantian backlash. His work should be read as a response to Habermas's resurrection of

a top-down approach to the history of philosophy. It affirms the historical thesis in the face of Habermas's neo-Kantian criticisms. Ricoeur does not dismiss Habermas's concerns. He does not simply side with Gadamerian hermeneutics and against the Habermasian critique of ideology. Instead, he argues that Habermas's concerns can be addressed within a hermeneutical framework. He claims that we can assign philosophy a critical and disruptive role while also viewing it as inherently historical. This is not to say that Ricoeur wishes 'to fuse the hermeneutics of tradition and the critique of ideology in a super-system that would encompass both' (*TA*, 294). But he does wish to steer a third path between hermeneutics in its Gadamerian form and the critique of ideology as Habermas describes it—albeit a path that is closer to the former than to the latter. In short, Ricoeur wants to show that there can and must be 'critique within hermeneutics' (*TA*, 295). To see how he does so, we must look more closely at his interventions in the Gadamer-Habermas debate.

In a series of articles on the debate,[17] Ricoeur argues that Habermas's hostility toward the hermeneutics of tradition is both incoherent and unwarranted. It is incoherent because the critique of ideology cannot 'be detached from hermeneutic presuppositions' (*TA*, 271). Habermas's ideal of 'an exhaustive critique of prejudice—and hence of ideology—is impossible, because there is no zero-point from which it could proceed' (*TA*, 278). Ricoeur argues that there are four respects in which the Habermasian critique of ideology has hermeneutic presuppositions that undermine it. First, he claims that 'the theory of interests that underlies the critique of ideologies' (*TA*, 302) rests on hermeneutical presuppositions. Habermas claims that all inquiry is driven by one of three cognitive interests: the technical interest of the empirical sciences, the practical interest that governs the humanities, or the emancipatory interest at work in critical social science. But which interest drives the theory of interests itself? To what sphere of inquiry does it belong, and on what basis are its theses justified? If the theory of interests belongs entirely to any one of Habermas's three spheres, then its claims 'would become regional theses as in any theory . . ., and [their] justification would become circular' (*TA*, 302). If we claim that the theory of interests is an empirically verifiable theory similar to those of the natural sciences, for example, we beg the question—we presuppose the distinction between empirical science and the other cognitive spheres, rather than legitimating it. We also risk restricting its claims to a single cognitive

sphere, rather than allowing them to cut across all spheres. Thus the theory of interests cannot be collapsed into any single cognitive sphere. We seem to have to say that the theory of interests articulates something more fundamental than any of Habermas's three spheres: namely, 'a philosophical anthropology similar to Heidegger's Analytic of *Dasein*, and more particularly to his hermeneutics of "care" ' (*TA*, 302). We must conclude that 'interests are neither observables, nor theoretical entities like the ego, the superego, and the id in Freud's work, but rather "existentiales" ' (*TA*, 302). In appealing to them, Habermas tacitly invokes a philosophical anthropology—an *interpretation* of human existence. Like the *Daseinanalytik*, this philosophical anthropology has hermeneutic presuppositions.

Second, Ricoeur argues that the goal of the critique of ideology—communication free of violence—is intelligible only on the basis of tradition. Critique tries to expose distortions in communication and liberate humanity from them. It conceives of communication that is free of distortion as a regulative ideal to be pursued, though this ideal may never be encountered in experience. But how, Ricoeur asks, can we conceive of this ideal at all, even if it is only regulative? He argues that this ideal is made intelligible by our experiences of successful communication, partial though they may be. He asks: 'If we had no experience of communication, however restricted and mutilated it was, how could we wish it to prevail for all men and at all institutional levels of the social nexus?' (*TA*, 304). He responds that we could not. We cannot anticipate a regulative idea at all 'unless that idea is exemplified' (*TA*, 304). Habermas's critique of tradition 'would be quite empty and abstract if it were not situated on the same plane as the historical-hermeneutical sciences' (*TA*, 303)—on the 'plane,' that is, of an encounter with tradition mediated by interpretive understanding. The emancipatory interest would be empty if it were not founded on the practical interest.[18] In this respect as well, the critique of ideology rests on a hermeneutic presupposition.

Third, Ricoeur argues that the specific criticisms of ideology that Habermas advances are made possible by tradition. Habermas is particularly critical of the distortions effected by one contemporary ideology: the 'ideology of science and technology' prevalent in 'modern industrial society' (*TA*, 304). He fears that the goals and values of this ideology have overrun all other spheres of culture. In particular, they have overrun the sphere of communicative action, distorting the political with the language of

bureaucratic efficiency. Habermas insists that this movement must be reversed, and that the sphere of communicative action must be restored to an earlier state of health. But Ricoeur asks Habermas: 'upon what will you concretely support the reawakening of communicative action if not upon the creative renewal of cultural heritage?' (*TA*, 306). Habermas's criticisms of the present in the name of past ideals shows that the critique of ideology speaks from a highly specific place. His criticisms—which he presents as a repudiation of tradition—are made possible by his ties to a specific tradition.

Finally, Ricoeur argues that '[c]ritique is also a tradition' (*TA*, 306). Criticizing authority to emancipate humanity is not something we do from nowhere. It is an activity with a long and highly specific history, and we can make no sense of it unless we are connected to this history. 'This tradition,' Ricoeur says, 'is not perhaps the same as Gadamer's; it is perhaps that of the *Aufklärung*, whereas Gadamer's would be Romanticism. But it is a tradition nonetheless'—perhaps 'the most impressive tradition' (*TA*, 306).[19] Ricoeur even suggests that 'there would be no interest in emancipation, no more anticipation of freedom, if the Exodus and the Resurrection were effaced from the memory of mankind' (*TA*, 306). We cannot engage in critique from nowhere. We cannot even make *sense* of critique from nowhere. Critique in the interest of liberation is a tradition, and when we enlist it to fight ideology, we continue this tradition. The idea of using critique to escape tradition altogether is deeply incoherent.

So Ricoeur claims that Habermas's hostility toward tradition is incoherent, because the critique of ideology rests upon a hermeneutics of tradition. But this hostility is not only incoherent; it is also unwarranted. It is unwarranted because Habermas is wrong to equate tradition with an unreflective endorsement of the past. Hermeneutics and critique are not simply opposed. On the contrary, the hermeneutics of tradition can, and indeed must, contain a critical moment. To participate in a tradition is not to accept a heritage passively, but to appropriate it critically. Just as the critique of ideology needs hermeneutics, hermeneutics needs critique. Ricoeur thinks the critical resources of hermeneutics have been overlooked because of the dominance of Gadamer's work. We tend to equate philosophical hermeneutics with *Truth and Method*, and to assume that everything in the former is also in the latter. Ricoeur thinks this is unfortunate, because Gadamer often expresses himself in ways that downplay

the critical resources of hermeneutics. The very title of Gadamer's *magnum opus* is misleading, since it suggests that hermeneutics is founded on an antithesis: truth *or* method, the humanities *or* the sciences, belonging to tradition *or* breaking with it. Such dichotomies are unhelpful. Gadamer's reliance on them prevents him from 'recognizing the critical instance and hence rendering justice to the critique of ideology' (*TA*, 297). According to Ricoeur, we must rethink the assumption that being embedded in a tradition is incompatible with distancing oneself from it and criticizing it. Belonging and distanciation must rather be seen as dialectically related. In short, we need to reinterpret embeddedness in tradition as an essentially critical stance. We can do this, Ricoeur thinks, if we shift the emphasis of philosophical hermeneutics away from the opposition between 'truth' and 'method,' and back toward its origin in the interpretation of texts. Viewing tradition as a text to be interpreted will allow us to see the criticism of traditions as necessary and productive.

Ricoeur outlines four ways in which viewing tradition as a text can help rehabilitate the critique of ideology. Each has to do with the notion of *distanciation* [*Verfremdung*]. When we criticize a tradition, we distance ourselves from it. We suspend our ties to it; we objectify the tradition and regard it as something foreign. This is the stance embodied by the 'method' of the natural sciences. In Ricoeur's view, Gadamerian hermeneutics sees distanciation as an 'ontological fall from grace' (*TA*, 294). It claims that to distance oneself from tradition is to disrupt the belonging that makes understanding possible. But distance is not necessarily an obstacle to understanding. When we interpret a text, certain kinds of distance actually make understanding possible. For one thing, distance is a condition of there being literary texts at all. Texts come into being only when discourse is fixed in writing and so rendered autonomous—autonomous 'with respect to the intention of the author; with respect to the cultural situation and all the sociological conditions of the production of the text; and finally, with respect to the original addressee' (*TA*, 298). To fix a discourse in writing and distance it from the conditions of its production is not to destroy it. It is what *makes* the text a text. Objectification helps realize the 'profoundest aim' (*TA*, 299) of discourse.

The second way in which interpreting something requires critical distance has to do with Dilthey's distinction between explanation and understanding. Gadamer would have us oppose these terms. For Gadamer,

explanation is what results from the 'method' of the sciences and the objectifying attitude they adopt toward their subject matter. Understanding—
and 'truth'—are accessible only when one puts aside this objectifying
attitude. To 'explain' a text in Dilthey's sense is to distance oneself from
it and therefore hinder one's understanding of it. Understanding is the
overcoming of distance. Ricoeur argues, however, that it is simplistic and
false to view explanation and understanding as dichotomous, since their
relation is actually more complex. Explaining a text by objectifying it can
help us understand it. Consider the literary critic who subjects a text to a
structural analysis, thereby disclosing the 'formal arrangement' (*TA*, 299)
of its elements. We need not be structuralists to see that analysis of this sort
can shed unexpected light on a text, and thereby help us to understand it.
'The *matter* of the text,' in other words, 'is not what a naive reading of the
text reveals, but what the formal arrangement of the text mediates' (*TA*,
299). If this is so, then treating a text as an object to be explained does not
hinder understanding. It helps make understanding possible.

The third way in which understanding a text requires us to adopt a critical stance toward it concerns the notion of reference. Texts point to something beyond themselves. Ricoeur identifies the referent of a text with 'the
world opened up by it' (*TA*, 301) and more specifically with 'the type of
being-in-the-world unfolded *in front of* the text' (*TA*, 86). When I read a
text, I open up 'a *proposed world* that I could inhabit and wherein I could
project one of my ownmost possibilities' (*TA*, 86). This proposed world differs from everyday reality. In opening it up, I effect 'a new sort of distanciation that could be called a distanciation of the real from itself' (*TA*, 86).
Because texts refer, understanding them involves a peculiar kind of distancing: the distancing that comes about when a text opens up a new world and
new possibilities for being-in-the-world. This shows that distanciation is not
always an obstacle to understanding it, but can complete understanding.

The final way in which distanciation makes possible the understanding
of texts concerns the capacities of the reader. A good reader is self-aware.
She reflects on her skills and limitations, and she recognizes her tendencies
to misinterpret texts in various ways. Just as a psychoanalyst must recognize
any tendencies she has to distort her analyses of others, so that she may
compensate for them, a good reader compensates for her tendencies to distort texts. Reading well requires a willingness to view oneself critically, to
subject one's capacities to impartial scrutiny. Reading demands an ability

to distance oneself from oneself. It demands 'a critique of the illusions of the subject,' a critique that Ricoeur likens to Habermasian critique of ideology (*TA*, 301). In this respect as well, the activity of critical distanciation is not an obstacle to understanding. An objectifying attitude is 'not a fault to be combated but rather the condition of possibility of understanding oneself in front of the text' (*TA*, 301).

For Ricoeur, then, hermeneutics and the critique of ideology are not simply opposed. We need not choose between an affirmation of our dependence on tradition, and a critical gesture that breaks with the past. Critique is possible only on the basis of hermeneutic presuppositions—that is, on the basis of its embeddedness in a highly specific historical tradition. At the same time, the hermeneutics of tradition must contain a critical moment. It must view its heritage as a text to be reinterpreted, and it must recognize that its ability to distance itself from this heritage is what makes reinterpretation possible. Ricoeur does not deny that there is a tension between the critique of ideology as Habermas describes it and philosophical hermeneutics as Gadamer describes it. He insists that hermeneutics must be *re*-formulated in a less Gadamerian way if its critical resources are to be made manifest. His point is simply that such a reformulation is possible. It is possible to acknowledge our dependence on the past *and* our interest in emancipation. We can address Habermas's demand for critique within hermeneutical philosophy. We can, in short, engage in critical hermeneutics.

What does all of this have to do with the history of philosophy? Ricoeur's call for a critical hermeneutics amounts to a response to the debate between Kant and Hegel—a debate that, as we have seen, is resurrected in the late twentieth century. Gadamerian hermeneutics continues the way of thinking about the history of philosophy that originates in Hegel. By affirming the need for contemporary thinkers to come to terms with tradition, Gadamerian hermeneutics articulates a version of the historical thesis about philosophy. It thus places itself squarely in the camp of Hegel and Heidegger. By contrast, Habermas's attack on hermeneutics is best seen as a Kantian backlash to this camp. In his attack on the hermeneutics of tradition, Habermas places himself squarely in the company of Kant and Windelband. Like his Kantian forebears, Habermas argues that philosophy must pass judgment on its history, and that contemporary philosophers must break with tradition and assess it critically. He thus rejects the historical thesis about philosophy. Ricoeur's work seeks to concede some of

Habermas's criticisms while retaining the historical thesis. It recognizes the legitimacy of critique, while insisting that philosophy is inherently historical. Ricoeur's work is important because it is a reformulation of the historical thesis that takes account of this most recent Kantian backlash. It is a contemporary restatement of the view that followers of Hegel have always advanced in opposition to followers of Kant: namely, that we can be critical of the past without seeing the past as dispensable. We can acknowledge the importance of tradition without falling into the traps of historicism and traditionalism. Ricoeur's interventions in the Gadamer-Habermas debate amount to a contemporary defense of the historical thesis about philosophy.

We now know what Ricoeur wants to do. He wants to reformulate and defend the historical thesis in a post-Heideggerian context. And he wants to do so in a way that does justice to Habermas's neo-Kantian demand for critique. If we accept what Ricoeur has said up to this point, we know that it is possible to do so, because Ricoeur's hermeneutical sympathies—for all their debts to Hegel and Heidegger—are compatible with critique. But we do not yet know *how* Ricoeur will carry out this project. In order to see how Ricoeur reformulates the historical thesis, we must look beyond his interventions in the Gadamer-Habermas debate, and beyond his programmatic remarks about the compatibility of hermeneutics and critique in the abstract. We must look at his attempt to articulate a critical hermeneutics. The centerpiece of this attempt is his discussion of the hermeneutics of historical consciousness in *Time and Narrative*.

Ricoeur's hermeneutics of historical consciousness

As we have seen, post-Heideggerian discussions of the history of philosophy tend to focus on tradition. Ricoeur accepts this way of framing the issue. But he does think that debates about tradition should be more subtle. He thinks contemporary philosophy has incorrectly viewed tradition as a monolithic concept, rather than the complex and multifaceted one that it is. As a result, contemporary thinking about tradition has become mired in some unnecessary confusions. The Gadamer-Habermas debate is one such confusion. Ricoeur argues that if we are to put tradition at the center of our understanding of history, we must recognize that

it is not a single phenomenon, but a cluster of interrelated ones. 'Instead of speaking indiscriminately of tradition,' Ricoeur claims, 'we need to distinguish several different problems that I will set under three headings' (*TN3*, 219). These headings concern *how* we are connected to the past, *what* we are connected *to* when we relate to the past, and the *legitimacy* of the past's hold on us.

To say that philosophy takes place in a tradition could mean three different things. On the first reading, it is to make a fairly thin epistemic claim. It is to say that philosophers are trapped within the hermeneutic circle, and that they must begin their enterprise by taking up problems and preoccupations from the past. Without these fore-meanings, we could never begin to philosophize. It is a necessary condition of the philosophical enterprise that we take our beginnings from tradition. On this first reading, however, there is no *particular* tradition with which contemporary thought must begin. All that is necessary is that we stand in relation to some tradition or other, and any number might fit the bill. In short, this first reading is a formal one. It sees the importance of tradition as a result of *how* we understand, or of the *manner* in which we philosophize. Tradition's importance is not a function of *what* is handed down to us in particular contexts. Our need for tradition is separate from what particular traditions happen to pass down to us. The second reading also sees the claim that we are dependent on tradition as an epistemic claim, but as a more robust one. On this second reading, tradition makes philosophical thought possible in a stronger sense: in the sense that there is some particular tradition, or some particular group of traditions, to which we must belong if we are to philosophize. It is not enough to stand in relation to some tradition or other. We must inherit some particular fore-meanings and not others. We might call this second reading a material one, since it sees philosophical thought as made possible not by our manner of belonging to some tradition or other, but by some particular transmitted contents. The third reading is even more ambitious. On this interpretation, tradition is not just a set of transmitted contents that governs our thought, but one that *legitimately* does so. To say that philosophers take their beginnings from tradition is not merely to say that they must do so, because of 'the unavoidable finitude of all understanding' (*TN3*, 225). It is to say that they are right to do so—that one particular tradition can claim not just a hold on us, but an *authority* that others cannot. A tradition in this sense is not just a set of fore-meanings

that governs our thought. It is something that governs our thought by right, something that binds us legitimately.

To keep these three notions separate—how we understand, what we understand, and the legitimacy of what we understand—Ricoeur distinguishes the concepts of *traditionality*, *traditions*, and *tradition*. Each term picks out an aspect of our link to the past, but a different aspect. 'Traditionality' is Ricoeur's term for the way in which we are connected to the past. It concerns *how* we are shaped by history, how our thought is made possible by the past. To speak of traditionality is to speak of 'a style of interconnecting historical succession' (*TN3*, 219). It is to speak of our embeddedness in 'the chain of interpretations and reinterpretations' (*TN3*, 220) transmitted to us from the past. Our thought is governed by traditionality in that we always take our beginnings from the past. This is an inevitable result of the finitude of human understanding. Regardless of what tradition we inhabit, regardless of what is transmitted to us from the past, we always think in the mode of tradition. Thus Ricoeur calls traditionality 'a transcendental for thinking about history' (*TN3*, 219). Traditionality, as the *how* of understanding, can be defined independently of *what* we understand. It is a 'formal concept' (*TN3*, 221), and refers only to a style or a manner of thinking. It can be 'filled in' with an indefinite number of contents. *What* we receive from the past varies with our cultural and historical situation. *That* we receive something, and *how* we receive it, do not vary. As a purely formal feature of our understanding, traditionality is a 'transcendental.'

Traditionality must be sharply distinguished from *traditions*. Traditions are the particular 'transmitted contents' (*TN3*, 223) we receive from the past. They are 'the things said in the past' (*TN3*, 222), or 'every received heritage within the order of the symbolic' (*TN3*, 227). Traditions are *what* we understand when we open ourselves to the past. They are the particular fore-meanings inherited at particular times in particular places. To speak of traditions is not merely to speak of a need to take our beginnings from some cultural heritage or other. It is to speak of particular cultural heritages that can play this role. Whereas traditionality is formal, traditions are 'material' (*TN3*, 221). Since our need for fore-meanings is purely formal, and since any number of different fore-meanings can fill in this form, there are inevitably 'rival traditions' (*TN3*, 224). There is more than one set of fore-meanings we can receive from the past. The ones Ricoeur receives from his cultural heritage are no doubt very different from the ones an

analytic epistemologist receives from hers, and both are very different again from the ones with which an eighteenth century philosopher might begin. It is not immediately clear how to adjudicate among these rival fore-meanings. While we must take our beginnings from the past, there is no particular set of fore-meanings with which everyone must begin. There are competing traditions, and any one of them might satisfy our need to begin somewhere. The most salient fact about traditions, then, is their multiplicity. Ricoeur therefore says that 'by "tradition," we shall mean "traditions"' (*TN3*, 221).

There is also a third side to our experience of traditions. Though traditions are essentially plural, and though there is no obvious way of adjudicating among them, we nevertheless accept and endorse them. When I speak of *my* tradition, I assign a certain legitimacy to it. I suggest that a particular heritage not only governs my thinking, but does so rightly. I acknowledge its authority over me. According to Ricoeur, the question of the legitimacy of traditions is unavoidable. Traditions are 'proposals of meaning' (*TN3*, 227), and 'the question of meaning cannot be separated from that of truth except in abstraction. Every proposal of meaning is at the same time a claim to truth' (*TN3*, 222). Traditions inevitably make truth claims. Each one presents itself not just as one tradition among others, but as *the* tradition. For this reason, Ricoeur finds it necessary to distinguish the concept of *tradition* from traditionality and traditions. By 'tradition,' he means an endorsed set of fore-meanings, a transmitted content accepted as legitimate. To pass from 'traditions' to 'tradition' is 'to introduce a question of legitimacy' (*TN3*, 224). It is to transform 'the Gadamerian prejudice in favor of prejudice into a position based on being right' (*TN3*, 225). This move is inevitable, given the finitude of human understanding. 'Taking a distance . . . regarding transmitted contents,' Ricoeur argues, 'cannot be our initial attitude. Through tradition, we find ourselves already situated in an order of meaning and therefore also of possible truth' (*TN3*, 223). Because of our need to begin somewhere, we have always already accepted some tradition as legitimate. This does not mean I cannot criticize my tradition. But the criticisms I eventually make of my tradition are in some sense made possible by it.

What could justify the move from traditions to tradition? Some justification is certainly necessary. That a tradition shapes my thinking does not show that it is right to do so. That I must begin somewhere does not prove

that I am right to start here. It is not at all clear 'what legitimacy can stem from what seems to be only an empirical condition, namely, the unavoidable finitude of all understanding' (*TN3*, 225). This is why Marx's followers have seen the need for a critique of ideologies. My tradition would shape my thinking even if it were not legitimate, and if it were not legitimate, I would have all the same reasons to consider it legitimate that I do now. Ricoeur responds to this worry with the notion of a 'presumption of truth' (*TN3*, 227). The truth claim that tradition makes on me is one I must initially accept, because I have no alternative. My initial attitude must be to accept the tradition as legitimate. But this is just a presumption. It is tentative, fallible, and subject to revision if new evidence should arise. 'In the face of criticism that devours itself,' Ricoeur writes, 'the truth claim of the contents of traditions merits being taken as a presumption of truth, so long as a stronger reason, that is, a better argument, has not been established' (*TN3*, 227). In the absence of a better argument, the truth claim stands. Tradition's legitimacy is in the first instance a presumed legitimacy. So 'if a transition is possible between necessity and right, it is the notion of a presumption of truth that assures it' (*TN3*, 227).

It is not hard to see why Ricoeur wants to distinguish traditionality, traditions, and tradition. Keeping these concepts separate seems to be the only way of avoiding a slippery slope to which hermeneutical philosophy is all too susceptible. When we speak of 'tradition' in the abstract, it is easy to slip from weak claims about the way human understanding takes place to much stronger claims about particular institutions and their legitimacy. It is one thing to point out that we always find ourselves in the hermeneutic circle, and that we must take our beginnings from somewhere. It is something else to say that we must take our beginnings from one particular tradition and not from one of its competitors. It is something else again to say that our tradition is legitimate in a way that others are not—that it is right to govern our thought as it does. Neither of the two latter claims follows comfortably from the first. To assume that they do is to fall victim to a romantic traditionalism. And it is to leave oneself vulnerable to the criticisms Habermas advances in the name of the critique of ideology. If our need to be connected to some tradition or other forced us to accept some particular tradition over others, *and* to see that tradition as legitimate or even immune from criticism, then Habermas would be right: hermeneutical philosophy *would* be ethically dangerous. Ricoeur's hope is

that in framing the issue as he does, Habermas's worry need not arise. On Ricoeur's view, our need for fore-meanings has to do with the formal concept of traditionality. This formal concept can be kept separate both from the contents that fill it in under particular circumstances, and from the question of the legitimacy of those contents. Ricoeur can argue that on his view, there is no slippery slope from a recognition of the role of traditionality in human understanding to the uncritical traditionalism feared by Habermas. 'Only the third' of Ricoeur's concepts—tradition—'lends itself to the polemic that Habermas undertook against Gadamer in the name of the critique of ideology' (*TN3*, 224). In this way, the Gadamer-Habermas debate rests on an insufficiently subtle understanding of what tradition is.

Ricoeur's hermeneutics of historical consciousness, then, is based on a sharp distinction between the form and the content of philosophical understanding. The form of philosophical understanding is what Ricoeur calls traditionality—a 'style' (*TN3*, 219) or a manner of thinking. We philosophize in the mode of tradition in that we inevitably take up certain projects and preoccupations from the past, and then continue them, modify them, or break with them. Philosophy has the form of traditionality because it takes place within the hermeneutic circle. For Ricoeur, our need to confront the past is a function of this form alone. The importance of history concerns *how* we think—the *way in which* understanding takes place. It is not a function of *what* we understand, the particular 'past contents' (*TN3*, 221) handed down through the 'chain of interpretations and reinterpretations' (*TN3*, 220). It is not the contents of our cultural heritage that force us to confront the past. It is the universal form of philosophical understanding that does so. Traditionality and traditions are separate. Of course, the particular past contents we receive are entitled to a presumption of truth. But this presumption of truth is not only tentative and revisable; it is itself required by the form of philosophical understanding, not by its contents. That our initial attitude toward our heritage must be acceptance is a function of how we relate to fore-meanings, not of any intrinsic merit those fore-meanings may have.

Ricoeur's discussion of tradition amounts to an argument for the historical thesis about philosophy. It implies that philosophy is an inherently historical discipline, and that those who engage in it must take their beginnings from its past. Like Gadamer, Ricoeur sees the importance of the history of philosophy as a function of our dependence on tradition. Like

Gadamer, Ricoeur thinks that inquiry takes place by means of the hermeneutic circle, and that philosophical inquiry is no different in this respect.
To do philosophy is to take part in a process of handing down, to be situated within an 'interconnecting historical succession' (*TN3*, 219). Unlike
Gadamer, however, Ricoeur emphasizes that philosophy's dependence on
tradition is a formal dependence. It results from how we think, from our
need to take our beginnings from some heritage or other. And it can be
described without making reference to the particular contents transmitted to us through this interconnecting historical succession. Philosophy's
link to the past is a purely formal schema. It must be filled in with some
tradition or other, but no one tradition is uniquely qualified to do so. In
that sense, philosophical thinking is similar to performing a mathematical function. A function has variables: x's and y's that must be assigned
values. But the function does not specify which values are to be plugged
into it in any given case. Similarly, philosophical thinking is dependent
on content—traditions—being fed into it. But it does not specify which
traditions, which fore-meanings, are to fill it in. Philosophy is dependent
on the history of philosophy in much the same way that a mathematical
function is dependent on the values that can be assigned to its variables.
Both are formal mechanisms that depend on content being fed into them
from outside. These contents are essentially plural.

   Ricoeur's defense of the historical thesis is particularly interesting in
light of the narrative I have been constructing. Ricoeur gives what I have
called a *form-based* argument for the historical thesis. He claims that philosophy is inherently historical because it has the form of traditionality—a
style of thinking that is essentially situated in a 'chain of interpretations
and reinterpretations' (*TN3*, 220). Ricoeur's view of the history of philosophy is important because it echoes a claim made by Heidegger half a
century earlier. Heidegger also argues that philosophy's historical character results from its form. As I have argued, this strategy amounts to a
reciprocal rejoinder to Hegel's content-based arguments for the historical
thesis. But as we have seen, Heidegger's reliance on form is deeply problematic, because he describes that form in a way that makes it hard to
distinguish it from philosophy's subject matter. Heidegger tries to ground
philosophy's historical character on its form, but fails to do so, because he
does not adequately separate form and content. Ricoeur's approach looks
like it might avoid these difficulties. Like Heidegger, Ricoeur grounds

philosophy's historical character in a conception of how philosophy proceeds. But unlike Heidegger, he takes great care to distinguish philosophy's form from its content, and to argue that philosophy's historical character has to do with its form alone. He carefully separates the formal concept of traditionality from both the material concept of traditions and the normative concept of tradition. And he insists that traditionality alone makes philosophy an essentially historical enterprise. He argues, for example, that Gadamer's apology for tradition in *Truth and Method* is really a defense of traditionality, not of traditions or tradition. When Ricoeur's discussion of traditionality is seen against the backdrop of the narrative I have been constructing, it becomes clear that there is more at stake in it than a quibble with Gadamer's terminology. Ricoeur's discussion of traditonality is nothing less than an attempt to articulate a form-based argument for the historical thesis that avoids the difficulties in Heidegger's argument. It is an account of philosophy's form that seeks to do two things: first, explain why philosophy is essentially historical; and second, define philosophy's form without referring to its content. This is the real significance of Ricoeur's sharp distinction between traditionality and traditions. This distinction is an attempt to keep separate what Heidegger did not, and thus to give a form-based argument for the historical thesis that is not a content-based argument in disguise. I am not suggesting that Ricoeur intends it as such, or even recognizes it as such. But regardless of whether Ricoeur intends his work to be a rejoinder to Heidegger, it can be read as one.

So Ricoeur continues a line of thinking that begins with Hegel and passes through Heidegger to more recent continental philosophy. And he does not simply continue this line of thinking, but develops it as well. Just as Heidegger's approach to the historical thesis responds to difficulties in Hegel's, Ricoeur's approach responds to difficulties in Heidegger's. Ricoeur's work can be seen as an attempt to rearticulate the historical thesis, and to defend it from both external and internal difficulties. The external difficulties are the criticisms of neo-Kantians such as Habermas, who would abandon the historical thesis altogether. The internal difficulties are the problems with Heidegger's way of approaching the historical thesis, problems that Ricoeur seems poised to solve by means of his distinction between traditionality and tradition. Ricoeur's hermeneutics of historical consciousness is both an answer to Habermas and an amendment of Heidegger.

What should we make of it?

The dependence of form on content:
Kant's revenge, part three

Ricoeur's argument rests on his distinction between the form and the content of philosophical understanding, or between traditionality and traditions. It is important to see that there is more at stake here than a mere conceptual distinction. Ricoeur is not just claiming that it is possible to distinguish the concepts of traditionality and traditions in a philosophical analysis. His claim is actually much stronger. First, Ricoeur is making a descriptive claim about how philosophy proceeds. He is saying that philosophy has the form of traditionality—that to think philosophically is to relate to one's cultural heritage in a certain way. Next, Ricoeur insists that traditionality is something universal, and that there is a single form of philosophical understanding to be found at all times and all places. There is one and only one manner of carrying out the philosophical enterprise, common to all particular philosophical projects. It consists in taking up the 'things already said' (*TN3*, 221) in the past in a certain way. This is why Ricoeur calls traditionality 'a transcendental for thinking about history' (*TN3*, 219). *What* we receive from the past varies according to our historical and cultural context. *That* we receive things from the past, and *how* we receive them, do not vary. As Ricoeur says in another context, this process of transmission 'presents a transcultural form of necessity' (*TN1*, 52). Finally, what *makes* traditionality universal is that it can be defined independently of the contents transmitted by it. As a transcendental, traditionality is independent of the particular traditions that instantiate it. The form of philosophical understanding is what it is independently of the contents that happen to fill it in at particular times and places. This is why traditionality is like a mathematical function. Functions have variables, and while these variables must be assigned some values or other, there is no particular value that must be assigned in any given case. By definition, different values can be assigned, and the function itself does not force us to choose one value over another. We can define the function without making reference to the particular values that will eventually be assigned to its variables. Ricoeur's concept of traditionality is similar. We always encounter it as filled in by some particular contents, but those contents do not make it what it is. The form of philosophical understanding can be defined

without making reference to those contents. They are, finally, attached to it accidentally.

So Ricoeur's claims about traditionality are more ambitious than they first appear. Instead of just distinguishing concepts, Ricoeur is advancing some ambitious claims about philosophical understanding: that it takes the form of an encounter with tradition, that this form is universal, and that its meaning is independent of cultural context. Ricoeur does not seem to argue for these more ambitious claims. He does not explicitly argue for the thesis that the form of philosophical understanding is separate from its contents, and that as a result it is universal. The closest he seems to come is to suggest that if we do *not* understand traditionality in this way, we will be unable to respond to Habermas's criticisms of hermeneutics.[20] But while the desire to answer Habermas may justify a conceptual distinction, it does not justify the more ambitious theory of traditionality that Ricoeur advances. So at the very least, Ricoeur's claims about the independence of form from content seem inadequately supported. They are not really defended, but asserted. This fact should make us uneasy. But the problems do not end there. It is not just that Ricoeur's attempt to separate form and content is inadequately supported by argument. It is an implausible distinction. There is good reason to think that form and content will not separate as neatly as Ricoeur wants. There is good reason to think that traditionality is not a transcendental form capable of being defined independently of any concrete traditions—not even 'in abstraction' (*TN3*, 222). On the contrary, there is good reason to think that traditionality cannot be defined without making reference to particular traditions, and that the form of philosophical understanding is intelligible only if reference is made to its contents. The concept of traditionality would be meaningless if we did not tacitly understand it as embodied in and inseparable from our experience of actual traditions. As a result, traditionality is not universal, singular, or 'transcultural.' Just as there are multiple traditions, there must be multiple traditionalities. Let me explain why.

One of Ricoeur's central claims is that tradition is something that *happens*. It is a process, an activity of transmission, an *Überlieferung*. 'Before being an inert deposit,' Ricoeur maintains, 'tradition is an *operation* that can only make sense dialectically through the exchange between the interpreted past and the interpreting present' (*TN3*, 221, my emphasis). As an operation effected between the present and the past, tradition is in the

first instance something we *do*. Moreover, the process of taking part in tradition is a *normatively structured* activity: an activity subject to standards of
correctness and incorrectness. There are better and worse ways of taking
part in a dialectical exchange with the past. This is shown by our ability
to criticize the ways in which others take part in this exchange. We level
criticisms at those who, in our view, are not performing this activity as well
as they should. If the process of receiving a heritage from the past were
not norm-governed, these criticisms would be unintelligible. There would
be no sense in calling someone's appropriation of the past wrong if there
were no standards distinguishing wrong from right.

Ricoeur clearly recognizes that participating in a tradition is a normatively structured activity. He clearly thinks there are better and worse ways
of carrying on a dialogue with the past. This is made evident by his own
tendency to criticize the ways in which others take part in tradition. His
work is full of examples of this tendency. In a short piece on the future of
Europe, for example, Ricoeur condemns in quite sweeping terms those
who identify belonging to tradition with simply preserving what is past.
The right way to belong to a tradition, Ricoeur argues, involves responding
to the past by interpreting it in novel ways. 'Tradition,' he says,

> means transmission, transmission of things said, of beliefs professed, of
> norms accepted, etc. Now such a transmission is a living one only if tra-
> dition continues to form a partnership with innovation. Tradition repre-
> sents the aspect of debt which concerns the past and reminds us that
> nothing comes from nothing. A tradition remains living, however, only if
> it continues to be held in an unbroken process of reinterpretation.[21]

How could Ricoeur make this criticism if he did not see the 'transmission of
things said' as governed by standards of correctness? If his charge is to make
any sense, participating in tradition must be a normatively structured activity. Consider as well Ricoeur's criticisms of Habermas. Part of what troubles
Ricoeur about the critique of ideology is its attitude toward the past—its
tendency to view history as nothing but a repository for ideology. Ricoeur
is adamant that this is the wrong way of relating to the past. The freedom
from history that Habermas seeks 'is condemned to remain either an empty
concept or a fanatical demand.'[22] Ricoeur could not criticize Habermas for
relating to the past badly if it were not possible to relate to the past well.

We can criticize the role someone plays in an *Überlieferung* only if we recognize standards of correctness governing this process of handing down. Here again, Ricoeur's willingness to criticize some ways of appropriating tradition shows that he sees this appropriation as an activity governed by norms.

Now, as Wittgenstein has shown, there are two ways of understanding normatively structured activities. There are two ways to make sense of what we are doing when we engage in activities that can be performed well or performed badly. One is to see behavior of this sort as capable of being understood apart from actual cases—that is, independently of a grasp of how a norm is instantiated in particular situations. On this view, performing a norm-governed activity is tantamount to *following a rule*, enacting a linguistically stable principle. One can follow this principle without any prior acquaintance with other examples of following it. Consider someone who counts '2, 4, 6 . . .' On this first view, the correct description of this behavior is that the person in question is following the rule 'add two.' One does not need to see others follow this rule in order to know how to follow it oneself. Grasping the rule is enough. Thus on the view being entertained, norms stand in an external relation to behavior in accordance with them. To obey the norm, it is not necessary to be familiar with actual cases of following it.

But as Wittgenstein points out, there is a problem with this way of understanding normatively structured behavior. No rule is sufficient to distinguish behavior that falls under the rule from behavior that does not. An indefinite number of actual cases might appear to accord with a given rule. The only way to distinguish those that do accord from those that do not is to examine the cases. Suppose someone announces that she is about to follow the rule 'add two.' She proceeds to count '2, 4, 6 . . .' So far, her behavior accords with the norm. But at this point, we have no idea how she will continue. She may continue by counting '8, 10, 12 . . .,' but she may also continue with '9, 18, 27,' or with '10, 15, 20 . . .,' or with any number of other series. Clearly, the first way of continuing is right, while the others are wrong. But how do we know this? The rule 'add two' does not explain *why* we must continue in the first way rather than another. What makes the first way correct? How do we know how to proceed?

Wittgenstein's answer is that following a rule of this sort—and indeed, engaging in any norm-governed activity—is 'exhibited in what we call "obeying a rule" and "going against it" *in actual cases*.'[23] Hence the second—and,

according to Wittgenstein, the correct—way of understanding normatively structured behavior. On this view, norms are not capable of being understood apart from a grasp of their embodiment in actual cases. The norm I am following as I count '2, 4, 6 . . .' is not as simple as the instruction 'add two.' Rather, it is something I grasp through an acquaintance with actual cases, and something I can grasp in no other way. To grasp it *just is* to know how to continue the series '2, 4, 6 . . .' correctly. More generally, to understand a norm *just is* to know how it works in practice, how it is instantiated in actual cases. As Gadamer might say, to understand a norm is to know how it is completed in application. Given the difficulties raised by the first way of understanding normatively structured behavior, we seem to have little choice but to accept this second one. Norms must be exemplified, and they are incapable of being understood apart from their exemplifications.

There is no reason to think that participating in tradition is different from counting in this respect. Like counting, participating in tradition is an activity governed by norms. It is an activity we assess with standards of correctness, and an activity we criticize when it is performed badly. Accordingly, there is no way to understand what we are doing when we participate in tradition without making reference to how this activity is performed in actual cases. The reference we make to these actual cases may be tacit and intuitive, but it must be there. Knowing what it means to participate in tradition just is knowing how this activity is exemplified in actual cases, knowing how some particular member of some particular tradition inherits and transforms some particular contents under some particular circumstances. A purely general account of how *one* participates in tradition is a pipe dream. Any account of how we receive a heritage must make reference to what we receive. But if this is the case, then Ricoeur's claim that traditionality is independent of traditions must be wrong. Traditionality cannot be a transcendental, a form whose meaning is independent of the contents that might fill it in. We cannot understand the transmission of a heritage unless we grasp how this activity proceeds in actual cases. Traditionality—the form of philosophical thinking—must derive its meaning from an acquaintance with the transmission of particular traditions.

Indeed, Ricoeur seems to admit as much. At certain points in his work—though not, it seems, in *Time and Narrative*—Ricoeur argues that our understanding of what it is to participate in a tradition is made possible

by, and is inseparable from, our experiences with particular traditions. Recall what he says about the tradition of criticism in 'Hermeneutics and the Critique of Ideology.' There, he argues that the process of criticizing tradition—which, as we have seen, he considers an essential moment of belonging to tradition—is made possible by our ties to a highly specific history. He suggests that there would be 'no more interest in emancipation, no more anticipation of freedom, if the Exodus and the Resurrection were effaced from the memory of mankind' (*TA*, 306). He rejects Habermas's claim that this freedom is merely a regulative idea, insisting that we can make no sense of a regulative idea 'unless that idea is exemplified' (*TA*, 304). He claims it would never occur to us to overcome distorted communication if 'we had no experience of communication, however restricted and mutilated it was' (*TA*, 304). At all of these points, Ricoeur suggests that our understanding of how tradition works cannot be separated from our experiences with particular traditions. He grants that the way in which we receive a cultural heritage cannot be divorced from what we receive. Yet he does not seem to recognize the problems that this fact causes for his view of traditionality.

Thus Ricoeur's version of the historical thesis rests on an untenable distinction. Traditionality cannot be neatly separated from traditions. The form of philosophical understanding cannot be specified in abstraction from the particular contents that instantiate it. On the contrary, our only access to this form is through content. The only way to understand what it means to participate in tradition is to be acquainted with some particular tradition or traditions. There is no universal form of traditionality in the abstract. There is only traditionality as it is manifested in the transmission of particular traditions. But if this is so, then Ricoeur's attempt to give an entirely 'form-based' argument for the historical thesis cannot work. As attractive as this argumentative strategy may be, it rests on an implausible separation of form and content.

But there is a deeper question here: why would Ricoeur *want* to separate the two so neatly? Why would Ricoeur want to claim that traditionality is a transcendental concept whose meaning is independent of particular traditions? He does this, I think, for reasons we have already encountered. Lurking in the background of Ricoeur's thought is a familiar view of the relation between truth and historical knowledge: the view that Hegel inherited from Kant, and that he transmitted through Heidegger to

contemporary thought. It is the view that truth cannot be in history. The truths that philosophers seek, the story goes, must be separate from history and opposed to the ontic. They must belong to another order altogether: to a spirit not identical with any of its historical manifestations, to a meaning gleaned from the whole of history but not reducible to any particular moment of that history, or something of the sort. For Ricoeur, the site of philosophical truth is traditionality. Traditionality is, after all, the form of philosophical understanding. And traditionality is independent of particular traditions—independent of particular cultural heritages, of particular moments in history, and indeed of anything ontic. Traditionality, as a transcendental concept, is ontological, whereas traditions are ontic. And philosophical truth is to be found solely in the former realm, not in the latter. In short, despite Ricoeur's impressive attempt to amend Hegel and Heidegger, his view of historical knowledge is in one respect not very different from theirs. Like them, Ricoeur tacitly assumes that truth cannot be in history.

What reason is there to think that Ricoeur shares this assumption? Consider that the reason he gives for separating traditionality and traditions is to give hermeneutics the resources to answer Habermas. We must distinguish our need for some tradition or other from the particular traditions we happen to be born into, if we are to avoid a dangerous romantic traditionalism. But to answer Habermas in this way, all that is necessary is that we draw *some* distinction between traditionality and traditions. There are less ambitious ways of doing so than the one Ricoeur chooses. We could, for example, explore the possibility that there is more than one form of traditionality. We could grant that the form and the contents of traditions are distinct, but insist that there are *several* such forms, or perhaps an indefinite number of them. We could argue that how a tradition is transmitted is inevitably shaped by what is transmitted, and that as a result, each tradition has its own form of traditionality. Doing so would still leave form and content distinct, and therefore give us ample resources for answering Habermas. Ricoeur goes much further than he has to. He does not merely argue that the form of philosophical understanding is distinct from its contents; he claims that there is only *one* such form. He argues that traditionality is a transcendental, a universal, and that its operations embody a 'transcultural form of necessity' (*TN1*, 52). Ricoeur's attempt to purge traditionality of any particular contents is so overzealous and so unnecessary

for his purposes that it must have a different motivation. The best explanation is that Ricoeur's motives are the same as those of the 'hermeneutical tradition to which [he] belongs' (*TA*, 1). Ricoeur wants traditionality to be separate from traditions because he wants truth to be independent of anything ontic. He wants the distinction between traditionality and traditions to map onto the distinction between the ontological and the ontic. The reason he does so is that he assumes—with Hegel and Heidegger—that truth is not genuinely in history.

But there is a twist to the story. In the case of the other thinkers we have examined, the conviction that truth is not in history goes hand in hand with a hostility toward mimesis. Truth cannot be situated in the ontic because if it were, then we could find truth simply by studying the philosophers of the past. Finding philosophical truth in this way is assumed to be impossible, because mimesis, the story goes, is unphilosophical. We encountered this view in Kant and Hegel, and we saw that for both, a low opinion of mimesis leads to an attempt to purge truth of the ontic. Ricoeur seems to break this pattern. Granted, he assumes that truth cannot be in history, and to that extent he is a successor to Kant and Hegel. But he does not share the view of mimesis that usually goes hand in hand with this understanding of history. He does not think mimesis is always passive or unproductive. On the contrary, Ricoeur understands mimesis as active. His writings on mimesis argue that to imitate something—whether in an art work or a philosophical position—is to act on it, to exert one's spontaneity over it, and to transform it.

Ricoeur's account of mimesis grows out of his theory of narrative. For Ricoeur, narrative is important because it is the medium through which we try to make sense of time. Ricoeur argues that time is essentially aporetic. There can be no satisfactory theory of what time is, or of how the various temporal ecstases are related. But we can lessen these aporias by telling stories, constructing narratives about events that take place in time. Narratives humanize time: 'time becomes human to the extent that it is articulated through a narrative mode, and narrative attains its full meaning when it becomes a condition of temporal existence' (*TN1*, 52). Narratives are constructed by means of 'emplotment' (*TN1*, 31), or the 'activity of narrating a story' (*TN1*, 52). In constructing a narrative, we actively organize events into a coherent structure with a beginning, a middle, and an end. This process is clearly mimetic, in that a narrative imitates events, whether historical

or fictitious ones. But it is also active in that it transforms the events to be imitated. Situating an event in a story changes it. It gives the event a significance it did not have before: the significance attached to the beginning, middle, or end of a story. In short, to construct a narrative is to engage in active mimesis. It is to imitate without simply mirroring a pregiven content. It is to place an episode into an organized whole, and thereby to change it. For this reason, Ricoeur argues, mimesis can involve 'production,' 'construction,' and 'dynamism' (*TN1*, 33). We should understand mimesis not as a 'structure,' but as an 'operation' (*TN1*, 33).

Ricoeur discusses three specific ways in which narration involves active mimesis. He calls them—both 'seriously and playfully' (*TN1*, 52)—mimesis1, mimesis2, and mimesis3. All three have to do with figuration, or with the imposition of structure on a collection of heterogeneous elements. Mimesis1, the first step in the construction of a narrative, involves picking out the events to be included in the story. It involves distinguishing events that are meaningful, and that can therefore be included in a story, from those that are not. It involves 'identifying action by means of its structural features' (*TN1*, 54)—where the 'structural features' in question are the properties events have by virtue of being mediated by language and other symbolic systems. Selecting the appropriate material for a narrative is an activity. Since it involves choosing the events to be ordered at a later stage, we might call it the activity of *prefiguration*. Next comes the 'configurational dimension' (*TN1*, 67), or mimesis2. Mimesis2 is the sort of imitation found in the construction of a plot proper. It is the organization of appropriate events into a story with a beginning, a middle, and an end. Constructing a plot 'transforms the succession of events into one meaningful whole' (*TN1*, 67). Configuring events in this way is obviously active. It transforms heterogeneous elements by synthesizing them into a unified story. The third kind of mimesis—mimesis3—is the activity performed by a narrative's readers. Narratives are not simply composed; they must also be read and interpreted. As Gadamer would say, they must be completed in application. The reader *refigures* the narrative by interpreting it with respect to her own situation. In this way, the reader also 'carries the burden of emplotment' (*TN1*, 77). The processes of prefiguring, configuring, and refiguring a text are all mimetic. But they are also active. Ricoeur's theory of narrative shows how one might understand mimesis not as passive copying, but as an active, productive process.

Thus Ricoeur occupies a peculiar place in our narrative. On the one hand, his version of the historical thesis is problematic. Though his form-based argument for this thesis looks like a promising alternative to the content-based arguments offered by Hegel and Heidegger, it is not, at the end of the day, a real alternative to them. It tacitly accepts the picture of historical knowledge shared by Hegel and Heidegger. Ricoeur's conception of the historical thesis merely reverses the terms of Hegel's and Heidegger's positions. It does not question their presuppositions in a sufficiently radical way. On the other hand, while Ricoeur assumes that truth cannot be in history, he rejects a view that usually goes hand in hand with that assumption: the view that mimesis is passive and unphilosophical. His theory of narrative shows that it is possible to think of mimesis as active and productive. He shows that one of the first principles of continental thinking about the history of philosophy is not obviously true, and may well be wrong. In doing so, he provides some fruitful resources for thinking about this history in a different way. Ricoeur's theory of active mimesis may help point the way out of the continental tradition's incoherent view of the history of philosophy—even if Ricoeur remains trapped in this view himself.

How could a theory of active mimesis lead to a more satisfactory view of the history of philosophy? That is the subject of the next chapter.

Chapter 5

Truth in History

In Chapter 1, I claimed that continental thinking about the history of philosophy is in crisis. I argued that the historical thesis is regarded as an article of faith in a great deal of recent continental philosophy. It is taken as obviously true, but without being adequately defended, or even understood. Specifically, I argued that three contemporary philosophical schools—Derridean deconstruction, Gadamerian hermeneutics, and Levinasian ethical thought—are all committed to the historical thesis. Yet in each case, this commitment is made deeply problematic by a variety of confusions and tensions. In the chapters that followed, I turned to history to make sense of these confusions. I traced the development of the historical thesis, in the hope of discovering how contemporary philosophy had arrived at its muddled state. It might now be helpful to summarize this development.

The crisis originates in Hegel's break with Kant. Kant claims that while studying the history of philosophy is important, it is not really part of philosophy. This is because the historian's standpoint is intrinsically unphilosophical. The philosopher as such is active with respect to her subject matter. She does not passively represent something handed to her from without. She *acts* on her subject matter, exerting spontaneity over it. Historians of philosophy, on the other hand, passively imitate positions found in past thought. And as Kant tells us, 'the imitative faculty is not itself productive' (*KRV*, A836/B854). Representing a position from the history of philosophy is diametrically opposed to arriving at that position through active reasoning. Kant assigns a subordinate task to the history of philosophy because he sees mimesis as passive and unphilosophical.

Hegel sets out to break with this Kantian model. He claims that the history of philosophy is not something we study only after constructing our philosophical system. We must grapple with it while doing philosophy,

and even while coming to understand what philosophy is. But while Hegel rejects Kant's view of the history of philosophy, he accepts the theory of mimesis that gives rise to it. Like Kant, Hegel sees imitation as passive and unphilosophical, even as he advances a conception of the history of philosophy that is incompatible with this view. In order to have it both ways—in order to maintain that philosophers must be historians while also claiming that the study of history is unphilosophical—Hegel advances what I have called a content-based argument for the historical thesis. He argues that the history of philosophy is important not because of anything to do with its particular stages, but because the history as a whole teaches lessons about a content distinct from it. He claims that the history of philosophy is indispensable even though there is no truth *in* it—only *beyond* it. This claim is deeply incoherent, and Hegel discovers as much over the course of his career. Thus a confused view of the history of philosophy grows out of Hegel's incomplete break with Kant. Hegel tries to reject Kant's conclusion while accepting the premises that give rise to it.

Later developments make this confusion worse. In particular, Heidegger transforms Hegel's incoherent view of the history of philosophy into a genuine crisis. Heidegger develops what looks like an alternative to Hegel's position. He claims that the history of philosophy is important not because of what it teaches about philosophy's content, but because of considerations involving philosophy's form. A confrontation with this history is required not by 'the *what* of the objects of philosophical research as subject-matter, but rather the *how* of that research' (*BT*, 50). As we have seen, though, Heidegger's form-based approach is never adequately distinguished from the content-based approach, or from a problematic conception of philosophy's subject matter. It looks like a break with the content-based approach, but is really just a disguised version of it. Heidegger therefore begins the practice of appearing to break with Hegel while not really doing so. This practice continues in more recent hermeneutical philosophy, which I take to be exemplified by the work of Paul Ricoeur. Ricoeur also tries to break with a Hegelian, content-based approach. He does so by sharply distinguishing traditionality—the form of philosophical understanding—from traditions—philosophy's subject matter. But again, Ricoeur's attempt to separate form and content does not go deep enough. It rejects Hegel's content-based approach while accepting the assumptions that underlie it. Like Heidegger, contemporary hermeneutical philosophy recognizes the need to move away

from Hegel. But it does not break with him in a sufficiently radical way, because what it takes to be the problem with his legacy is really just a symptom of the problem. It breaks with Hegel's content-based approach without questioning the view of historical knowledge that gives rise to it.

So it is not surprising that the three schools examined in Chapter 1 understand the history of philosophy in ways that are confused, even incoherent. It is not surprising that their discussions of the historical thesis founder on internal tensions. All three of these schools belong to the tradition of post-Kantian philosophy extending from Hegel through Heidegger to more recent thought. This tradition claims that philosophy is an essentially historical enterprise, while accepting a view of historical knowledge that is incompatible with this claim. In light of this tradition's history, we should not be surprised by the tensions in the work of its most prominent representatives. We should not be surprised by Derrida's suggestion that the history of philosophy both is and is not indispensable. Nor should we be surprised by Gadamer's claim that radical breaks with the past both are and are not possible. Finally, we should not be surprised that Levinas says that philosophy is inherently historical, but does philosophy in a way that is at odds with this claim. If the story I have told is right, we should expect such tensions to arise. If post-Kantian philosophy has developed in the ways I claim, then we would expect it to be in crisis today.

Now that we know how the crisis developed, we should ask whether it *had* to develop in this way. Was it inevitable that continental thought would adopt an incoherent view of the history of philosophy? Could things have unfolded differently? Are *we* forced to accept the tradition's problematic way of thinking about the history of philosophy? Or are there alternatives? Of course, if my narrative has taught us anything, it is that we should be suspicious of radical breaks with the past. Attempts to leave the past behind have a funny way of failing to do so. Still, if we can show that a number of these problems have a common assumption as their source, *and* that this assumption is not forced on us, then it may be worthwhile to look for an alternative and see how far it takes us. As I have repeatedly suggested, there *is* a common assumption at work in each of the philosophers we have examined. It is the Kantian view of mimesis. Kant maintains that mimesis is passive and unproductive, since it is a mere imitation of an external content, not an exercise of spontaneity. In one way or another, this understanding of mimesis surfaces in each of the thinkers we have discussed. We might

therefore call it the *received view of mimesis*. To call this view of mimesis the received one is not to say that all of the thinkers we have examined explicitly endorse it. Some do not discuss it in so many words; some, such as Ricoeur, even advance theories of mimesis that are incompatible with it. But even the thinkers who reject Kant's discussion of mimesis tend to accept the consequences it has had in other areas. For example, though Ricoeur gives a decidedly un-Kantian account of mimesis, he continues to think of the history of philosophy in terms of the concepts of form and content. He also continues to assume that truth cannot be in history, and that the concept of traditionality must be purged of everything ontic. These ways of thinking are manifestations of the received view. So if we want to look for a way out of the crisis, we need to ask a more basic question: Is the received view the only possible view of mimesis? Or is it possible to understand mimesis differently—not as passive, unproductive, and unphilosophical, but as *active?*

I believe that it is, and so in this chapter, I subject the received view to critical scrutiny. I want to show that it is not the only possible way of understanding mimesis, and that there are alternatives to it. Indeed, I want to show that the received view is implausible in many respects, and that this fact has important implications for the way we understand the history of philosophy. My argument falls into three parts. The first surveys some recent work in aesthetics, a field in which the received view of mimesis has long been considered dubious. These developments show that it is possible to reinterpret mimesis as active. Next, I argue that the reinterpretation of mimesis found in contemporary aesthetics can be extended to history with little difficulty. Doing so shows that while historical knowledge is mimetic, it is not on that account passive or unproductive. On the contrary, the sorts of imitation found in the historian's work are in important respects active. In the third and final section, I argue that adopting this new view of mimesis comes at a price, because it forces us to rethink what it means for a history of philosophy to be true. Importing active mimesis into history requires us to see truth as something that can be genuinely *in* history.

Active mimesis in aesthetics

The classic discussion of mimesis in aesthetics appears in Book 10 of Plato's *Republic.* Near the end of the *Republic,* Socrates advances a series of criticisms

of imitative art. Mimetic art, he claims, does not belong in the education of the guardians, since it is 'inferior with respect to truth,' and 'appeals to a part of the soul that is similarly inferior.'[1] The artist is merely an 'imitator of what the others make.'[2] He represents things of which he has no particular knowledge—he can 'paint a cobbler, a carpenter, or any other craftsman, even though he knows nothing about these crafts,'[3] and he can write tragedies though he knows nothing of the fates of great men. Unlike a craftsman, the artist is free to take up an object about which he knows nothing, and passively mirror it. That which his art works imitate—to take an example that Socrates gives, a bed—is both independent of the imitation, and more real than it. The bed is in no way constituted by the activity of the artist who depicts it. The artist does not produce anything but images. He simply mimics real things.

It is this view of mimesis, or one very much like it, that underlies Kant's first *Critique*. And it is easy to see why Kant would believe that mimesis of this sort cannot yield philosophical knowledge. For Kant, one knows through the 'free use of [one's] reason.'[4] Knowledge is not a passive mirroring of an object, but an exercise of spontaneity. Indeed, there is a sense in which knowledge constitutes or produces its object, in so far as all cognition involves some active contribution on the part of the subject. But mimesis as described in the *Republic* does not allow for a contribution of this sort. Mimesis passively represents a given object; knowledge, on the other hand, constitutes an object that is dependent on the knower. Surely this is what Kant means when he claims that one *produces* one's knowledge, that it has '*arisen* . . . out of reason' (*KRV*, A836/B854). This is why he says that 'the imitative faculty is not itself productive' (*KRV*, A836/B854).

Of course, it is far from clear that the discussion of mimesis in the *Republic* should be taken at face value. It has long been suggested that Plato was not really endorsing the words that he put in Socrates's mouth—that he was being ironic, or playing devil's advocate, or something of the sort. But it *is* clear that Book Ten of the *Republic* is not an adequate account of contemporary art. The sort of mimesis described in the *Republic* will not go very far toward helping us to understand the painting, literature, and music of the past century. No one would deny that the most important and influential art works of the past century have been nonimitative (or 'nonobjective'), in the sense that they do not simply take up a content and reproduce it

passively. What, after all, does a cubist painting represent? Even when a painting by Picasso or Braque has an identifiable subject matter, it does not mirror it passively, in the manner of the picture of a bed described in the *Republic*. Instead, it presents a series of diverse perspectives that must be actively synthesized by the viewer. Similarly, what does a painting by Jackson Pollock represent? Or, for that matter, one by Andy Warhol? I am not suggesting that these questions have no answers. But it is far from clear *how* we are to answer them, and the *Republic*'s discussion of mimesis will be of little help in doing so. If questions of this sort are pressing in the visual arts, they are even more pressing in other genres. What is represented by a Schoenberg cantata? Or by *Finnegan's Wake*? The received view of mimesis can tell us little about the most important works of contemporary art, and almost nothing that is interesting. If mimesis is merely the passive reproduction of pre-given contents, then the past century has had little use for it. So we might expect aesthetics to turn its back on the concept. We might expect the philosophy of art to relegate mimesis to the dustbin of history, and to take up new concepts with more relevance in the contemporary world.

Interestingly, though, this has not happened. Instead of abandoning mimesis, contemporary aesthetics has tried to reinterpret it. The sort of passive imitation described in Book 10 of the *Republic* is of little use in making sense of contemporary art—and for that matter, a great many other types of art as well. It is typically argued, however, that imitation of this sort has never defined mimesis, but only one form of it, and a shallow and uninteresting form at that. Mimesis is broader and deeper than simple copying or mimicry. A common way of arguing this is to try and retrieve an older and more basic meaning of mimesis. The *Republic*'s interpretation of mimesis, it is argued, actually distorts the concept's original meaning, and while this distorted interpretation cannot be usefully applied to contemporary art, the more original sense of mimesis may be. This more original sense, whatever it is, generally sees mimesis as more dynamic than does Book 10 of the *Republic*. On this view, mimesis does not simply copy an independent object, but transforms this object. In short, the notions of copying and reproduction are of little use in making sense of contemporary art. But it does not follow that the concept of mimesis is of little use as well, because it might well turn out to mean something deeper. Contemporary aesthetics tends to agree with Gadamer when he says that 'anyone who thinks that art

can no longer be adequately grasped using Greek concepts is not thinking in a sufficiently Greek way.'[5]

Let me turn to Gadamer's discussion of mimesis, because it is a good example of how recent philosophers have tried to salvage mimesis by reinterpreting it. Gadamer maintains that it is wrong to think that nonobjective art cannot be understood in terms of mimesis. It is easy to see why one would make this mistake, because mimesis has long been taken to be the mere copying of a pre-given object. But according to Gadamer, 'the concept of mimesis can be grasped in a more original fashion.'[6] Indeed, it *ought* to be grasped more originally, since the received view of mimesis distorts the concept's meaning. 'No special historical investigations are required,' Gadamer claims, 'to recognize that the meaning of the word "mimesis" consists simply in letting something be there without trying to do anything more with it.'[7] Mimesis originally refers to the presentation of things, especially 'the presentation of order' in things.[8] To engage in mimesis is to make a thing present in such a way that it is capable of being recognized. This is why Aristotle illustrates mimesis with the example of children dressing up. We enjoy seeing children in disguise even when their costumes are poor. The pleasure we take in mimetic activity comes not from the accuracy of the copy, but from the fact that mimesis allows us to see something we know in a new context. It lets us recognize the familiar in the unfamiliar. 'When I recognize someone or something,' Gadamer writes, 'what I see is freed from this or that moment of time. It is part of the process of recognition that we see things in terms of what is permanent and essential in them.'[9] In this sense, the mimetic art work does not copy a thing, but *presents* the thing, 'in the only way available to it.'[10] Properly understood, mimesis is a dynamic process. It consists not in the passive reproduction of things, but in their presentation, 'in terms of what is permanent and essential in them.'[11] Mimesis acts on things, and, in presenting them, transforms them.

There is much more to be said about this understanding of mimesis. But Gadamer's discussion shows that the received view of mimesis is not obviously right. It is possible to see mimesis as something that transforms—and in some sense constitutes—its object. Indeed, there is some evidence that this understanding is closer to the original meaning of mimesis than is the received view. Of course, it does not follow that Gadamer's reinterpretation is right. But it does follow that we should reinvestigate mimesis. It may be

worthwhile to look more closely for elements of activity in the mimetic process—that is, to look for specific ways in which mimesis transforms an object by acting on it. So *are* there specific ways in which mimesis transforms or constitutes its object? If we can answer this question in the affirmative, then we will have gone some way toward showing that the received view of mimesis is not just dubious, but wrong. And I think we *can* answer in the affirmative. There are at least three specific ways in which mimesis involves activity. There are at least three senses in which mimesis is a productive process that transforms its object. Let me discuss each in turn.

The first way in which mimesis is active concerns the *composition* of a mimetic art work. This composition is never wholly passive. No matter how faithfully a painting or a poem depicts its subject, it is never simply a reproduction of something given. In order to compose a mimetic work, one must first select its subject matter. One must determine what is to be represented and what is not. In selecting her work's subject matter, the artist must actively distinguish it from other candidates for representation. Before Van Gogh can paint the 'Room at Arles,' for example, he must focus on his bedroom and not on some other room. He must focus on his bed and not on some other object in the room. And he must select one perspective on the bed from an indefinite number of other possibilities. No matter how faithfully 'Room at Arles' depicts Van Gogh's bed, no matter how good a copy the painting is, it is not a purely passive reproduction. It is the result of a string of decisions and selections, each of which shapes the final product. Thus whenever an artist imitates something, a certain ordering activity has already taken place: the activity of distinguishing her subject from other possible ones, and of viewing it from one perspective rather than another. This activity makes certain objects stand out in relief and others recede into the background. It turns certain objects into a figure and others into a ground. In this respect, it transforms what is to be represented.

The second way in which mimesis is active has to do with the synthetic character of the work itself. Not only can the work be composed only after its subject matter has been selected; the work itself is a collection of heterogeneous elements that must be grasped together. And this grasping together takes place by means of a 'synthetic act,'[12] both on the part of the artist, and on the part of the audience. Indeed, there is no unified work apart from this synthetic act. Any art work obviously consists of several diverse elements. A painting is made up of many different brush strokes,

perhaps ones that depict different objects, or different facets of the same object. A narrative describes several different events, or perhaps different perspectives on the same event. And a piece of music consists of many notes and chords that unfold successively over time. But in none of these cases is the art work just a diversity of elements. Both the artist and the audience grasp the different elements as elements of a single work. We view the work as unified. Confronting a work of art is therefore an exercise in what Louis Mink calls 'comprehension'—the ability to 'think together in a single act, or in a cumulative series of acts, the complicated relationship of parts which can be experienced only *seriatim*.'[13] More specifically, it involves that particular form of comprehension that Mink calls 'configuration,' or 'the ability to hold together a number of elements in just balance.'[14] To 'read' a painting, or a narrative, or a piece of music, is to configure it—to organize the diverse elements in such a way that they make up a unified whole. This is a task for the work's audience as well as for the artist. The work does not force us to 'read' it in one way rather than another. Configuration is something we do, an activity we perform. The unity of a work of art is something we achieve, not something that is simply given to us. In so far as the work is a collection of elements that must be thought together, its being depends on my configurational activity. In this sense, we might say that it is constituted by me.

The third way in which mimesis is active has to do with its reception by an audience. A mimetic work is essentially indeterminate. No matter how faithfully it depicts its subject matter, it cannot copy everything. It must leave open spaces that will be filled in by those who encounter it. Roman Ingarden has called these open spaces 'spots of indeterminacy.'[15] And the work is incomplete until its spots of indeterminacy are filled in—that is, until the work is supplemented by another synthetic act performed by its audience. In this way, a mimetic work must be completed in application. To see how this is so, consider an example given by Gadamer. Any reader of *The Brothers Karamazov* will recall the staircase down which Smerdyakov tumbles. The passage that describes it is obviously mimetic, in that it depicts an object, albeit a fictional one, and strives to do so accurately. Reading it creates a picture of the staircase in my mind's eye. But my picture of the staircase will not be exactly the same as anyone else's. It will not be quite the same length, or have quite the same sort of banister, or be lit in quite the same way as it is for another reader. Any of Dostoyevsky's

readers 'will "see" the staircase in a most specific way and be convinced that he sees it as it really is.'[16] The passage describing the staircase is not complete until I have filled in its indeterminate spaces through an act of imagination. This act does not leave the passage as it is. It transforms the work by applying it to my unique situation. Moreover, it is not just literary works that are indeterminate and that must be filled in through a synthetic act on the part of the audience. A painting or a sculpture must be read in much the same way. Though works of this sort are mimetic, they are not on that account unproductive. They are not simply copies of a pre given reality. There is an important sense in which the objects they imitate are fully realized only in them.

So there are at least three specific ways in which every mimetic art work is active, three ways in which depicting something transforms it. In keeping with Mink's terminology, we might call them *prefiguration, configuration*, and *refiguration*. Prefiguration makes something a candidate for representation; configuration is the process of representing it; and refiguration completes the representation by applying it to the audience's situation.[17] Of course, I did not choose these terms by accident. They were introduced earlier, during my discussion of Ricoeur's theory of narrative. Ricoeur argues that a narrative is always the product of a 'threefold mimesis' (*TN1*, 52). The first stage, which he calls mimesis1, is the process of selecting the action to be described by the narrative. Mimesis2 is what happens when the author brings together the narrative's diverse elements into a single plot. And mimesis3 is the process through which readers fill in the narrative's gaps by applying it to their own situation. I suggested earlier that these three kinds of mimesis could be described, respectively, as kinds of prefiguration, configuration, and refiguration, and that is why I have retained these terms here. But the terms 'prefiguration,' 'configuration,' and 'refiguration,' as I am using them, are not identical with Ricoeur's three kinds of mimesis. Ricoeur seems to restrict his three kinds of mimesis to the study of literary works. This is not an unreasonable restriction, given that *Time and Narrative* is *about* literary works, and is not explicitly concerned with other genres. I, on the other hand, will use the terms 'prefiguration,' 'configuration,' and 'refiguration' more broadly. I will use them to refer to activities that occur in *all* mimetic art works, not just in literary works. On my reading, Ricoeur's 'threefold mimesis' is just one example of a process that takes place in all

artistic genres. To say this differently, my discussion of active mimesis is an attempt to generalize Ricoeur's study of literary mimesis to mimetic art as a whole.

The received view notwithstanding, then, mimesis need not be seen as a passive, unproductive process. It can be understood as a dynamic process that transforms its subject matter. Up to this point, we have confined this view of mimesis to aesthetics. But can it be extended to history? Could it be the case that, although the historian's task is mimetic, it is also active, productive, and transformative? Since Aristotle wrote the *Poetics*, it has been common to think there is a sharp division between the tasks of the artist and the historian. Aristotle claims that poetry is more philosophical than history, because the historian describes things as they are, whereas the poet describes things as they might be.[18] I want to suggest that the historian's work is more poetic than Aristotle acknowledges. Properly understood, history is active and productive in many of the same ways as poetry. History may not be more philosophical than poetry, but it might be *just as* philosophical.

Active mimesis in history

In what sense is the historian's work mimetic? And in what way does a history *of philosophy* involve mimesis? The simple answer is that a history of philosophy describes what other people have thought. When I study the history of philosophy, I am concerned with descriptions of philosophical positions that have been advanced by other people. I construe what Hegel says, or what Heidegger says, or something of the sort. In doing so, I depend on historical data that I do not produce and that are handed to me from without: books they wrote, records of their lives, and so on. This is why Kant calls historical knowledge '*cognitio ex datis*' (*KRV*, A836/B854) or knowledge from data. And this is why Kant says that a familiarity with what other philosophers have thought is 'unproductive' and 'merely historical' (*KRV*, A836/B854). Reproducing data and describing the positions of others does seem rather passive. It does seem to be a mere copying of what others have said. In light of Kant's claim that genuinely rational knowledge involves active synthesis, it is not surprising that he calls the historian 'merely a plaster cast of a living man' (*KRV*, A836/B854).

Kant's criticism is a natural one, and it is bound to appear compelling to those who accept the received view of mimesis. If mimesis were nothing more than the copying of existing objects, then history would be a passive and unproductive enterprise. And if we agree with Kant that philosophical thinking is active, then history would be a decidedly unphilosophical enterprise as well. As we have seen, though, the received view of mimesis is dubious. There is good reason to think that mimesis is not just the reproduction of existing objects. There is good reason to think that mimesis involves the activities I have called prefiguration, configuration, and refiguration. Since Kant's verdict about history presupposes the received view of mimesis—a view we can no longer accept—we should rethink it. In particular, we should ask whether the activities of prefiguration, configuration, and refiguration have analogues in the sphere of history. If they do, then studying the history of philosophy will be in important respects like composing a mimetic work of art. Like mimesis in aesthetics, mimesis in history will turn out to be dynamic and transformative. Thus it will be possible that the study of the history of philosophy involves the same kind of active synthesis that Kant thinks is found only in a smaller subset of cognitive acts. It will be possible that even by Kant's standards, its study is philosophical. Let me discuss each of the three activities in turn. And let me illustrate them by means of a history of philosophy that we have already encountered: the one Kant gives in his *Lectures on Metaphysics*.

What role does prefiguration play in the history of philosophy? In art, prefiguration is the process of selecting a work's subject matter, and of distinguishing that subject matter from other subjects that might have been chosen. Before I paint a bed, I must single out a bed, and focus on it rather than on something else. I must also view the bed from one perspective rather than another. Something analogous happens when a narrative about the history of philosophy is composed. Narratives are selective: they describe some things and not others. They are also perspectival, in that they reflect one standpoint rather than another. Before we construct a narrative about the history of philosophy, we must decide what it is about. We must select the events to be described by our history, and we must describe them from one perspective and not from another. It is impossible to describe everything that has happened in the history of past thought, so we select some periods for discussion and ignore others. Similarly, we cannot

discuss everything that happens in any particular period, so we select certain figures rather than others, and certain books by those figures and not others. We need not be aware that we are doing so. The choices we make in selecting our subject matter may seem so uncontroversial that we do not even recognize them as choices. No doubt tradition shapes how we carry out the task of prefiguration; it may well be that, as Gadamer puts it, history 'determines in advance both what seems to us worth inquiring about and what will appear as an object of investigation' (*TM*, 300). But even if the task of selecting our subject matter is not one we consciously control, we still carry it out. The history of philosophy should not be regarded as a body of facts 'out there' waiting to be copied by the historian. That about which the historian writes is, in some sense, dependent on her narratives about it.

The history that Kant gives in the *Lectures on Metaphysics* obviously bears the stamp of this prefigurational activity. Kant does not describe everything that has ever been thought or said. Rather, he composes a short and highly selective story that focuses on some periods and ignores others. Kant divides the history of philosophy into three periods: those of the Eleatics, the Athenians, and the moderns. He ignores periods a contemporary historian might consider crucial: Hellenistic philosophy, for example, as well as the entire medieval period. Indeed, he acknowledges that he is doing so, as when he dismisses medieval philosophy as 'muck' that was 'swept away by the Reformation.'[19] Moreover, Kant obviously discusses the history of philosophy from a highly specific perspective. His philosophical interests and preoccupations lead him to focus on certain topics and not others, as when he discusses Plato's metaphysics and epistemology but not his ethics.[20] Even a history as paltry as Kant's is more than a passive copy of a given body of facts. It is a highly selective story told from a highly specific perspective, not one that passively duplicates its subject matter. As such, it is a product of the activity that I have called prefiguration.

The second kind of activity involved in mimesis is what I have called configuration. It is the process of unifying diverse elements into a single work by thinking them together. In art, configuration is the act of transforming different elements into *a* work of art—a variety of brush strokes into a single painting, a variety of events into a single story, and so on. Similar things happen in historical narratives. Just as fictional narratives combine a variety of fictitious events into a single plot, historical

narratives combine a variety of elements into a single history. A history of philosophy is an attempt to think diverse elements together. Any number of elements might be thought together in such a history. There are obviously multiple philosophers to deal with, and in most cases, multiple works by each. There are numerous events to be described: fateful meetings, the publication of important books, and so on. Numerous philosophical themes must be discussed, as must different branches of the discipline. There are also cultural factors to consider: the historian may put a philosopher's work in the context of political, scientific, or artistic developments, for example. In all of these ways, and in many others, a history of philosophy deals in diversity. But it also unifies this diversity by combining its elements into a single history. It is, essentially, a product of configurational activity.

Kant's history is an instructive example of how this sort of configuration takes place. Despite its brevity, Kant's history covers an enormous amount of ground. It discusses a great many centuries, a wide range of philosophers, and a large number of theses advanced by those philosophers. But Kant's history is not just a collection of heterogeneous elements. It is a coherent narrative that unifies its elements in a variety of ways. One of the ways it does so is through its talk of philosophical movements or schools. Kant does not, for example, discuss Parmenides, Zeno, and related figures individually. Instead, he lumps these thinkers into a single movement—the Eleatics—unified by one thesis. A second device Kant uses to unify his subject matter is causality. Kant's history does not simply list a series of thinkers who advance unrelated claims. Instead, it traces chains of influence among the major figures. Kant argues that Leibniz is best understood as a modern version of Plato, Locke as a modern version of Aristotle.[21] By tracing influence in this way, Kant brings together a wide range of very different philosophers. Finally, Kant helps unify his history of philosophy by tracing thematic continuities. He tells us that Parmenides, Aristotle, and Locke are not simply different thinkers engaged in diverse projects. Each poses the same questions; each seeks solutions to a common set of problems. And of course, each of these thinkers anticipates a major insight of the critical philosophy. Thematic continuity is thus another tool Kant uses to unify the diverse elements of his history. It is another way in which Kant's history is an exercise in configuration.

Finally, narratives about the history of philosophy involve what I have called refiguration. As Gadamer would say, they must be completed in application. In aesthetics, refiguration has to do with the essential indeterminacy of a mimetic art work. Such a work has 'open spaces' that must be filled in by the audience—open spaces such as the staircase in *The Brothers Karamazov*, which each reader must visualize in his own way. The same sorts of open spaces are found in narratives about the history of philosophy. Like a painting or a novel, a historical narrative is essentially indeterminate, and must be completed by a synthetic act performed by the reader. As an example, consider the function that a history assigns to background information. No history can explicitly state all the information that is needed to understand it. Certain things must remain unstated. These things are left to be filled in by the reader. Someone writing a technical history of twentieth-century ethical thought will probably not say explicitly what ethics is, or how it differs from other branches of philosophy. Nor will she describe most important ethical debates, or say what is at stake in them. Nor, finally, will she tell us what human behavior is, or how it can be distinguished from other phenomena. All of this will be presupposed. While her narrative is intelligible only in the context of certain background information, the historian typically does not give this background information explicitly. She assumes that the reader will fill it in. And as with the visualization of the staircase, there is no guarantee that different readers will fill in this gap in the same way. Like a refigured work of art, a refigured history is largely constituted by its audience.

Kant's history of philosophy is no different in this respect. It too is essentially indeterminate; it too presupposes a certain amount of background information. And it too must be refigured by the reader who provides this information. Consider the way Kant describes the ancients and their theses. Eleatic thought, he tells us, is preoccupied with the deceptiveness of the senses. It discovers that our experience of the world is both 'sensitive' and 'intellectual.'[22] It further maintains that 'there is no truth in the senses.'[23] Kant's history does not explicitly say what sensation is. It assumes that we know this much, and that we understand what it means to say there is no truth in the senses. Thus we must supplement Kant's narrative with our own understandings of what sensation and intellect are. It is important to recognize, however, just how active this supplementation is, and just how much the reader must contribute to Kant's history. There is not one and

only one way to fill in the gaps in Kant's text. There is not just one under-standing of sensation that can complete the open spaces of his history. Our concept of sensation is surely not that of Kant's contemporaries. When Kant uses the term 'sensation,' it has a whole range of connotations and reverberations that it need not have for us. Kant's understanding of sen-sation is closely linked to Humean sense impressions, Enlightenment psy-chology, and a Newtonian view of the world. Ours is bound up with what we know of Hanson, Sellars, and an Einsteinian, relativistic universe. This is not to say that these two views are incommensurable, or that it is impos-sible for a twentieth-century reader to understand sensation in a Kantian way. Perhaps the gap between Kant's framework of background informa-tion and ours can be bridged. The point is simply that there is a gap to bridge. There is a difference in the ways in which two different readers fill in the blanks of Kant's text. There is no guarantee that different readers will carry out this process in the same way. So the claim that historical nar-ratives must be completed in application is not trivial. The refiguration of such a narrative requires us to do a great deal.

The upshot of all this is that studying the history of philosophy is a much more creative enterprise than one might think. Granted, history is mimetic, in that it describes what others have thought. To someone who holds the received view of mimesis, it is bound to appear passive and unproductive. But if we reject the received view—and as I have argued, we should—then the historian's task begins to look more interesting, more active, and more philosophical. The study of history can no longer be understood as the passive copying of a pregiven reality. Instead, it must be understood as a constructive activity similar in many ways to the production and reception of a mimetic art work. That which the historian of philosophy studies is constituted by her narrative about it, in three ways. The object of her stud-ies invariably bears the stamp of prefiguration, configuration, and refigu-ration. To this extent, the past she describes depends on her own activity. Once we reject the received view of mimesis, we must also abandon the myth of a past in-itself, independent of us and waiting to be copied as it really is.

Talk of this sort has an important consequence. I have been arguing against the idea of a past in-itself. If 'there is no such thing as *the* text apart from its interpretation,'[24] then there is also no such thing as *the* his-tory of philosophy apart from our narratives about it. Instead, that which

historical narratives describe is in important ways shaped by those very narratives. If this view is right, then it poses difficulties for our understanding of what it means for a history of philosophy to be true. There is a natural tendency to think of a true history as one that gets the past right. On this view, a history of philosophy is true if it represents the thought of earlier philosophers correctly—that is, if it discovers what Hegel or Heidegger really thought. In other words, it is tempting to think that a true history of philosophy is one that provides what Alasdair MacIntyre calls an 'external representation'[25] of the past. External representation, as MacIntyre uses the term, is 'the relationship which holds between a passport photograph and its subject: one can inspect the two items independently and inquire as to the degree of resemblance between them.'[26] With internal representation, on the other hand, 'it is by means of the representation that we learn to see what is represented.'[27] If the view I have advanced is right, then a true history of philosophy is not one that gives a correct external representation of past thought. On the contrary, it is only by means of the historian's narratives that we 'learn to see' the past. The past cannot be compared to our narratives about it in the way I can be compared to my passport photo. So if we understand the historian's task as an active and productive one, we must reinterpret what it means for a history to be true. And we must do so in a way that is compatible with the claim that there is no past in-itself waiting to be copied.

Can we reinterpret truth in this way? I believe we can. What follows is a sketch of how we might reinterpret truth in order to make room for active mimesis in history. It is not a fully developed theory of truth, but a discussion of some of the criteria that an account of truth would have to meet to be compatible with the preceding view. It takes its beginnings from Gadamer's notion of effective history [*Wirkungsgeschichte*].

Truth in history

Gadamer's notion of *Wirkungsgeschichte* grows out of his critique of Romantic hermeneutics. He first introduces the notion as a way of criticizing Schleiermacher. For Schleiermacher, Gadamer says, hermeneutics aims at a '*reconstruction*' (*TM*, 164) of the past. Before we can understand the texts that have been handed down to us by tradition, we must overcome the ways

in which they have been 'wrenched from their original world' (*TM*, 166). We must recognize that the true meaning of these texts becomes apparent only when they are viewed in historical context. Since a text 'enjoys its true significance only where it originally belongs' (*TM*, 166), its interpreter must reconstruct its world in thought. She must learn all about the author's circumstances: the cultural context in which he wrote, the intentions he had for his work, the influences on his thought, and so on. Having done so, she is in a position to understand the text as the author did, or perhaps better. Indeed, for Schleiermacher, to understand a text just is to 'reproduce the writer's original process of production' (*TM*, 166). Only by mentally reconstructing the author's world as it really was can we discover what his text means.

Schleiermacher's hermeneutics assumes that we *can* reconstruct the world of the author as it really was—that it is possible to determine what the author did and did not think as she composed her text. Gadamer calls this assumption 'historical objectivism' (*TM*, 300). It is the view that we have access to what I have called a past in-itself, a past that is independent of our interpretations of it. In other words, it is the view that the past is an object that can be grasped theoretically, and that learning about the past is a matter of representing this object accurately. Gadamer does not think this assumption is plausible. 'Reconstructing the original circumstances,' he argues, 'is a futile undertaking in view of the historicity of our being. What is reconstructed, a life brought back from the lost past, is not the original' (*TM*, 167). Any attempted reconstruction will be shaped by our own historical situation, and so the goal that Schleiermacher assigns to hermeneutics cannot be realized. But according to Gadamer, the implausibility of historical objectivism does not mean that understanding the texts handed down by tradition is impossible. It simply means that this understanding does not reconstruct a past in-itself. More generally, it means that interpretation is not to be understood as a relation between a subject and an object, or as a process in which an autonomous interpreter in-herself strives to reconstruct the past as it really was. According to Gadamer, hermeneutics must abandon the myth of a past in-itself waiting to be reconstructed—or, for that matter, that of an interpreter in-herself waiting to do the reconstructing. Neither the subject nor the object of interpretation is an in-itself capable of being understood apart from the other.

Gadamer's solution to this problem is to reject historical objectivism, and thus to deny the antithesis on which Romantic hermeneutics is based. 'Our line of thought,' he claims, 'prevents us from defining the hermeneutic problem in terms of the subjectivity of the interpreter and the objectivity of the meaning to be understood. This would be starting from a false antithesis that cannot be resolved' (*TM*, 311). Interpreter and interpreted must not be understood as a subject and an object, entities capable of being defined independently of one another. Instead, they must be understood as poles of a complex historical process—a process of '*thoughtful mediation with contemporary life*' (*TM*, 169). At one end of this process is the 'past,' but it might better be described as the *past for us*—the past *as we understand it*, a past that has been filtered through our biases and preoccupations. At the other end is the 'present,' but a *present affected by the past*—a present that is itself the product of historical forces. The past and the present mutually shape each other. Neither pole can be adequately understood in abstraction from this historical process. The history to which they belong is an *effective* history [*Wirkungsgeschichte*] in which each pole conditions and is conditioned by the other. 'The true historical object is not an object at all,' Gadamer says, but rather 'a *relationship* that constitutes both the reality of history and the reality of historical understanding' (*TM*, 299, my emphasis).

Understanding the past, therefore, does not involve a correspondence between an interpreter in-itself and an interpreted in-itself. In fact, it is better not to think of it as a relation between a subject and an object at all. Understanding the past involves an *interplay*—'the interplay of the movement of tradition and the movement of the interpreter' (*TM*, 293). Gadamer characterizes this interplay as a *fusion of horizons*. A horizon is 'the range of vision that includes everything that can be seen from a particular vantage point' (*TM*, 302). To say that we understand history from within a horizon is to say that we have no access to the past that is not already shaped by our historical situation. This situation, however, is not something fixed, or something within which we are forever enclosed. Our horizon moves with us—'"to have a horizon" means not being limited to what is nearby but being able to see beyond it' (*TM*, 302). Likewise, that which we seek to understand in the past has a horizon. A text can be understood only by an interpreter transposed into its 'range of vision.' The text exercises a range of historical effects, and to understand it is to open

ourselves up to these effects. This is why Schleiermacher speaks of the need to 'see the past in its own terms,' or 'within its own historical horizon' (*TM*, 302–303). Gadamer's thesis, however, is that 'into this other situation we bring, precisely, ourselves' (*TM*, 305). That which we transpose into the horizon of the text also has a horizon. Understanding takes place when these horizons fuse, or when the range of vision afforded by our historical situation overlaps with the range of effects brought about by the text. Understanding is 'not a method which the inquiring consciousness applies to an object it chooses and so turns it into objective knowledge' (*TM*, 309). It is something that happens. It is, 'essentially, an historically mediated event' (*TM*, 299–300).

Indeed, *truth* turns out to be a historical event as well. Gadamer is adamant that the *Geisteswissenschaften*, and especially philosophy, attain truth. Though this truth is not accessible to the 'method' of the natural sciences, it 'must—*and really can*—be achieved by a discipline of questioning and inquiring, *a discipline that guarantees truth*' (*TM*, 491, my emphasis). There is truth to be had by the disciplines concerned with tradition, the disciplines that study texts handed down through history. But if Gadamer's account of understanding is right, this truth cannot be the sort that arises when we describe past thought as it really was. The idea of a past as it really was—what I have called a past in-itself—is incompatible with Gadamer's account of understanding. If Gadamer is right about the ways past and present affect each other, then there *is* no past in-itself to be reconstructed in the way Schleiermacher would like. Strictly speaking, there are no historical objects for inquiring subjects to represent, whether correctly or incorrectly. There is only the interplay that Gadamer calls *Wirkungsgeschichte*: a web of historical effects whose fluid poles we call 'past' and 'present.' The humanities attain truth not when the present correctly mirrors the past, but when horizons fuse. Whatever truth is, it cannot be a relation between theories about tradition and a tradition in-itself. Truth can only be something that happens under certain historical conditions—that is, within the movement of *Wirkungsgeschichte*.

Clearly, this is not an exhaustive treatment of Gadamer's account of truth. There is a great deal more to be said here. But it does show what *kind* of thing truth must be, given Gadamer's account of understanding. For Gadamer, truth cannot be anything other than a historical event. The humanities do not attain truth by representing past thought correctly. Instead, they

attain truth by taking part in the movement of *Wirkungsgeschichte*, and by allowing their horizons to fuse with those of traditional texts. The truth that they seek—and that they '*really can*' attain—is something that happens in a historical process. So for Gadamer, truth is *in* history in a way that it is not for a number of the other figures we have studied. For Kant, and perhaps for his contemporary followers such as Habermas, history is at best the medium through which we discover truth. But while philosophical truths happen to be discovered at particular points in history, we can acquire those truths without knowing anything about their historical genesis. Moreover, we *should* acquire them in this way, because if we do not, our knowledge of them will not have 'arisen *out* of reason' (*KRV*, A836/ B854). Though we must turn to history eventually, in order to make our knowledge systematic, we do so only after constructing our philosophical system. Constructing a philosophical system is not an inherently historical undertaking.

Hegel, of course, goes further than Kant. He argues that we must consult history while doing philosophy. He also claims that it is impossible to understand philosophical claims without knowing how they have emerged from their histories. Nevertheless, Hegel insists that the subject matter of these claims is not reducible to any moment of this history, but is in some sense beyond it. That is why it is possible to grasp these claims with the consciousness of necessity as well as without it. For Hegel, history is a medium that teaches lessons about a content separable from it. The truth that philosophy seeks is in this content, not in history. Even Ricoeur, for all his debts to Gadamer, refuses to place truth squarely in history. Rather, he situates it in the sphere of traditionality, and argues that this sphere is separable from particular traditions—that truth is independent of everything ontic. For all of these thinkers, history is important, but only because it allows us to discover truths that are *not* historical. For Gadamer, however, truth just *is* a historical event. It is not merely discovered through a fusion of horizons. It *is* this fusion of horizons. Gadamer is different from most of the figures we have examined because he does not merely claim that we reach truth as a result of the interplay of historical events. He argues that truth *is* such an interplay. Gadamer therefore understands truth as something that is genuinely *in* history.

It might be useful to appropriate Gadamer's account of truth, or one very much like it. His account shows how one might reinterpret truth as

something that can be in history, in a way that the key figures of the tradition have been reluctant to allow. Gadamer argues that the study of history gives us access to truth. But he argues this without invoking the myth of a past in-itself, and without claiming that a true history is one that correctly represents the past as it really was. Perhaps Gadamer's account of truth could be fruitfully applied to one particular kind of historical knowledge: knowledge of the history of philosophy. Like Gadamer, I have argued against historical objectivism. I have claimed that historians of philosophy do not passively reconstruct what the thinkers of the past 'really thought.' Instead, they are engaged in an enterprise that, while imitative, is constructive and productive as well. Their narratives prefigure, configure, and refigure the history of thought, and to that extent transform it. Gadamer agrees that the study of history is 'not merely a reproductive but always a productive activity as well' (*TM*, 296). So he might be able to help us understand what it would mean for histories of philosophies to be true, in the context of the account I have offered. He might give us the resources to view truth not as something that results from a correct imitation of past thought, but as an event that unfolds within history itself.

Reinterpreting truth along these lines would clear the way for us to see the history of philosophy as an inherently historical enterprise. It would allow us to see a study of this history not just as a postscript to philosophy, but as a part of philosophy. As we have seen, continental philosophers since Kant have been reluctant to see the history of philosophy in this way, despite their claims to the contrary. They have tended to maintain that truth cannot be in history in any meaningful sense, because if it were, then we could attain truth simply by copying the philosophical positions of the past. Since they have also tended to accept the received view of mimesis— the view that mimesis never attains truth—they have found this conclusion unacceptable. These assumptions have led them to see the history of philosophy as a cognitively inferior enterprise, often despite their stated intentions. If, however, we rethink our accounts of mimesis and truth, this conclusion is no longer forced on us. If truth is genuinely in history, it can be obtained through a study of the history of philosophy. If truth is an event that unfolds within the history of philosophy, then there is no reason to think that studying this history is unphilosophical, or inferior to some other kind of thinking. If truth is in history, then studying the history of

philosophy can be a genuinely philosophical undertaking. In short, if we want to accept the historical thesis, we would do well to embrace Gadamer's account of truth.

This is all very tentative. I have not given anything like a detailed theory of truth, let alone argued for one. I have, however, outlined some of the criteria that any account of truth would have to meet to be compatible with the historical thesis about philosophy. If we are to understand the history of philosophy as a genuinely philosophical enterprise, truth must be *in* history in a very robust sense. If the continental tradition wishes to subscribe to the historical thesis—as it has for the better part of two centuries—then it must reinterpret truth as something in history. It must also rethink the nature of mimesis and the status of historical knowledge. In short, if we are to accept the historical thesis about philosophy, we cannot simply graft it onto our existing epistemological and metaphysical frameworks. We must revise these frameworks—radically, in some cases—to make them compatible with the historical thesis. Gadamer is important here because he helps show how one might carry out this project. He shows how one might reinterpret truth as something that is in history. He therefore shows how to clear the way for the historical thesis to be true. Gadamer's way of doing so might not be the only way. Perhaps there are other interpretations of truth that are different from Gadamer's, but equally compatible with the historical thesis. But at the very least, Gadamer shows that we can view truth as something genuinely within history, and that it is possible to arrive at truth through a study of the history of philosophy. This is an important discovery.

We now have some idea of what must be done, if we are to accept the historical thesis. But is contemporary philosophy willing to do it?

Conclusion

The truth in contemporary continental philosophy

This book began in the present. I examined three contemporary philosophical schools, each of which is committed to the historical thesis about philosophy. I argued that in each case, this commitment was undermined by a wide range of confusions and tensions. The later stages of this study focused more on earlier episodes in the history of post-Kantian philosophy. But they did so in order to make sense of the present—that is, to find the source of contemporary philosophy's confusion about the historical thesis, and to look for alternatives. Now that I have diagnosed the problem and suggested a remedy, it is only fitting to return to the present. What light does this study shed on the state of contemporary philosophy? Could it be used as a way of assessing contemporary philosophical positions, or of adjudicating among alternatives? Now that we know what continental philosophy must do to make its account of the history of philosophy more coherent, is there some contemporary school that is particularly well-suited to do it?

In posing these questions, I do not mean to suggest that the thought of Derrida, Gadamer, and Levinas is without problems. As I argued in Chapter 1, the work of each of these thinkers is fraught with difficulties, difficulties that must be addressed before we can consider Derrida, Gadamer, or Levinas an ally. But while these thinkers suffer from the crisis in contemporary continental thought, their work might nevertheless contain resources for coming to terms with this crisis. More specifically, I have argued that in order to come to terms with the crisis, the tradition must reinterpret truth as something that is in history. It must also rethink the nature of mimesis and the status of historical knowledge. Now the question is this: Can Derrida, Gadamer, and Levinas help us to see how truth can be in history? Or to rethink mimesis as an active process? Or to reinterpret

historical thinking as genuinely philosophical? Does their work contain resources for remedying the very confusions from which it suffers? To put it crudely, can this study help us find some truth in contemporary continental philosophy?

Perhaps. There seem to be promising strands in Derrida's thought. Derrida's work contains some resources that might help us reinterpret truth, mimesis, and history in the ways I have claimed are necessary. One such resource is a hostility to the project of reconstructing the past as it really was. This hostility is particularly apparent in Derrida's discussion of Husserl's *Origin of Geometry*. Derrida argues that while we must study the history of mathematics in order to clarify our own mathematical claims, we cannot hope to reconstruct the past with any finality. The 'origin' of geometry, Derrida argues, cannot ever be made fully present to the historian's gaze. It is an origin that 'presents' itself only by withdrawing from every attempt to recapture it. Derrida's work on origins shows that he does not see historians as engaged in the task of reconstructing the past as it really was. He is hostile to the very idea of a past in-itself. To that extent, his work might help the tradition free itself from a dangerous myth.

There are also promising strands in Levinas's thought. Levinas's well-known critique of the theoretical standpoint might be of some help in overcoming what I have called historical objectivism. Levinas cautions that there is something inevitably totalizing, and thus inevitably problematic, about the enterprise of turning things into objects for a subject. He reminds us that there might be other ways of relating to alterity that are not as objectifying or as totalizing. Levinas's thought might therefore be of some help as we rethink historical objectivism and look for alternatives to it. I have argued repeatedly that we must view the history of philosophy as something other than an object to be accurately represented by subjects. Levinas's critique of *all* objective thought could show us ways of overcoming one particular kind of objective thought. To be sure, there are other strands of Levinas's thought that will make it difficult to appropriate him for my purposes. His low opinion of historical thinking, and his suggestion that it inevitably totalizes, are serious obstacles. So Levinas's work may contain resources for coming to terms with the crisis, but exploiting them will be an uphill battle.

Of the three figures I have discussed, Gadamer looks like the most promising ally. His thought seems to offer the greatest resources for coming to terms with the crisis. There are three themes in Gadamer's work that might

help us develop a more coherent account of the history of philosophy. The first is his account of mimesis. Gadamer offers a sustained critique of the received view of mimesis. He explicitly attacks the view that mimesis is simply a passive copying of existing objects. And he offers an alternate interpretation—one that not only sees mimesis as active, but that seems compatible with the concept's Greek origins. We cannot come to terms with the crisis until we develop a theory of active mimesis, and Gadamer may be able to help us here.

Second, Gadamer offers a sustained critique of the myth of a past in-itself. I have claimed again and again that we will misunderstand the history of philosophy as long as we see it as a reconstruction of past thought as it really was. The history of philosophy is not an object waiting for us to interpret it. To a large extent, it is constituted by our own figurational activity. Gadamer's critique of Romantic hermeneutics advances a similar thesis. It argues that the goal of hermeneutics is not to reconstruct the past, but to mediate between traditional texts and contemporary life. The result of this process is not an adequation of interpreter and interpreted, but a fusion of two fluid horizons, and an interplay of which past and present are only moments. I have also argued that historians must be seen as doing something other than simply getting the past right. Gadamer could of great help in explaining what this something else is.

Finally, Gadamer shows that rejecting these two myths—the received view of mimesis and the idea of a past in-itself—is compatible with the existence of truth. It is possible to deny that mimesis is passive, or that history reconstructs the past as it really was, and still maintain that the history of philosophy is a source of truth. Gadamer does this by reinterpreting truth as a historical event. His discussion of *Wirkungsgeschichte* shows that it is possible to understand truth as something that is genuinely in history. He shows that we need not view truth as something that is discovered at particular points in history, but that is itself outside this history. This is exactly what contemporary thought needs to do in order to defend the historical thesis about philosophy. Of course, I have not defended this thesis here. What I have shown is that if philosophy is an inherently historical enterprise, then it is so not just as a repository for past contents, but as a rational inquiry that preserves truth. And I have shown that if we do view philosophy in this way, we must refine our understanding of what truth is. Gadamer shows one way of doing so. It might not be the only way. Perhaps there are other ways

of seeing truth as something that is in history, ways that are just as compatible with the historical thesis as Gadamer's. But Gadamer shows that it is possible to view truth in this way. There is an interpretation of truth that is compatible with the historical thesis about philosophy. In demonstrating this, Gadamer shows that the tradition's problematic view of the history of philosophy is not forced on us. The crisis in continental thinking about the history of philosophy is not inevitable. There are alternatives.

So if we had to endorse a contemporary position on the basis of this study, it would be Gadamerian hermeneutics. This is not because Gadamer's thought is free of problems. Rather, it is because his work contains rich resources for addressing these problems, including the very problems it itself creates. Gadamer does not always take advantage of these resources, but there is no reason his sympathetic interpreters cannot. Besides, it would be churlish to conclude without endorsing any position in contemporary thought. One of the themes of this book is that philosophy cannot begin in mid-air. We have to begin somewhere. Gadamer's thought is as good a place to begin as any, and better than most. Like the tradition that it describes, Gadamerian hermeneutics is best seen as a starting point, a promising place to begin. It is not immune from criticism. Nor is it without tensions. But like tradition, it is something that, despite its tensions—or perhaps, in some way, because of them—'guarantees truth' (*TM*, 491).

Notes

Introduction

[1] Jonathan Bennett, 'Critical Notice of D. J. O'Connor (ed.), *A Critical History of Western Philosophy*.' *Mind* 75 (1966), 437.

[2] See, for example, Vance Maxwell, 'The Philosophical Method of Spinoza.' *Dialogue* 27 (1988), 89–110.

[3] Edwin Curley, 'Dialogues with the Dead.' *Synthese* 67 (1986), 33.

[4] Louis Dupré, 'Is the History of Philosophy Philosophy?' *Review of Metaphysics* 42 (1989), 466. My emphasis.

[5] Lesley Cohen, 'Doing Philosophy is doing its History.' *Synthese* 67 (1986), 51. My emphasis.

[6] Charles Taylor, 'Philosophy and its History,' in *Philosophy in History*, ed. Richard Rorty, J. B. Schneewind and Quentin Skinner (Cambridge: Cambridge University Press, 1984), 18.

[7] Taylor, 'Philosophy and its History,' 17.

[8] Stanley Rosen, *The Limits of Analysis* (New York: Basic Books, 1980), 259.

[9] Alasdair MacIntyre, *After Virtue*, 2nd ed. (Notre Dame: University of Notre Dame Press, 1984), 69.

[10] Karl Ameriks echoes this point when he says that 'even if historicists cannot find an Archimedean point from which to resolve this question, they can still reply that they cannot help but hold on to their own historicism, for it is simply a fact that they do not see how they can commit themselves to any positive alternative.' See Karl Ameriks, *Kant and the Historical Turn: Philosophy as Critical Interpretation* (Oxford: Oxford University Press, 2006), 3.

Chapter 1

[1] Brian Leiter, 'Introduction,' in *The Future for Philosophy*, ed. Brian Leiter (Oxford: Oxford University Press, 2004), 12. For further discussion of the problematic nature of the label 'continental philosophy,' see Simon Critchley, 'What is Continental Philosophy?' *International Journal of Philosophical Studies* 5 (1997),

347–365; and Peter Simons, 'Whose Fault? The Origins and Evitability of the Analytic-Continental Rift.' *International Journal of Philosophical Studies* 9: 3 (2001), 295–311.

2 In an 1840 essay on Coleridge, originally published in the *London and Westminster Review*, Mill speaks of 'Continental philosophers' and 'the Continental philosophy.' I am indebted to Simon Critchley for pointing this out. See 'What is Continental Philosophy?' 361.

3 Leiter, 'Introduction,' 15.

4 Martin Heidegger, *Identity and Difference*, trans. Joan Stambaugh (New York: Harper and Row, 1969), 41.

5 Edmund Husserl, *The Crisis of European Sciences and Transcendental Phenomenology*, trans. David Carr (Evanston: Northwestern University Press, 1970), 369.

6 Martin Heidegger, *The Basic Problems of Phenomenology*, trans. Albert Hofstadter (Bloomington: Indiana University Press, 1988), 23.

7 Jacques Derrida, *Positions*, trans. Alan Bass (Chicago: University of Chicago Press, 1981), 186.

8 Robert Bernasconi, *The Question of Language in Heidegger's History of Being* (Atlantic Highlands: Humanities Press, 1985), 1.

9 Jacques Derrida, 'Structure, Sign and Play in the Discourse of the Human Sciences,' in *Writing and Difference*, trans. Alan Bass (Chicago: The University of Chicago Press, 1978), 280.

10 Derrida, 'Structure, Sign and Play,' 280.

11 Friedrich Nietzsche, 'On Truth and Lie in an Extra-Moral Sense,' in *The Portable Nietzsche*, trans. and ed. Walter Kaufmann (New York: Penguin Books, 1954), 46.

12 René Descartes, *Meditations on First Philosophy*, in *The Philosophical Writings of Descartes*, Volume Two, trans. John Cottingham, Robert Stoothoff, and Dugald Murdoch (Cambridge: Cambridge University Press, 1984), 12.

13 Jacques Derrida, *Positions*, 42.

14 Derrida, 'Structure, Sign and Play,' 280.

15 Derrida, 'Structure, Sign, and Play,' 284.

16 Derrida, *Speech and Phenomena*, 99.

17 Derrida, *Speech and Phenomena*, 102.

18 Derrida, *Speech and Phenomena*, 25, my emphasis.

19 The terms 'sediment' and 'sedimentation' are Husserl's, but Derrida makes extensive use of them in his commentary. See *OG*, 98–99.

20 Husserl, *Crisis*, 369.

21 Derrida, *Speech and Phenomena*, 85.

22 Derrida, *Speech and Phenomena*, 82.

23 Derrida, *Speech and Phenomena*, 85.

24 Derrida, *Positions*, 17.

[25] Hans-Georg Gadamer, *Reason in the Age of Science*, trans. Frederick Lawrence (Cambridge: The MIT Press, 1981), 56.

[26] G. W. F. Hegel, *Philosophy of Right*, ed. Alan Wood, trans. H. B. Nisbet (Cambridge: Cambridge University Press, 1991), 68.

[27] Gadamer, *Reason in the Age of Science*, 111.

[28] Here, I argue that Gadamer's discussion of how *all* understanding proceeds implies a certain view of how *philosophical* understanding in particular proceeds. This way of putting the point is contentious. Not everyone agrees that Gadamer's thought is compatible with distinctions among different kinds of understanding, or among different academic disciplines. Alasdair MacIntyre, for example, argues that Gadamer's work is incompatible with our practice of compartmentalizing academic activities into disciplines such as philosophy, literature, and so on. MacIntyre writes: 'If Gadamer's argument, as I understand it, is correct, we cannot develop even a minimally adequate view of the particulars—for instance . . ., the English language as used by Pope—until we have drawn on materials—philosophical, historical, literary, linguistic—which are now allocated to what are now taken to be different disciplines. There is *no* enquiry which ought not be comparative from the outset' (Alasdair MacIntyre, 'Contexts of Interpretation: Reflections on Hans-Georg Gadamer's *Truth and Method*.' *Boston University Journal* 24: 1 (1976), 46). Even if MacIntyre is right about this, however, I do not think it affects my point. Even if we believe that there is a firm distinction between understanding in general and philosophical understanding in particular, Gadamer's work still implies that philosophy is inherently historical. If, as MacIntyre claims, there is no such distinction, then we need not even *try* to show that what is true of understanding in general is true of philosophy in particular. It is enough to point out the historical character of all understanding and leave it at that.

[29] Hans-Georg Gadamer, *Hegel's Dialectic: Five Hermeneutical Studies*, trans. P. Christopher Smith (New Haven: Yale University Press, 1976), 3.

[30] Gadamer, *Reason in the Age of Science*, 46.

[31] Joseph Flay, 'Hegel, Heidegger, Derrida: Retrieval as Reconstruction, Destruction, Deconstruction,' in *Ethics and Danger*, ed. Arleen Dallery and Charles Scott (Albany: SUNY Press, 1992), 200.

[32] Gadamer, *Reason in the Age of Science*, 43.

[33] Gadamer, *Reason in the Age of Science*, 45.

[34] Gadamer, *Reason in the Age of Science*, 56.

[35] Gadamer, *Reason in the Age of Science*, 105.

[36] Gadamer, *Reason in the Age of Science*, 105.

[37] Note that my discussion is restricted to Levinas's ethical thought—especially to *Totality and Infinity* and *Otherwise Than Being*—and not to those parts of his work

focused more on other topics. I do not, for example, discuss his Talmudic writings.

[38] Levinas's readers have generally had little to say about his view of the history of philosophy. An important exception is John Caruana, 'The Drama of Being: Levinas and the History of Philosophy.' *Continental Philosophy Review* 40 (2007), 251–273.

[39] Despite his willingness to engage in phenomenological description, Levinas understands this enterprise quite differently than earlier phenomenologists such as Husserl. In particular, he rejects the Husserlian notion of a transcendental subject, and he denies that phenomenology uncovers meanings that are essentially related to such a subject. See, for example, *TI*, 122–127. This rejection of a transcendental subject seems to be the reason Levinas occasionally says that he is not a phenomenologist: see, for example, Emmanuel Levinas, *Time and the Other*, trans. Richard Cohen (Pittsburgh: Duquesne University Press, 1987), 92. Presumably, Levinas is not denying that he is engaged in a systematic description of lived experience. What he is denying is that there is a transcendental subject of the sort Husserl describes. When he says that he is not a phenomenologist, he means that he is not a *Husserlian* phenomenologist.

[40] Gary Gutting, *French Philosophy in the Twentieth Century* (Cambridge: Cambridge University Press, 2001), 358.

[41] Emmanuel Levinas, *Otherwise Than Being or Beyond Essence*, trans. Alphonso Lingis (Dordrecht: Kluwer, 1991), 20.

[42] Levinas, *Otherwise Than Being*, 20. For a more detailed discussion of the type of drama at work here, see Caruana, 'The Drama of Being.'

[43] Robert Bernasconi, 'Levinas and Derrida: The Question of the Closure of Metaphysics,' in *Face to Face with Levinas*, ed. Richard Cohen (Albany: SUNY Press, 1986), 194.

[44] Bernasconi, 'Levinas and Derrida,' 194.

[45] See Emmanuel Levinas, 'God and Philosophy,' in *Basic Philosophical Writings*, ed. Adriaan Peperzak, Simon Critchley, and Robert Bernasconi (Bloomington: Indiana University Press, 1996), 148. Levinas is here responding to the criticisms advanced in Derrida's essay 'Violence and Metaphysics' (in *Writing and Difference*).

[46] Stephen Watson, *Tradition(s) II: Hermeneutics, Ethics, and the Dispensation of the Good* (Bloomington: Indiana University Press, 2001), 68.

[47] Levinas, *Otherwise Than Being*, 20.

[48] Levinas admits as much in *Otherwise Than Being*, where he says that my responsibility toward the Other 'cannot serve as the point of departure for a demonstration, which would inexorably bring it into immanence and essence' (12).

[49] Adriann Peperzak, *To the Other: An Introduction to the Philosophy of Emmanuel Levinas* (West Lafayette: Purdue University Press, 1993), 23. The 'earthly paradise' Peperzak mentions is described in Section II of *Totality and Infinity*. See in particular *TI*, 109–121.

[50] Gutting, *French Philosophy in the Twentieth Century*, 358.

[51] Rudolf Bernet, 'The Subject's Participation in the Game of Truth.' *Review of Metaphysics* 58 (2005), 806.

[52] Aaron Preston puts the point this way: 'an adequate *philosophical* understanding of the social landscape of philosophy, whether current or historical, must include a grasp of how philosophical views factor into the mix. Moreover, from the genuinely philosophical perspective, those views will be the most salient ingredients in the mix, and will be granted explanatory primacy wherever possible.' See Aaron Preston, *Analytic Philosophy: The History of an Illusion* (London: Continuum, 2007), 66.

[53] Husserl, *Crisis*, 23.

[54] Husserl, *Crisis*, 362.

Chapter 2

[1] R. G. Collingwood, *The Idea of History*, revised edition (Oxford: Oxford University Press, 1993), 93.

[2] Heinrich Ritter Srbik, *Geist und Geschichte vom Deutschen Humanismus bis zur Gegenwart* (Salzburg: Otto Müller Verlag, 1950), 146.

[3] Not all of Kant's readers agree that the popular style of these pieces precludes them from being serious philosophy. One who explicitly attacks this view is Emil Fackenheim. See his article 'Kant's Concept of History.' *Kant-Studien* 48 (1957), 381–398.

[4] Immanuel Kant, *Lectures on Metaphysics*, trans. and ed. Karl Ameriks and Steve Naragon (Cambridge: Cambridge University Press, 1997), 121.

[5] Kant, *Lectures on Metaphysics*, 121.

[6] Kant, *Lectures on Metaphysics*, 122.

[7] Kant, *Lectures on Metaphysics*, 124.

[8] Kant, *Lectures on Metaphysics*, 125.

[9] And this is no accident. Kant dismisses medieval philosophy as 'muck' that was 'swept away by the Reformation.' See Kant, *Lectures on Metaphysics*, 305–306.

[10] Again, this omission is no accident. Kant seems to think that metaphysics and epistemology are the only branches of philosophy that have progressed enough to have earned places in the history of pure reason. 'In moral philosophy,' he claims, 'we have come no further than the ancients' (Kant, *Lectures on Metaphysics*, 306).

[11] Lucien Braun, *Histoire de l'histoire de la philosophie* (Paris: Editions Ophrys, 1973), 205, my translation.

[12] Karl Reinhold, 'Über den Begriff der Geschichte der Philosophie,' In *Beiträge zur Geschichte der Philosophie*, ed. Georg Gustav Fülleborn (Züllichau: Friedricj Frommann, 1796), 3–36.

[13] As Braun has pointed out, critical history was a radical challenge to earlier approaches to the history of philosophy in Germany. Before Kant, the dominant approach to the history of philosophy had been Tiedemann's. Tiedemann argued that historians of philosophy have an infinite task, since a philosophical system can take any one of an unlimited number of forms, and it is the duty of the history of philosophy to investigate them all. For Kant and his followers, by contrast, the task of historians of philosophy is not to explore the diversity of philosophical positions, but to reduce it. Their aim was not to extract an endless series of philosophical principles from the data of history, but to extract a handful of such principles from reason itself, and then make the data of history conform to them. See Braun, *Histoire*, 212.

[14] Immanuel Kant, *Logic*, trans. Thomas Abbott (Westport: Greenwood Press, 1972), 12.

[15] Immanuel Kant, *Prolegomena*, trans. Paul Carus (Chicago: Open Court, 1988), 1.

[16] Kant also draws the distinction between rational and historical knowledge elsewhere. See, for example, his *Logic*, 12–13.

[17] Kant makes a similar claim in the *Critique of Judgment*, where he argues that artistic genius is opposed to 'the *spirit of imitation*.' The genius does not simply imitate existing works—the works of the ancients, for example—because to imitate is merely 'to learn and follow a lead.' Imitation of artistic models is unproductive and therefore incompatible with genius. See Immanuel Kant, *Critique of Judgment*, trans. James Creed Meredith (Oxford: Clarendon Press, 1952), 169. The status of mimesis in the third *Critique*, however, is more complex than these passages suggest. What complicates the issue is Kant's claim (in sections 46–49) that while the genius does not simply imitate other works of art, her work is mimetic in the deeper sense that she imitates nature's productive capacities. She does not copy artistic models; rather, she copies nature's ability to create in the absence of models. For a discussion of the status of mimesis in the third *Critique*, see Jacques Derrida, 'Economimesis,' trans. R. Klein. *Diacritics* 11 (1981), 3–25.

[18] Kant, *Logic*, 13. To be sure, matters are more complicated than I have suggested here. It is misleading to say that Kant sees mimesis as *simply* passive and unproductive, because he also sees imitation as an exercise of the productive imagination, and the productive imagination is a faculty of spontaneity. But in so far as the spontaneity of the productive imagination is wholly prescribed by the categories, imitation is still *ultimately* passive for Kant.

[19] To say that spirit is philosophy's subject matter is not to reify it. It is not to assert that spirit has an existence independent of particular human beings and their actions. It is simply to say that any complete account of what philosophy does must make reference to the notion of spirit. As Frederick Beiser puts it, it is to

say that the notion of spirit is 'first in order of explanation, if not first in order of existence.' See Frederick Beiser, 'Hegel's Historicism,' in *The Cambridge Companion to Hegel*, ed. Frederick Beiser (Cambridge: Cambridge University Press, 1993), 292. In other words, the claim that philosophy's subject matter is spirit is not a claim about spirit's ontological status.

20 Beiser, 'Hegel's Historicism,' 275.

21 Charles Taylor, *Hegel* (Cambridge: Cambridge University Press, 1975), 43.

22 Taylor, *Hegel*, 40.

23 Taylor, *Hegel*, 41. Taylor's approach is unpopular today. Contemporary readers of Hegel generally insist that, as John McCumber puts it, 'Hegel is not making silly claims about some present entity (such as the *Zeitgeist* or the Absolute),' but is doing something far less grand—'teaching us how to validate the present by reconstructing a certain sort of past,' for example. See John McCumber, *Reshaping Reason* (Bloomington: Indiana University Press, 2005), xiii. Be that as it may, notions such as 'spirit' and 'the absolute' play a crucial role in the *Phenomenology* and other works, and that is why I have retained them in my discussion. These terms may not refer to a 'present entity,' and Hegel may not wish to make 'silly claims' about such an entity. But the terms themselves still play important roles in Hegel's discussion of philosophy's historical character.

24 One might object that it is inappropriate to read a distinction between form and content into Hegel's work, since dialectical thinking is incompatible with distinctions of this sort. The central claim of the *Phenomenology*, after all, is that any attempt to characterize the objects of consciousness (its 'content') as independent from the acts of consciousness (its 'form') lapses into incoherence, since there is no sharp distinction between consciousness and its objects. Other Hegelian texts undermine the form-content distinction in similar ways. But this objection oversimplifies a complex issue. While Hegel does undermine the form-content distinction in some contexts, he endorses it in others. Section 133 of the *Encyclopedia Logic*, for instance, describes the form-content distinction as an indispensable part of our thought (*EL*, 202). Sections 55–56 and 121–125 of the *Philosophy of Right* also depend heavily on a distinction between form and content. Hegel does not reject the form-content distinction across the board. While he is leery of it in some contexts, his view is much more ambivalent than this objection suggests.

25 I am not suggesting that 'idea' is simply another name for spirit. Clearly, the two are different. But the function of the idea in the *Lectures on the History of Philosophy* is similar to that of spirit in the *Phenomenology*, at least in so far as both terms name philosophy's subject matter. The *Phenomenology* suggests that philosophy is about spirit; the *Lectures on the History of Philosophy* suggest that it is about the idea.

26 This formulation comes from G. W. F. Hegel, *Science of Logic*, trans. A. V. Miller (Atlantic Highlands: Humanities Press, 1989), 755.

27 Hegel, *Science of Logic*, 755.

28 Hegel, *Philosophy of Right*, 28–34.

29 G. W. F. Hegel, *Hegel: The Letters*, trans. Clark Butler and Christiane Seiler (Bloomington: Indiana University Press, 1984), 392–393.

30 G. W. F. Hegel, *Philosophy of Mind*, trans. A. V. Miller (Oxford: Oxford University Press, 1971), 302.

31 On this point, see Beiser, 'Hegel's Historicism,' 275–276.

32 Hegel, *Philosophy of Mind*, 224.

33 Hegel, *Philosophy of Mind*, 59.

34 Hegel, *Philosophy of Mind*, 59.

35 Hegel, *Philosophy of Mind*, 62.

36 Hegel, *Philosophy of Mind*, 60.

37 Hegel, *Philosophy of Mind*, 61.

38 G. W. F. Hegel, *Aesthetics: Lectures on Fine Art*, Volume One, trans. T. M. Knox (Oxford: Clarendon Press, 1975), 300.

39 Hegel, *Aesthetics*, 300.

40 Hegel, *Aesthetics*, 301.

Chapter 3

1 Wilhelm Dilthey, *Introduction to the Human Sciences*, trans. Michael Neville, ed. Rudolf Makkreel and Frithjof Rodi (Princeton: Princeton University Press, 1989), 48.

2 Mary Pickering, *Auguste Comte: An Intellectual Biography*, Volume One (Cambridge: Cambridge University Press, 1993), 279. There is some dispute about whether this is true. See, for example, Mary Pickering, 'New Evidence of the Link Between Comte and German Philosophy.' *Journal of the History of Ideas* 50 (1989), 443–463.

3 Pickering, *Auguste Comte: An Intellectual Biography*, 611.

4 Wilhelm Windelband, *A History of Philosophy*, trans. James Tufts (New York: Macmillan, 1893), 9.

5 Windelband, *History of Philosophy*, 681.

6 And to give Windelband his due, Hegel does sometimes speak this way. In the *Lectures on the History of Philosophy*, for example, Hegel argues that we should avoid accounting for philosophical positions with non-philosophical factors, such as 'political history, forms of government, art and religion' (*LHP*, 54).

7 Windelband, *History of Philosophy*, 14.

8 Windelband, *History of Philosophy*, 12.

[9] Martin Heidegger, *History of the Concept of Time*, trans. Theodore Kisiel (Bloomington: Indiana University Press, 1992), 138.

[10] Gail Soffer, 'Heidegger, Humanism, and the Destruction of History.' *Review of Metaphysics* 49: 3 (1996), 569.

[11] Charles Guignon, *Heidegger and the Problem of Knowledge* (Indianapolis: Hackett, 1983), 225.

[12] Heidegger, *History of the Concept of Time*, 138.

[13] Soffer discusses this tendency of Heidegger's in some detail. See 'Heidegger, Humanism, and the Destruction of History,' 568–569.

[14] Soffer, 'Heidegger, Humanism, and the Destruction of History,' 568.

[15] Soffer, 'Heidegger, Humanism, and the Destruction of History,' 569.

[16] Soffer, 'Heidegger, Humanism, and the Destruction of History,' 569.

[17] Soffer, 'Heidegger, Humanism, and the Destruction of History,' 569.

[18] *Auslegung* (or 'interpretation') is not to be confused with *Interpretation* ('Interpretation'), a term Heidegger reserves for more scientific inquiries.

[19] Heidegger gives a somewhat different description of phenomenological method in *The Basic Problems of Phenomenology*. There, he says that the process of studying something phenomenologically has three steps. The first, reduction, consists in turning one's attention away from a particular being and toward the Being of that being. The second is construction, or 'the projecting of the antecedently given being upon its Being and upon the structures of its Being' (*Basic Problems*, 22). The third is destruction, or the process of tracing our ontological concepts back to their sources. But this description is consistent with the one given in *Being and Time*. The three steps of phenomenological method correspond roughly to the (projected) stages of fundamental ontology. Reduction corresponds to the *Daseinanalytik*, or to the attempt to explicate Dasein's Being. Construction corresponds to the ontological interpretation of the *meaning* of Dasein's Being. And destruction corresponds to the process of dismantling the history of philosophy in accordance with 'clues' gleaned from steps one and two.

[20] Heidegger, *Basic Problems*, 20.

[21] Martin Heidegger, *Parmenides*, trans. André Schuwer and Richard Rojcewicz (Bloomington: Indiana University Press, 1992), 134–135.

[22] Heidegger, *Parmenides*, 135.

[23] Heidegger, *Parmenides*, 135.

[24] That said, the problems of fate and destiny remain notoriously underdetermined in *Being and Time*, particularly in sections 67 and 74. To determine them, I am arguing, would require that Heidegger sufficiently distinguish form and content—something he never did. Moreover, while Heidegger invests a good deal in the independence of destiny in his later work, there is still considerable

continuity between his early and late accounts. Specifically, in his later work, Heidegger still understands destiny as *phenomenological* from beginning to end. See, for example, 'My Way to Phenomenology,' in *On Time and Being*, trans. Joan Stambaugh (San Francisco: Harper and Row, 1972), 74–82.

[25] Heidegger, *Parmenides*, 135.

Chapter 4

[1] Bernard Dauenhauer, *Paul Ricoeur: The Promise and Risk of Politics* (Oxford: Rowman and Littlefield, 1998), 3.

[2] Derrida, 'Structure, Sign, and Play,' 280.

[3] Derrida, 'Structure, Sign, and Play,' 280.

[4] Levinas, *Otherwise Than Being*, 20.

[5] Levinas, *Otherwise Than Being*, 20.

[6] Levinas, *Otherwise Than Being*, 20.

[7] Gadamer, *Reason in the Age of Science*, 56. Perhaps confirming my claim that Heidegger's historiography is continuous with Hegel's, Gadamer also describes his discussion of tradition as a continuation of Hegel. See *TM*, 164.

[8] Hans-Georg Gadamer, 'The Universality of the Hermeneutical Problem,' in *Philosophical Hermeneutics*, trans. and ed. David E. Linge (Berkeley: University of California Press, 1976), 3.

[9] Jürgen Habermas, *On the Logic of the Social Sciences*, trans. Shierry Weber Nicholson and Jerry A. Stark (Cambridge: The MIT Press, 1988), 170.

[10] Habermas, *On the Logic of the Social Sciences*, 170.

[11] Jürgen Habermas, *Knowledge and Human Interests*, trans. Jeremy Shapiro (Boston: Beacon Press, 1971), 196.

[12] Habermas, *Knowledge and Human Interests*, 53.

[13] Habermas, *Knowledge and Human Interests*, 283.

[14] Habermas, *On the Logic of the Social Sciences*, 170.

[15] Habermas, *On the Logic of the Social Sciences*, 170.

[16] Habermas, *On the Logic of the Social Sciences*, 170.

[17] The relevant articles are: 'Ethics and Culture: Habermas and Gadamer in Dialogue,' in *Philosophy Today* 17: 2 (1973), 153–165; and 'The Hermeneutical Function of Distanciation' and 'Hermeneutics and the Critique of Ideology,' both in *From Text to Action*.

[18] On this point, see Ricoeur, 'Ethics and Culture,' 162.

[19] To be fair, Gadamer denies that his view of tradition is romantic. See *TM*, 273–274.

[20] See, for example, *TN3*, 219.

21 Paul Ricoeur, 'Reflections on a New Ethos for Europe.' *Philosophy and Social Criticism* 21: 5/6 (1995), 8.

22 Ricoeur, 'Ethics and Culture,' 165.

23 Ludwig Wittgenstein, *Philosophical Investigations*, trans. G. E. M. Anscombe (Oxford: Basil Blackwell, 1953), 81. My emphasis.

Chapter 5

1 Plato, *Republic*, trans. G. M. A. Grube (Indianapolis: Hackett, 1992), 276.

2 Plato, *Republic*, 268.

3 Plato, *Republic*, 268.

4 Kant, *Logic*, 13.

5 Hans-Georg Gadamer, 'Poetry and Mimesis,' in *The Relevance of the Beautiful*, trans. and ed. Robert Bernasconi (Cambridge: Cambridge University Press, 1986), 122.

6 Gadamer, 'Poetry and Mimesis,' 117.

7 Gadamer, 'Poetry and Mimesis,' 119.

8 Hans-Georg Gadamer, 'Art and Imitation,' in *The Relevance of the Beautiful*, 103.

9 Gadamer, 'Art and Imitation,' 99.

10 Hans-Georg Gadamer, 'The Relevance of the Beautiful,' in *The Relevance of the Beautiful*, 35.

11 Gadamer, 'Art and Imitation,' 99.

12 Gadamer, 'Relevance of the Beautiful,' 27.

13 Louis Mink, *Historical Understanding*, ed. Brian Fay, Eugene Golob, and Richard Vann (Ithaca: Cornell University Press, 1987), 50.

14 Mink, *Historical Understanding*, 53.

15 Roman Ingarden, *The Literary Work of Art*, trans. George Grabowicz (Evanston: Northwestern University Press, 1973), 246.

16 Gadamer, 'Relevance of the Beautiful,' 27.

17 Since refiguration involves what Gadamer calls application—that is, rendering a text determinate in a specific situation—it is tempting to think of it as a process of *interpretation*. But this does mean that prefiguration and configuration are not interpretive as well. They do not involve application in the way refiguration does, but they do involve interpretation in a broader sense: namely, in the sense of 'seeing as' that Heidegger describes in section 32 of *Being and Time*. Prefiguration is interpretive in that, before something can be singled out for imitation, it must already have been encountered as meaningful. It must already have been seen *as* something. Otherwise, it would never occur to us to single it out in the first place. Configuration is interpretive in that, before a diversity of

elements can be grasped together in a single act, they must already have been grasped as amenable to this configuration. Otherwise, it would never occur to us to grasp them together. In short, when we prefigure and refigure, 'we already do so understandingly and interpretatively' (*BT*, 189). So we must be careful in thinking of refiguration as the interpretive moment of the mimetic process. If by 'interpretation' we mean 'application,' then it is. But if we take interpretation to mean 'seeing as' in the broadest possible sense, then all three stages of the mimetic process are interpretative.

[18] Aristotle, *Poetics*, trans. J. Bywater, in *The Collected Works of Aristotle*, Volume Two, ed. Jonathan Barnes (Princeton: Princeton University Press, 1984), 2322–2323.

[19] Kant, *Lectures on Metaphysics*, 306.

[20] Kant, *Lectures on Metaphysics*, 305–306.

[21] Kant, *Lectures on Metaphysics*, 125.

[22] Kant, *Lectures on Metaphysics*, 121.

[23] Kant, *Lectures on Metaphysics*, 121.

[24] MacIntyre, 'Contexts of Interpretation,' 43.

[25] MacIntyre, 'Contexts of Interpretation,' 43.

[26] MacIntyre, 'Contexts of Interpretation,' 43–44.

[27] MacIntyre, 'Contexts of Interpretation,' 44.

Bibliography

Ameriks, Karl. *Kant and the Historical Turn: Philosophy as Critical Interpretation.* Oxford: Oxford University Press, 2006.

Aristotle. *Poetics*, trans. J. Bywater. In *The Complete Works of Aristotle*, Volume 2, ed. Jonathan Barnes. Princeton: Princeton University Press, 1984.

Beiser, Frederick. 'Hegel's Historicism.' In *The Cambridge Companion to Hegel*, ed. Frederick Beiser. Cambridge: Cambridge University Press, 1993, 270–300.

Bennett, Jonathan. 'Critical Notice of D. J. O'Connor (ed), *A Critical History of Western Philosophy.*' *Mind* 75 (1966), 437.

Bernasconi, Robert. 'Levinas and Derrida: The Question of the Closure of Metaphysics.' In *Face to Face with Levinas*, ed. Richard Cohen. Albany: SUNY Press, 1986, 181–202.

—*The Question of Language in Heidegger's History of Being*. Atlantic Highlands: Humanities Press, 1985.

Bernet, Rudolf. 'The Subject's Participation in the Game of Truth.' *Review of Metaphysics* 58 (2005), 785–814.

Braun, Lucien. *Histoire de l'histoire de la philosophie*. Paris: Editions Ophrys, 1973.

Carr, David. *Time, Narrative, and History*. Bloomington: Indiana University Press, 1986.

Caruana, John. 'The Drama of Being: Levinas and the History of Philosophy.' *Continental Philosophy Review* 40 (2007), 251–273.

Cohen, Lesley. 'Doing Philosophy is doing its History.' *Synthese* 67 (1986), 51–55.

Collingwood, R. G. *The Idea of History*. Revised edition. Oxford: Clarendon Press, 1993.

Critchley, Simon. 'What is Continental Philosophy?' *International Journal of Philosophical Studies* 5 (1997), 347–365.

Curley, Edwin. 'Dialogues with the Dead.' *Synthese* 67 (1986), 33–49.

Dauenhauer, Bernard. *Paul Ricoeur: The Promise and Risk of Politics*. Oxford: Rowman and Littlefield, 1998.

Derrida, Jacques. 'Différance.' In *Margins of Philosophy*, trans. Alan Bass. Chicago: University of Chicago Press, 1982, 3–27.

—'Tympan.' In *Margins of Philosophy*, ix–xxix.

—'Economimesis,' trans. R. Klein. *Diacritics* 11 (1981), 3–25.

—*Positions*, trans. Alan Bass. Chicago: University of Chicago Press, 1981.

Derrida, Jacques. 'Cogito and the History of Madness.' In *Writing and Difference*, trans. Alan Bass. Chicago: University of Chicago Press, 1978, 31–63.

—'From Restricted to General Economy: A Hegelianism without Reserve.' In *Writing and Difference*, 251–277.

—'Structure, Sign and Play in the Discourse of the Human Sciences.' In *Writing and Difference*, 278–294.

—*Edmund Husserl's* Origin of Geometry: *An Introduction*, trans. John P. Leavey. Lincoln: University of Nebraska Press, 1978.

—*Speech and Phenomena*, trans. David Allison. Evanston: Northwestern University Press, 1973.

Descartes, René. *The Philosophical Writings of Descartes*, Volume Two, trans. John Cottingham, Robert Stoothoff, and Dugald Murdoch. Cambridge: Cambridge University Press, 1984.

Dilthey, Wilhelm. *Introduction to the Human Sciences*, trans. Michael Neville, ed. Rudolf Makkreel and Frithjof Rodi. Princeton: Princeton University Press, 1989.

Dupré, Louis. 'Is the History of Philosophy Philosophy?' *Review of Metaphysics* 42: 3 (1989), 463–482.

Fackenheim, Emil. 'Kant's Concept of History.' *Kant-Studien* 48 (1957), 381–398.

Flay, Joseph. 'Hegel, Heidegger, Derrida: Retrieval as Reconstruction, Destruction, Deconstruction.' In *Ethics and Danger*, ed. Arleen Dallery and Charles Scott. Albany: SUNY Press, 1992, 199–214.

Forster, Michael. *Hegel's Idea of a Phenomenology of Spirit*. Chicago: University of Chicago Press, 1993.

Gadamer, Hans-Georg. *Reason in the Age of Science*, trans. Frederick Lawrence. Cambridge: The MIT Press, 1981.

—*Truth and Method*, 2nd ed., trans. Joel Weinsheimer and Donald Marshall. New York: Crossroads, 1992.

—'Art and Imitation.' In *The Relevance of the Beautiful*, trans. and ed. Robert Bernasconi. Cambridge: Cambridge University Press, 1986, 92–104.

—'Poetry and Mimesis.' In *The Relevance of the Beautiful*, 116–122.

—'The Relevance of the Beautiful.' In *The Relevance of the Beautiful*, 1–53.

—*Hegel's Dialectic*, trans. P. Christopher Smith. New Haven: Yale University Press, 1976.

—'The Universality of the Hermeneutical Problem.' In *Philosophical Hermeneutics*, trans. and ed. David Linge. Berkeley: University of California Press, 1976, 3–17.

Guignon, Charles. *Heidegger and the Problem of Knowledge*. Indianapolis: Hackett, 1983.

Gutting, Gary. *French Philosophy in the Twentieth Century*. Cambridge: Cambridge University Press, 2001.

—*Pragmatic Liberalism and the Critique of Modernity*. Cambridge: Cambridge University Press, 1999.

Habermas, Jürgen. *On the Logic of the Social Sciences*, trans. Shierry Weber Nicholson and Jerry A. Stark. Cambridge: The MIT Press, 1988.

—*The Philosophical Discourse of Modernity*, trans. Frederick Lawrence. Cambridge: The MIT Press, 1987.

—*Knowledge and Human Interests*, trans. Jeremy Shapiro. Boston: Beacon Press, 1971.

Hegel, G. W. F. *Lectures on the History of Philosophy*, Volume One, trans. E. S. Haldane. Lincoln: University of Nebraska Press, 1995.

—*The Encyclopedia Logic*, trans. T. F. Geraets, W. A. Suchting, and H. S. Harris. Indianapolis: Hackett Publishing Company, 1991.

—*Philosophy of Right*, ed. Alan Wood, trans. H. B. Nisbet. Cambridge: Cambridge University Press, 1991.

—*Science of Logic*, trans. A. V. Miller. Atlantic Highlands: Humanities Press, 1989.

—*Hegel: The Letters*, trans. Clark Butler and Christiane Seiler. Bloomington: Indiana University Press, 1984.

—*The Difference Between the Systems of Fichte and Schelling*, trans. Walter Cerf and H. S. Harris. Albany: SUNY Press, 1977.

—*Faith and Knowledge*, trans. Walter Cerf and H. S. Harris. Albany: SUNY Press, 1977.

—*Phenomenology of Spirit*, trans. A. V. Miller. Oxford: Oxford University Press, 1977.

—*Aesthetics: Lectures on Fine Art*, Volume One, trans. T. M. Knox. Oxford: Clarendon Press, 1975.

—*Philosophy of Mind*, trans. A. V. Miller. Oxford: Clarendon Press, 1971.

Heidegger, Martin. *Plato's* Sophist, trans. Richard Rojcewicz and André Schuwer. Bloomington: Indiana University Press, 1997.

—*Aristotle's* Metaphysics *1–3*, trans. Walter Brogan and Peter Warnek. Bloomington: Indiana University Press, 1995.

—*History of the Concept of Time*, trans. Theodore Kisiel. Bloomington: Indiana University Press, 1992.

—'Phenomenological Interpretations with Respect to Aristotle,' trans. Michael Bauer. *Man and World* 25: 3 (1992), 358–393.

—*Kant and the Problem of Metaphysics*, trans. Richard Taft. Bloomington: Indiana University Press, 1990.

—*The Basic Problems of Phenomenology*, trans. Albert Hofstadter. Bloomington: Indiana University Press, 1988.

—'My Way to Phenomenology.' In *On Time and Being*, trans. Joan Stambaugh. San Francisco: Harper and Row, 1972, 74–82.

—*Identity and Difference*, trans. Joan Stambaugh. New York: Harper and Row, 1969.

—*Being and Time*, trans. John Macquarrie and Edward Robinson. San Francisco: Harper Collins, 1962.

Husserl, Edmund. *Ideas Pertaining to a Pure Phenomenology and to a Phenomenological Philosophy*, trans. F. Kersten. Dordrecht: Kluwer, 1982.

—*The Crisis of European Sciences and Transcendental Phenomenology*, trans. David Carr. Evanston: Northwestern University Press, 1970.

Ingarden, Roman. *The Literary Work of Art*, trans. George Grabowicz. Evanston: Northwestern University Press, 1973.

Kant, Immanuel. *Lectures on Metaphysics*, trans. and ed. Karl Ameriks and Steve Naragon. Cambridge: Cambridge University Press, 1997.

—*Prolegomena*, trans. Paul Carus. Chicago: Open Court, 1988.

—*Logic*, trans. Thomas Abbott. Westport: Greenwood Press, 1972.

—'Conjectures on the Beginning of Human History.' In *Kant: Political Writings*, trans. H. B. Nisbet, ed. Hans Reiss. Cambridge: Cambridge University Press, 1970, 221–234.

—'Idea for a Universal History with a Cosmopolitan Purpose.' In *Kant: Political Writings*, 41–53.

—*Critique of Judgment*, trans. James Creed Meredith. Oxford: Clarendon Press, 1952.

—*Critique of Pure Reason*, trans. Norman Kemp Smith. London: Macmillan, 1927.

Leiter, Brian. 'Introduction.' In *The Future for Philosophy*, ed. Brian Leiter. Oxford: Oxford University Press, 2004, 1–23.

Levinas, Emmanuel. *Basic Philosophical Writings*, ed. Adriaan Peperzak, Simon Critchley, and Robert Bernasconi. Bloomington: Indiana University Press, 1996.

—*Otherwise than Being or Beyond Essence*, trans. Alphonso Lingis. Dordrecht: Kluwer, 1991.

—*Time and the Other*, trans. Richard Cohen. Pittsburgh: Duquesne University Press, 1987.

—*Totality and Infinity*, trans. Alphonso Lingis. Pittsburgh: Duquesne University Press, 1969.

MacIntyre, Alasdair. *After Virtue*. 2nd ed. Notre Dame: University of Notre Dame Press, 1984.

—'The Relationship of Philosophy to its Past.' In *Philosophy in History*, ed. Richard Rorty, J. B. Schneewind, and Quentin Skinner. Cambridge: Cambridge University Press, 1984, 31–48.

—'Contexts of Interpretation: Reflections on Hans-Georg Gadamer's *Truth and Method*.' *Boston University Journal* 24: 1 (1976), 41–46.

Makkreel, Rudolf. *Dilthey: Philosopher of the Human Studies*. Princeton: Princeton University Press, 1975.

Maxwell, Vance. 'The Philosophical Method of Spinoza.' *Dialogue* 27 (1988), 89–110.

McCumber, John. *Reshaping Reason: Toward a New Philosophy*. Bloomington: Indiana University Press, 2005.

Mink, Louis. *Historical Understanding*. Ithaca: Cornell University Press, 1987.

Nietzsche, Friedrich. 'On Truth and Lie in an Extra-Moral Sense.' In *The Portable Nietzsche*, trans. and ed. Walter Kaufmann. New York: Penguin, 1954, 42–46.

Passmore, John. 'The Idea of a History of Philosophy.' *History and Theory* 5 (1965), 1–32.

Peperzak, Adriann. *To the Other: An Introduction to the Philosophy of Emmanuel Levinas*. West Lafayette: Purdue University Press, 1993.

Pickering, Mary. *Auguste Comte: An Intellectual Biography*, Volume One. Cambridge: Cambridge University Press, 1993.

—'New Evidence of the Link Between Comte and German Philosophy.' *Journal of the History of Ideas* 50 (1989), 443–463.

Pippin, Robert. *Modernism as a Philosophical Problem*. Oxford: Blackwell, 1991.

Plato. *Republic*, trans. G. M. A. Grube. Indianapolis: Hackett, 1992.

Preston, Aaron. *Analytic Philosophy: The History of an Illusion*. London: Continuum, 2007.

Reagan, Charles E. *Paul Ricoeur: His Life and Work*. Chicago: University of Chicago Press, 1996.

Reinhold, Karl. 'Über den Begriff der Geschichte der Philosophie.' In *Beiträge zur Geschichte der Philosophie*, ed. Georg Gustav Fülleborn. Züllichau: Friedricj Frommann, 1796, 3–36.

Ricoeur, Paul. *The Just*, trans. David Pellauer. Chicago: University of Chicago Press, 2000.

—'Reflections on a New Ethos for Europe.' *Philosophy and Social Criticism* 21: 5/6 (1995), 3–13.

—*Oneself as Another*, trans. Kathleen Blamey. Chicago: University of Chicago Press, 1992.

—'The Hermeneutical Function of Distanciation.' In *From Text to Action*, trans. Kathleen Blamey and John Thompson. Evanston: Northwestern University Press, 1991, 75–88.

—'Hermeneutics and the Critique of Ideology.' In *From Text to Action*, 270–307.

—'On Interpretation.' In *From Text to Action*, 1–24.

—'Phenomenology and Hermeneutics.' In *From Text to Action*, 25–52.

—*Time and Narrative*, Volume Three, trans. Kathleen McLaughlin and David Pellauer. Chicago: University of Chicago Press, 1988.

—*Time and Narrative*, Volume One, trans. Kathleen McLaughlin and David Pellauer. Chicago: University of Chicago Press, 1984.

—'Ethics and Culture: Habermas and Gadamer in Dialogue.' *Philosophy Today* 17: 2 (1973), 153–165.

Rorty, Richard. 'The Historiography of Philosophy: Four Genres.' In *Philosophy in History*, 49–75.

Rosen, Stanley. *The Limits of Analysis*. New York: Basic Books, 1980.

Simons, Peter. 'Whose Fault? The Origins and Evitability of the Analytic-Continental Rift.' *International Journal of Philosophical Studies* 9: 3 (2001), 295–311.

Smith, P. Christopher. *The Hermeneutics of Original Argument*. Evanston: Northwestern University Press, 1998.

Soffer, Gail. 'Heidegger, Humanism, and the Destruction of History.' *Review of Metaphysics* 49: 3 (1996), 547–576.

Srbik, Heinrich Ritter. *Geist und Geschichte vom Deutschen Humanismus bis zur Gegenwart*. Salzburg: Otto Müller Verlag, 1950.

Steinbock, Anthony. 'The Origins and Crisis of Continental Philosophy.' *Man and World* 30 (1997), 199–215.

Taylor, Charles. 'Philosophy and its History.' In *Philosophy in History*, 17–30.

Watson, Stephen. *Tradition(s) II: Hermeneutics, Ethics, and the Dispensation of the Good*. Bloomington: Indiana University Press, 2001.

Windelband, Wilhelm. *A History of Philosophy*, trans. James Tufts. New York: Macmillan, 1893.

Wittgenstein, Ludwig. *Philosophical Investigations*, trans. G. E. M. Anscombe. Oxford: Basil Blackwell, 1953.

Index

411244493R00104

Behind the Scenes

of a Calling

by

Tyra Smith

ISBN- 979-8-218148-08-9

Liberation's Publishing LLC
West Point - Mississippi

Behind the Scenes

of a Calling

Table of Content

✎ Introduction

There is an age-old tactic that the enemy uses, and the best way to explain is to share my life story. As you read and turn these pages, you'll notice that I start with the background history of my mother and father. I share their lives and how those two lives formed my own. When I tell you that the enemy dropped a stone of pain and trauma into the life water of my family that caused generations of ripple effects, it did. I walked through life jumping here and jumping there not realizing that by doing that I was seeking validation from others. I came to understand that this meant that I didn't know who I was. It was a plan of the enemy. I tell you, he comes to steal, kill, and destroy, your very identity. The very thing that is rightfully yours from the beginning, he takes away. if you find yourself reading this book it means that there are going to be some parts that you can relate to. What have you been fighting with? Or what has been fighting against your life?

There comes a time when you get so tired of fighting that you feel defeated. I promise you, I have been there, but God has the last say! So, I encourage you to keep going and work this thing out. Make the enemy mad! Have you ever wondered why is it that when you start going to church or you start praying, the stakes get a little harder? I know you've experienced it, because I have. The more you start seeking God; the more you pray, God starts to reveal to you to you. He reveals who you belong to. I have found that the heavier the anointing the more you go through in the area you are anointed to walk in. I know that all the hard trials and the tribulations we go through are specifically designed to build us up. James 1:1-4 *Consider it pure joy, my brothers and sisters, whenever you face trials of many kinds, because you know that the testing of your faith*

produces perseverance. Let perseverance finish its work so that you may be mature and complete, not lacking anything. (NIV)

The joy we should be considering during the hardship seems so far away when we are going through a trial. Even farther away when you get out of one hardship and enter another. I must be honest. It seemed as if every time I thought I was getting a break something else sprang up almost immediately. Let's not forget then the trials come in multiples at one time. I encountered multiple trials at once. The key is to know who you are, and that you're not alone. Most times I felt I was going through my trials alone, but God was there shielding me so that the weapons did not prosper. God will take your messy life and do a new thing. He will take the shame of your past and weaponize it against the enemy. Your shame will become his downfall. You will be anointed to bless God's people and walk them through trying situations. The enemy's weapons are guilt, shame, and condemnation, God's shield is love, forgiveness, and reconciliation. He does not care how crappy your life has been. He was there through it all. He is the fixer of all things broken. It only takes you submitting to him. When I tell you that I am unashamed of my past, and I chose to walk in my purpose.

🎬 Chapter One

As I'm driving down the highway, I'm listening to a sermon by Bishop T. D. Jakes. He is so blessed in the word of God, and whenever he teaches I'm captured and often feel as if he's speaking directly to me. Today was one of those days. I heard him speak these words, "A WOUNDED MOTHER GIVES BIRTH TO A WONDERING DAUGHTER." My God! Right then and there I started to examine my life. I thought to myself, "Hummm." I began putting somethings together. As I continued to think back over growing up in a small town outside of St. Louis Missouri. I remembered how I was fifteen years old when my mother shared her life story with me. As I look over it now at thirty-eight years old, I see I was a wondering daughter of a wounded mother.

Mom opened up to me about being sexually assaulted by her stepfather from the time she was a little girl well into her teenage years. My heart literally dropped. Could anyone ever imagine their mom being hurt in this way? She went on to share that he even built a shed in the back yard specifically for these torments. I believe that my grandmother knew about this but did nothing to stop him from hurting my mom. My mom could do nothing to protect my grandmother from his domestic violence. I believe that my grandmother was scared and terrified to do anything about what was happening. Whenever he was angry and wanted to beat on someone my grandmother was his punching bag. I tried putting myself in her shoes to sympathize with her. I could only imagine how bad it really was. It didn't help me put aside the reality she had inflicted on me. So no matter how bad of a picture mom painted of her childhood, my reality and present pain would not let me feel mercy. I will explain more in a moment.

I want to first, tell how my life was when I was about eight years old. My childhood was good. My mom kept me busy with many activities in school, girl scouts, batons, anything a girl could participate in I was in it. Now, I don't remember many hugs or "I love you's". I do remember her making sure I had opportunities. She was the oldest out of five kids, as well as my dad. He was the oldest out of five kids. Both of them experienced some horrible things in life. My dad was left to pretty much raise his younger siblings. His mom was a partier and wasted the little they did have to feed themselves. She would often waste the family's allotment of food stamps, and he would end up going to food pantries to find food. He was often abused physically and verbally, and always got the stick for anything the younger children did. Both my parents suffered unthinkable trauma.

In contrast, it seemed through my young eyes that my mother's mom spoiled me. She walked me to my bus stop every day, and whenever I was at her house we played this card game called Pity Pat. My favorite thing was her buying me Tootsie Rolls for a penny each whenever we went to the store. I remember one morning we were walking to the bus stop as usually, but this time we kept going we didn't stop. I asked her why we weren't stopping and she replied, "You aren't going to school today. We're going to the store so we can buy some candy and play Pity Pat." I was so excited to skip school and play with my granny all day.

When we made it to the store, I grab as many handfuls of candy my small hand could hold. As we approached the counter my grandmother leaned over to me and said, "Give me the money out of your pockets." I reach into my pocket and gave her the money and replied, "Grandma, my mom told me to take this to school with me." She leaned back down and said, "Your mom isn't going to find out." So, Granny goes up to the register and puts all of the candy I grabbed on the counter. She then proceeds to say, "Give me a half pint of Vodka, please?" She paid for it all with the money I gave her.

Once we got home and the liquor was in her system she started

talking out of her head. At least I thought it was out of her head. She said things like, "No bet to me. No bet to the rabbit." Whatever that meant I had no idea. I remembered her falling all over the place, yelling and cursing. I was little and I remembered running to help her. Or, at least trying to help her from the floor and asking, "Grandma, are you okay?"

I also remember her buying me my first pager. Man, I thought I was cool. I just knew I was loved by my grandmother. She used to let me put dish soap all over the kitchen floor so I could pretend to be ice skating. Thinking back on my grandmother off and on over the years I realized she was an acholic. I'm not sure how long she had been an alcoholic, but it had to be several years.

The root of it could stem from some type of trauma. My grandmother had burns on her body from head to toe. The source of those burns was the beginning of trauma for both of us. The beginning of trauma for me was me remembering when I was three years old. My mom and I pulled onto a street with all of these lights from ambulances and fire trucks. There was so much smoke going up to the sky. I remember my mom getting out of the car running toward the smoke and I was left in the car by myself. Even though I didn't understand what was going on at that age I knew something was not right. And little did I know that the two little cousins that I once played with would never return, and the memory who they were would fade. My grandmother made it out, but she didn't know my aunts two children were upstairs hiding in a closet. They were scared and didn't know what else to do.

When the fire department found the remains upstairs they were hugging each other in the closet. I believe that my grandmother carried a lot of guilt and pain from the pain her daughters suffered. On top of the domestic violence from a man she thought loved her, was added not protecting her daughter and her grandchildren. When I was thirteen she passed away from cirrhosis of the liver.

My father wasn't there much when I was little. He would pop up on occasion but never constantly. I remember being seven or

eight and hearing his voice over the phone and being so excited to talk to him. One day he told me that he was coming to pick me up for the weekend. I would spend the entire week packing my things for the stay. He would call and say he was on his way, and I would spend the entire day sitting at front of the door looking out the window with my bags ready to go. After I would realize how late in the day it was the tears would start rolling down my face. By that time, I knew he wasn't coming. I would still hang on to a little ounce of hope that he would pull up any minute, and the tears would be for nothing. Each time I would wake up the next day in my bed and my bags by my door in my room. I would lay in my bed and look out the window and feel so hurt. I didn't understand how my father could tell me something and not follow through with it. What could be more important than me.

Even though my dad was hardly there my mom always took me to his mother's house. While there we went to church every Sunday. So, I did grow up knowing his family. I grew up in church being in the choir and ushering at a young age. On the occasions my dad did pick me, up of which I can count on one hand, we would always stay at some woman's house. Her kids would be there, and I would not be along with my dad. We never spent quality time together. I always had to share him with other women's kids. He was always attending to the women instead of me.

There was one time when I heard my dad on the phone and I was trying to get his attention. I overheard him tell the person on the other end of the phone that I was his niece, not his daughter. His denial of me at this young age took root in me. It started a distorted need of wanting attention from a man. I really can't say that I was mad about it at that time. I think I was just happy to be in his presence. The seed was still planted though.

To make up for my father being gone, my mother would spoil me with things. One year I asked for a bunk bed. I was an only child, but for some reason I wanted a bunkbed. It could have been because I collected a lot of stuffed animals and I needed somewhere for them

to sleep. I think my mom gave me so much because she knew how hurt I was when it came to my father. One year I had a father and daughter dance, and I asked my dad to come. He could never tell me no so he left it up to my mother to be the barer of the bad news. He never showed up. I think my mom just wanted me to have someone there, so she sent my uncle. She didn't want me to be the only one there without a father. I remember seeing my uncle walk through the door of the dance. I was happy while at the same time hurt. I was crushed by my dad's absence. I was also embarrassed when other kids asked me was that my dad and I had to tell them he was my uncle. I just hung my head down.

We all know how mean kids can be to other kids. I thought that I was not important enough for him to show his face. I remember off and on hearing my mother say that my father was too busy chasing Jason. I didn't even know what that meant at the time, but I was sure I would find out sooner or later. All I knew was that my dad and my uncle were both chasing Jason. Maybe, they were chasing him together. And I thought that if they could catch Jason together then maybe they could be around more often than they were. Maybe they were these big-time bounty hunters catching criminals on the run. Later on, as I got older, I found out what chasing Jason meant. According to my mom it meant they were chasing and smoking crack cocaine. Finding out that my dad was a drug addict was one of the hardest things I ever heard or had to accept. I didn't want to believe it. Crack cocaine is what had been keeping him out of my life and away from me. It was easier to believe that instead of him not wanting me. Deep down knowing that my dad was on drugs made me even madder and more angry with him.

9

 *Chapter Two*

As I got older, I had this best friend named Heather who would spend almost every weekend with me. Her mom and my mom were best friends. We grew up together from pampers. She and I got into so much trouble together it was crazy. We went to so many parties in high school. Once I got my license my uncle on my dad's side bought me a car. Wait, no, this car was not cute at all, but it did what it was supposed to do. It got me and Heather around to all the parties. I was about seventeen when I started going to high school parties and smoking marijuana. Mom worked nights and would be gone from eleven at night until seven in the morning.

During this time, we did the most. Mom would always wonder why we slept all day. It was because we worked the same hours, lol. We would be tired from our all-night benders and adventures. When there wasn't a party to go to, we went to a place called Mecham park aka Chocolate City. We met up with friends there. It was also where I met a guy named john.

Sometimes we had small parties after mom went to work. If we were having a party at home, we would start planning it early in the week. By Thursday, we would have the exact plans, and it was going down Friday and Saturday. We would wait to hear mom walk out of the front door, and listen for her to walk down the stairs. We would crawl army style into the living room and look out the window to make sure she pulled off. If we were having friends over we would call them and say come on. If we were leaving then we would wait a good thirty-minutes before we would leave out.

One night we were almost caught. Mom let me have a little sleep over, and it was three of us all together. We invited these boys we had met at Mecham Park, John being one of them. I don't know what it was about john that struck my interest. I don't know if it was because he was a drug dealer or because he seemed like someone

that would never let anything happen to me. He was a skinny little guy and wasn't very tall. I stood 5'2 and he stood a couple inches taller than me so he was maybe 5'4 or something like that. He had a hot temper that went right along with his height. Anyways the boys came over and soon as we all got settled in the house, something told me to look outside. When I did, I saw my mother walking up the sidewalk. I yelled at the girls and informed them, and we shoved all the boys into my bedroom closet. We hurried up, laid down, and pretended to watch movies. We asked as she came in what happened, "You decided not go to work?" She replied, "No, I forgot my wallet." And walked out of the door. OMG that was scary. We made the boys stay in the closet until the coast was clear.

Heather and I had good times and broke lots of rules. There was one time my cousin and this big-time drug dealer came to visit me. My uncle and his girlfriend brought along a friend of his named Nate. I remember my uncle and his girlfriend in the living room watching tv and my cousin and this friend were in my bedroom. This friend of his tells my cousin to leave the room. At the time I didn't know that he was the biggest drug dealer in Mecham Park. My cousin gets up and leaves, but when he shuts the door I get a little nervous. I didn't know Nate very well.

Anyway, he precedes to ask me if I liked him. At the time it seemed safe for me to say yes, I do. Immediately, he grabbed me by the back of my head. With my hair rapped tight in his hand he shoves me face into his groin area. As I start to scream, he jerked my head toward him with his fist in my face and said, "if you make a sound I will beat your face in." I was beyond scared. When I tell you I squirmed trying to get out of the tight grip he had on my hair, but he was not letting go.

Now Nate was about 5'7 and 278 pounds so he was a very hefty man, one that I didn't not want to keep pissing off. He still had my face shoved in his private parts when he leaned down and said "if you bite me, I will kill you." I had to find a way out of this. I thought to myself. I kept squirming and he slapped me in my face and said,

"Stop moving and put it in your mouth." I knew someone had to hear all this commotion coming from my room. I politely told him that I had to go to the restroom really bad, and if he let me go I would come back and do whatever he wanted me to do. He let me go.

The way our apartment was designed, the bathroom had a door to mom's room and the hallway. I went into the bathroom and locked that door. Then went into my mother's room and locked that door as well. I hid in the corner in a ball in the dark and cried. I just knew that my cousin had to have known and that he brought this man to my house to rape me.

The next day I called John and told him what happened. By that time, we were dating. He asked, "who did this?" I told him Nate did and he had nothing else to say about it. They were all scared of him. This incident was never talked about ever again. I never told it to my dad or my mother. My uncle never said a word about what he heard that night.

A couple of weeks later my Mom tells me that she has decided to marry my dad. OMG I can't with her. I threw a fit and told her not to marry him. But I'll be darned if she didn't. I was so mad. Mostly I was mad at the fact that I wouldn't have the house to myself. I wouldn't be able to sneak out to parties anymore. Even though Heather and I had just got in trouble the weekend before with my mom. We took her car to a place in the city she had told us not to. As we were coming back, we got pulled over. I didn't get a ticket or anything, so we thought we got away with it. Somehow, she found out about it. I think I was more upset at the fact that my father thought he was going to come and start trying to run things.

Standing in the courthouse and watching this wedding go down was horrible might I add. I was not happy about this at all. I made sure they both knew my opinion about it. The first thing I remember telling him after they got married was "don't come in here trying to act like my dad, because I been doing just fine without you. You have not been a dad so don't start now. I am almost grown." Yup those were the words I said. Looking back on that I was hurting so

bad. What daughter doesn't want to be a daddy's girl? I sure did. So anyways my dad moves right on in and starts making himself at home. The remorse and anger I had toward him came rushing back. I was bitter, hurt, angry, and longing for a father all at the same time.

One night there was this party that Heather and I wanted to go to. I got dressed. As I was about to walk out of the door he says, "Don't forget your mother said that you had to clean up and do the dishes." I turned around and looked at him with the most hateful look on my face and said, "she is not here; you do the dishes." and walked out the door. I went and picked up Heather and another friend named Sara and we rolled on to the party.

This party was one of those where, if you were not there you were not cool at all. I just knew I had to be there. Not to mention that I was a cheerleader, and it was a must to be there. I was a cheerleader all through high school except for my senior year. This party was lit as they say. By the time we got ready to leave we were all drunk as a skunk. When we left the party Sara was so drunk that she couldn't walk. Heather and I had to sit her on her porch, ring the doorbell and run. After that I dropped Heather off. By the time I walked through the door at home my dad was on the phone with my mom. All I heard was him saying, "no she is not drunk." This led me to believe that Sara's mother had called my mother at work and told her that we left her daughter on the steps drunk, and that we were all drunk. Which we all were obviously.

Now when my mom married him, she knew that he was still on drugs, yet she still married him. My dad wrecked my mom's car, and my car. When he wrecked my car, they didn't' tell me at the time he had done it. They both told me that my car broke down, but I found out the truth later. I had my mom's car one day riding down the street. I was going pass the town's junk yard and out of my peripherals I see this car that looked like mine. I pulled over and looked around. What do you know? It was my car totaled out, not even drivable. Just a couple of weeks after he had wrecked mom's car. I was furious about my car.

Something strange happens. A week later I was chilling in my room. My dad comes in, gets on both of his knees, and tells me how sorry he is for not being there for me. He said how he wishes he could change having not been there for me. Now this is where most people would have given forgiveness and would have fell weak to the tears. Not me. I looked at him like he was crazy. With all the lies he had told me when I was younger there was no way I believed the words that were coming out of his mouth.

I don't know the whole depth of the relationship with my mom and dad. One day I woke up and he was gone. My mom had taken him to rehab. I do not remember if I went with them. It was almost like I kind of remember a road trip going an hour away from home, but I'm not sure if that was to take him or pick him up. Either way I definitely did not care as long as he was out of our house. Maybe things would go back to how they were before he came in and messed up everything. Well at least that's how I felt. I have to say this before I continue.

I have to be honest with how I felt at that time in my life and the situations that were going on at that time. After my dad left, I still felt every bit of the anger, sadness, bitterness, and this big hole in my heart that was never going to be filled. So, I filled that void with boys and marijuana. I went to more and more parties and smoked more. My friend Heather and I was always in St. Louis and other not too nice places. We were going to the inner hoods meeting guys and smoking. The guy John I talked about earlier was still very much in the picture.

 *Chapter Three*

Oh, how I thought I was in love with John. John was about 5'4 not too much taller than me. He was light skinned. Don't judge me. I was going through a light skin phase back then. I don't think he weighed too much, because it looked like if the wind blew too hard he would fly away. He had a head full of hair that he never kept combed. When he did get it done, he was sexy as could be. In hindsight, I don't know how I thought I was in love. The brotha didn't even have a car or a license to drive. Heather and I would go down to John's hood and chill with him and his drug dealer friends on the corner. I thought we were cool too. I was so cool that I ended up pregnant! Yup at 18.

Let's talk about how I was so cool that I was terrified to tell my mother that I was going to walk across that graduation stage pregnant. I know exactly when I got pregnant too. We were all at a friend's house Heather, John, one of his friends, and another girlfriend of mine who had her own place. John and I were … yeah you know already what we were doing. The condom broke. We were so smart that neither one of us knew where this liquid running down my leg was coming from. A month later I was lying at home in my bed wondering why I was feeling something floating in my stomach. I also wondered why I kept having this reoccurring dream.

The dream was me standing on the side of some street just waiting on the corner just standing there. Every time this dream came something was different. The anticipation of something or someone coming would get stronger and stronger. I am having the dream for about the seventh time. I am in my bed. There I was again standing on the corner waiting with so much anticipation. I look down the street and I see a man walking toward me with all of these people walking behind him. After seven dreams he finally gets to me. He grabs my hand and I walk beside him. I knew that maybe

this was Jesus. Even though I had heard and read of him, I didn't know him at that time. I really didn't know what that dream meant. I just knew that these dreams were coming periodically from the age of fifteen to eighteen.

The next day I got up and went to Birth Right. For those of you who don't know what Birth Right is, it's a place where you can go if you think you're pregnant to get a free test. They help you with things you may need during and after pregnancy. They gave me a test and yup I was in fact pregnant. I didn't know exactly how I was going to tell my mom, but I knew I had to. I went home in fear. I was hoping she wouldn't be home so I would have more time to get my words together, longer than just the car ride to plan out how I would execute this. It was going to be execution that day for me.

When I got home I pulled up looking at her car like, "oh crap ok." Then I thought, "She could be sleep for work tonight. Yes, let's hope for that." My luck couldn't get any worse; she was wide awake. As I walked back and forth past her room, she looked at me and said, "what's wrong? Why do you keep walking back and forth in front of my door?" As I stepped into her room I said, "Mom, I need to tell you something."

"What is it? What's wrong with you. Spit it out!" She said.

"Mom I am pregnant." A long silence came between us simultaneously.

To my surprise, my mom was excited. Her only concern was making sure that I graduated high school, and I did. I walked across the stage to graduate at four months pregnant. After my graduation everything was ok for a little while. My mom and I ended up moving from the town we were into the city of St. Louis. We moved into a nice house down there before my baby was born. After my baby was born. I decided to go to college, but my mom had other plans for me. I had to go to school for what she wanted me to go for. I was not allowed to choose. Fall of 2004 I started classes to become a dental assistant. I finished my class, and all I needed to do was my internship.

I thought more about my dad after my baby was born. I remember wanting to talk to him a little more. I wanted to know who he was for myself and determine if he was the type that just didn't care about his kids. So, I did just that. I called and he came to pick me up from the house and I put some gas in his van. Yes, he had a van. The kind that had a bed in the back. I just wondered at the time if I was sitting in a seat where his picked up prostitutes sat. No I don't really know if he did or not but at that time I really couldn't put it past him. We rode that day. I wasn't sure if he picked me up because I had gas money or if he really wanted to spend time with me. All I know was when I got home my mom was pissed. She tried to beat me with a baseball bat that night.

I noticed that since the move something had changed in her. It was like she was ok one minute and yelling and cussing me out the next. I packed up the baby and my things and left. I moved back to my old town with one of my friends who had gotten their own place. I left because mom was changing, and I could see it. I didn't know what it was. I didn't know if she didn't want me to know my own dad, or if she was still hurt from all the problem that came with the decision she made to marry him. I think we were both suffering from the way my dad left us both with a heart full of pain. I know that she loved him so much that she didn't care that he was a drug addict. I was his daughter and left without a father's loves.

I left and stayed that one friend. I stayed with her for a while and got a job at a cleaning service. One day I remember my friend and a couple of other friends were sitting at the kitchen table talking and laughing, and we heard a knock at the door. So I jumped up and walked to the door. I opened the door, and I got snatched up by my shirt. It was my mother. She flings me around and tries to throw me down a flight of stairs. I was so terrified. She told me that I had to move back in the house with her asap. So, I gathered my things and went back. If I was not in prison then I don't know what it was.

My mom and I didn't have a relationship when I grew up, only when I was a little girl, before she started drinking. She was a great

mother when I was little. Even to this day, I don't talk to my mom about a lot and for the most part we have very different views. She started getting lost in alcohol at a time I needed her the most. Going into adulthood and being a single mother with no direction and no one to give me a little nudge in the right direction was hard. I often wondered what did I do wrong? I know now that everyone has their own demons they must fight. Everyone has their own trials and tribulations going on. I just so happened to be born by two parents who both had their own trauma. The generational curse needed to stop so why not with me.

Time passed and I ended up dating this guy named … Ok, I will call him Brad. Brad was a truck driver not too cute. When I say not too cute he was not at all. He was tall, about 6'2, dark skinned and weighed about two hundred eighty pounds. Even though he wasn't too cute he could appear a little cute after he grew on you. He did have money and was big on romance. He took me to go and check on an apartment I had heard about from one of my cousins. The apartments were called Castle Park. Oh yeah, you would know about these apartments if you were from St. Louis. Back then they were low-income apartments. They were in the hood off St. Charles Rock Road.

So, he took me there and I ended up moving in. When I tell you I couldn't wait to move out into my own place. After I moved in, I thought my mom would show up and try to throw me down another set of steps. She was so upset about me moving out that I was fearful of her rage. She never came. Back to the apartment. You would never know that these apartments were there if you weren't from St. Louis. You drive through this neighborhood up a little hill. All the way at the back after rounding a corner a big castle appears. When I say a castle, I literally mean a castle. It was awesome. It looked like they took a castle that was already there and made it into an apartment complex.

You walk up these big steps into a grand entrance door. It was a grand entrance alright. When you walk through the door there was

this big desk where the police would sit. If you were not a resident, you would have to give them your licenses. I moved in. When I say my mom was not a happy at all about that. Before I moved out she had started drinking more. It was like one minute she was ok, and the next she would come out of her room yelling and cussing. I would never let her drink anything, but when she disappeared and went to her room, bet money, she would come out yelling and cussing.

At first, I was wondering what was happening to her. Was she still hurt about the situation about my dad? Was it the trauma from the marriage? Little did I know that this was coming from a long line of family hurt. At the time I didn't understand that hurt people hurt other people. I never put the two together. I could never make it, make sense. So, I left. Don't get me wrong I love my mother to death. We just didn't make good roommates. I know we were not roommates. She was my mother. I just couldn't understand why we didn't get along. Sometimes I thought she was battling with empty nest syndrome. I was older and maybe she didn't want to live alone. Whatever the case, I was just ready to be on my own, so I could breath.

My mom would come over every once and a while but not often. That was ok with me. I kind of needed a break from the drama. One day she called me wanting to pick me up so we could have dinner together as a family. I agreed. She came and picked me and the baby up and took us to her house. She did in fact cook dinner. We sat and ate. I really don't remember any conversation we had that night. I do remember her slowly getting tipsy and me asking her to take us home. Instead of being like, "Yeah Tyra, I will take you home." She told me to walk home, and referenced that the baby stroller was still downstairs. I remember begging her to take me home. She wouldn't take me, but went on to tell me to get out of her house. I got the stroller out and put my baby in it and I began to make my way home.

Mind you that yes, I didn't live far from her by car, but it was

one hell of a walk. The baby and I were walking and crying at the same time. Twenty-minutes into my walk a car pulls up. It just so happened to be my grandmother coming to get me. All I could do when I got in her car was break down and cry. I asked her how she knew that I was walking. Keep in mind it was ten o'clock at night. She said that my father called her and asked if she could come pick me up. It was later in life, but I did get a chance to ask my dad how he knew I was walking. He told me that my mom called and told him that she put me and the baby out and that we were walking home. All I could do was cry. I didn't know what I did to make her treat me this way. I wondered why my mother grew to dislike me so much. Even though these questions always ran through my mind, I always carried hope that she would return to the loving mother I knew when I was a girl. On the other hand my dad and I were still talking a little. Not as much as I wanted, but we were talking.

Dad ended up having this live in girlfriend and stayed in Salem Missouri. She was nice, and I liked her. She had some daughters that were about my age. I remember her coming to get me and the baby. We stayed with her for a little while. It was a three to four hour drive, and my boyfriend Brad was headed that way to pick up a load in three weeks. He would pick me up while he there so I could go back home. While I was out there her daughters and I had a blast. We hung out a lot and we kicked it hard. When it was time to leave, I took a cab to meet up with my boyfriend who was securing a load at this scrap metal yard.

When I got there he and his workers were loading the trailer up with tons of scrap metal. I remember telling him that I wasn't comfortable with riding with him. He had been drinking some beers. I wanted to ride in the van with his workers. He wouldn't let me because it was a van full of men. When I tell you I was so uncomfortable riding with him. I had this crazy creepy feeling. I get in the tractor with the baby. We started on the road, and I noticed something when we were riding. We were taking all back roads and I wondered why so I asked. He told me that the trailer was

overweight. I didn't know what that meant at the time. I knew nothing about tractor trailers. We were on this narrow back road and a car was halfway in our lane. He tried to move the trailer over a little and the back tire of the trailer went into the ditch. He was trying to ease the tire back up onto the road, but when he did, the tire started to skid back and forth. That's when I see it coming. I jumped back on the bed where my baby was sleeping and covered him as the whole tractor trailer started flipping. We flipped a total of three times. All I remember is holding my son so tight and closing my eyes and praying that we would make it through this alive.

When the tractor finally stopped flipping, I was standing on my feet with the grass in my toes. So picture this tractor was on its side and the windows are down on the driver and passenger side. There is a window above me, and through the window below me I am standing up on both feet holding my baby. I was looking to see if he was bleeding. I saw blood everywhere. I looked at Brad and said my baby is bleeding I couldn't find where all the blood was coming from. As I continued to feel every inch of my baby's body. My boyfriend says, "no babe, that's you bleeding." Brad and his workers got my son out of the tractor first and then they took me out. We had to climb out of the window of the truck. I thank God that my son came out of that accident without a scratch on him. For me I had a cut going down my eyebrow.

After everyone was out of the truck we hopped into the van. Brad took me and my son to a hospital that we had passed about a mile back. We walked in and everyone was rushing around because they heard the accident from down the street. I guess all the blood that was running down my face sent people in a panic. They put me on a gurney and my neck in a brace. They thought my neck was broken. They ended up putting me on a helicopter and flew me back to St. Louis. I remember getting in the helicopter and it taking off but after that I was knocked out. I did not wake up until the next day. When I opened my eyes, I saw a lady putting stitches in my face. I wanted to know where my son was, but I was so drugged up that I

fell back to sleep. Finally, the next time I woke up I was able to leave the hospital. I couldn't wait to get back to my apartment.

When we got home my son and I settled in and healed. I sued his insurance company, and won a settlement. Then what do you know Brad shows up wanting the money that I got from the lawsuit so he can get a new tractor. "Oh no buddy! Who do you think you are I asked him. "I need the money you got, because I don't have a tractor anymore." He said. I told him he should have filed his own lawsuit, but you can't because you had alcohol in your system."

 Chapter Four

As time went on my mom did not get any better; she was getting worse with the drinking. I remember receiving a phone call from my mom to come over her house. On my way … wait. Let me pause right here and say this. Yes! Honey, I bought a car with some of the settlement. It was a nice car, white with a sun roof. Your girl finally got some wheels. No more being put out and told to walk home. I was swerving home, lol. Anyways let's get back to the story. I received a phone call to come over. As I was on my way, I got off on the Brentwood exit. I saw a car. I'm going to stop right here and try my best to explain exactly what it was I saw. So, you know how when you get off an exit ramp, and it has the metal guard rail going up the side. Well the car I saw was on the guard rail. Two tires were up in the air on the guard rail and the other two were on the ground.

When I saw it, I started talking cash money stuff about the person that just ran their car up on the rail. As I get closer to this car I'm like, "Dang, that look like my momma car." I get closer and well I'll be. It was her car. I pulled over so I could try find her. I didn't see her, but a police officer walked up to me and says, "Is your mother named beep, beep." (not trying to use her name). I said, "Yes sir. It is." He says, "Your mother wrecked her car and fled the scene of an accident. She will be going to jail." Let me stop right here. What was going through my mind at the time was, "Dang, I thought I did some crazy stuff when I was younger, but she is old and running from scenes of accidents and stuff." I just had to be real with what I was thinking and feeling at that moment, which was the exact moment she decided to call my phone. I politely walked off in the distance so the police officer wouldn't hear that I was on the phone with her.

"Tyra where are you?" She asked.

"I am at the scene of your accident, and the police are telling

me that you can be arrested for leaving the scene. What where you doing? Why did you run?"

As she explained why she ran, I heard the alcohol in her voice. She said that she was coming back from work and accidently ran up on the guard rail. I believed she had been drinking before work, and they sent her home because she was intoxicated. I also believe that was the last time my mom worked as a CNA. I think she was fired for continuing to show up for work intoxicated. The police officers were really nice. They told me if I could get her to come back, they would not arrest her. They would just give her a ticket. So, I called her back and let her talk to the officers. They told her to let me come and get her and bring her back to the scene. So, I went and picked her up. She had only ran down the street to a gas station. I pick her up and took her back to the scene. They gave her a ticket but impounded her car.

About three weeks later mom seemed like she was doing better after her criminal escapade. She was able to get her car out. I even let her take my son for a weekend. It seemed like my son gave her hope when he was around. Boy was I wrong. I remember coming home to a police department and family service card on my door. I instantly went into panic mode, because I didn't understand what was going on. I called Maplewood police which was in the city where my mom lived. They told me that my son had been picked up by his dad, and my mom was in jail.

I couldn't understand for the life of me what exactly happened. The police told me that my mom and my son went to Walmart. She had been drinking and somehow lost my son in Walmart. The Walmart protocol was after looking for a lost kid for a certain amount of time they call the police to come and assist them in the search. My mom ended up finding my son before the police came, and decided to walk home from Walmart. She left her car sitting in the parking lot. In searching for her, the police found mom in a ditch passed out and my son was running around in the street. My heart dropped and my body filled with anger. After that I had to sign a

document form from child protection serves that my mom could no longer have my son without supervision. They also had to check my home as well and make sure that there was food in the fridge, and I had a safe home for him to be in. When I tell you I was furious with my mother. OMG! That doesn't even begin to scratch the anger I had at that time. I couldn't understand why mom was going downhill and so fast.

I really started to miss the mother I knew as a girl. I spent nights just crying, wishing I could go and just hug her, cry on her shoulder. At the same time I knew that was not how she raised me. I was to show little emotion, suck everything in and toughen up. I didn't know then how much I would long for the love of a loving mother that could hug and cry with me when thing where going bad. I wanted her to teach me about self-worth, what to expect from men, and just how to walk through this life as a woman. How could she teach me what she had not learned herself. I didn't know then that I had a long road ahead of me before I learned what self-worth was.

Time passed and I met this guy named Jacob. Jacob was 5'5, dark skinned, and kind of cute. He had good skin with a mouth full of gold that always fell out of his mouth when he talked. He was a sweet guy and seemed really nice. We started hanging out and talking. Then one thing lead to another and I ended up pregnant. By this time my son was three, and Jacob and I decided to get married. We went to the courthouse. Let me tell you! When we were standing in line to get our marriage license everything in my gut was telling me to turn around and run. I was too scared to do it. The shame and embarrassment, of running out and leaving him standing there out weighted my gut. So, I stayed in line. We got our license and moved through the line towards the judge. The fear kept growing. You know how people say swallow your pride. I was literally trying so desperately to swallow my fear and everything that was telling me to run for the hills. But I pushed down and sucked up the feeling to run. When I tell you that God will still move even if you don't know him like you should. I know now that the fear I was feeling was Him

telling me to walk away. This is going to take you down a road you do not want to walk on.

After marriage I realized that Jacob was the kind of man who didn't want to work for nothing. He was always lying to get out of work so he could stay home and drink. Once he called me from work and said that he had been throwing up and I needed to come and pick him up. So, I went and picked him up. Immediately he say, "Stop by the gas station." We stop. He goes in and comes out with a case of beer, cracks one open, and starts drinking. I was like, "Yo! What's going on!"

"I didn't feel like working today so I was ready to go." He replied with no remorse at all. He went on to say how he had taken three days off. By day two, his job started calling me and asking was he ok cause he hasn't been to work and hadn't called in. So, his supervisor started sending his work schedules to me instead of him. His supervisor thought he wasn't old enough to handle his own schedules.

My desire is to give you a transparent testimony with no filter. We shouldn't lie about or be ashamed of what God has brought us out of. You never know how telling your truth can help someone else. And this is my truth and I pray to God that this helps someone else make it through. Our stories may not be the same, but I can bet they are relatable. So please don't think this is a book to bash people because it's not. I refuse to be a victim of my past.

Ok! Now, let's get back to this marriage, because I have a lot to tell you. Jacob and I continued to live in the Castle for a while and we had a beautiful baby girl. So I was a stay at home mom and still smoked a lot of marijuana. Just being real again. My husband worked sometimes and wasn't very consistent with work. So let me tell you about the time I had a nervous breakdown with my kids. My oldest son was about four years old. When I tell you, this little dude was hyper. I remember he used to run around the house climbing and jumping off of things. OMG!

In the castle all these apartments had high ceilings and I had this

entertainment center that just about touched that celling. I was coming out of the bathroom and looked around, because it was too quiet. So I just knew he was into something. I came around the corner and he was all the way at the top of this thing. I saw him out of my peripherals just as he jumped off. I almost died that day. LOL. When it came to school he used to run from the teachers, and they would call me to come up to the school so I could catch him. By time I got there, the teachers would be so tired and worn out they would already have his things ready so I could take him home. This last incident I'm going to share brought it all in to perspective. I was in the kitchen cooking, and he was just too quiet. I walked around the corner he came running out of the bathroom screaming, "IT BURNS! IT BURNS!" I was like, "What happened!" This boy had Vicks vapor rub all over his face. That's when the doctors diagnosed him with ADHA.

After that, we were looking for a place to live back in my old town I grew up in. My uncle helped us find a place, and we moved from St. Louis to Pacific. This was a big change for me. Neither Jacob or I had lived there since I graduated from high school. I was kind of happy to be back to a familiar place. All my friends where here and some of my family as well. We moved and got settled in, everything was good for a while. I got a job at the one place that knew my whole family. I was sure that they would have me work for them. It was a nursing home that my family had worked for years. My mom worked there for years and the people there watched me grow up from a little girl. Both of my aunts worked there and one was still work there when I applied for work. Our family history with this place went way back.

So, I started working there in dietary serving food. Many of the people that worked there I knew from school. So I was not a stranger. Eventually I moved from dietary aid to being a certified nurse's aide. I loved working there. On the wall by the nurse's station there was a star with my name on it for a perfect employee. When I tell you if I could go back to working at that one place I

would be excited. That's how much I loved it there. And no my husband at the time, Jacob, still couldn't keep a job. I was trying to cope with everything that had happened, so I thought.

Some very weird things were going on in the house with my husband. To this day, I believe that he was drugging me. It got to the point where I would wake up the next day and know and feel that my body was so off, violated. I didn't know what was going on. I just knew that it was something weird. I remember feeling the same when we lived in the castle, but I shrugged it off. I thought I was going crazy. He would always get my weed for me and sometimes make me drink. I started to wonder if maybe he lacing the weed and putting something in both. I started to watch the way he moved and took mental notes of everything. Then I thought, "No, Tyra you're thinking too much into this. He wouldn't do anything to hurt you. You're his wife. He knows what you've gone through in your past, being rapped at seventeen. He couldn't be drugging me." I just know we took vows. So as I always did I shrugged it off and just thought maybe I was really going crazy.

I sat him down and explained in a caring way that I understood his need for sexual attention. I wanted to be a part of it, and I wanted to be alert when he started, so please wake me up. He said that I was trippin and nothing was happening to me while I slept. I believed him, and me waking up feeling violated stopped for a while. Then out of nowhere it started again. This particular time I was able to open my eyes. I was trying so hard to get my vison together, because it was so cloudy. I was able to open them long enough to see him pulling off my panties. Whatever he was putting in my tea had me so loopy that I couldn't keep my eyes open. Before I knew it I was knocked back out. When I woke up the next day I just laid there with this disgusting feeling all over my body. I didn't know what to say to him. I did cry and plead for him to stop. Once again it stopped for a little while but happened again. This time it was awful.

I woke up in so much pain, and when I went into the bathroom and saw blood all over my butt. I remember calling his mother and

talking to her about the situation, and what she said blow my mind. His mother said, "You are his wife and whatever he wants to do to you is his right." I immediately hung the phone up with tears in my eyes. That was the last straw. I couldn't live like that anymore. I put him out. Yep, I did. So, when I put him out he moved into the apartment behind mine with one of his friends. This wasn't good at all. One night I was cooking, and he called me and started telling me what I was wearing and what I was cooking. He was watching me. Whenever I left my house he would call or text and ask where I was going or what did I think I was doing. I was terrified. I went and got a restraining order on him. A couple days after I filed the order Franklin County sheriff's office came and knocked on my door to tell me that he was trying to purchase a gun.

 *Chapter Five*

I started working more of hours, and I remember I was at work and I wasn't feeling good at all. One of the nurses took my blood pressure and it was to the roof. They sent me home, and the next day I went to the doctors. My doctor said that I was working too many hour and was stressed. He gave me some migraine pills because I was having headaches all of the time. The third time I went to the doctors he finally did an MRI on me. I left the doctor's office heading to work for a meeting. Mind you the doctors is a thirty minute ride from my job. By the time I pulled up to work, my doctor called and said I needed to come back right away. I did but not without complaining. Ooh I complained all the way there. When I got there, they were there waiting for me. They admitted me as soon as I got there. They said that I had pseudotumor cerebri, which is meant that I had too much fluid around my brain, and it acted as a tumor. I was in the hospital for a while and they drained the fluid off my head through my spine. It most defiantly was not fun.

All that time I spent in the hospital, my mother came to see me once. My dad was traveling for welding. He was getting himself together. So, I was happy for him even though we still were not too close. Just before this happened, I had gotten back with John. I thought he would be there for me since we had a baby together but as I started getting sick and was in the hospital, he took my car and never came to see me unless I needed clothes or something like that. Also before I got sick I had gotten close with my uncle and his girlfriend, Jill. Jill was so sweet. She had this long pretty blond hair and a little girl that was the same age as my daughter so we became pretty close. When I got sick I couldn't depend on my own family to be there. God gave me Jill. She ended up moving in with me and she cared for my kids for me while I was working. She was great with all the kids and a great friend to me. While I was sick and, in

the hospital, she took care of the kids while John avoided all responsibilities, for everything in life.

When I got out of the hospital, I had to take medicine every day. The medicine that I had to take I couldn't be in artificial light or direct sunlight. So, when I got home, I covered all the windows in my room and stopped using lamps and I only went outside when the sun was going down or it was completely dark outside. You are talking about the darkest time of my life. The doctors had prescribed me a lot of meds I had Percocet's, methadone's and Xanax. Why they gave me methadone I'm not sure because I have never used meth in my life. The only drug that I used in life was marijuana. So, I was taking these pills daily. I felt so trapped and in the dark, and I mean that literally.

I ended up getting addicted to all of this medicine. It was crazy. After I came home from the hospital life was more difficult than I could ever Imagine. I ended up losing the job that I loved so much. Before I lost my job I tried to go to work and push through, but every time I went and was moving around, I would have to run to the bathroom and throw up. I always ended up being sent home. So finally, I stopped trying to go back. It's like I gave into the darkness that was surrounding me at that time. I got fired from the job. From there, it seemed like everything started going downhill. I got rid of John because he was doing no earthly good for me. How he was calling himself a drug dealer, and never have money to help me with anything was beside me. So, I felt he had to go. On top of that he wasn't supportive while I was sick and going through all of this. So, yeah, I kicked him to the curb asap.

My life was still dark and gloomy, and it was pulling me down in this hole. So, I started getting addicted to the pills and I started selling them to try and make ends meet. When I started selling these pills, OMG! I never knew that there was so many people who were addicted to pain pills. I was getting so many pills a month. I mean a crap tone of them. So I started separating the pills I would keep for myself from the ones I would sell. I was making money. Even more

money than John was making. I was brand new to the game, and he was in the game for years and had nothing to show for it. He was still living with his momma or living off of women to make it through life. That's how I felt at the time about that. So, I very much thought that I was living my best life.

That's what I thought, until, I started having suicidal thoughts. I sure tried to follow through with them. Once, I thought I could cut my wrist with this big knife that I was using to cut up raw chicken. I stared taking three pain pills at once. From there I started bumping up the number of pills I was taking. I so, desperately wanted to take my life at that time. I remembered one day I made the decision to take eight pills at once. I just knew that was going to get the job done. I took the pills and I laid across my bed. The feeling of being high as a kite and the feeling that death was right at the doorstep seemed a pleasant relief. In a matter of seconds I would be floating off succeeding this death mission. I froze and cried out, "Wait, no, I don't want to die yet! Hold on Jesus! No!..." In mid-sentence I passed out and woke up later pinching myself thinking that I had died. I was still very much alive. I had just been sleeping for two days, smh.

I had no Idea exactly how rough everything was about to get. After my near-death experience, I still kept selling my pills and taking them. I just never took that many again. I was still addicted to them. I was losing my apartment, so I helped Jill move back in with her parents, and I went home. I packed up my car with as much stuff as possible and drove off. I left everything in the apartment. I had this cousin that lived a couple builds away from my old apartment. I went to his place, he and his girlfriend let me and the kids stay with them for a little while. One day they were at work and the landlord came and knocked on the door. I opened it and she was furious that I was there, because I had been evicted from my apartment and the property as well. I didn't want my cousin and his girlfriend to get put out on my account. I decided that my cousin would keep my kids for a while, so I could try and get somethings

sorted out.

I went and stayed with a friend that lived about seven minutes away her name was Lucy. Now Lucy dated a real drug dealer. He was well known and had the money to back up his name. I had stopped selling pills, and was partying hard. No I didn't start selling any other drugs. I just partied a lot, going to clubs and smoking a lot of marijuana. I stayed high as a kite on the pills and alcohol. I did this mostly to cope with the pain. Not the pain from a physical wound but a mental and emotional wound. I was hurting and bleeding so bad on the inside. I was wounded from the inside out if that makes sense. I didn't know that then, but I sure know it now. Looking back over my life I often thought why did I have to go through this? why did I have to endure so much pain? And why is it still an ongoing pain? did I do something to make God mad at me? Is this a punishment for something I didn't do correctly? Or was this stuff I deserved to go through? I mean there was always so many questions floating through my thoughts. It's crazy. I did wonder at one point why does God hate me so much. Don't worry I will most defiantly answer or give my conclusions to these questions at the end.

I partied like I thought I was a rock star, bleeding and leaving blood trails everywhere. There was so much blood pouring out of me that if you were trying to find me it wasn't going to be hard at all just follow the trail that I was leaving behind. During the party stage I would go see my kids and drop money off for them to eat. I know I was not a good mother at all at that time. Sometimes I felt like I was bleeding all over them. I didn't even realize at the moment that I was doing that.

After my party and drunken stage I got back to reality about my situation, and the reality was that I had no one to turn to and nowhere to go. What was I going to do? Where was I going to go? I realized that I had to breakdown and call my mother. Oh, how that was the hard part, because it was obvious that she couldn't stand me. We really didn't talk much to be honest about it. But, I had no one else

to turn too. So, I got my kids and I went back to St. Louis. As I pulled up to my mother's apartment my heart was beating so fast. The fear and nervousness of seeing her face to face, and asking if I could stay with her for a little while, sent pulses through my body. The fear of her being drunk played a big part of my fear. I wasn't always afraid of her. She created this fear in me.

Mom was amazing when she wasn't drinking, but when she was drinking it was pure hell. She would be mad at the world and didn't care who she took it out on. Staying with her at that time, I learned that I wasn't the only one she hated when she drank. I learned that she hated Jack as well. Jack was her boyfriend who I was not fond of. I didn't like him simply because I felt my mother could do better. Jack was tall about 5'8 maybe weighed about 200 pounds, and he didn't have a home. He lived at bus stops and begged for money and change in front of gas stations and grocery stores. I always thought that her drinking didn't start until he came into the picture. But I was lying to myself and didn't want to face the truth. She had always been drinking before he even came in the picture. When she was sober, we were all her friends. You were her best friend if you had money and could buy her a drink.

While I was staying with them it was so hard. Some nights the kids and I had to sleep in the car, because she would put us out. Jack would always yell at her about it. But he had no control over her. She would remind him of the fact it wasn't his house, and he could get out too. That's when I started looking at him differently. He would try to talk sense into her, but she never listened. Every day would start good but never end well. By nighttime it always ended with her drinking and putting me out of her house. Most of the time she would only put me out and sometimes it was all of us. It would start with her telling me that I think I am better than her and that I need to stop acting white. Then it went from that to she wished she never had me. On to, I was a drug addicted because I smoked marijuana day in and day out. I wondered why I smoked so much ummm ... Yeah, because this was my life. I felt like I needed to

cope.

The whole suicide thing didn't pan out too well so I smoked as much as I could. And Jack and I became smoke partners together. I think we both needed the escape to be honest. So during my stay between my moms and my car, I really didn't know what to do or where to go. I remember one night while sleeping in my car, I had a couple of dollars so I went to this chicken place to get something to eat. I ran into this guy I knew from when I was 15. I was best friends with his little brother. The guy was about 5'7 and weighed about two-hundred-thirty-five pounds and had a neck like a tree stomp. He was cute and not cute like a baby monkey. He had a caramel completion, thick eyebrows, and a gap in between his two front teeth but he was cute.

He wanted my number so we could catch up. We exchanged numbers and started talking. It took me a while to tell him what was going on and explain my entire situation, but I did eventually. I did let him know I was staying at my mom's house. Going forward, when my mom put me out, I went and stayed with him. He started talking to me about moving to Georgia with him and how it was this great place to live. I told him that I would think about it. And I did. I had so much to think about when it came to moving. It would mean leaving the very place where I experienced the most hurt and pain. Eventually I agreed to go, and we started plaining the move.

I didn't tell anybody that I was moving I just left. My family didn't care what I was going through and my mother didn't realize how much pain she brought me. Or, how she was bleeding over me. so I thought why not go it's not like anyone would notice that I was gone. St. Louis was a very hurtful place for me. Even now when I go back to visit and see that arch and ride across that bridge, I feel some kind of way. When we left, I remember looking at the arch in my rear-view mirror. I felt all the weight of everything I encountered and endured leaving from me, and a new start was on the rises.

This ride from St. Louis to Georgia was about an eight hour drive. It could take longer depending on how many stops you took

along the way. Everybody was sleeping in the car, so I had time to reflect on my life. I had so much running through my mind. The biggest shock was that I had just left my home town and had never lived outside of Missouri. I was nervous I thought we had a plan, but as we left Missouri I realized we had no plan of how we were going to survive. I had two kids. How would I take care of them? Where would we sleep? Well, it's definitely not like we never slept in the car before. As we came into Georgia coming down high on I-20 passing six flags, it was such a beautiful view at night seeing the lights of Atlanta's downtown buildings lit up. I was so amazed at the beauty of it. I just knew that life was going to be turned around for the good, even though I was already getting home sick. Finally we came to a stop at a hotel off Fulton industrial.

Now anybody who is familiar with Georgia knows what goes down over there. But anyway, we stopped that night so I couldn't really see what the area was about. We checked in and went to our room and slept. When I woke up the next morning and looked outside, my first thought was, "What the heck is this? Are we were prostitutes walked?" We were dead in the middle of a drug town with two kids. We ended up staying at that hotel for a while maybe a week or so. You don't want to know the thoughts that ran through my mind at the time, but I know you're just dying to know. The first thought that ran through my mind was, "I know this ninja didn't think that he was about to put me out here, with him being my pimp." Let's just be honest for a moment and recognize that sex trafficking is real. But that's not what happened. We moved on from there to Marietta where we found a homeless shelter to stay at for a while. During the day we would ride around and find something to do. I was basically taking him around to look for jobs.

I think I messed up when I told him everything about my past. He took some of those things and used it to put fear in me. My entire life had been looking for the love of my parents in the men that I dated. I wish I knew that back then, but I didn't. I defiantly know that now. At some point he knew that he could place the fear in me

and that's exactly what he did. Have you ever felt the feeling of being safe, while at the same time being afraid? The feeling safe part came from knowing that he wouldn't let anyone do harm to me, and the afraid part comes from knowing that he could do harm to me. Let me give you some background. I remember when I was seventeen, I was at Chucks house visiting his brother. I always knew that Chuck liked me. I also knew his girlfriend was there and he was abusive to her. He said that he had changed, and I wanted to believe that because he said it so gentle and nice. That could have been because he felt bad for my situation. Maybe he could relate to me not having anyone there for me because his mom had passed away. I don't think he knew his dad at all, and I walked a lot of my life mourning a mother and a father that weren't dead, but still walked the earth.

Now listen when I tell you it wasn't love that brought Chuck and I together. I think it was just comforting for the both of us to have someone at each other's side. I can't say that I honestly was in love with him. I think it was more of the fact that he did something nobody else was doing and that was protecting me and looking out for me. The feeling of all of that made me feel warm and loved, for a little while at least.

 *Chapter Six*

The feeling I had before of feeling safe and afraid started to increase. It started to show its ugly head. While in the homeless shelter he started to talk about getting married. I really wasn't interested in being married again. I put up a battle about it. I tried to be strong in my stance. I wasn't strong in the last marriage I was in. Trying to be strong got me thrown up against the wall, yelled at nose to nose. If that wasn't intimidating, and scary at the same time. It scared me so much I married him. I almost peed my pants and the last time I peed my pants was when I was sixteen. My mom came in my room at two in the morning and grabbed me by my ankles and flung me out the bed, and started punching me like I was a stranger in the street. I was terrified and scared, lying there covering my face as her punches came flying for every direction. I just laid there and pissed myself. I stayed in the fetal position in my own urine for a while even after she had stopped punching me and left.

I was glad he didn't punch me, because he was a big man. His hit would have been fatal to my face. I didn't want to find out if it would even go that far, so I agreed to do what he was asking of me. I agreed to get married. I heard someone say, "what takes you fifteen minutes to get into, but years to a lifetime to get out of?" I didn't hear that saying until now, and it is a true statement. I had to learn that the hard way. We ended up in another homeless shelter in downtown Atlanta called the Salvation Army. Chuck had found a job in Marietta, so I had to take him back and forth from Atlanta to Marietta every day. We finally found a place to live in Marietta, Cobb County. It was a small apartment two bedrooms inside of a four unit building. There was a whole circle of these building. We were happy to finally have a place called home.

He would go to work and I was a stay at home mom with my two kids. I would send my son off to school and it would be me and

my three-year-old daughter at home. I would sometimes sit at the window to look outside. I loved to just look outside and just stare at the trees as the wind blew. This particular day I noticed someone moving in upstairs, it was a young girl and some old man. I couldn't tell if it was her dad or her grandfather. So I just watched them as they moved their stuff in. I thought it would be nice to have someone to talk to. I was an only child so I was used to being by myself. Having friends wasn't really a must, but if you spoke to me I would definitely speak back. I wasn't the type of person that would walk up to people and start a conversation. So, I just watched from the window. I guess it was safe to say I was like a neighborhood watch cause I kind of knew what would go down in the neighborhood during the day. I guess I can say I was just nosey too, lol.

A couple of days after the young lady moved in upstairs, I noticed the old man leaving and not soon after that I heard a knock at the door. I opened the door and the young lady that I watched moving in was at my door. She introduced herself and said her name was Amy. She proceeds to ask if she could sit with me and watch tv because she didn't have her tv yet. I agreed, I also thought that it would be nice to have a friend to talk to. So, from that day forward we became friends. I also found out that the old man was not her grandfather or dad, but her man, hummm, yeah.

I'm not sure how that worked, but ok if you like It, I love it, I guess. After finding that out I asked no more questions about their sex life. I had a thousand and one questions going through my brain. I really did want to know about their sex life thou. I had wondered if he could still perform. Could this old man still get it up? You know what? Y'all don't judge me? If you would have seen the same old man that I saw walking in the building with this cane and looking like he just came out the senior citizen home, you would be wondering too. Amy and I became close especially since she was my first friend that I made in Georgia. She kept me company while my husband was at work. I introduced her to Chuck and we all smoked marijuana together. After a while Chuck started bugging me

about having a baby. I really didn't want any more kids. I had my girl and boy. I most definitely didn't want anymore, but he had a certain way of manipulating me. I didn't know it back then, but as I look back on it now, he did it a lot. I had birth control in and I remember going to the doctor to have it taken out so we could try having a baby, even though I didn't want to. At the time I was still taking Percocet's even thou I didn't need them anymore. I was still addicted to them. I would go into the pain management center and say that I was hurting so I could still take them. When I got pregnant I stopped taking them. I remember me wanting to look for a church to go to. I felt like I was missing somethings in my life. What If I could find out what it was by going to church.

I had been taught a little and knew about the man upstairs, but I didn't know him quit yet. I stared wondering about him and the kind of life that I was really supposed to be living, thinking and wondering was there a better life for me out in this world. So, I found this church down the street from our home, and we started going. It was a really nice church. I loved the pastor and the first lady. We walked to church on Sundays, and then I would come home and cook. I remember us getting really close with the pastor and is wife they were very helpful. I started praising and worshiping at home while Chuck was at work. I mean I really had nothing else to do and I needed answers and clarity so that's what I did.

One night I had a dream that I was taking a nap during the day and I saw myself sleeping. I was wearing some gray capris and a red tank top. I heard Chuck yelling for me to wake up. His voice was coming from the living room. In this dream I woke up and ran to the living and as I entered the living room there where three police officers standing there with him in hand cuffs. When I looked down at my stomach I looked like I was about six months pregnant and then I woke up. When I woke up, I was terrified about this dream, so I told Chuck about it. He got mad at me and said I was burning bread on him and walked out.

I was pregnant and getting bigger. There was this one Sunday

that I will never forget. We argued dead in the middle of church. When the collection plate came around to us I put in everything we had. Boy was he mad. He yelled at me right in the middle of church service. "Don't put all of our money in church!" He then proceeded to try and take the money out of the plate, because I had never let the money actually fall from my hand he grabbed my hand away from the plate and I pulled my hand back to the plate. Finally I won this battle and took the money out of his hand and hurriedly passed the plate before he could try to grab it again. When I tell you the feeling of being yelled at in church in the middle of service was embarrassing. Everybody turning around and looked. The pastor stopped his message, and looking up. It was too much. I was so humiliated I didn't even know how to talk to the pastor and his wife after church that day. I just walked out. So after the episode in church he cussed me out all the way up the block. He didn't have a job anymore and we hand no money because I decided to put all the money in the offering. I didn't think about how we were going to survive without any money. I really I think he was just mad because it was his weed money. He couldn't smoke or buy any. I put his weed money in church. My feelings where if I can't smoke because I am pregnant then you can't either. He was mad. As we continued to walk up the street with him yelling at me, his phone rang. It was someone offering him a side job to make eight hundred dollars for the next day. That phone call made him happy, and it was way more money offered then what we, well I, put in the offering plate at church.

Chuck never stayed at the same job for a long time. He ended up getting a new job at some nice restaurant. And it was all good for a while. One day we were both home and I was taking a nap while he was in the living room listing to music. I remember being in a deep sleep and sleeping so good. At six months pregnant all you want to do is eat and sleep. As I slept, I heard him yelling my name and it felt like it was a dream. I opened my eyes and realized that he was really calling my name. So I jumped up and ran in the living

room and there it was my dream was playing out play by play to the tea. My living room was then filled with police officers. As they handcuffed him he yelled, "You set me up! You set me up!" At that moment, I didn't understand why he was saying that I set him up until I looked down at what I was wearing. It was the gray capris and the red tank top. My belly was the same size that it was in my dream.

When I tell you that I felt like I was in the Twilight Zone. I didn't know what to do or say. They took him and locked him up for skipping out on probation. Yes, he left St. Louis without permission from his probation officer. He, well I guess we, were on the run. When I tell you all I could do was cry. At that time I was so confused about what was happening to me. My dream just played out step by step in front of my face. I had told him the dream six months prior. I could only assume that he never forgot the dream that I told him. That's why he was saying I set him up. At that time, I called the only person I could I call, the pastor of the church that we were attending. He was such a great man of God. He went down to the jail to see what was going on. The pastor told me that they were going to be sending Chuck back to St. Louis so he could answer to a judge there. Later that night Chuck called and we talked. I told him that I wanted to stay in Georgia. I didn't want to go back to St. Louis, but he wasn't having it. The pastor had talked to him about the same thing and my pastor and his wife was willing to take me in and video the birth of his son.

After Chuck was able to take care of everything in St. Louis he could come back to Georgia and I would be there waiting for him when he returned. He kept saying no to me and the pastor. I often wondered what my life would have been like if I stayed in Georgia anyway. Being around the pastor and his wife, would my life have turned out different? Or would it have been the same? I definitely wondered about that time to time. When I tell you I hated the mere thought of going back to a place that was so traumatizing. I cried so hard, and the fact that I had to leave everything behind was crazy

and hurtful. I wasted no time. I got to work with trying to clean as much of the apartment out that I could and packing as much of the kids clothes and mine that I can carry on a greyhound. I gave it one more attempt to get him to let me stay. He wasn't budging at all. He told me if I didn't get my butt on that bus I was grass. So, I did. I carried so much stuff along with being six months pregnant with two kids and bags and bags of clothes. I got on that bus and headed back to the place I dreaded so much.

 *Chapter Seven*

On the bus ride back all I could do was wonder where I was going to stay. How were we going to make it. I was making phone calls while on the bus to try and find somewhere for me and the kids to stay. I was in luck because my girl that I used to ride with saved the day. Lucy had set up shop in the Lou. The Lou was a short way of saying St. Louis. She had moved out of the small town we had once lived in. She offered my kids and me a place to live, so I took it. Let me say this, no one in my family or my friends liked Chuck at all. I was used to being with him and having him around, Lucy was this tall white girl with long blond hair and pretty blue eyes. She was very beautiful and she wasn't too fond of Chuck either. She was kind of glad that being around him was limited.

Chuck had to stay in this place that looked like a prison, but he was allowed to come outside walls on certain days but had to go back in at certain times. It was like a halfway house kind of. And the feeling of entrapment with Chuck was on a whole different level since we were back in St. Louis. the fact that he needed to know where I was, and who I was with, was very over whelming to go through every day. There was one thing that Chuck dangled over my head. That one thing that frightened me to no ended. So whenever I talked about me not being happy and wanting to end it he would dangle that one thing and he knew it would shut me up. This thing was something I would carry for years. It was a secret that only he knew. When I tell you I was honest with him about everything in my past, he took this thang and used it to hold me hostage to him and only him. To think that this was his whole plan all along to entrap me. He manipulated me into believing that I would never be brave or have the audacity to be strong enough to leave him. I believe he thought of me as being a weak individual, which at that time of my life I was. I was desperate for someone to love me and

protect me in a way my parents didn't.

I think letting everyone know that I was back was the hardest thing to do. I banked on not never coming back to this place. A few days after being there I saw my mom and her response to me being pregnant was she didn't believe that she could love this grandbaby as much as she loved the others. That ended up being a lie because till this day that baby is her heart. But anyway. I stayed with Lucy for a while until my mom's boyfriend Jack helped me find a place to live. It was a house over in Berkley MO. The kids and I moved in, and Chuck eventually got out for good and was off probation as long as he stayed out of trouble. I think I was about eight months pregnant. This house was right on time for the coming of the baby.

The baby came, and Chuck finally got a job. We ended up getting a truck, a nice one too. I overheard him telling people that, it was his truck, and that I had no say so over anything. The truth was I always paid for everything even when we had that apartment in Marietta. I did have some income every month it wasn't a lot, but it paid for whatever roof we had. It most definitely wasn't his truck he didn't even have a license to drive it. as I am writing this, I am realizing that I was involved with men that didn't have a license to drive anything but swore that they ran everything. The truth was the only thing they had was a license to run was their mouths. They were barely educated enough to run that. Anyways let's get back to the story. I had the baby, and everything was ok for a while.

Chuck, and I loved to throw gatherings. Mother's Day that year we had a big gathering and we had a blast. After everybody left it was my mom, Jack, Chuck and I at the house. I was sitting there minding my own business and the next thing I know my mother punches me in the back of my head. I didn't know why. Chuck was livid when I tell you it broke out into the biggest argument. Chuck most definitely had my back and wouldn't allow anyone to put their hands on me. My mom wanted me to let her and Jack stay with me, but at this point I refused to let her stay in my house and get abused when she needed a punching bag. Yes, she was still an alcoholic. I

could never understand why she hated me like this, to just walk up behind me and do this.

I wouldn't let her live or stay with me, so she leaves and walks up the street. As I stood on my porch smoking a cigarette, I looked up the street I see her standing there on the phone. I wasn't trying to figure out what she was doing. At the moment I was too mad to try and figure out what she was doing. The next thing I know Berkley police comes flying down the street. Chuck and I look at each other like what is happening. The police get out and say they got a phone call that we had pounds and pounds of marijuana in our house. Now I have to stop here when I tell you at the time, I was livid. As I am writing this right now I am cracking up because what she did was stupid on so many levels. The police didn't search our home and by the way we didn't have pounds of marijuana in our home. The police said it sounded like the woman that called had been drinking. I pointed up the street and told the officer what had just happened between my mom and I. The police ended up leaving.

I felt like she was trying to get my kids taken from me. So, let me say this. She has asked a lot throughout my life, to let her have one of my kids, and not to have one to file taxes on, she meant to have and raise as her own. SMH, what!!!???? Who does that? She made that sound like she was in a candy store or something. Most of the time when people give their kids to someone, that person is more well off or more established then they are. How do I give a kid away to someone that is at the same level as me? I wasn't established but I was giving my kids the best life that I could. Please understand, life and raising kids is not like you going to the store and buying a coffee maker. A coffee makers comes with an instruction manual, life does not.

So anyways after that I was very angry at my mom for what she did. Being who I was I did forgive her, but I was damaged by it. It did nothing but create an even bigger wound then what I already had at the time. Looking back on this particular incident, it has made me not to trust anyone. If my mom could do this to me, no one would

have a problem just throwing me to the dogs. I often think over the mommy and daddy issues that I once carried, I say once, because now it's not as hard. I still see the lack of commitment, trust, and mother issues that I may or may not have when it comes to my kids, I don't want to bleed over my children like my mother and father did me. How do I do better than them? How do I change the effect of my traumas so there are not passed on to my kids? How can I be the best mother I can be? The traumas that I have endured were passed down to me. I got what was handed down to my parents. How do I make sure these traumas aren't continually passed down and continue to overtake this family of my kids, kids? Have I already passed some trauma down to them? I worry about this as a mother every day. I have always had one eye open to people that just claimed to want to help me out of the kindness of their heart and wonder what their alternative motives are.

Now I try to look at all of this differently. There are some good people out here in life that just honestly want to help. I am definitely not writing this book to put people on blast or to talk bad about anyone. The thought that I am not the only one in the world that has dealt with trauma like this and has walked though most of their life being bled on our bleeding on others brings some comfort. I don't believe that my parents knew any better. They exhibited what they had seen their entire life. I have learned that it could take eighteen to two-hundred and fifty-four days to create a new habit. Sixty-six days for a new behavior to become natural, so what does that mean when you go a couple of decades of the same thing? There is no wonder why we're all imitating, and being taught to cover it up with this fancy pretty rug.

My heart goes out to my mother and father for trying to overcome their past, but I was bleed over so bad that I lost so much in life. I am going to do what my family has not been able to do and that is share my pain with the world. And, use my shame as a testimony to help encourage others to break free of being a victim. I have prayed and prayed to God to help me discover my purpose. In

writing this book I think I have found it. I have woken up from sleep walking in life, now it is time for me to walk and navigate through these traumas and the pain. I had an awaking and came to the understanding of the cause and effect. This has made me want to take accountability and be transparent about my life. We often go into "he did this and she did that, my family did this my mom did that" and I am a victim. We often wonder why we haven't made it anywhere in life. We are too busy pointing fingers and asking why. We haven't gone anywhere in life or done anything meaningful with it. We all have and are able to make decisions in this thing called life and it's up to us individually to decide if we will be a victim or victorious. Guess what I am deciding? I am more than a conquer and I will triumph through and over this. I know I am not the only person who has had trauma and pain interfere with their life.

🎬 Chapter Eight

When I think about my parents and what they encountered as they were growing up, I see how they both got the short end of the stick. It makes my heart hurt for them and to think I spent most of my life being mad and angry at them for what they did or allowed to happen in my life. I blamed them for every wrong turn and decision that I made in life. Somehow, they were the ones who placed me in horrible situations, but I made the decisions. I had to learn and understand that my parents did and showed me what they were taught. So now the challenge and the question is can I unteach myself the things I was shown and teach myself from the fairytale parents I envisioned for myself? I wanted to give this to my children.

So how could I really be mad at them if this was something that they suffered also. Hey, I don't have this answer yet, but just giving my thoughts. Now my dad has done well for his self. He had been clean of drugs for years and had been traveling as a welder for years. I am so very proud of the man he is today. It's not easy or fun to dig yourself out of a lifetime of trauma and stand up and take accountability for actions you did when you bleed over everyone including you children because you inherited these issues from your parents. I often wonder what my great grandparent's parents did to cause all these traumas to take root. Where did it all come from.

I do apologize my thinking runs deep sometimes. My mother, I believe worries me the most, because it's like she's in this deep hole and my arms aren't long enough to pull her out. I love my mother with all my heart and it's hard to watch her dig herself deeper and deeper in this never ending pit. She just got tired of trying to get out. It's almost like she has no more fight left in her. Her fight has been at everyone else instead fighting to live. When I say live, I mean really live freely, no longer as a victim. Some of us at some point, or well I will just say for me, I have wanted to give up on life on

multiple occasions. I have told my story of wanting to die and took that action of really trying to end my life. I got for real sacred when death was at the door knocking. I can't help this right now, but I sound like little Richard keep knocking but you can't come in lol. Ok, sorry I couldn't help that. That was what it was like for real. Death was knocking but I was too scared to let it in. BUT GOD had other plans for me even in the mist of all the bad decisions I was making and probably will still make. This time I won't make them without walking in accountability for my own actions.

This part was solely about me and the decisions I have made in life. I hope you guys are ok with me being totally transparent with you. I want to tell you all the tea about things I have done in life. So, kick back and get your comfy blanket and get you a cup of tea cause I'm about to tell all. Well not all. Because I would like to have another book after this one. I will tell you most of the tea. You can pour a full cup of it because you'll need it. Let's get with it.

The situation where my mom called the police on me, we moved on from it , but. I'd like to say it left me feeling some type of way. I continued talking to my mom and let her come back over, but not without a bit of a distance thought. Not too long after that I got sick, because all I did was smoke weed and eat up stuff that wasn't good for me. Let me mention I was like three hundred and something pounds at the time. I was so depressed about life. But I ended up being diagnose as a diabetic. I remember going into the hospital with an over six-hundred sugar level. My friend Lucy helped me to become more active, move around and exercise more. I ended up losing some of the weight and not needing to take the medications. It took hard work and changing my diet.

Just when I thought I was starting to get ahead in life everything broke out we were behind in bills and couldn't afford our truck note. We were slowly losing the house. We had to trying and find a way to save everything we had. So as always, we came up with what we thought then was a great idea. We could sell drugs. Not just any kind of drugs, but we thought we would sell crack cocaine. We could take

it out to the town I knew best to sell it and make a little profit from it. So, we did. We found someone to buy large amounts from in St. Louis and took the drugs to the city I grow up in and sold it. We found someone's house to be in and that's where we cut everything down, bagged it up, and sold it. Please understand that I am not proud of that at all. That was a low point in my life, and that wasn't the only low point I had.

This was all a part of the bad decisions I have made in my past when I blamed the world and everyone in it but myself. So I thought I was doing something back then. We really had no idea what we were doing. Chuck knew a little something and I knew a little something. Chuck didn't have a license so I drove and carried the drugs on me. When I say I carried the drugs on me I mean I had to put all of what we had in my privet part. I remember being scared that all the bags would bust and I would die of an overdose. How would I know if they did burst. I wouldn't until it was too late. We would pull up to the house we used to setup and everybody would already be there waiting on us.

We pulled up and would grab whatever we had brought with us. They would clear the way as we walked in the door and went straight to the back room to break everything down and start handing out whatever they wanted to order. This is one part of my life that I don't like admitting to. Yes there is more that I really don't want to put in here. We have all done things that we aren't proud of, things that we feel would bring a load of shame over us. I know I have. I will most definitely tell the truth and shame the devil. After our Bonnie and Clyde moments of drug dealing eventually, we did stop. At that time, I think I felt like I was this big-time drug lord like on cocaine cowboys or something lol. I didn't like where I had to carry it sometimes. I don't have to spell it out for you. I think Chuck and I felt like a couple of Bonnie and Clyde's being that ride or die couple. But in reality, that was not how a marriage should have been at all. And still as every day came, I always had in the back of my mind that I was married to two men.

After the days of driving a getaway car and being big drug lords and running from the law lol, we retired that profession. I remember one day storms came through the St. Louis area and a tornado was coming. I mean the drills where going off and the sky's where green and all you could hear was this loud noise like a train. Now I knew what that meant, because one of my favorite moves then was *Twister*. Man when I tell you that movie taught me so much about tornados it wasn't funny. So I started running around the house opening windows so no windows would break. Chuck and I started taking the kids downstairs so they could be safe. We were just trying to grab everything that we could use just in case we got trapped in the basement.

When we all finally made it to the basement Chuck and I realized that we hadn't grabbed any water. So, I ran up the stairs to grab some and I guess I was so distracted by being scared that when I came back down the stairs all I had was a cigar and some weed to smoke. I really thought that was a part of my survival kit without water smh. The things I did then. But by that time Chuck and I had realized what I had in my hand the whole house was shaking really bad. Thankfully, our house didn't get hit. But when it was over, we walked outside and the whole block was messed up. There where trees everywhere and we noticed that the neighbor was missing half of his roof. That was so frightening to go through that my heart goes out to anyone who has been through such a catastrophic situation like tornado's.

During the time of Chuck and I, I believed I tried to leave him on multiple occasions, I always went back. Let me ask you a question real fast. Have you ever been in a position where you have grown to love someone and you know that they are not for you and, you know you need to walkway but, you have gotten so used to them being there next to you, but also know that the relationship is toxic and needs to come to an end? Yeah, that's what that relationship was with Chuck. I had grown to love him, because as I said in the beginning that I wasn't in love with him. He was just there. The

person who gave me a sense of protection. I felt this way because my parents weren't doing it.

They thought they were protecting I guess, but I don't think they thought they needed to protect me from them. Their bleeding became my blood that I was bleeding out. I remember packing up the kids one day and telling Chuck that I was going to drop the kids off at my mom's house and I would be back. Yeah, I had no thought of coming back to that house. At least that's what I thought. I got some of the kids things together and left and went to the house that mom and Jack had. I stayed there for a while, and trust that didn't go without him blowing up my phone for hours. Eventually, I went back and we tried to save the house that we were living in. We weren't able to save it, so we started cleaning out the house. I tried to find another house to move into but couldn't. At this point in life I felt like a failure, a failure to my kids and myself. I didn't know what to do to get myself out of this situation. So I called my cousin, Jen.

Now I want to believe that everyone has people that were so close to the family that you claimed them as family. That's what Jen and her family were to our entire family. We had had been around each other for so long that we grow up calling each other family. So anyways I called Jen and she offered us all a place to stay, for a little while at least. So we packed up everything and went to stay at her house. I had started looking for a job and couldn't find one. I hadn't worked since I had got sick a few years back. It was so hard to find one. I wasn't even getting any interviews. It was like I was being black balled. So, no jobs even Chuck he wasn't working at the time. Eventually something came in for him, but I wasn't having any luck at all. It was like the world was against every move Chuck and I made. We were getting pushback at every turn we made.

So I started secretly talking to someone else. Now before I tell you what I did and was doing, let me say this. For many years of my life I was lost, confused, hurt, broken. I was at a crossroads in life like we often have and like everyone I did a lot of things I am most

definitely not proud of. I started sneaking away from husband number two to meet up with a girl. Yes I said a girl. I was curious about the other sex, so I thought that since all of my relationships with men were horrible and maybe the reason being was I was supposed to be with a woman. So I remember going to meet up with her at this point just trying to see if this was where I belonged.

So I remember trying to take another attempt at leaving Chuck and to hopefully not return again. Like before I packed up the kids and my things. I told him that I was leaving him and that this wasn't working for me. Oh, he was furious. Even though he tried to stop me my cousin Jen stopped him and told him to let her cool off. I had already put the kids in the truck and was backing up when I see this two-hundred-sixty-five pound running back charging at the truck. Shhhhhhh! That was enough to scare the crap out of anyone. I hurried up and threw the truck in drive and pulled out the parking lot. When I tell you that I have never seen a big man like that running so fast. I hit the gas even harder and by this time I thought he had given up, but as I looked out the passenger side window he was right there running and looking at me and screaming at me to stop. The look on my face was so terrified that I looked at the mph gauge and I was going like forty-five miles per hour.

Now in my head, I'm like what the hell? Why and how is he running so fast? I accelerated even faster and now I'm thinking if I look back over there and he is still running at the side of the truck I just wouldn't even know what to do with that. So I took one more look and if he was still able to make eye contact with me, I would just pull over at that point. When I looked he was then at the back window so that meant his legs was getting tired. I accelerated once more and he was then in the rearview mirror, and I kept going. Not even all the way down the street my phone rings. It's my cousin calling. I hesitate to answer the phone I just waited to the last ring to pick up the phone cause I just already know what she is going to say to me.

I pulled over at a gas station down the street and answered the

phone. She was like, "you know you are wrong for this right!" In my head I'm thinking no he is wrong cause I am terrified, at the fact that I just watched a two-hundred and sixty-five pound man run as fast as the car I was driving. Now that was wrong. I didn't say anything I was thinking, I just listened to what she had to say and hung up. I sat for a minute in the parking lot and just cried, because I didn't know what to do about my life. My life was chaotic and I didn't know how to begin to fix it. So I went back to Jen's house.

Chuck and I talked and we decide to go back to our house. We didn't formally have an eviction notice yet, so we went back and stayed there for a little while longer. I did eventually leave and stayed with my mom until I found another apartment. I left Chuck at the old house, and I moved in with the girl I had started dating. Yes, we moved in together, and at the same time Chuck kept calling trying to get me to come back to him. He kept trying to talk me into to us going back to Georgia. I loved being in Georgia it was something about that place that gave me relief from my past. It was like in Georgia I didn't have all the pressures of the things that I endured. So, I kind of kept what he was saying in the back of my mind.

The girl I was dating, her name was Toni. We moved in together in this little apartment in downtown St. Louis. I remember one morning she was gone and it was just me and my kids at the house. I was standing at the window looking out at all the snow. I did this often I would stand at the window to look out at the trees. This particular morning it was beautiful outside and snow was everywhere. Just gazing out and pondering about life I heard this deep voice saying to me GET OUT, YOU DON'T BELONG HERE, GO NOW. When I tell you the absolute fear of GOD came over my whole body and I was terrified. When I tell you I ran, packed my stuff, and called Chuck. I said, "OK I'm in. let's go back to Georgia." I loaded my truck up and left. And I felt bad because I never told Toni why I up and left.

Please let me explain and say this I have no problem with

anyone that may be gay or bi but I just don't think or believe that, it's for me. I am not here to judge anyone. What you choose to do with your life is not my business. I have my belief in GOD the LORD, JESUS, the HOLY SPIRIT. But at that time, I was not reading or worshiping at all I was still new to and trying to get an understanding about God. He still spoke to me and had me leave that relationship.

Chuck and I hit the road and I didn't look back. I remember her calling me as I was going down the highway. I felt so bad, but not that I left, but the fact I didn't tell her that I was leaving, and I just left. When I tell you that I was so lost in life, Can't you tell? Yeah, tell the truth. So as we are riding down the highway I called my old friend up Amy to see if she was still located in Georgia. She was. We most definitely stayed in touch off and on while I was back home. I wanted to see her when we made it there. When we got into Georgia, we got a hotel and rested up.

 *Chapter Nine*

The next day we went to see Amy. Our kids where happy to see each other and we definitely enjoyed the visit. She invited us to go to church that Sunday. When we got back to our hotel room, she called and asked us if we could come and stay with her until we found a place. We packed our stuff up went to her house the next day. We stayed with Amy for a little while I think three or four months, and then we moved into our own house. This time we started to attend church and try to change things. Chuck found a job that was like an hour away. Why he did that I will never know? We tried to make things work and they did for a little while.

I remember our tire being so bad on the truck and I was scared to drive it. Mind you this entire time I was with him he never had a driver's license. I had to take him wherever he needed to go. The tire was bald and we had no money, but I had to go pick him up from work. I made it there and on the way back the tire blew on the highway. We had to call someone to pick us up and leave our truck on the highway. We had just given offering in church and we had no money. We called the pastor at the time and he told us there was nothing he could do for us, but he did come and pick us up from the side of the highway, took us home and dropped us off.

Not knowing what to do at the time we paced the floors trying to figure out what to do. I remember the next day the water got shut off. So we didn't have any running water either. We went back to check on the truck and get it moved off the side of the highway people had broken into it and taken everything out of it from under the hood. I think I lost it at that point. When I say we were going threw it. We was all at the same time, it was like there was no break in between all the crazies. All I could do was cry and pray. I remember after going a whole week without water we finally was able to get it back on. We still lost our vehicle. Two-weeks I cried

in the shower and just kept asking God can you even hear me, telling him that I felt like I was praying for nothing. After those two weeks of praying the same prayer in the shower and just sitting in the bathroom crying, I went to church that Sunday. This lady at the time I didn't know said, "I was told to tell you that he says that he can hear you". My eyes got big, and I said "what did you say?" And she said it again and then added "you keep asking him if he hears you and he told me to tell you that he can hear you." When I tell you my faith shot out the roof and I cried even more. At that point I knew he was listening to me when I spoke to him. I thought change would come asap, but no that's not how that works. It does take time for things to come into the physical realm. So I tried so hard to work throw this messed up situation that I was in. I was still smoking weed but I soon stopped.

So let me tell you this funny story about how and why I stopped. Do you remember the year I think it was 2013 or 2014 when we had the blood moons? Yeah I remember not really knowing about them like that. It was my first year really trying to be devoted to God. So anyways that night of the first blood moon I was high as a kite. I had just finished smoking and saw somethings on the internet about this blood moon. I started watching them. I don't think that's a good combination for anyone to be high as a kite and then start looking at testimonies of how the Lord was coming back on the night of the blood moon, which happened to be that night. When I tell you I was running around the house trying to get under the bed and splashing water on face trying to figure out how to get sober before the blood moon peaked at its highest.

This was not funny at the time, when I tell you from that night right there, I have carried the fear of the Lord. I did not smoke anymore after that night cause if he would have come, he would have caught me slippn. After that we ended up losing that house too. We went back to stay with Amy. We stayed there for a while and while we were there Amy decided that she was going to move back home. We ended up finding another place right down the street from

Amy's house. We moved in and Chuck ended up finding a really good job as at city worker. He started to get abusive to me. He was slamming up against the wall and screaming at me. He was mad because I didn't have a job, and at the same time he couldn't keep one. When he didn't have one, I was the one that made sure rent was paid. During this time, I was still going to church and he didn't like it at all. He stopped going to church with me and started telling me that he believed in a higher power, but not exactly Jesus. We were in this house for a while. Things got a little better but not really. I remember one day he was yelling at me, and I went to take the baby outside for some air. He locked us both out the house. My other kids were at school.

Chuck definitely made other people feel like and know that he was abusing me. And he did sometimes but mostly mentally. I started going to church every time I got the opportunity to. I joined the choir, went to bible study, anything at church that would get me out the house and out of his sight. I was going to church so much that he accused me of sleeping with all the deacons of the church even though they were all past the age of sixty. Apparently, I was sleeping with all four of them if you left it to him. I really wasn't allowed to really go anywhere like that. He didn't even like it when I went to church. I remember when I finally sat down and told him I wanted us to go our separate ways, he said no and took my phone and kept it for three or four days.

I had become very close with this older lady at church and she became a great friend named was Ms. Gina. I also became friends with this young lady name, well we will call her Tiff. She actually became one of my greatest friends. We are still friends until this very day. But anyways the older lady at the church that I became good friends with stopped by my house cause she had been trying to call me. Chuck had took my phone so she wanted to stop by and check on me and make sure I was ok. This is why I say Chuck gave off the impression that he was a little abusive. I already knew what happened with the girlfriend that he beat. I definitely tried to tread

little when it came to making him mad. I think some of his anger came from me trying to and kept running off, so he always watched my every move. And I don't know why I kept taking my dumb self-back cause I knew at some point that this was not love. I believe it was control and manipulation.

And during this time where he had my phone I could go to church but I could only take one kid with me so it reassured him that I would come back. He knew that if I took all the kids with me I probably wouldn't come back. He would tell me often that nobody wants me and if I left him again he would tell the police that I was married to two men and I would get locked up and never see my kids again. He was really good at putting the fear in me that was always one of the reasons I would go back because he made sure I didn't forget that. When I stopped smoking, he told me that I had to keep smoking. We had nothing in common because that was all we had together. As I was going through all of this in the back of my mind I am praying that God would give me the strength to leave and never look back.

Trying to come up with a plan to leave was hard, because I knew he would be watching like a hawk this time. He knew he had me cornered because I was in a state with no family. Who was going to rescue me. I didn't know anyone like that I didn't have anyone's house to run to and nobody here to have my back. Even back home my uncles knew him, but the way Chuck would carry his self no one could touch him. He wished they would try. He was a big guy and was a running back for a college team back home until he got hurt and had to leave the team. The older lady Ms. Gina at church could tell something was going on but I would never say anything.

She would just always say please don't hesitate to call me if you need anything, and she would look at Chuck if he was around. Now Ms. Gina was grade A crazy, but a very sweet lady and would do anything for anybody at any time. I got so much closer with some of the people there at the church I was attending and the pastor I loved so much like he was my dad and he moved as such too. I

remember in a last attempt to save my marriage we counselled with the pastor. Now this was my last attempt, but I made sure he didn't know that's how I felt. So, we had counseling and at this point I really didn't think that anything was going to help our situation.

Tyra Smith

 *Chapter Ten*

So let me tell you guys a quick story about something that happened when I lived in St. Louis. One day my mom calls and tells me she needed me to help her and Jack move. They had moved mostly everything except their bed. They needed me to help move their bed to the new house. At the time I had this gold SUV that had the bars at the top carry strapped down loads. So, I agreed to help. I go over there and Jack straps the bed to the top of the truck. I walk around the truck to make sure it was tied down. We all get in the truck my mom, Jack and I. We pull off to head to the new house, which was not far maybe about a ten minute drive. It was just a couple of blocks so I had no problem helping them.

We're going down the street we're having a great talk and laughing on the way. I was taking my time and driving slow, maybe about twenty-five to thirty miles per hour. You know how people get mad and start honking there horn because you're going too slow. Yeah, that's how slow I was going. Anyways we are letting them hunk and all of a sudden I hear a noise "boom,bammm!" I looked out my review mirror and the mattress that was on top had flown off knocking this mad off of his Moped. He was on the ground. I slammed on my brakes and jump out the truck to see and make sure the guy was ok. I helped him get up and when I turn around the police were already coming down the street. When I tell ya'll I was so scared. There were no words to express the amount of fear that was racing through my body. The look that was on my face would have said that I just killed someone in cold blood murder and got caught in the middle of the act. I mean the man did fly about five-feet back from his Moped.

Standing there in amazement and shock of what just happened and the police pulling up, I turned around and was looking for my mom and Jack. The police come up to me and the man and ask what

happened. The only thing I could say at the moment was I don't know. I mean I know but I'm just in shock right now. I proceed to tell the officer that I was helping my mom move and her boyfriend tied the mattress to the top of the truck. We thought it was tied up tight. I continued to explain that I was driving as slow as possible and that I wasn't going any faster than thirty miles per hour and the mattress flew off. The police officer ask, "So if your moving your mom is she here with you?" At this point I look behind me and took one step backwards to see if they were in the truck. I noticed that neither one of them were in the truck. I begin to look around like I was trying to find where's waldo, and what do you know? I see my mom and Jack standing on the corner two blocks aways looking down at me and watching me like they were innocent bystanders witnessing an accident. Let me tell you I was furious on the inside.

So anyways I ended up getting a ticket for improperly tying down the mattress and for injuring a bystander. I don't know how that was possible, because he wasn't standing around he was riding his Moped, but ok. I get in the car and I ride down the street to pick up my mom and Jack. All I could do was be mad and ask them why they left me by myself. There answer to why was, "We had warrants man!" My thought at the moment was I should have left yall standing on the corner and acted like I didn't see you or know you. That's what they had just done to me. I had to tell that because when I think back on it I burst out laughing. I just couldn't laugh at that moment. I ended up getting the bed there for them.

Let me tell you the awesome thing about this story. Months later I called to get my court date and I missed the date. I didn't have a warrant yet so I was able to pay the fee to reschedule the date. They rescheduled, and months later I forgot about it again. I called to see how much it would be to take the warrant off and low and be hold I had no warrant. There was no ticket on file for my name and birth date. Praise God ya'll I was so excited about that.

In the last chapter I left off with talking about my husband and us getting counseling. It was obvious that it wasn't going to work. I

was right it didn't. I have a question for you, have you ever been with or in a relationship where every move yall tried to make together as a couple just didn't work? Every corner you turned there was a brick wall stopping you from getting around the corner. Well, I hope some of you guys said yes. That was my husband and I all the way. Now I want to tell you my secret that I was carrying for years with me. This was a secret that my husband made sure that I stayed bound to him with. He used it to keep me in my place and make sure I would never try to or actually get the courage to leave him. When I left St. Louis and moved to Georgia, I married Chuck, and it wasn't really by choice it was from fear of Chuck. Chuck knew everything about me. I had told him everything. I was married to two men for six to seven years. When I say I thought I was stuck for real. That's how I felt, dealing with that thought of being married to two men for that long had hunted me every day, most days.

Some days I was able to push it to the back of my mind, but most days I couldn't. I knew it wasn't right and I didn't know the first thing of how to fix it or get out of it. I struggled with this for years, it wasn't till I started praying more and seeking God more and asking him what to do and how to fix it. So first let me says this. When Chuck and I got married, I never changed my last name. I didn't change my name with my first husband. With both husbands I felt trapped to them. I could have stood strong and walked off. But that fear had me shook to where I entrapped myself. Yes, I said entrapped myself. So the last couple of months that I was with Chuck all I did was pray and praise. I needed an answer.

I needed to know what to do and how to do it. One day I was standing in the window talking to God and I heard this loud voice saying YOU ARE NOT SUPPOSED TO BE HERE. I was so terrified I didn't know if he was talking about being in the house or maybe I wasn't supposed to be In Georgia. So, I asked, "where should I be Lord and what do I do? If you give me a way to leave I will leave." I also knew I was scared of leaving Chuck. He just put so much fear in me it was crazy. I didn't think about how the devil

tries to keep us trapped in bondage, but I know that now. I told God to make a way for me to leave and I would. So, remember I told you that he would not let me too far out of his sight because I told him I wasn't happy and I wanted to leave.

Well a few days later after I asked God to please make away for me to leave, he did. Somehow this man got a check in the mail from the last job he had. What do you know he had to leave the house to walk up the street and cash it. That meant he had to leave me there. When I tell ya'll I played that card so good. I mean I had too otherwise he would have never left me there alone. He came to me and said " Hey babe I just got a check in the mail, so I have to walk up the street and cash it."

"Ok babe, what do you want me to cook for dinner?" I asked him.

"It doesn't matter." He replied and walked out the door.

As he walked out the door, I was watching out the blinds for him to walk around the bend so he wouldn't be in sight. As soon as I seen him disappear around the corner I started throwing clothes in a trash bag. While I was putting things in the trash bag I called Ms. Gina and told her that I was calling a cab and going to a hotel. I would call her when I got there. I didn't want her to worry about me because she did she checked on me a lot. When I would talk to her it was almost like she knew the kind of abuse that was going on. But as I was telling her this, she immediately said, "I am leaving work I'm on the way." When I tell you she made it there in no time. As I was waiting on her my body was filling up so fast with fear that he was going to walk around that door and catch me.

I was watching out the blinds to see if I would see him coming around the corner. My whole body was shaking. I had kids asking me what we was doing as I was putting their clothes on them and I couldn't give them an answer at that moment. I was more concerned with getting back to the window so I could see if he was coming. Shortly after getting the kids clothes on Ms. Gina pulled up. When I tell you I had to run and put the kids in the car, run back to the

house and try to get as many bags as I could to take with us. This was crazy and scary. At the same time I just hoped and prayed that he wouldn't walk around the corner and see us. I knew from past experience that he could run his butt off if he needed to. He would probably catch up to the car. I was able to get at least three bags of clothes and I hear Ms. Gina say leave the rest and come on before he comes. We will try to get the rest another time.

So I got In the car and just cried I was so terrified. I was trembling and the only thing Ms. Gina could say was you made the right decision and it's going to be ok. All I could do was look in the rear-view mirror with so much fear. Just because I was in the car with Ms. Gina didn't mean I was safe or at least that's how I felt at the time. Ms. Gina seen the amount of fear I had and she knew there was nothing she could say that would make me feel safe at that moment. She took me back to her house and told me she had to go back to work, so she dropped me off.

Now Ms. Gina lived far from where I had lived Chuck and I had lived off of Cleveland Avenue and she lived in Riverdale which was a drive from where I lived. She dropped me off and the only thing I could do was sit in a corner, look and watch the phone. I knew that when my phone rang that would be the moment he knew I was gone. I went from watching my phone to watching out the window and hiding in that order, back and forth. After about thirty-minutes of that the phone rings and its him. The moment that phone rang and I see his name flash across the screen an instance rush of even more fear took over me. I didn't know what to do because if I answer it I would be even more scared. If I didn't answer it I was still even more scared I was confused. I was too scared and filled with too much fear to pray. I was too afraid to sit down. I was too afraid to do anything let alone got to sleep and take a nap and feel comfortable.

So, I didn't answer the phone. I just cried and then my phone rings again. Now I felt like I needed to answer it, because he would get so mad if I didn't. I answered it and all I could feel was the fear. I swallowed so hard that I would have thought I had a Adams apple.

As I put the phone to my ear, I hear him yelling and cussing "where is my son? You had no right to take him!" I hung up. He called back and told me that he was going to beat the crap out of me and kill me. After that I tried not to answer. He would call back and say he was sorry and didn't mean to scare me and to come back home. I spent so many nights not sleeping because I was scared to go to sleep. I thought he would find me somehow and beat the crap out of me. Eventually I got up some nerves to pray again. Some days I would be ok but other days I was not. I would even think what will I do without him? Nobody is going to want me. I was this fragile, scared, weak minded girl that didn't know where to go from that point. I had been beaten some physically but most of it was mentally. All abuse in any form is bad but that mental abuse is a booger. I say that because that is the first thing the devil will attack is your sanity, your will power to hope and believe for better. He may have had me for a minute, but God is all I can say.

I stayed with Ms. Gina for maybe a couple of months and then finally found a place of my own. I was a little nervous about being for real on my own. I finally made it to a space in life where I wasn't too scared or afraid anymore. But I still had a lot of pain in my heart. I don't think I realized it back then. I think I had gotten so used to pushing it down and dressing it up and not allowing myself to think or feel any of it. I remember the first day moving in Ms. Gina took me to a dollar store. I stood in the toilet paper aisle for about twenty minutes. Ms. Gina came in the store and was like "What's wrong?" The only thing I could say to her was, "I don't know."

She said "don't know what?"

I stood there and cried because I didn't know what kind of toilet paper to buy. I didn't know anything about what I wanted to use for my house. I was so used to getting everything he required that I had lost me. I had no clue what I liked. I wrapped myself up in him so much that I didn't know who Tyra was anymore. Did I ever at any time of my life know who she was? This is the point in my life I believe I was having a spiritual awakening. I also didn't know that

either at the time. It's crazy how God allows somethings to unfold in life. But here I was crying in the middle of an aisle in the dollar store having an epiphany about the fact I don't know or that I didn't know who I was or what I wanted to buy to clean my home. I mean I went to the store to buy some simple things and it turned out that doing that simple thing lead to a big thing of who am I?

From that point on I didn't know would continue to ask myself the same thing over the next year and a half. After I left that dollar store my life changed. I wanted to know who I was and what I wanted. So, I did the only thing that I knew to get answers, I prayed and worshiped. Yes, praying gave me peace and serenity but I still wanted to know what does Tyra want? Who is she? What does she want out of life? I mean there were so many questions racing through my mind all the time. It wasn't a racing that made me uneasy or anything. I was calm and I still had peace. Every Sunday I went to church I sat in the same pew and just cried. My heart was hurt from my marriage not working even though I knew that I was still married to two men. I was still hurt.

70

Tyra Smith

 *Chapter Eleven*

My heart was finally healed after all the months of crying. Things were looking a little better, but I was still married to two men. That, I could not shake off my mind or heart. I still prayed for God to help me figure out a way to divorce both of them and finally be free of the guilt. I wanted to finally be able to stop being afraid of the police coming to lock me up for being married to two men. Not long after I left Chuck, he started to talk to some women from back home that he used to date in high school. He ended up moving back to St. Louis to be with her. Trust, I was not hurt or sad about that. I kind of wondered if she knew what she was getting herself into. At the same time it wasn't my business. I just stayed in my lane. Chuck and I finally got to a point where we could talk over the phone.

One day I asked if I could get his new address so I could send him some divorce papers in the mail to sign. We needed to get this over with and done. He was moving on and I wanted to as well. His response to that was, "No you can't and you don't need a divorce from me. You're not going to get one. And if you try to divorce me I will tell the courts that I just found out that you're married to another man as well." In my head I was thinking ok here we go again trying to pull this mess and all because he still wanted to run me all the way from Missouri. So, I polity said, "OK that's fine." I went back to the drawing board and prayed and kept praying for months about this divorce and asking God to give me the strength to do it and not to be afraid of what man will say or do.

At the same time I was a little sad that Chuck had left Georgia. My kids and I where down here alone for real. The thought of that hurt and the fact that he was with someone else. The fact that the kids and I where here with no family was just the push I needed to get me through this. One day I picked up the phone and called a

divorce attorney and told them my situation. I told them that Chuck didn't and wouldn't sign the divorce papers. I told them my first husband was willing to let me serve him with court papers. So they gave me an appointment to come in so we could talk about it. The next day I caught the bus down town Atlanta and had my meeting. As I sat in the office waiting for the lawyer to come in, I was so nervous and afraid to tell my story again, but I did. The lawyer looked at me and said "Well the bad news I have for you is, I can't help you because you don't have a job or get enough money to pay for my services." At that moment I didn't know what to think, but he continued to say, "I know that I can walk you through a cheaper process, and you're going to need to write it all down. You will have to file both of them a week apart."

"Wait. What?" I thought in my head, "This man is crazy. I will for sure get caught up doing it like that." Ya'll when I tell you I looked at that man like he was crazy. I took all the instructions down like he told me too and I left. The whole bus ride home I was just in fear of doing it like the man had told me to but I did. The next day I went back down town and filed the first one, and then I waited a week and went back to file the second one. When I tell ya'll I was so scared when I went back to file the second one. When I walked in the building I just knew someone was going to remember me from last week and be like "oh back so soon" laugh out loud. I was told that both divorces would take thirty-days.

After I came back from filing the last one, I just prayed and cried that I wouldn't get found out. It took about a month in a half to get divorced from both of them. I remember the day I got the first divorce decree. I was so happy, but I knew I wasn't out of the woods just yet. There was one more to tackle before I could get my cake with the picture of shackles falling off the ankles. The last one I was waiting on was the divorce from Chuck. When I say I was waiting I was checking emails every day to see what was poppin. As I was waiting on this decree to be final, I was telling all my kid's schools that they were not coming back the next year because we were

moving.

The school asked, "So where are you moving to so we can send documents over to the new schools?" I polity told them I didn't know. I just know they will not be back, and I would get the paperwork when I found out. When I tell ya'll I was walking in the crazy faith. Sometimes God has you do some crazy things that don't make sense at all to you but makes perfect since to him. So let me explain this a little I was not looking for any houses online. I just knew that we were moving and that was all I could say about that. I didn't have anything preplanned. I wasn't shopping around. I wasn't doing any of that normal stuff we would do to organize a move. June 21, 2017 at two-thirty in the afternoon an email goes off. At the same time my friend and sis in Christ pulls up. I'm waving to her as I am opening up my email. It's my divorce decree for Chuck. I was so happy that it was finally over. I could get my cake ya'll.

As I was jumping up and down my friend walks up and says I need you to come with me on a ride real quick. So I was like, "Ok." I get in the car and we ride to the other side of town to a little city called Rex, Georgia. We pulled up at this beautiful house and I ask why are we here. She proceeds to tell me that I needed to see this house, and they guy that owns it. We get out and we walk in this beautiful house. The guy was so awesome that he worked out a deal with me. Ya'll I was negotiating with no money about how much I could pay a month and we came up with a great deal. So I was to pay him sixteen hundred dollars by the next week. This was a three-bedroom, bonus room, and 2 bathrooms home. It also had a bonus room with a jacuzzi tub. When we left that house, I had no clue how I was going to pay this money. I wasn't worried about it either.

My friend dropped me off back home. Not even four days later a different friend gave me a check for the exact amount I needed for that house. We moved in on July 1st, do you yall know that I waited five-months before I gave Chuck the divorce decree. When I did he was so mad that he cussed me out in front of his girlfriend. He said, "Who do you think you are getting a divorce behind my back. I

didn't give you permission to do that." You guys his girlfriend had a look on her face that said everything she was thinking. Her face was like, "NO YOU DIDN'T!" And I am looking like, "YES HONEY HE JUST DID THAT."

I believe he was madder at the fact that he had nothing else to hold over my head. I was finally free after seven years of bondage, of being stuck. When I tell you that every day I woke up in my new house I was like, "YES I am all the way free from both marriages." I was finally in a place in my life where I had never been before. I knew it and I loved it. I started to know me, who I was and what I wanted out of life. Everything was finally clear in my life. By this time it had been seven or eight years. So when I tell you I was so thankful for this brand new life. After I got a job, about three months later I had a new car, well not brand new, but it was new to me. God was moving in my life and I could see him doing these beautiful things for me.

So I went on living the best life I possible could. The job I had was driving in a school. That was a whole mental process for me. Let me tell you guys the process it took for me to even think about getting my CDL'S to work for a school district. My friend that connected me to the new house called me one day and was like" you should study for your CDL's because there is a school district that is hiring for bus drivers. I believe you can do this because you're good with kids." My response to that was, "NO oh nonononono!"

She was like, "why not Tyra?"

"Because I don't even like my own kids sometimes. And you think that me driving a school bus with kids, and then come home to kids is going to be good for my sanity, you are sadly mistaken."

I have never been so adamant in my life. Her response was, "Just take this to God in prayer and talk to god about it."

"No I don't want to because I already have my answer for you and that's no." All she could do was laugh at me. But I did take it to God he was like, "Yes do this." So, I did but when I tell y'all I fought hard not to do this job. I did for real. When I tell you that I loved

hard on the kids I had as a bus driver, and they loved me just as hard. It was to the point they would call me if I wasn't at work. "Ma'am where are you? We didn't approve your off day today." Is what I would get for missing days. "Whoever this other driver is today is horrible. When are you coming back?" So, because of them I hardly ever took a day off because I loved my babies. This was my first job since I had gotten sick and lost my job as a CNA. So, I was really in a place where everything was brand new, to me at least.

Now I was doing really good. I mean I thought I was. Let me tell you guys what happened. I feel like I am doing that black people thing of see what happened was. Then you just know because they started with that this has to be a lie, lol. But no, for real I backslid like I don't know what. I started wanting to date. The next thing you know I am in a place I didn't want to be. I didn't intend to be there. One of my good friends from the school district ended up leaving and going to a freight company to get her class A CDL's which was great for her. She was talking to me off and on about coming to her job because they really didn't have women drivers. My response to that was like before NO, NO, NO I'm not really interested in driving semis. The fact that I would get dirty every day on the job didn't not make it pleasing for me.

We would talk every couple of months and she would say come on up here sis. At this time COVID had come and tore up things. I was still telling her no and I'm good on that. But yall I ended up filling out an application for a part-time dock worker. It was part-time for the simple fact that I wasn't going to stay on the dock long. I was going to go into their driver program. When I say I was set up when it comes to this job. I mean I was set up and not by my friend that referred me to the job. The good kind of set up. You will understand as I keep going. Anyways my first day was training and I walked on to this dock that was huge and had over two-hundred doors for these tractors to back trailers up in. It was for loading and unloading all kinds of freight, and people riding around on forklifts everywhere.

I mean they were moving on these forklifts with a purpose for real. When I tell you that it was so many men on this dock, there was no women on this dock, and the women that was working on the dock they were playing for the other team. if you know what I mean, no judgement on that do you boo. I just know where I stood on that I loved men. When I tell you this was not the place to be if you truly are trying to stay away from temptation of sex and men. I had no business being in a place like this, all men. The first thing I thought walking on this dock with all these men was help me Jesus!

There were so many men in this place and when I tell you most of them where very good looking. I mean this is not a place for single women in destress over finding love. When I tell you I was that one. All I could do was pray as I walked down this dock on the day of training. As the trainer was walking me around and showing me all the doors that was there, I felt like a T-bone steak that was being waved in front of a pack of wild hungry wolves that had never seen such a thick well-preserved kind of meat before.

So, I had to go through three days of training and when I tell you I had come up with such a lie to tell these men. They kept asking if I was single, and so I decided to keep myself out of trouble and buy a fake ring and tell these men that I was married with six kids. I sure did. But that only worked for a short time. Only my trainer knew my true store, and he never did tell anyone my truth. Finally, after three days I was released from training and I was on my own. That made me even more nervous because now I was by myself. That meant that these men could approach me without the defense of my trainer being there to tell them to not bother me.

So let me tell you every time I looked like I might be in distressed a guy would pull up and ask if I need help. Sometimes I would say no, but if I really didn't feel like working and doing any work I would put on the damsel in distressed role and help would come from everywhere. When I tell you it always worked like a charm. There was this guy that I met who introduced himself as freight master. Why he called himself that I didn't know at the time,

but I soon found out. This man pulls up to me and asked, "hey do you have a man?" I was ducking behind freight. He went on to say, "I see you and I haven't had the courage to ask you out. I had to amped myself up to ask you."

When he approached me it was something different about him that I just couldn't shake. He had these brown eyes that if you looked in them too long and hard you would probably fall in love. He had this nice brown skin complexion with some thick eyebrows, beautiful smile, pretty teeth with these dimples that only showed up when he smiled. All I could think was or Lord here I go again.

 # In Closing

I was going through so much while this book was being put together by my publisher. I started writing it in the beginning of October 2022. The second week in writing the book I was taken out of service by the company I worked. Let me explain what being put out of service means. It means that I cannot drive or be behind the wheel of the tractor until I am released by my doctor. Which in turn means I can't be a driver for dispatch. I found out later that I had a bulging disc the was pinching the nerve and my spinal cord on my left side of my shoulder. When I tell you it was so painful driving that tractor trailer, backing it up, and parking trailers in spots. The pain started to get worse even with driving my personal car. When I say that I acted a monkey's butt. I really acted a monkeys butt when my company put me out of service. I was in tears. I ran out of the building just crying.

You know how you can do something and realize later that the scene you created in front of a lot of people was maybe a little dramatic and over the top. Yeah, that was me all day. Don't sit there like you have never done it before. Tell the truth and shame the devil. We be talking about keeping it real, so let's be real. When I replayed that part back in my head, I laugh so hard, and shake my head at myself. Those of you who know me personally know that I can be a little bit dramatic at times, but that is beside the point. I want to address something. I just said, the hard thing about keeping it real and being 100 has to first start with yourself. It is vital that we are 100 with ourselves first. Once we're 100 with ourselves, we can be 100 with others and more importantly with God.

This pain that we encounter throughout our life ends up being this big ball of trauma. This trauma affects us and causes us to become stagnant in life. The pain has made us numb to feeling anything. Some people may appear to encounter pain, whip it off,

and keep going. The struggles are not to harm you, but to build you up in such a way that you build character and persevere. You become an overcomer and the very things that you fear, the fear of the greater you, the fear of the best you, you become. This here was my very problem, allowing the pain and trauma to ruin my life and tell me that I would never be what my dreams and vision told me I could be.

I would often lose myself in the pain that I carried and would often convince myself that they were just dreams. I would never be better than the pain I endured. I would always be subjected to the pain. I didn't want to confront the pain I carried, because I was always taught to press it down. When we were younger, someone told us how to be, or it was modeled in front of our faces. I watched my mother carry her pain and never really be able to conquer it. I watched her struggle with it for years. She would talk about it every once and a while, but she never overcame it. My struggle ended up being identical to hers. I let it ruin me and I let it tell me what I wasn't. I let it tell me that I couldn't make a difference or change in my life. I'm sharing this because there are so many people out there in the world who struggle because of what they saw. Who better to talk about this than someone who has overcome it.

Let me not get started on rejection that goes along with the trauma. I say trauma because the very meaning of trauma is "a deeply distressing or disturbing experience," and the enduring of pain after pain. It is an invitation into a world of trauma that you carry with you everywhere you go, I will get more into this later.

So, after being put out of service the first week of being home after five to six years of going to work every day and working ten-to-fourteen-hour days, I now saw myself pacing the floors trying to figure out how I can I get back to work by any means necessary. When I tell you I wanted to lie to my doctor and tell him guess what I had a miracle healing, and I am ready to get back to work. I am so for real ya'll. But at the same I think what made me so not at ease was the fact of going into the unknow. Not knowing what was going

to happen or if something was going to happen. So, by the second week of being out of work I decided to continue to write, as I continued to write the book, I would find myself on my living room floor crying so hard. as I keep going, I found out that I was learning how to allow the pain to resurface and not consume me. I learned to navigate through it all.

A couple of months before I even started writing I started seeing a therapist. The reason I started to see a therapist was because I was coming out of a relationship that hurt me to my core. When I say hurt me to my core that's exactly what I meant. Those of you that know pain you know that when you get hurt to your core that new pain just adds on to the old pain that you have already been carrying. The pain you were already carrying hurts even more and it begins to feel like a double offence against your heart. You find yourself being angry at the person that caused that last hurtful offence and I say offence because that's exactly how it felt to me. I suffered so much in love, but mustered up the nerve to give another person that space. That too ended with the same fate. I asked myself, "Why can't I find love. Why am I not good enough? What's wrong with me? Why can't I find love?"

This is everything that ran through my head as I sat in the therapist office. She just didn't know how deep my pain really ran when it came to matters and issues of my heart and love. I remember she told me to start writing a book, because she I knew I had a lot to say and that I had been through so much. When she told me this my first thought was, "Yeah lady. I have tried to write a book before years ago and it didn't quit work out. I got all of one page typed and was like this is not it." I didn't see myself writing a book or sitting in one place long enough writing all day. But I did take her advice and I started writing, not even knowing exactly what to write, or how to write it.

I remember she just keep telling me just write whatever you want to talk about. Write whatever comes to mind, just write your story. She said that you can write a novel and who knows you may

end up writing a second book. That is how my journey began with writing. Boy, when I tell you it has been a tough journey. It really has. But the more I wrote the more I cried. I would allow myself to ball up on the floor or on my couch and just let the tears flow. I did this for all of about ten to twenty minutes. Then I would try and pick myself up, wipe my tears and push through the day with some self-care. This self-care was usually walking the park and taking in nature or treating myself out to lunch alone. When I tell you guys that it is vital when navigating through the pain you learn to love and embrace yourself. Don't let the voices of pain tell you that you're doing it all for no reason. When you have been in/through so much pain/trauma it's like it sets up its own defense mechanism of walls that wasn't there before.

Made in the USA
Columbia, SC
10 October 2024

43448960R00135